2006
CLINIC NOTES

Lectures by
Premier High School Coaches

Edited by Earl Browning

COACHES
CHOICE™

www.coacheschoice.com

ISBN: 1-58518-982-0

Library of Congress Control Number: 2006926696

Telecoach, Inc. Transcription: Earl Browning, Jr., Kent Browning, Tom Cheaney, Bill Gierke, Dan Haley, Kevin Wallace

Diagrams: Steve Haag

Book layout and cover design: Studio J Art & Design

Front and back cover photos of Todd Dodge: Courtesy of Sports Editor Zack Wallace and the *Southlake Journal*. Photos by Robert Hughes.

Back cover photo of John McKissick: Courtesy of Summerville High School Athletic Department

Special thanks to the Nike clinic managers for having the lectures taped.

Coaches Choice
P.O. Box 1828
Monterey, CA 93942
www.coacheschoice.com

Contents

Contents

BUILDING THE DEFENSIVE GAME PLAN

Memphis University High School, Tennessee

Thank you very much. It is nice to be able to come out and exchange some ideas about football. Since the University School was re-founded in the 1950s after being closed for a little while, I am only the third head coach the school has had. I spent 20 years as an assistant coach there before becoming the head coach.

My wife loves the fact that we did not have to move. One of the few things in coaching that keeps your wife happy is when she does not have to move.

I started going to clinics many years ago. I remember at one clinic, hearing a coach say if you could get one thing that would help you win a game, it was a successful clinic. That is what I have tried to do over the years.

As a speaker, if I can say one thing to help somebody win a game, I will have done a good job. If I do that, I hope you call me and tell me. That way, maybe I can evaluate and see if we are doing anything right.

My father was a pastor. He talked a lot about getting the call by the Lord to be a pastor. My prayer every night was: "Please Lord, do not call me to be a pastor." As you might know, God has a sense of humor because I became a football coach. There is only one thing worse than being a pastor and that is a coach.

Everything you do is being evaluated by people who do not know what they are doing, let alone what you are doing. We have had some very good years. However, two years ago we were 4-7. Everyone was mad at me, and a few people thought it was time for me to do something else. It was a fight and it was not very pretty. It was not fun being the coach.

My only goal, from when I started coaching to this day, was to teach the important life lesson that football has to offer to our players. I want my players to come back 20 years from now and tell me that I taught them something that made a difference in their lives. That is the greatest thing that can happen to a coach. That is what matters to me.

The irony about football is you do not get to teach those lessons unless you win. Winning is the only insurance that allows you to do what you want to do. Winning is important. If you coach at a place that does not care whether you win or lose, you are probably trying to get out of there.

If you are realistic about the attitude of players, you have to win. If you do not win a big percentage of the time, the players will not listen to you.

With that as a backdrop, we are going to talk about game planning. What I am going to do is take you through the week before we played in our tenth state championship game. I will cover all the things we had to do to prepare for that game. Before I do that, I feel I have to tell you something about our philosophy.

I believe the most talented team wins 90 percent of the time. There are some good coaches in the game, but I believe that the team with the best players wins the games. If a coach talks about winning three state championships in a row with inferior talent, I do not believe him.

There is a winning formula in football. The first thing you have to do is have the best players on your team on the field. That sounds simple, but I have to fight with our coaches to do it all the time. I do not want the back-up linebacker to be one of the best 11 defensive players we have. I want him on the field somewhere even if he is not one of our best linebackers.

I do not want a back-up defensive lineman to be one of our five best offensive linemen. That means he is not on the field on defense or offense. Do something to get the best players on your team on the field. I do not want to hurt the players we need on Friday night in practice during the week. It does us no good if they are on the sideline in a cast. We will do everything we can—structurally—to get the best players on the field.

Secondly, I want the best player in my school on my team. If they want to play another sport or some school activity, I have no problem with that. I think it is smart to have the best players in the region or state in your program. If you have a good player, and he is smart, I want him to come to our school.

We have a great weight and conditioning program at our school, which helps in our recruitment of students. I want the best coaches teaching our players. I want the best coaches in our school coaching football.

In the coaching model, I am looking for coaches that are good teachers. I want coaches that are honest evaluators. I want our coaches to have competitive spirit. They are the coaches that put the team first.

Our coaching staff coaches all of our teams. We coach grades nine through twelve. We put all our players in the same team. I want my best defensive back coach coaching all our players from the "get-go."

Every coach in our program has a different on-the-field assignment. My offensive coordinator coaches the running backs and all the kick-return men. The offensive line coaches coach the special teams and especially the kickoff-return team.

My wide receivers coach is the freshmen offensive coordinator and calls the plays for the freshmen team. He also coaches our punt teams. Our assistant offensive line coach coaches the

snappers. The quarterback coach is the JV offensive coordinator. He calls the plays for the JV team.

We do the same thing with our defensive staff. Our defensive coordinator coaches our linebackers and the punt-protection team. Our defensive-corner coach also coaches our punt gunners. Our defensive line coach calls the defense for the JV team and coaches the field-goal team. Our defensive safeties coach calls the defense for the freshmen team and handles the punters and kickers.

The amount of coaches you have in your program is not important, but you have to have as many as your opponents. In our league, everyone has as many coaches as we do. If you have three assistant coaches and the teams you have to beat have six, you better be knocking on your principal's door. If you want to win you must have help. All of our coaches have other duties, but that is the way we break it down on the field.

I want everyone on our staff to know what is going on. That is why I have three levels of coordinators within the program. I am training coaches to be coordinators and head coaches. When you allow everyone to have that type of input into the program, they work harder to prepare.

When we look at our team personnel there are certain models we have in mind. We want to play two-platoon football. I do not want anyone going both ways. I struggled with that point for several years. I discovered something after we went to the platoon system. We have great athletes on one side of the ball that cannot play on the other side.

A good example of that fact is a player that played for us last year and is now a wide receiver at Ole Miss. We stayed mad at him for two years because he would not hit people on defense. He was not a defensive player. He could cover ground and do some good things, but he would not strike people.

I have had athletes who were great players on defense and screwed up everything they did on offense. He made eight tackles on defense, but could not block a soul. I want to get the personnel on the side of the ball that suits their abilities and personality.

Our coaching staff has a draft on our team for the talent. We have a draft day. The first three picks go to the offensive staff. They pick the quarterback first, the running back second, and the wide receiver third. The next 17 picks go to the defense. The only thing they cannot do is pick someone who cannot run. My best defensive teams have been the ones that did not have anyone over 200 pounds. I do not want anybody playing defense that cannot run. Putting a 280-pound player on the defensive line is the worst thing you can do. You are wasting his time as well as yours.

The next picks (18 through 24) are the offensive linemen. That group will probably be all of the fat, slow players. Pick number 25 is the back-up quarterback. Picks 26 through 30 are our receiver corps. Pick number 31 is our back-up running back.

After we pick 31 players, I let the remaining players choose what they want to play. If we have a dispute, I mediate.

When our players come in as freshmen, we make them pick a position. For three weeks, they try to make the varsity team. If they can play that position at the varsity level, we practice them at that level.

In practice, we do the majority of our drill work in groups. When we go to team period, we split the squad and they go in different directions. When we play a freshman game, we do not platoon. We are not a big enough school to have that many skilled players. We want to win at that level and play the best players on both sides of the ball. In our school, we have 400 boys in grades 9 through 12.

Before you talk about players, you must have coaches. If you have enough coaches, the number of players in the program will not be a problem. That is our program game plan.

We have a season game plan. After we pick the team and have been honest in our assessment, it is time to determine the playing style. Bill Belichick had a great statement about "honestly assess your team." The year after they won the Super Bowl, they missed the playoffs. They almost got there but failed to make it. The first team meeting after they did not make the playoffs, he made a statement that was an honest assessment of his team. He told his team, and I quote, "We have one of the bottom five teams defensively in the league. We suck at stopping the run. We're bad in the red area and we can't get off the field on third down."

I think we all have trouble honestly assessing our team. Either we are too negative about what kind of players we have or we are too positive about our team. I have coaches on my staff that go all week and never see anything except the bad things that are happening. I also have coaches on my staff that see nothing but the bright side of things.

After that, I think you pick your poison, as to what you run on offense. To me there are three types of offenses—regardless of what formations you align in. You are a smash-mouth team, a take-what-they-give-you team, or a wing-and-a-prayer team.

When we play a team, I want to know if they are a smash-mouth team. You can play smash-mouth football with three backs in the backfield and two tight ends. You can play smash-mouth football with one back and four wide receivers. Smash-mouth football to me is the type of team that gets in the huddle and runs the play the coach calls. It matters little what the defense does because they will run that play. They will run it because they think they are better than you are.

If we have the best player, we play smash-mouth football. The take-what-they-give-us teams do what their name says. They are not better than the defense and they run plays to get yardage that the defense will give up.

The third category is what we get into when we are not very good. A wing and a prayer is when the offense throws the ball up and hopes something good happens.

On defense, there are only two kinds of fronts. It does not matter where they line up. They are a read-and-react defense or an act-and-reread defense. Those defenses play only two types of coverages. They play either zone or man. That is what we want to decide about our team and our opponents as well.

The week before the championship game required a tremendous amount of planning. Bill Belichick says this about game planning: "Planning the issues around the game is as important as planning the game itself." That is a profound statement. It does not have to be a state championship game; it could be the game that gets you into the playoffs. You cannot just let things happen. You have to plan what will happen.

We played our semi-final game on Friday and the championship was the next Saturday. In that game, we were playing our biggest rival, which was approximately two miles from our school. Both of our teams were going to pay $8000 to load on buses and drive 252 miles to play in Murfreesboro in the championship game.

The first challenges we have to face are the travel to the game, a practice schedule, and how to handle the hoopla surrounding the game.

When we travel, we do it the same way every time. When we were getting ready to travel, I wanted to see what Christian Brothers was going to do. I was hoping they had planned to travel on Friday and spend the night before the game.

How many high school teams spend a night somewhere before they play a game? Not many of them do. We are not going to do that. I will do anything to get there on the day of the game. The players do not want to spend the night before they play the game. They want to be home in their beds going through the same routine they did during the season.

Since the game is on Saturday, we have the extra day to practice during the week. I want to keep the routine of practice and travel the same as it was all season. We do not want to do anything special. Make everything the same. If we can do that, our players will play better.

Any time you get to a state championship game, there is always hoopla surrounding the game. Having a TV camera show up at your practice will be a distraction. The big problem I have is with the parents. I have to calm them down and convince them that this is not going to be the biggest event in their sons' lives.

I want the kids to just play football. I do not want the parents having special events like team breakfasts and things of that nature. If we win the game, we can do something special. If we can handle the hoopla, that gives us the best chance to win. We do not want to make the game more important than it is. I always tell our kids after the game that there are a billion Chinese people in the world that do not give a crap whether we played or not.

They put our game on the Internet and we had one guy from Tennessee who lived in China and listened to our game on the Internet. We had to revamp our comments about the Chinese. We used to say there were 999,999,999 people in China that did not care whether we played.

The next thing we wanted to do going into this game was to evaluate the match-ups honestly. I do something every week that I have never heard anyone talk about. I evaluate the coaching match-ups. We were playing Christian Brothers and I wanted to know if I was a better coach than Kevin Locastro. I wanted to know if our coordinators were better than Christian Brothers' coordinators.

The next thing is to evaluate the players. We want to know where we have an advantage and where they have one. We want to try to create mismatches with their players. We have to decide how to get our best defenders on their weakest blockers.

When I evaluate a team, I look at their stats. I want to know what they are doing statistically. Most of the recorded stats lie, but I have faith in a few stats. One of those stats is red-zone efficiency.

In 2001 and 2002, we got in the red zone 44 times in both years. We scored 30 times in 2001 and 28 times in 2002. That was 68 percent in one year and

64 percent in the other year. That was terrible. However, if you look at the 2004 and 2005 seasons, we won the state championship both years. We were in the red zone 40 times and scored 32 times in 2004. In 2005, we were in the red zone 41 times and scored 34 times. That was 80 percent in 2004 and 83 percent in 2005.

In those same years, our red-zone defenses allowed nine scores in 20 times in the red zone in 2004 for 45 percent, and 14 scores in 31 times for 67 percent in 2005. Those statistics are very telling. I look at that and see how our opponent does in the red zone.

In a track meet, if I can get your sprinters to run 110 meters and my sprinters to run 100 meters, our team stands a good chance of winning the race. I want to do the same thing in a football game. I want to play field-position football and play on a short field. I want the opponent to play on the long field and to have to go further to score than we do.

In our first football game this year, we had to go 46 yards on average to score a touchdown. They had to go 78 yards to score. We won that game. We want to punt the ball and play field position. This year our opponents had to go, on average, 75 yards to score a touchdown. We had to go 63 yards to score. I want to take advantage of our punting game. We had an excellent punter and we used him to swing the advantage in our favor.

If we could avoid the turnovers, we would end up with the best field position and the shorter field. Field position is a quick way to gain two to three first downs.

I look at our efficiency on offense as one of the indicators of how well we played. If you take the number of sacks, the number of turnovers, and the number of penalties, add them up, and find what percentage of your offensive plays that represents, you will know whether you played well. If the percent is 12 percent or less, that is not bad.

We look for one touchdown for every 100 yards of total offense. The third down is an important down. On third-and-long, you will not pick that up

much. The thing we try to do is to not screw it up and punt the ball. On third-and-medium, we hope to make it 40 percent of the time. However, the most important down is third-and-short. You have to win that down. This year, the opponents on third- and fourth-down-and-short made the first down at the rate of 53 percent. We made that situation 70 percent of the time.

You must have a play in your offense that can pick up the first down on third-and-four to go for the first down. In the championship game, we were six for seven in our attempts in that situation.

Our short-yardage play is the quarterback keep from the veer fake. We are about 90 percent with this play. We run this play on the goal line. We fake the running back and the quarterback finds a crease to pop through.

It is demoralizing to come off the field after not making a short third-down conversion. Find a play that will pick that yardage up a high percentage of the time. We chart the plays we run on third-and-four. If the play gets the first down, it is an efficient play. I do not worry about yardage-per-carry on a play.

When we get in the red zone, it is important to me to score touchdowns. It is more important to score touchdowns than it is to kick field goals.

The last offensive stat that is important is big plays. Are you getting more than you are giving up? When you are good, you get the big plays and do not give them up.

That gives you a background about how we feel about preparing for the big game.

We were playing the crosstown rival that we played earlier this year in the state championship. I evaluated the coaching match-ups and there is no advantage for either team. I know their staff and Kevin has done a good job of upgrading his assistants. We are not going to outsmart them in the game.

On defense, we start out each week by looking at the other team's personnel. I want to know if they have a prime-time player. I am hoping they have none, but if they have two, we are in trouble. When I talk about a prime-time player, I mean a player we cannot tackle one-on-one.

Unfortunately, Christian Brothers had a prime-time player. They had a little running back that was very good. We struggled to tackle him in a one-on-one match-up. If they blocked us and we got one defender to the hole, I was not sure we could tackle him.

If the offense has that type of player, for you to stop him you have to get more people to the ball. To do that, you have to give up something.

That reminds me of a story about a state championship game we played in the mid-1990s. We played against a team from Nashville. They had three or four prime-time players. Among them was a player by the name of John Henderson, who went on to have an NFL career as a defensive tackle. He played tight end for this team. They had a center that went on to UT and a two-time Back of the Year in Tennessee playing in their backfield.

We played hard and got up with very little time to go in the game. They had the ball and needed to score to beat us. They split out John Henderson. He was 6'8" and everyone in the stadium knew what was going to happen. They threw the ball down the field to Henderson. He went up and rebounded the football for a 20-yard gain.

They did again and got the ball to the 15-yard line. We called time-out and set our defense. We loaded up on him and told the linebacker to tackle him coming off the line of scrimmage. We were not going to let him catch another pass. The next play they ran a quick trap and scored.

The point to the story is if you gear your defense to stop one player, you have to give up something. When you give up something, you have to know where the weakness occurs and how to shade the defense to that weakness.

If we play a team that does not have a prime-time player, that does not mean they are not a good team. Sometimes you can look at a team without a

prime-time player and gain a false assurance that you will win the game. It does not mean the team is bad, it means they do not have someone you have to stop on every play.

When we play teams like that, we play down-and-distance and run-and-pass. We take away the two or three things they do best. We play the percentages when we play a team with no PTP.

When we practice defense, we practice our first team against our first team. We do not take anyone to the ground, but everything else is full speed. We line the first offense on one hash mark and the second and third offenses on the other hash mark. We have cards drawn with the plays we want to run.

The first defense goes against the first offense. When that play is over the second and third offense breaks the huddle on the other hash mark and starts to the ball. The first defense has to run to the other hash and play against the seconds and thirds. When that play is over, they have to go back to the other hash marks and do it all over again. If we do the drill right, we can run 35 to 40 plays in a 15-minute period. It is a conditioning drill as well as a team-defense period.

We practice for an hour and a half and I do not want anyone standing around watching. Everybody moves and we get off the field. The first team runs the most complicated plays, and the second team runs the base offense.

On Tuesday, we run the opponent's base or normal offense. On Wednesday, we run their special plays that they like to run. If you have enough players and coaches to work in this form, I would encourage you to do it. You can get a lot of work done in a small block of time. It also gives the offensive groups time to look at the cards to see what they do.

In practice, we work on our play for getting off the field on third down. We go over each down-and-distance situation for the third-down defense. If the offense has a big playmaker, stop him and get off the field.

On offense, we felt the two teams were evenly matched. We were not going to outsmart them. They had three great linebackers and good defensive backs. Their defensive line was the weakest element of the defense. They were not bad, but were not as talented as the other parts of the defense.

The offense wants to take what the defense gives them. We design our normal plays to get four yards. We did not want to signal in plays in the opening drive. Actually, we only run two running plays. We run the zone play and the stretch play. We run them from a lot of different formations and call the play something different, but it is the zone or stretch plays.

In normal situations, we felt we could run the zone play. If the defense packed the box, we ran the three-step passing game. The zone play is the greatest play ever run. It allows your offensive linemen to come to practice every day and practice on one thing. The fewer things you practice on, the better you become at those skills.

I have some plays on video of the zone play. We run it from under the center and out of the shotgun. Our running back is our back-up quarterback. We slated him to be the starter but he got hurt last year. He sprained his ankle in practice trying to run a play we have never run in a game. All we are looking for is run-efficiency. We want four yards on the play.

Their defense was a heavy blitzing team. We had a play to make them pay if they blitzed. We ran the tunnel screen against their blitz. We can run the tunnel screen from both sides based on our alignment. The first time we played Christian Brothers, we threw the tunnel screen to our X-receiver. He can catch the ball, but he cannot make anyone miss a tackle. We decided in this game to throw the ball to our running back. We flared the back and brought him underneath the coverage for the tunnel screen.

In our first game, we did not make them pay for blitzing us. We completed this early in the game and got a big play on it. That slowed them down for the entire game with their blitz package. We ran the same play and threw it to our best receiver.

On third down, the offense has to be tough. You have to make the short-yardage, third-down play. We were six of seven on third-and-short in this game. We are a one-back team most of the time, but in short yardage, we go to two backs. The play we hang our hat on is the veer option with the quarterback carrying the ball. At some point along that line of scrimmage, he finds a crease to get into for the yardage. He takes the ball inside and outside. On occasion, he follows the diveback into the hole. It has been successful 90 percent of the time.

I believe you must have one or two trick plays in your offensive game plan. The timing of the trick plays is critical in a game. On our first trick play, we ran it one play late. If we had thrown the play on second down instead of third it would have scored. The trick was to fake the ball to the running back and throw it to him down the field. The third-and-eight situations were not the time to use the play.

When it comes to winning games, you do it with talent. I believe that is definitely true. If you have talent and work it right, you will win 90 percent of your games. That may be all you need to keep your job. If you want to win championships, you must have character. The best team does not always win the championship.

The most important thing the head coach does is build character in his team. All of the other mechanics of the game are important, but the most important thing is teaching character development in your team. In the championship game, we were down four points, and Christian Brothers was driving to go up two scores. Everyone on our team believed our defense was going to make the play.

They made the play and I do not think there was any doubt in anybody's mind that we would drive 84 yards and score. Of the three minutes, it took us two and a half minutes to get to midfield. We made three fourth-down plays in the drive.

If you have a team you think is championship caliber, make sure you teach your leader to have character.

This is what I wrote to our players the week of the championship game.

MUS vs. CBHS

2005

Series Record

(14-11)

Last Meeting 2005

MUS-10 CBHS-14

Heroes win championships. So how does one go from being good or great to heroic? I would like to suggest it can be found in the verses from 1 Corinthians 13:13.

"So faith, hope, love abide, these three; but the greatest of these is love."

Saturday presents a great challenge, but more importantly, a great opportunity. Each of you can be a hero this week—whether in practice, in the locker room, or on the field Saturday. Faith in your team, hope realized by your commitment throughout the year, and love for each other will allow us to play courageously and unafraid. Knowing that we have the love of our teammates, regardless of our performance, gives us the freedom to make those plays that we will remember forever.

Our defense took this to heart and the player who made the interception was not one of our strong players. He had not played well the entire night. He made the interception, but when we graded him after the game, he graded out the worst game of his season. I do not think he would have made the interception if he did not know that his teammates were behind him no matter how bad he had played. That allows your players to make those types of plays. We made several in the last drive of that game.

Thank you all for listening. If there is anything we can ever do to help you, please contact us. I will send you tape and help any way I can. Thank you very much.

ELITE OFFENSIVE BLOCKING RULES

West Valley High School, Washington

I have been coaching for 29 years. I was the defensive coordinator for Coach Joe Ortolf for several years. Years ago, I wrote an article and made a video on the 20 gap defense based out of the 4-4 or 4-2 defense. Our 20 gap defense is based on the philosophy of "bend but don't break."

In the 20 gap defense, players read and react to offensive reads. Each player has his gap responsibility. Linemen keep the offensive linemen from getting to the linebackers, and they make the majority of tackles. However, the 20 gap defense is still an attacking defense. The 20 gap defense is easily adapted to all of today's complex formations and plays, making it easy for players and coaches to be successful.

That experience proved very successful. I met and heard from coaches all over the country. Also, it opened a number of doors for me throughout the country with college and high school coaches.

In the last five or six years during spring break, I have gone somewhere related to football. I want to share a few of those experiences with you. A few years ago, I was selected to go to Canton, Ohio, to the Pro Hall of Fame for the program the NFL has for the high school coaches. My expenses were paid for that trip. I was able to share a lot of ideas with coaches from across the country. I met a lot of the pro players and coaches. I got to see the hall-of-fame inductions. I just had a blast.

I try to do something different each year. I try to include my wife in the trips. It is hard to do that all of the time, but I think it is very important. One year my wife and I went to a clinic in Los Angeles and had a lot of fun. We went to a lot of the attractions and spent three days going to the clinic and having fun.

One year I went to Iowa but I did not take her with me. She did not figure there was a lot to do in Iowa. I spent almost a week with the Iowa Hawkeyes going to their defensive staff meetings and going to their practices. Norm Parker, the defensive coordinator at Iowa, is an awesome person.

One year I went to Nashville, Tennessee, to visit with the Titans. I wanted to study their blocking rules. In the evenings, we were able to go to some of the events and my wife enjoyed that trip. We had a great time and it was a great way to spend a spring break.

Last year, some of our assistant coaches took our wives to Pennsylvania. We made it a New York trip. We ended up going down to West Chester University to visit with Bill Zwaan, who has done a lot of work with wing-T camps. We spent some quality time with him because of our interest in the wing-T offense the last few years. We spent four days there watching practice. We were able to sit in the meeting and to talk with their coaches. Later on that trip, we ended up going to Washington, D.C., and had a great time.

I am here today, but my wife is not with me. She is down at Disney World now, and she did not invite me to go with her. She did not want to sit in the hotel room all day while I went to the clinics.

One of my contacts is Glenn McNew of Morgantown, West Virginia. He is retired now, but we spent a lot of time with him and have been on the phone a lot picking his brain.

When I was in Tennessee, I wanted to learn about blocking rules for the wing-T. While I was there, I went to visit with a high school coach by the name of Roger Holmes. The person who told me about Roger was Herschel Moore, who was the head coach at Cumberland University of Tennessee. Herschel started coaching in 1952 and ran the wing-T with great success. He was running the wing-T and the jet series in 2000. I spent a lot of time with Coach Moore and learned a great deal about his offense.

I went to see Coach Holmes, who had a unique blocking system. It was inside-out for the blocking rules. He was running the basic wing-T offense, and he ran the jet series as well. He gave us his blocking rules on a tape. He said, "If you do not get anything from your trip but this tape, it will be worthwhile."

When I got back home, I put the tape on and looked at it. My first reaction was, "Holy smokes. This is different than what I have been used to seeing." Now, after coaching for a number of years, it is difficult to change things as dramatic as the blocking rules for your offense. I did not think much more about the tape until two weeks later when I watched the tape and really was able to concentrate on what he was doing. I decided what he was doing was very good. It may be a little confusing at times today as I explain what we are doing on offense.

During the first 23 years of my coaching career, our teams always ran I formation and spread sets on offense, and we were very successful. In 2000, we put in the Delaware wing-T system. As a head coach, I spent a tremendous amount of time attending wing-T clinics and watching available wing-T videos. I thought it would be a simple offense to teach my players and assistant coaches. It was not. While we have made the playoffs each year running the wing-T offense, I really felt that using all of the tag terms for plays was still difficult to teach.

We basically had different rules for every play and had to memorize the play. It also limited our game planning and adjustments during the game. In the 2002 season, we only had one starter back on the offensive line and none on defense. I knew I had to do something better to streamline our teaching techniques for learning blocking rules.

I also wanted more flexibility on offense to make blocking adjustments during the game. In the spring of 2002, I gave each coach, lineman, and running back a copy of the *Elite Blocking Rules Video and Workbook* to complete before we went to camp. This included two JV quarterbacks who I was moving to the offensive line. I told the players that they needed to complete the entire playbook and know all the rules for each position.

At first, my line coach and some of the players were upset about changing the way we called our plays and rules for line blocking. Why change? We were league champs and placed third in the state playoffs the year before. After watching the video, doing the workbook, and applying the superior rules, our line coach would never want to switch back. This is the best system for teaching and learning blocking rules I have ever seen, and they apply to any offense. It is truly the cutting edge.

We do offer the video and workbook for your offensive lineup on our website. You can go to: www.nwinfo.net. Our e-mail is: 20gap@nwinfo.net.

Elite Interactive Blocking Rules Video and Workbook

- It saves valuable time as a head coach.

- It is a superior way to teach blocking rules.

- Learn by video, complete the rules in the workbook, and then apply the rules by drawing the blocking schemes.

- It is a superior way of applying blocking rules to today's complex defenses.

- It offers flexibility to game plan blocking schemes without confusing players or changing the rules for new defenses.

- It saves time by having coaches and players complete their interactive video workbook on their own time.

- It is a sound way of implementing the same blocking system within your entire football program at all levels of play.

Following are some facts about our video outline. It is approximately one hour in length.

- It teaches numbering system on the line.

- It teaches call system.

- It includes rules on each play for all linemen.

- It teaches the playside puller his play rules (down).

- It teaches the backside puller his play rules (traps).

- It teaches two backside pullers their play rules (counters and reverses).

- It teaches the weakside isolation play.

Odd/Even or 1-through-9 Numbering System

You must indicate whether you are an odd/even front or a Delaware 1-through-9 hole-blocking team. This system can be applied to any offensive scheme.

In our workbook (playbook) outline, we include the following information:

- We provide instructions on how to diagram in the workbook.

- We make it easy to read.

- You fill in terms and numbering system.

- You fill in playside puller rules for each position and then draw in the blocking for all players on four given plays calls versus an odd and even defense.

- You fill in two backside puller rules (counter/reverse) for each position and then draw in the blocking for all players on six given play calls versus an odd and even defense.

- You fill in blocking rules for the weakside isolation play (X-block play) for each position and then draw in the blocking for all players on four given play calls versus an odd and even defense.

- We have an index of blocking calls how to call double-team blocks and fold blocks.

The high school coach I met in Tennessee was Roger Holmes, and he was 39 years old. He was making 42 grand as a teacher-coach in Tennessee. When I talked with Herschel Moore of Cumberland University, he told me I needed to go to visit the high school coaches in Georgia if I really wanted to learn about the wing-T because they are a lot more serious about football in Georgia. He said they pay very well in Georgia. So the next year, Roger Holmes moved to Dublin High School in Georgia to coach high school football. His salary was $81,000 in Georgia.

In his first year in Georgia, he went all the way to the state championship game. I asked Roger what he was going to do next. He replied, "I am going to see the athletic director to see if I can renegotiate my contract. I am going to ask for 100 grand." This past year, his team set the scoring record in Georgia using the same rules he used before.

I want to go over our PRIDE chart that we use to motivate the players in everything they do for our team. We spell out the word P-R-I-D-E.

P-R-I-D-E

- P – Pay the price. Everything that is worthwhile has a value. Give every bit of talent to see our team to be successful.

- R – Respect. We must respect our opponents, teammates, and coaches. Sometimes it will be necessary to sacrifice personal desires for the welfare of the team.

- I – Intelligence. Understand our system thoroughly so that we can attain maximum benefit from it. Poised teams are the ones that come through in the clutch and win the close games. Know your rules on each play.

- D – Discipline. Self-discipline is the greatest discipline. In order to be successful, it is important that the team be disciplined in its approach to the game. Coaches set rules and adhere to them.

- E – Execution. Learn to execute fundamental football skills. Learning these skills depends on repeating them over and over. Your ability to out-technique your opponent will allow you to beat stronger and faster foes. Work at it.

Offensive Line Blocking Rules

0-X (Trap)

8 – Running lane

7 – Fill block for #6. If even call, check and block linebacker.

6 – Trap first man on the line of scrimmage past the center and #6.

C – Post. If not there, lead (block back). Choke call if the line-of-scrimmage defender is on center and #6.

4 – Lead. If not there, load linebacker. If not there, influence out after #7 has cleared. Mike call (#3) block linebacker.

3 – Block first linebacker on square.

2 – Running lane

1-Special

8 – Running lane

7 – Release flat for running lane.

6 – Pull right up hole. Block Sam linebacker.

C – Ace to area, then block back over #6.

4 – Pull right two and a half yards deep. Block first man outside wingback block.

3 – Down block.

2 – Down block.

3-GX

8 – Running lane

7 – Fill for #6. If even call, check and block linebacker.

6 – Pull right and lead up hole.

C – Ace to area, then block back over #6.

4 – Pull and trap from #2 (end) out.

3 – Down block.

2 – Lead. If not there, block linebacker. Block zero. If he is not there influence and block outside (game plan).

5-X (Trap)

8 – Running lane

7 – First linebacker on square

6 – Lead. If not there, loaded linebacker. If not there, influence out after #5 has cleared. Mike call (#7) block linebacker.

C – Post. If not there, lead (block back). Choke call if the line-of-scrimmage defender is on center and #4.

4 – Trap first man on line of scrimmage past 5 edge.

3 – Fill for #4. If even call, check and block the linebacker.

2 – Running lane

9-Special

8 – Down block.

7 – Down block.

6 – Pull left two and a half yards deep. Block first man outside the wingback's block.

C – Ace to area, then block back over #4.

4 – Pull left up in the hole. Block Sam linebacker.

3 – Release flat for running lane.

2 – Running lane

7-GX

8 – Lead. If not there, block linebacker. Block zero. If not there, influence and block outside (game plan).

7 – Down block.

6 – Pull and trap from #8 (end) out.

C – Ace to area, then block back over #6.

4 – Pull left, then lead up in the hole.

3 – Fill for #4. If even, call check and block the linebacker.

2 – Running lane

I am going to cover the 1-through-9 rules. We number each person, and not the gaps. If the play is going to the right, we call it the playside (Diagram #1). Away from where the play is going is called the backside.

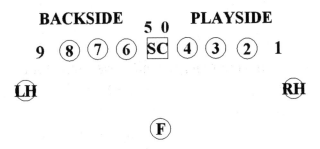

Diagram #1. Playside Numbering Right

If the play is going to the left, it becomes the playside (Diagram #2). Away from that side is called the backside.

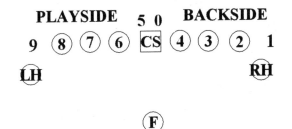

Diagram #2. Playside Numbering Left

We can run our offense out of different formations. I give the players a workbook and video of the blocking system.

Our players on the playside are the center, guard, tackle, and end. On the backside we have our X, our W, and the offside guard. If we pull both guards, we call it "special" (Diagram #3). We use

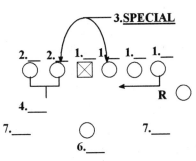

Diagram #3. Both Guards Pull – Special

this on our buck-sweep play and we call it 21 special. I will cover more on that as we go through this system.

If both X and W pull, such as a counter trey play, we call that Z. If the tight end pulls and we are stacked the other way, we call it R for reverse. A crisscross for us would be X reverse. The X would pull and the reverse would go. The fullback is lettered with Y, and the halfback is the K.

We read the play and number the man in our blocking calls. We play a number on the man called. This is the edge (Diagram #4). The call is 82 G-Bob. We are going to the 2 man, which is our tight end.

Diagram #4. 82 G-Bob - 2

We ask the players to draw all kick-out blocks going uphill toward the defensive player. Remember to kick-out just past the edge (Diagram #5).

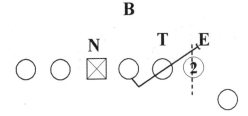

Diagram #5. 82 G-Bob – Kick-out

After the players understand this rule, we have them draw in the blocking for the other offensive players.

We run our plays in series. The linemen only need to know the last number of the play called. When he has a player pulling to the playside, the rule is for everyone else to block down on the play. Bob means we are pulling the guard and we are blocking B-O-B, which means "back on backer."

If you are a player behind the puller, the rule is to scoop block and climb to the next level. If the player does not encounter a linebacker, he goes ahead to the secondary to block.

The second one on the video, this is what we have the players fill out:

- Playside lineman player letters are C-G-T-E.
- The backside lineman player letters are X and W.
- If both guards pull, it is called special.
- If both X and W pull, it is termed Z.
- If the tight end pulls, it is termed R.
- The fullback is a backside puller and his letter is Y.
- The halfback's letter is K.

I am going to show you some diagrams of how we block the plays. First is the 82 G-Bob play (Diagram #6).

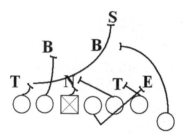

Diagram #6. 82 G-Bob – Blocks

To change the play up, we can call 83 G-Bib. Now we are running the back inside to the linebacker (Diagram #7).

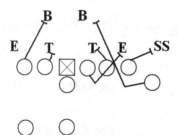

Diagram #7. 83 G-Bib

This is simple to the kids once they understand the concepts. If you have a playside puller, and in this case it is the guard, we block down. It is a simple rule that you can add to any offense.

Now I want to go over the rules for the playside and backside pullers. The rule is to pull and gain depth. We like them to pull getting two and a half yards deep. We want them to pull and get up the alley. The rule for men ahead of the playside pullers is to block down. The rule for the players between the two pullers is to block man. If they are behind the backside puller, the rule is to scoop block. An example is our 21 G-X special (Diagram #8).

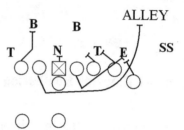

Diagram #8. 21 G-X – Special

We have a simple rule when we use two letters in a play. The first letter indicates who is pulling and coming up the alley to take the linebacker. The first letter is always the blocker that kicks out. The second letter is for the block that is coming from the side. We can change our blocking assignments very quickly if we are having a problem with the blocking on a play.

We must make a special point for the backside guard to get depth when he pulls. If he does not get depth, he will run into the block by the wingback.

On our 21 EX play, it is a little different. The first letter indicates the man pulling and the second letter indicates the man blocking on the side. If we call 29 TX, we would pull the tackle first and have the X block to the side. On 29 KG stretch, we pull the fullback and guard. We scoop the backside.

Our one backside puller is our trap play. Here is an example. We call the play 20 X. The center is the number-5 man, but he is also the zero man. We make the center's right shoulder the zero and the left shoulder a 5 call. If we call 20, we know the play is going to the right shoulder of the center. If we call 25 trap, we know it is going to the center's left shoulder. He is called the "call man." Here are the rules on the play.

The rule for the players behind the backside puller is to scoop block. The rule for the backside puller is to pull and kick-out. The rule for the called-man blocker is to post, and then to lead. The first player past the hole on the edge is going to lead, load to the linebacker, and influence (Diagram #9).

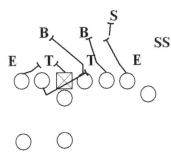

Diagram #9. 20 X

I know you will not be able to follow me on the blocking on the overhead. I am going to go through these fast and if you have questions, I will visit with you.

On the counter and reverse plays, we have similar rules. The rule for the man behind the pullers is to scoop block. The rule for the first backside puller is to kick-out. The rule for the second backside puller is to block the alley. The rule for the called-man blocker is to post, or lead block. The first player past the hole, or the edge, is to lead, load block, or influence block on the play. The blue rule is to block down.

There are many different ways of running the counter and reverse plays with two backside pullers. The rules on two backside pullers on counter/reverse plays remain the same. The man behind the puller has the scoop rule. The rule for the first backside puller is to kick-out. The rule for the second backside puller is the alley. The man called

has the post or lead block. The rule for the first player past the hole (edge) is to lead, load block, or influence.

If we have trouble blocking on the rules, we can call blue. If we add the word blue, everyone is to block down. We block down all the way to the pulling guard and he kicks out. We could run the 82 Z blue play and block down. We can run jet motion or no motion at all on the play.

A point I want to make is that our fullback is considered a backside puller at all times. Our line knows this ahead of time.

We got away from calling crisscross and just started calling the plays reverse. We can change the blocking a lot easier on the reverse plays. On 36 Y reverse, the Y and R are backside pullers. The call man is the left guard and he is number 6. His rule is post-lead. Here he has to lead block. The Y reverse is the fullback. He is going to kick-out. We can use jet motion or we can run it without motion.

On the isolation plays, we are looking for the old X-block plays. The rule for the called man is gap, down, or pull and kick-out. The tackle's rule is to block down, or to block onside. The rule for the players behind the blockers is to scoop block. We define the TUG call: tackle, under, and guard.

We use some terms to make the plays simple. We have the waggle plays, and we used to call it 21 waggle. Now we just call that play boot at 1. On the waggle for us, both guards are going the opposite way, or the wrong way.

My time is up. I want to thank you for your attention.

THE 3-3 STAND-UP DEFENSE

Byrnes High School, South Carolina

Thank you for that introduction. It is a pleasure to be here today. I appreciate you guys being here. I am going to make this very informal. I am going to talk about our defense. I hope you get something out of it. What we do is a little different, but it fits our players and it fits me as a coach. On our defense, all 11 of our players stand up.

That may seem as if we are unsound, but we have won four state championships in a row. I do not want to come off as if I know everything. I do not know anything except what we do at Byrnes High School. I do not know if we can take this defense anywhere else and win. I have no idea. To play this defense, you must be able to run. If you cannot run and all 11 of them are standing up, the offense will run over you. Our defenders will run around blocks to get to the football.

I want to show you the general idea via a PowerPoint presentation, and then I will go into more detail to explain the defense. At the end I will show the defense on film.

Building the Program

- We had 28 players in 1995; now we have over 100.
- In 1995, 10 players ran sub-4.9; now over 45 do.
- We scored 138 points in 1995; we scored 776 points in 2005.
- We allowed 32 points in 1995; we allowed 9.5 points in 2005.
- We threw nine touchdowns in 1995; we threw 73 in 2005.
- Our budget was $20,000 in 1995; it was over $100,000 in 2005.

When I came to Byrnes High School, we started with 28 players on the team. I won one game the first year and two games the second year. Over the last four years, we are 56-1. I do not know what we are doing, but we are doing something that our players believe in. We now have 260 players in the program.

We play Glades Central High School of Florida on ESPN at 12 noon on August 26. They have a well-established program. They have 27 ex-players in the NFL. We had one player make it to the pros and he plays in the NFL in Europe. They are a lot better than we are. We go to Cincinnati to play Moeller High School on TV on September 16.

In 1995, which was my first year, we had 10 players run under 4.9. Right now, we have 25 players who run under 4.9. I cannot take credit for all of that because all of our players run track. In 1995, we scored 138 points on offense. Last year we scored 776 points. In 1995, we allowed 32 points per game. Last year we averaged 9.5 allowed points per game. We threw for nine touchdowns in 1995 and 73 last year. In 1995, when we gave up 36 points per game, we were everyone's homecoming game. Now we cannot get anyone to play us. We have to play Glades Central High School from Florida, and we have to go up to Cincinnati to play Moeller High School to get games. Not many teams in our area want to play us.

In 1995, our football budget was $19,800. In 2005, our football budget was $102,000. Our touchdown club raised over $100,000 last year. I do not say that to be bragging, I say this because we have many loyal people in our program. They are going to install a $350,000 scoreboard next year.

The first year I taught seven out of eight periods in the school day. Next year I will not teach any classes. I am telling you this to let you know you need to be patient in your program.

In our program, we started out by focusing our entire program on offense. When we get to the championship season, we focus on defense. We focus on defensive alignment. Before practice every day, we put our players through R-and-R. They work on reaction and recognition. We want our players to be able to recognize certain formation and certain tendencies.

Just for curiosity's sake, how many of you have an editing system in your school? Can you break down films of the opponents? I know it is a big investment and it costs a lot of money to begin with, but it is worth it. We give our players a DVD of the opponents and their tendencies on Sunday. When they come to practice on Monday, they know what the opponents' best plays are. In high school football, most teams have strong tendencies in certain formations. Our players will know those tendencies and they will know the plays the offense is likely to run. We recognize and react to certain formations.

This next thing I learned from Coach Nick Hyder. He was a coach at Valdosta High School in Georgia. I heard him speak at this clinic many years ago. He talked about being a collision expert. When I was younger, my thoughts were you had to be an X-and-O expert. He changed our entire terminology. To play the game of football, you have to be able to block and tackle. Those are the most fundamental skills, and if you cannot execute those skills, you will not win.

In 1998, we had a state championship team's defensive coordinator come to watch us practice. I could not wait until practice was over to see what he had to say. I said, "Mike, what did you think about our practice?" He told me this. "I saw you run a bunch of plays, and a lot of drills, but I did not any blocking and tackling."

I told him we had done those drills earlier in the week. He told me that to be a good football player,

you have to tackle every day. The moral of that story is this: today in our practices, we block and tackle every day. We have board drills for our offensive and defensive linemen every day.

We run our nitro drill every day for ten minutes. We run the old Oklahoma drill every day. We go one-on-one everyday. We have offensive linemen against defensive linemen and a linebacker. We work a tackling circuit every day. We are probably the only team that has a tackling drill on Thursday before our games on Friday. We have become collision experts. Our players have become successful at tackling and they get better every year. In our circuit we head-on-tackle, angle tackle, tackle on the sled, and many other drills.

Be Good at Something

- Focus of all workouts/practices
  - ✓ Speed and agility
  - ✓ Passing game
    - ○ Protection
    - ○ Quarterback development
    - ○ High-percentage passing
  - ✓ Defensive alignments
  - ✓ Collision technique (tackling and blocking)

We want speed and agility at all positions. If you cannot run, you play offensive line for us. It does not matter the size of the player; if he cannot run, he cannot play defense in our scheme. Even in short-yardage situations, we do not believe in putting some big player in the middle of our defense. We do not do it.

Rebel Defense

- Focus on tackling.
- Work the tackle strip circuit.
- Focus on speed and agility at all positions.
- Create an atmosphere of wanting to play for the strike force.
- Stop the run; we gave up four rush touchdowns in 15 games in 2005.

We want to create an atmosphere for our players for the strike force. We do all kinds of things to motivate our players about playing defense. When we started our program, we concentrated on the offense. We had all of our good players on the offensive side of the ball. We had to change our way of thinking.

We give a helmet every Sunday for the Player of the Week. We give a green-beret helmet that we have painted silver and which have the words "strike force" on it. It is a big deal for our kids to get that strike-force helmet. Also, we give them "dog tags" with their names on them if they are selected as a Player of the Week. We give them a chain with a dog tag similar as the dog tags used in the military. We give a dog-tag award every week for the Defensive Player of the Week. Our players love to get those dog tags with their names on them. We try to point out to them, "You win games with offense, but you win championships with defense."

Key Thoughts on Defense

- A defense cannot do everything.
- Attempt to stop or neutralize the greatest offensive threats.
- Move around on defense.
- Attack the quarterback. (The best pass defense is a strong rush.) Try to send five to eight rushers.
- Team quickness and reaction time are critical to our defense.
- Size is not an issue.

On defense, we want to stop the run. We pride ourselves on our ability to stop the run. We want our players to know how many yards they are giving up per rushing down. We play 4A football in South Carolina. We have won four state championships in a row. In 2005, we gave up four rushing touchdowns the entire year. That amounts to 15 games in the season. That is tough to do, especially when we are playing with a three-man front three-quarters of the time.

Building the Defense

- Play linebackers at defensive line.
- Play larger defensive backs at the linebacker positions.
- Play the most agile/hostile athletes at defensive back.
- Practice one position for one hour and 45 minutes
- We were successful with our offense; we won championships with our defense.

Here is what we do on defense. We play linebackers in our defensive alignment. Not one kid on our defense weighs over 198 pounds. We play larger defensive backs at linebackers. We play the most agile and hostile players as defensive backs. The biggest and meanest hostile defensive backs play at the strong-safety position. We call the safeties "swords." They are savers and they are mean—and hostile. The corners have to be fast because we play a lot of man coverage. However, we can play cover 3 and cover 2.

We practice at one position for one hour and 45 minutes. For a player to become good on defense, you have to put him at one position and coach the fire out of him. He has to understand what other teams are trying to do to him in this defense.

We practice one hour and 45 minutes on defense, and 20 minutes on special teams. We want to be off the field in around two hours, or two hours and five minutes.

We were successful with our offense, but we won championships with our defense. We believe this very strongly. We have a sign in our locker room that has that written on it. Our defensive coordinator works hard and the players have a lot of respect for him. They work hard for him.

The 3-3 Stand-Up Defense

- Defenses should appear to be distortions of reality.
- Schemes do not win games; people do.

- Great defenses have speed and quickness, and play with emotion.
- How we win on defense:
- Neutralize the offense's best plays,
- Tackle well.
- Run to the ball on every play; demand it.

Our defense is a distortion of reality. When we line up on an offensive tackle—and we align head up, that offensive tackle should never know where the defensive man is going. We very seldom line up in a gap. We may end up in the gap, but we are not going to line up in the gap.

The offensive tackle does not know if we are going inside or outside. If we line up in the gap, we do not stay there. If we line up inside the offensive blocker, we probably will go outside of him. However, he will not know that.

Our defensive linemen get down on all fours and scramble around on the line of scrimmage. Before the offense snaps the ball, the defenders stand up. We work hard the week before the game to find out the offense's snap count. We will find a way to figure that out a week before the game.

Schemes do not win games. I had to learn that the hard way. I always thought that meant something about X's and O's and alignments on defense. To play defense, you must have speed and quickness and play with emotion. We harp on running to the football. To play defense, you must run to the ball like your life depended on you getting there.

When we have a seven-on-seven drill, it is for one simple reason. We can coach our players to get to the ball. When we are in a seven-on-seven drill, we can coach them on the line. We do not worry about formations. We are going to get the quarterback. We are not going to sit in coverage.

What We Base Our Defense On

When we come in for our meeting on Sunday, we break down the opponent's film. We want to stop the offense's best plays. We view the opponent's tape and we rank the opponent's best plays. We put them in rank order of their best plays. Usually they have three plays they are good at running. If they are a good team, they may have five top plays. We set our defense to stop those plays. If the tailback is the key to their offense, he is the player we want to stop. It does not matter what defense we are playing.

If we play a wing-T team and the tailback is their best player, everyone is going to be reading on him. If the wingbacks are the best players, we cross key them and take them out of the equation. If the fullback is the man, all three linebackers will be keying him. We are going to take out your best play. We are going to take out your best player. We are going to make sure we can tackle him. We are going to get to the football and make sure we gang tackle. I think the difficulty of open-field tackling is overrated. I played safety in college. I practiced open-field tackling in practice, but in the games, I always found myself turning the runner into the pursuit.

The strong safety wants to build a wall so the back does not cross his face. He knows he has a corner outside and he has nine other players coming from the inside on an angle to make the tackle.

What Is Our Defense?

- *What is it?* An eight-man front defense with most, if not all, defenders standing up and constantly moving. Defensive end is up or down, his option.
- *From where does it come?* It is not new; it began in the late 1960s and early '70s in high school football.
- *Why use it?* It has evolved into an excellent way of attacking a shotgun-snap offense. Players love it! It is a great scheme for little, quick people to showcase their talents.

Our defense is an eight-man front (Diagram #1). Most of the time we have all eight of the defenders in a two-point stance. The defenders are standing up and most of the time there is constant movement. The defensive ends are always in a two-point stance. People may refer to our defense as a 3-3-5, or a 3-5-3. The thing we are going to do is have an eight-man umbrella around the football.

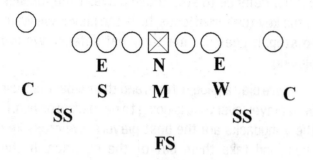

Diagram #1. Eight-Man Front

It is basically a 3-3 alignment, but we do not call it a 3-3 because all the defenders are standing in the umbrella. We can put the Mike linebacker and end up in a 4-2 look, but the entire eight-man front is going to be in the box on most of the defense we play.

Where Did This Defense Come From?

I had a coach that used to coach with me who is now 67 years old. His name is Mike Martin. He saw the defense at Salem College in West Virginia. He showed me a lot of tapes on this defense. Mike gave me a lot of tapes to watch because two or three teams from up in the mountains were running this defense.

They designed the defense to disguise the pass rush. The players on the defense were shifting and jumping around all over the place. They tried to get the offensive line to jump offside and keep them confused. They wanted to mess up their blocking schemes. They would jump all over the line of scrimmage. They would drop down, do a push-up, hop back up, and fake a blitz in one of the gaps.

We started using this defense against shotgun teams. We used the defense on third-and-long situations. We stood everyone up so we could rush the quarterback. We stood them up so they could see the ball.

When you think about the cadence in the shotgun snap, the center is the one calling the snap.

The quarterback is raising his leg, but the center is in charge of snapping the ball. We played four teams that used the shotgun offense and we gave those shotgun teams fits with the defense.

It looked so good we thought we should be doing this on every down. We looked at our roster and discovered we had only 12 players over 200 pounds. However, we had a bunch of fast players. We decided to use all of the fast players, put them around the line of scrimmage, and mess with people. We could score a bunch of points on offense and it might be fun.

We gave our little, quick players a chance to be successful. We gave them a chance to play and they were really aggressive. Our nose guard weighed 160 pounds in 2002. He could power-clean 360 pounds. We want to get him playing for us. He ended up as our nose guard. It is amazing how the defense evolved with a bunch of little kids running around and chasing the football. It was great for our high school.

What Are the Strong Points?

This defense gives the offense many different "defensive looks" and does not broadcast the stunts and coverages. You can move the defense on each down because all the players are almost all interchangeable. The movement and stunt disguise any intentions. We can put all eight of the defenders on the line of scrimmage, each one with his outside foot back. That is so they can bail off the line. We do not want the inside back. This drives offensive linemen crazy. The defense operates on speed and quickness, and not size and strength. It allows for easy adjustments.

What Are the Weak Points?

The weakness of the defense is short yardage and goal-line situations. What do you think we practice the most on? Short yardage and goal-line situations. When we get into those situations, we have to get into something to plug more gaps. Playing this defense, we gave up 2.9 yards per rush on this defense last year.

Why Do We Run This Defense?

- We experimented with various forms of the rebel defense in the 2000 football season at Byrnes versus shotgun/one-back offenses. Since that time, it has evolved into our primary defensive package.

- We run a basic eight-man-front scheme with eight defenders on or near the line of scrimmage in constant movement.

- All or most of these defenders are standing up. It allows us to read or penetrate with an attacking style. It is subject to change on a weekly basis to give us the best personnel match-ups and to ensure our ability to defend what the offense does best.

- The rebel defense has helped us produce four straight 4A state championships (with a four-year record in South Carolina of 56-1)

This is our primary defense. We run eight men on or near the line of scrimmage. We have constant movement on the defense. All of our defenders are standing up. This allows us to read and to penetrate the offense. When we say "read" in this defense, it is not like the read in the old 50 scheme. We work on the match-up and defend what the offense does best. We are a big-sweep team so we put the strong safety outside along with the outside linebacker. We slant the nose guard in that direction and blow the Mike linebacker through the B gap. We are coming to get you. We make sure we take away the sweep.

When we line up, we know the defense is not good against the pass. If we are in man free, the defense is not good against the pass. We have to get to the quarterback in order for us to be successful. If you have a great receiver, we put a corner in his face, and we are going to put a safety over the top.

The defense is always on the move, because we want the offense to have to hit a moving target. We are going to attack the quarterback. We make sure the quarterback does not have a lot of time to throw the ball. We want to hit him on every play. By the third quarter, he is not looking to pass; he is looking to pull the ball down and run. We want to get

many defenders in his face. We send five to eight rushers in our pass-rush scheme. We are not going to sit back in coverage and try to cover receivers. We are going to go get the quarterback.

Key Thoughts on Defense

- A defense cannot do everything.
- Attempt to stop or neutralize the greatest offensive threats.
- Move around on defense.
- Attack the quarterback. (The best pass defense is a strong rush.) Try to send five to eight rushers
- Team quickness and reaction time are critical to our defense.
- Size is not an issue.
- Rarely run the same defense two times in a row.
- Script and practice third-down situations every day. Hold opponents below 35 percent of third-down attempts.
- 2005 opponents converted 29 percent of third downs.
- Prepare for and practice against the unseen and the unexpected.
- Keep something in your pocket for the second half.
- Move around four different fronts.

In our defense, size is no issue. We do not care how big the defenders are. Our left defensive end to our left side is 6'0" and 185 pounds. The right defensive end is 6'0", 215 pounds, and runs a 4.5 in the 40. The nose guard is 5'8" and 180 pounds. The three linebackers are clones. The Mike linebacker is 6'2", 190 pounds, and runs 4.6 in the 40. The other two linebackers and 5'9" and 200 pounds, and the other one is 190 pounds, but they both run 4.5 in the 40.

One of the savers, or strong safety, is 5'8", 130 pounds, and runs 4.38 in the 40. He was in Texas over the past week and ran at that time out there. The other saver is 5'7" and 150 pounds. The free safety is a big defensive back. He is 6'3" and 180 pounds. The corners are 5'8" and 150 pounds, but they can run.

The other thing we do to find our defensive players is to do our agilities. If a player can run better than 4.7, and they can cut and change direction, they can play defense for us. We practice the third-down situation every day. Very seldom do we run the same defense. We want to hold our opponents to 35 percent efficiency rate on third down. If you feel like you are not doing a good job on defense, go back and check your third-down plays. If you cannot compete on third down, you will not win many games. This past year we held teams to 29 percent on third down. We have stats people that gives us the percentages in all our defensive categories after the game.

You need to prepare for and practice the unseen and unexpected plays. Make sure you go over trick and gadget plays in practice, especially on Wednesday and Thursday. On Monday and Tuesday, practice the defense that stops what the offense hangs their hat on. On Wednesday and Thursday, throw in the wrinkles. Run the reverses, halfback passes, and anything you think the offense might do. Make sure you try to do something with the unbalanced line.

This scheme is a balanced defense. Put in the unbalanced look to make sure you match up correctly with the formation. Run both unbalanced run formations and pass formations.

Always keep something in your pocket for the second half. If you have done a good job stopping the offense in the first half, keep something new for the second half. The offense will adjust to things that have been successful for you in the first half. If they solve their problems, have something they have not seen for the second half. We want to let our kids know we are saving something for the second half.

Move around in your defensive front. We try to use four different fronts. Those are the types of defense we run.

I have shown you the base 3-5 earlier in the lecture. In the 3-4 defense, we have a Sam linebacker that gets into a tilt 9 technique on the tight end (Diagram #2).

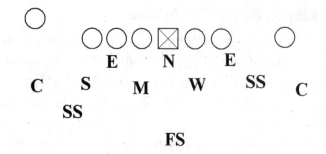

Diagram #2. 3-4-4

We align in a regular 3-3, with the strong safeties on the outside helping on the number-one receivers (Diagram #3).

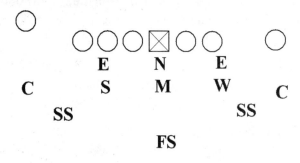

Diagram #3. 3-3-5

We align in a regular 3-3, with the strong safeties on the outside helping on the number-one receivers (Diagram #4).

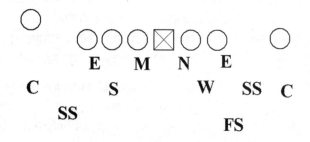

Diagram #4. 4-2

We can get into a 4-3 defense. When we go to that defense, we substitute a fourth lineman for a strong safety (Diagram #5).

In the 4-4 alignment, we put the Mike linebacker down and stack the strong safeties behind the defensive ends aligned on the tight ends (Diagram #6).

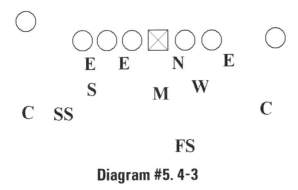

Diagram #5. 4-3

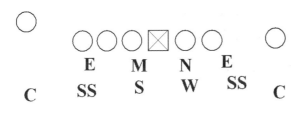

Diagram #6. 4-4

The last defense is the bear front, in which we let the linebackers do the adjustments (Diagram #7).

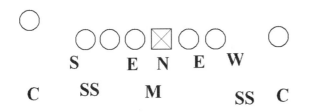

Diagram #7. Bear

We go through those schemes every single day because we do not run a base defense. I want to show you how far we have come with our personnel.

This defense has endless possibilities for stunts. You can run any combination of stunts from all of the alignments. You must be able to communicate the stunt. Let me cover a few of our favorite stunts. You can create your own terminology to name the stunts.

In the first stunts, both outside linebackers blitz the B gap with the strong safety coming off the edge (Diagram #8).

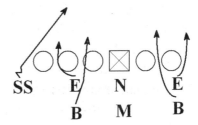

Diagram #8. Linebackers and Strong Safety Blitz

The next stunt is similar to the first stunt. We reverse the blitz pattern of the linebackers and the ends (Diagram #9).

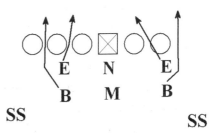

Diagram #9. Linebackers Stunt to C Gap

Here the down line slants to the tight end (Diagram #10). Both strong safeties come off the edges, and the strongside linebacker blows the B gap.

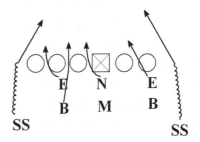

Diagram #10. Double Bullets Blitz

The defensive line slants to the openside of the formation on this next blitz (Diagram #11). The weakside linebacker shoots the B gap and the strongside safety comes off the edge.

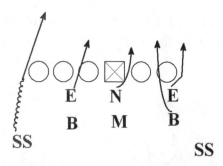

Diagram #11. Slant to the Weakside

The next stunt is the pinch blitz (Diagram #12). The defensive ends pinch inside to the B gap. The weak safety blitzes from the edge, and the strongside linebacker fires the C gap. The noseguard slants to the weakside A gap.

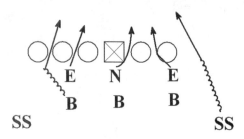

Diagram #12. Weakside Pinch Blitz

This stunt is the opposite of the stunt run to the weakside (Diagram #13).

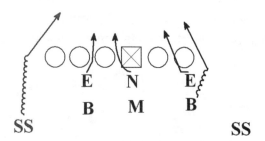

Diagram #13. Strongside Pinch Blitz

We use two primary schemes on this defense to get maximum coverage in the secondary. The first is cover-3 zone utilizing five under defenders (Diagram #14).

You can run the next scheme by bringing the strongside safety or the weakside safety (Diagram #15). This gives us a four-man rush and seven defenders in the secondary. We play three-deep, and the linebacker to the side of the blitz covers the flat.

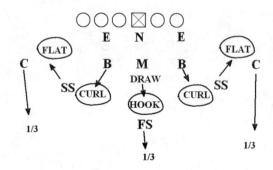

Diagram #14. Cover 3 — Drop Eight Defenders

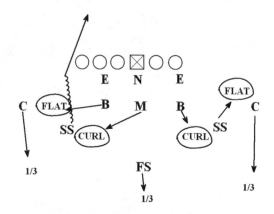

Diagram #15. Cover 3 — Strong Safety Blitz

In this defense, we try to call them by city names. South Carolina was using this defense when Charlie Strong was coaching there. Also, Mississippi State was using the defense. We went to Memphis State to study Joe Lee Dunn to see what he was doing on defense. We thought we could get something from him.

At first, we thought we could sit our linebackers inside and let them play like they play at South Carolina. We thought we could take the fullback on with the inside shoulder and make the play. We figured out we could not play it that way. We were not good enough to sit in our base defense. We ended up with the Mike linebacker covering the B gap. The Sam and Will linebackers became cover linebackers. The cover linebackers did not have to take on the isolation play. That gap was taken care of. The ball was bounced to the outside. He was able to take on the fullback in a glancing shot instead of straight on.

We figured out that we only had one linebacker in our scheme that had to plug the gap and that was the Mike linebacker. The other defenders just went to the football. We needed our strong safeties to be the run-support players. We found out that was not the way it was, because we played a lot of man-free coverage.

When we played man-free coverage, we decided to put the big, strong safety in the blitz package. He lined up six yards off the ball and one yard outside the tight end. We put our corners that really like to hit, as savers. All of a sudden, the defense started to fall into place. We have a plugger, two strong safeties, and two free safeties that can play man coverage.

What kind of front are we going to use in our defense? We are going to look at the personnel. If we have a running back that "has no hands," we put him at the nose-guard position. He understands what offenses are doing. Here is an example. If the offense runs a sweep, the nose man can make the play a lot of the time. He understands what the offense is trying to do and he can get outside and make the play. Most defensive linemen get tied up inside and chase the play. The nose man can flatten out and get outside coming down the line of scrimmage because he understands the purpose of the play.

The defensive ends are bigger, stronger, linebacker-type players. I hope this helps you. I wish someone had told me about this defense two years ago. It would have saved us a lot of time and perhaps we could have won more games.

I hope you got something out of this lecture. I appreciate your attention. God bless all of you, and good luck next year.

THE SPRINT-OUT PASSING GAME

Opelika High School, Alabama

Today I am quite certain that I do not know as much about football as some other people, but I have done a good job of taking things from other coaches. Someone once told me that if you steal everything you know from one person, it is plagiarism. If you steal everything you know from a number of coaches, it is research. Our offense is a product of good research.

My coaching career underwent a big change last summer. I met Dennis Parker, a 31-year veteran of high school coaching in Texas. Coach Parker had been a very successful coach in Texas and has retired. He has written a character-education book, Changing Lives. If you would like to know more about the book, you may go to his website: www.coachingtochangelives.com.

Coach Parker retired and put together this manual for coaching. We have all heard that athletics build character, and as coaches we want to believe that. The thought that athletics teach character is not necessarily true. What Coach Parker says is that if athletics teach character, then the highest form of athlete would have the highest form of character. We all understand that would not be true. Athletics in itself does not teach character; coaches do. We all want to teach our players the lessons of good character, and we want to teach them how to be better people. However, none of us ever had a class in character-building. His book is a program that actually teaches one how to teach character. Coach Parker is 68 years old and has decided to take a coaching job in Mesa, Arizona. He is an amazing person and is winning games now at a place where no one wanted to coach. We took his program and instilled his ideas into our team.

Two years ago, we went 6-4 and we were not very good. We also had a large number of players who were not a great deal of fun to be around. We had numerous problems, including grade problems. We had to remove five of our starters from our football team. One of those five was a Division I prospect. He could not keep himself out of trouble.

We introduced character education into our program this summer and we did not have one player receive an office referral during this season. We have talked to our teachers about this program and twelve teachers in our school have begun to teach character education. Those teachers have been a part of a large reduction in office referrals in our school in comparison to last year. I don't know how much of that is due to character education, but I do know that 70 of our 85 players did not make a grade below a C level this season. I believe that made a difference in our level of success this season. We went from a 6-4 team to a squad that made the city finals and lost in the final 22 seconds of the game.

I am going to talk about our sprint passing game. We have developed into a team that does a large number of things. We have been a double-slot offense that runs the midline option. We tend to build our offense around what personnel we have. We are the 41st-largest high school in Alabama and we are playing against the largest schools in the state. We don't get a chance to pick our own players and we have to find a way to best use the level of talent that we have. Hoover High School is the second-largest school in the state and has won the last four championships in a row in Alabama, and we have to compete against schools like that. I think the sprint passing game gives our kids a chance to be successful, and the way we teach it makes sense to our players.

The first thing I will talk about is our eagle route. Everyone in here runs curl-flat schemes. Our eagle route is our curl-flat scheme. It is a great route package against teams that play cover 3. We are a running football team, so we see a great deal of eight-man fronts with a cover-3 shell. I am our offensive line coach and I am going to try to stay away from talking about protection. If I begin to talk protection, we will never get to the remainder of our passing game.

The way we call our sprint game is that we will number our receivers from the sideline in to the football. In our eagle series, our number-one receiver will run a 12-yard curl route. He is going to start upfield, sell the vertical, and then work to an open curl area. He is taught to come back to the football. While it is a 12-yard route, we do not always break the curl at the same place. We try to recognize where the underneath coverage is located.

Where we go with the curl may depend greatly on the linebacker. If he is hanging inside, we may sit the curl down and work directly back to the ball. If the linebacker is flying into the flat area, we may have to work the curl back inside. Our playside number-two receiver is going to run the flat route. If we are in a slot formation, we run this as a bubble route, four yards from the sideline and two yards down the field, and then we teach him to sit down.

If we are in a tight alignment, we run a shoot-flat route. If we get any type of man coverage against him, the number-two receiver will turn his flat route into a wheel and go upfield. I am sure we are teaching the same things that many of you are telling your players. If it is zone, sit down in the open area. If it is man, keep going. If we have a number-three receiver on the playside, he will run a corner route. We very seldom run this route with three receivers to the playside. Our backside rules are the same on every sprint pass that we have.

If we are in a wide alignment, our receiver runs a skinny post. If we are in a tight alignment, the receiver will run a drag route. If we see something that makes us think that the defense is overrotating, we can give our quarterback a signal to throw to the backside post (Diagram #1).

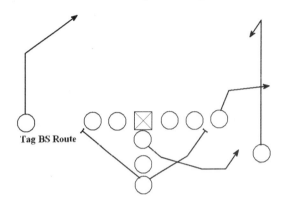

Tag BS Route

Diagram #1. Backside Throwback

We teach our quarterback to pre-snap read the coverage. In terms of throwing the ball, we teach him to read receivers. If our primary receiver is open, throw him the ball. On the eagle sprint-out, we will be reading curl-to-flat. We also teach that if the defense loses outside contain, we can run the football. We will start our spring practice in our base formation, which is a pro formation.

In that formation, the flanker would be running the curl route and since the tight end is tight, he would be running a flat. The backside is wide, so his route would be a post.

That post can be good for you if the secondary really takes off running toward your sprintside. If we are in a double-slot offense, it would be the same rules on the sprintside, but the backside has changed since it now has two receivers (Diagram #2). The inside slot is tight, so he would run a drag route. The split receiver would follow his rule and run a post. No matter what set you begin with, there is a place for this in your offense.

When we were a double-slot offense, we used a lot of motion in our option and jet-sweep game. We ran a lot of jet sweep. If we ran this with the motion, the motion receiver would be the person to

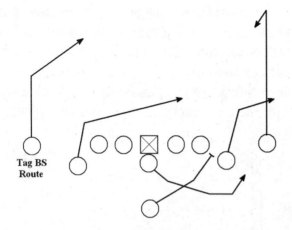

Diagram #2. Double Slot – Post Route

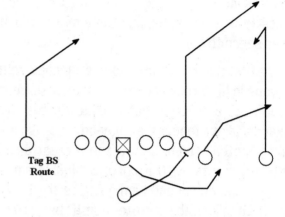

Diagram #3. Smash Concept

run the number-three rule, and to run the corner route. We have also spent time in shotgun formations and we worked hard on running the number-two receiver on the bubble route. It is very important that he keep his route at least four yards from the sideline. We would like him to get two yards up the field, sit down, and look back. We have found that it is an easier throw and an easier catch to allow the receiver to get upfield and sit down for the ball.

I realize this is nothing mind-boggling, but we spend a great deal of time in the summer working this route. Many times, we will take multiple quarterbacks and work multiple routes with balls being thrown to all of the receivers. This allows us to get more repetitions than if we were only throwing one ball at a time. We really like our eagle route against eight-man-front teams. Those teams are limited in their coverage schemes and will usually be cover 3, or some sort of man coverage.

The next sprint-out we teach our players is our smash concept. Our playside number-one runs a flat route, depending on coverage and alignment (Diagram #3). If we get soft coverage, we run a hitch. If we have any type of press coverage, we run a pivot route. We start with a slant look and pivot back out to the flat. The playside number-two receiver runs a 10-yard corner route. We tell him to run toward the flag and let the quarterback lead him to the sideline with the ball. The playside number-three receiver runs a vertical.

We really like to do this against a cover-2 look so that the safety has to hang inside on the vertical. That also allows the backside post to be important if the backside safety runs to the vertical and the frontside safety runs to the flag (Diagram #4).

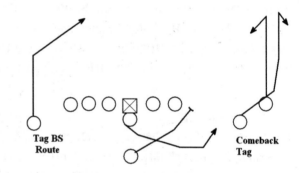

Diagram #4. Switch Route

As I said earlier, our backside rules are the same for our entire sprint-out package. We read this route flat-to-corner (Diagram #5). From time to time, we like to call switch on this route. If that

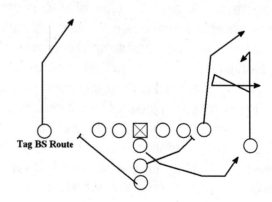

Diagram #5. Flat-to-Corner Route

occurs, the number-one and number-two receivers switch routes. The number-one receiver would run a post-corner route while the number-two receiver would run a flat route. If we get into a bunch set, we do have rules that would have the number-one receiver run a corner, the number-two receiver would run a vertical, and the number-three receiver would run the flat.

If we are in double slot, the motion back gets outside the slot and runs the corner. This is a route that complements the jet sweep very well as it will slow down the safety support on the jet sweep (Diagram #6). It was even effective out of the shotgun because it made it difficult for the defense to play the inside flat route.

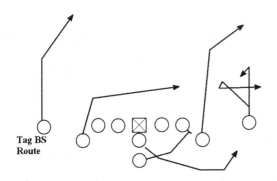

Diagram #6. Double Slot

Once again, the only rules that are different for our routes are in our bunch sets (Diagram #7). The number-one receiver runs the corner route in the bunch set. The number-two receiver will run the vertical, trying to hold the safety.

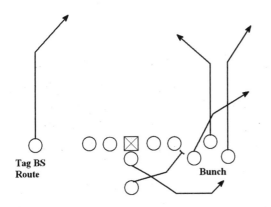

Diagram #7. Bunch Set – Corner/Vertical Route

Also, on the release, the number-two receiver is trying to rub off the number-three receiver, who is running the flat. We do not see many defenses playing us with man coverage in our bunch sets because of the number of pick routes that we run. Even though we change the rules for our bunch sets, the rules are still very simple. You just need to be able to count to three to understand what you are supposed to do in our sprint passing game. We can use different sets and use the "switch" tag to change up the routes and give the defense different looks.

Our protection is hinge protection. It ends up being a combination of man and gap principles. We block number one and number two on the playside. We tell our guard he has to reach number one unless he is an A-gap player. If that is the case, we will hinge to him. Our playside tackle must reach number two.

If we have a great deal of trouble reaching the 5 technique, or if we have defenders coming off the end, we can set a third receiver on that side and keep him in to block. If number two is so wide that our tackle cannot get there, he can make a "wide" call so that the fullback knows he has to get the number-two defender. We start our fullback to the outside. If the defense brings any type of blitz from the outside, our fullback is to pick that up. If there is no force contain coming at the fullback, he will turn and look for any pressure trailing the quarterback. Everyone else would be in hinge protection. If the defense brings four people from the sprintside, the quarterback is taught to get the ball out to the flat route immediately.

Our next route concept in our sprint package is the flood route. This is my favorite package. We will run this against any man or zone coverage. We have always run the flood into a trips set. The playside number-one receiver runs the vertical. We coach him to outside release his defender to create proper spacing. We also want the corner to turn and run with his back to the inside so he is not facing the ball.

Playside number two is the flat route. It is the same rule as previously stated. If he is outside, he runs the bubble. If he is tight, he will run the shoot route. Playside number three runs the 10-yard out route. We get that play open very often. The backside rules are the same as the previous packages. We teach the quarterback to peek at the vertical route as he begins his sprint. If the vertical is open, he can set his feet and throw the vertical. If the vertical is not open, we are reading flat-to-out as a high-low read on the outside linebacker.

If we switch the routes on the flood, we let number two run the out and number three run the flat (Diagram #8). The number-one receiver will continue to run the vertical. We also use these sprint-combination packages with our play-action game. That makes the route teaching very simple.

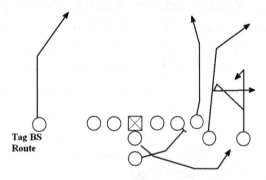

Diagram #8. Flood Route - Switch

In our bunch set, we automatically "switch." In our bunch sets, we want our number three to run the flat (Diagram #9). We feel like that creates a good pick situation. We are just trying to flood the zone and get good separation in our routes.

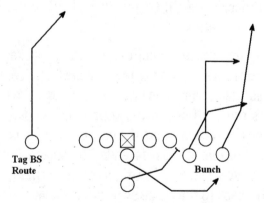

Diagram #9. Bunch Set - Switch

We have several ways of getting three receivers to the same side. We can use our pro set

and offset the fullback to allow him to be the number-three receiver (Diagram #10). We would switch that since the fullback would need to run the flat route. This allows us to get a large number of reps at doing these combinations.

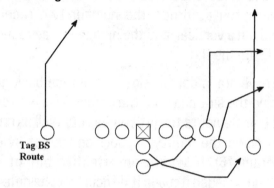

Diagram #10. Bunch Set - Combinations

Our players learn what we want on these concepts, and we are not trying to run a million things in an attempt to outsmart the defense (Diagram #11). We know what we are doing and we can just go play. It does not matter how much you know as a coach; it is how much your players know when they go on the field.

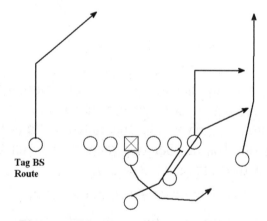

Diagram #11. Flood Route Offset Backs

We can run motion to get into the trips set and run the same route (Diagram #12). It is a matter of deciding what you want in the game plan.

Since we run so much flood package with our trips sets, we love to run the comeback route to the weakside. The defense tends to rotate over to our trips and it leaves us a good look at the comeback route. We do not see a great deal of underneath coverage on our routes to the weakside of trips.

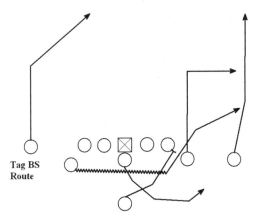

Diagram #12. Motion to Trips – Floor Route

We like to put our best receiver on the weakside of bunch trips and run the comeback. We will also call a three-step-drop slant route to him on the weakside of the bunch set. We give our quarterback the ability to call the slant if he sees that there is no underneath player on the weakside.

Let me get into how we teach our quarterbacks. My brother, Ben, who played quarterback at Troy State, is our quarterback coach. We work with our quarterbacks to be able to throw the ball off the sprint phase by moving and throwing the ball with a big chest turn. This is the way we warm up our quarterbacks.

We start with them moving and throwing. We tell them to run through the throw. This will help their follow-through. Running through the throw is what creates the velocity on the throw. Quarterbacks who do not have great arm strength must run through the throw to get the ball out on time. We start with the quarterbacks making sprint throws at 15 yards, and then we move it to 20 yards.

The next drill we start at 10 yards, jog down a line, turn, and throw. The coaching point here is to make certain that our shoulders are turned to our target. We want to make sure we get a big chest turn and that we run through the throw on the follow-through. Our quarterbacks understand the purpose of this drill and it is something that they can do on their own in the off-season when we cannot work with them.

The next drill is to get the sprint downhill before the throw. On this drill, we really emphasize how fast we get into the sprint from the snap. We want the quarterback to pick a spot to throw the ball. We want him to "aim small and miss small." We want to specify exactly where on the receiver's body that we want the ball to arrive. We want the quarterback to get to a depth of six yards and begin to head downhill.

For our younger quarterbacks, we will work with cones so they can get a good feel of exactly where they need to go. We set the cone at six yards right behind our tackle. When we run out of the gun, we are already at five yards, so we only get one more yard of depth. We do not use those with our older quarterbacks because we do not want them looking for the cones. We want them to have their eyes downfield.

We begin to teach our quarterbacks this technique when they are in middle school, so hopefully by the time they get to us, they will not need to look for the cones to get their eyes downfield. We do a good job of working with our middle school coaches to make certain they are running what we run.

I hope you have learned something from this presentation. Coaching is a great profession. We have to take the time to teach, to review, to correct, and to encourage. Thanks so much for your attention, and if I can do anything to help you, please contact me.

THE INSIDE- AND OUTSIDE-ZONE PLAYS

Franklin Regional High School, Pennsylvania

It has been 24 years since I first came to this clinic. In those 24 years, I never had the chance to win a state championship. However, we did win the state championship this past season. It was truly a miracle review for us as a staff.

It takes the whole package in order to win a state championship. Not only does it take a good offense, defense, and special teams, it takes a great staff. We were able to add a few young coaches this year, along with some of our coaches who had come up through our system. I knew at the beginning of the football season that we had something special. We took it on the chin three years ago when we were 3-7. We had five players that started as sophomores. By the end of the year, we had seven sophomores starting. Some of the people wanted to get rid of me as a coach. It is tough to please everyone when you are not winning. Some of the parents were upset because I had those seven sophomores playing. We were hopeful it would pay off in a couple of years.

They started weightlifting in early November. From that point on, we just caught fire. The thing I had to do was to get a staff with a year's experience coming back, and I did that. I did not do all of this by myself. I think I had some help from upstairs. We have 13 staff members and we all work together. I have an offensive coordinator and a defensive coordinator. I have the third phase of the game, which is the special teams.

We had a good football team this year. We had 13 players that will go on to college to play football. We had four players that signed with Division I schools. It is about the X's and O's, and it is about the scheme, but it is also about the athletes. We had a tremendous group of kids this year.

One thing I want to leave with you before I go on to the topic is this: it is very important to believe in your system and your staff. Empower your coaches to do what they need to do. If you do that, things will work out for you.

How many of you in this room run the zone plays? How many of you are here because you want to learn something that will help you defend the zone plays? I am going to go over the quarterback on the inside and outside zone offense. Coach Anthony Botti will go over the running backs and wide receivers. Coach Rich Johns will cover the line play.

In 1995, in my second year as a head coach, we ran a power offense. We faced 9- and 10-man fronts constantly. We lost to a team that was 0-3 and we were 1-2. They beat us and we had some great athletes, but we did not win many football games. I talked to the coaching staff and we decided to go to the zone offense.

We went to the zone offense for a couple of reasons. First, we could go against bigger, stronger players. Second, this offense would help us against any type of blitz package we would see. We ended up winning our next eight games and lost out in the playoffs. We were 1-3 when we changed to the zone, but made a great run to Three Rivers and the playoffs. From that time on, we went to the zone offense. Anyone that was added to my staff had to know something about the zone offense.

Coach Anthony Botti has taken it to another level with the shotgun look and the one-back look. We have made our offense a lot more diversified. We can do a lot of different things in our offense with the zone. I believe in this offense and we are going to stay with it because of the many different things we can do.

Coach Chuck Klausing mentioned the jet plays. We run some of the jet with the motion. It gives us another tool that gives our opponents something else to prepare for when they play us.

I am going to start with the two-back I formation. Our quarterback is where it all begins. We had two good quarterbacks this past year. One of our quarterbacks is going to Northwestern. He is 6'3", and 215 pounds. Not too many people gave us a chance against Thomas Jefferson High School. We were ahead early in the first quarter and our first quarterback was injured. He had to leave the game. We brought in our junior quarterback, but he had a lot of experience. All year we had been able to overcome adversity. We did not miss a beat in that game because we had a backup quarterback who had experience.

The responsibilities of our quarterback are very similar to what most teams do. He reviews his pre-snap checklist as he prepares to give the cadence. First, he must check the alignment. Next, he must identify the fronts. Then, he must identify the coverages in the secondary.

We want the stance where the quarterback is comfortable. His heels are on the ground. His right hand is underneath the center. The first step in our outside-zone play is always a big step at 45 degrees. As soon as he receives the snap, he must get as much depth as possible. He must make the handoff on the third step about five yards deep. Any fumble on the exchange on the handoff is the responsibility of the quarterback. He takes his first step as deep as he can. As he does that, he seeds the football in the mesh. We want to protect the football as we go back for the handoff.

On the second step, he is still gaining depth and he shows the football. We want him to show the ball because we want to do a couple of things out of this set. This is to set up the bootleg later on. By showing the football at this point, it holds the linebackers inside.

On the third step, he is five yards deep. We have put in the S-H-H-H call. That is show-hand-head-hand. On the third step, as he gives the ball off to the running back, at five yards deep he goes S-H-H-H. He is going to show the ball, show the hand, show the head, and show the hand again. We want everyone on defense to have their eyes on the quarterback, and we want them to be aware that we can hand the ball off to the back, run the bootleg, or set up and throw the play-action pass.

We can do a couple of things off the fake by the quarterback. We run a lot of naked plays. After the first step, we want depth, the second step show, and then the hand, head, and we run the bootleg. The decision to show the bootleg or step and show the play-action is predicated upon the defensive end and what we want to do against them. At times, we will show play-action to freeze the linebacker. That is our outside-zone play for the quarterback.

The quarterback's responsibilities on the inside-zone play are similar to the outside zone. He must make his pre-snap reads. The stance is the same as well. On the inside zone, his first step is at six o'clock directly behind him. As soon as we get the snap, the first step is as deep as we can make it for the midline at six o'clock. On the second step, we come off the midline still gathering as much ground as we can. We want to make the handoff at five yards deep. On the third step, we hand the ball off and run as deep as we can to show the "waggle" action on the play. The quarterback always wants to hide his hands. We want the inside linebackers guessing if the quarterback has the ball or not on the fake.

We have been very successful running the zone play. We have averaged more yards on the zone play than anything we run. We have had a 1,000-yard rusher for the last 12 years, except one year. Gentlemen, I was 0-9 once in my coaching career. We believe in the zone plays because they have been good for us.

Now Anthony Botti will go over the running backs and receivers, and their roles in the zone plays.

Coach Anthony Botti

A lot of coaches think you must have a great running back to run the zone offense. We have found that is not necessarily the case. You need coachable running backs. You need someone that is going to follow your directions and someone who is able to understand the concepts of what you are trying to do up front as well as what is needed from the running back. Over the last few years, we have had running backs who have bought into our system and have shown a great deal of patience on the play. They have been able to look for the things they need when they run the play.

The first point I want to cover is the depth and stance of the running backs. Our tailback is lined up seven yards deep behind the quarterback. Most of the time we run the two-back zone offense. Our fullback is lined up five yards behind the quarterback. There is also a reason he is so deep off the ball.

The reason the backs are so deep is because the zone play is slow-developing. Lining up deep, as we do with the backs, allows our linemen up front to do what they need to do. The deeper the tailback is, the better the blocking will set up for the play. The best blocker on the team in this concept is the tailback. By lining up deep as he does, it allows him time to read what he is looking for. He must decide if he should make the play with a playside bounce, if it is vertical now, or if it is a backside cutback. The deeper he is, the more vision he is going to have, and the better he is going to be able to make his cuts on the play.

The stance is as follows. The tailback is in a two-point stance. The fullback is in a three-point stance. We tell our tailbacks to have their weight on their heels in their stance. We do not want them leaning forward on their toes. If they do that, sooner or later they will be called for moving too quickly before the snap. By having the weight on the heels, it allows the tailback to make his first step.

We do not want a wide stance. We want the feet shoulder-width apart. This stance allows lateral movement. It allows him to take his steps and not get overextended. We want to be relaxed in our stance. We want to be comfortable. We do not want to be tense. We want to be able to move right or left.

The steps for the tailback are important. We use three steps, depending on who the running back is. We call the third step the 45-degree aiming-point step. The first step is at 45 degrees on both zone plays. That first step is going to lead the tailback upfield. The second step is going to come downhill on the aiming point.

The third step is a drop step at the aiming point. The reason we have three steps on the play is because each running back is different. The second step takes us downhill toward the play. We want the shoulders square to the line of scrimmage. Some backs can be fast behind the line of scrimmage and some backs can be slow behind the line of scrimmage. One thing that is always constant is the speed of our quarterback getting to the mesh point. At five yards, he has to mesh with our tailback. If we have an anxious tailback, and he takes the downhill step too soon, it causes fumbles on the exchange at the mesh point. He must take a lateral step to get the timing down on the play. If we have a slow tailback, we are going to tell him to take the 45-degree step and look for the aiming point. Because he is slower, he can take that first step downhill.

Next, I want to talk about the inside- and outside-zone rules. The first player is the fullback. The inside and outside zone are the same play. They do the exact same thing on both zone plays. He will be sent to the playside or he will be sent to the backside on the two plays. This is predicated upon the technique of the backside defensive end.

If we face a defensive end to the backside who is containing and is working up the field, we send the fullback to the playside. If that defensive end is slashing down inside, and is a threat to make the play on the tailback, we send the fullback to the backside and he picks up the end. He is responsible for anything that leaks outside the defensive end.

Our depth for the fullback is five yards. He is in a three-point stance. He must be sure to take the same steps as the tailback. He must step laterally because he must work with the offensive line on their blocks. He must be able to stretch out so he can get around the defensive end. By taking that first step, it gives him a better aiming point to get outside and block the defensive end.

If we feel the backside defensive end is such a good athlete that he can run the play down from the backside, we will send our fullback to block him on both of our zone plays. He must aim tight off our quick tackle to pick up the end if he is coming down inside hard. He must cut off all penetration by the defensive end and force him to go around the block. If that defensive end can run around the block by the fullback and make the play on the tailback, we are going to put in a new tailback because he is not doing what he is coached to do.

Next, I want to discuss the rules for the tailback on the outside-zone play. The first thing we talk about with our tailback is his aiming point. He has two different aiming points. When we run the outside zone, the aiming point for the tailback is one man removed from the line of scrimmage. If we are running the play to the tight-end side, he is aiming for one man outside the tight end. If we are running the play to the split-end side, he is going to aim for one man outside our quick tackle. The reason we aim wide is because of our blocking schemes. By aiming one man removed, when our linemen offset, he is already lined up with the tight end, and he can read the blocks and the flow on the play.

His first step is a short, six-inch lateral step. On his second step, he must make sure he gets width. We do not want to squeeze the tailback. This should be a dead sprint to get the ball to our running back. If it takes a sprint, it means the tailback is too tight. If our tailback is too tight, he is not going to see the outside cuts and he is going to cut everything tight.

The inside-zone play is a little different. The aiming point is at the outside leg of the guard. We key off the block on the guard because when he makes his move we have a clear picture of what is going on in the middle. He takes the short step first, and then on the second step he gets some width. We do not want him to squeeze the midline. If he is tight on the midline, we have a collision in the backfield and we lose yardage. We must be aiming at the outside leg of the guard. We want to make

sure we are not too tight on the quarterback. His second step takes us to the landmark, which is the outside leg of the guard and his movement.

The tailback must be patient. He must be slow to the line of scrimmage. This cannot be stressed enough. All year long our tailback coach yells, "Patience, patience, patience!" We tell the tailback, "Slow to, fast through." We want the tailback to be as slow as he can to the line of scrimmage, and when he sees the seam, we want him to be as fast as he can through the hole. By being patient, this allows our blocks to develop. As I said, the most important blocker on offense is our tailback. The slower he is getting to the line of scrimmage, the better the blocking will be up front. By being patient, the outside zone can hit four different places along the line of scrimmage. If he is too fast on the play, and a big hole opens up on the backside, he is not going to see that hole. Patience will allow him to see the cuts he needs to make.

Our tailbacks spend a lot of time watching film. They get a lot of the plays of the defense by watching film. They can read the flow on the film and have a good idea of how the play is going to develop.

If we get flow over the top, which means the linebacker floating over the defensive line, we know that the tailback needs to cut upfield. We have found the linebackers outrun the offensive linemen most of the time. So when we see flow over the top, we tell the tailback to cut back.

If we see flow underneath, we want to bounce the play outside. Flow underneath comes when the linebackers jab up the middle of the line.

We tell the tailback that once he makes his decision on the seam that he should get vertical. Once he sees the hole opening up, he must get vertical and get much yardage as possible. We do not want him to stop and try to make another cut on that play.

For our wide receivers, the coverage dictates the style of blocks. We have them use the stalk block or we have them run off. We make it very simple for our wide receivers. Most of the time we stalk block. We want to get in the face of the defender we are working against in both zone and man coverage. When we are running our zone play, the ball could very easily cut back to the wideside of the field. We do not want to come down inside to block because that leaves the backside corner free to make the tackle. At times, if we face man coverage, we give the receivers the option to run the defender deep or to get in their face and stalk block them.

This is how we teach the zone plays. We start with this on day one and we pound it day in and day out. Now, Coach Rich Johns is going to talk about the offensive-line play.

Coach Rich Johns

As most of you know, zone blocking has become a very trendy thing. A lot of pro and college teams are using the zone-blocking schemes. The scheme is not just limited to our offense. I talk with other teams that are trying to incorporate the blocking schemes with their offense. You do not have to run the I formation or the shotgun look like West Virginia runs. There are a lot of different teams using this scheme.

I am going to go over technique first and then get into some X's and O's. The techniques we are using are a direct result of what scheme we are using on offense. If we were a man-blocking-scheme team, we would do something completely different. Do not let the techniques you use dictate what you run on offense. Let the offense you are running dictate your technique. The techniques we are using on the line fit into our offense.

The first point is the stance. The weight is on the inside of their feet. The reason we want the weight on the inside of their feet is as follows. Most of the time, the first step we take is a lateral step. We do not want them wasting time pushing off laterally. We want to be loaded in our stance where we are very efficient.

We prefer a balanced stance. We will allow a staggered stance of toe to mid-foot. If a lineman cannot get to where he needs to be, I will allow that player to drop his foot to get to the block.

We want the linemen to have a flat back. We want to stress weight on the inside of the feet, and the keeping back straight or flat. We want the hand extended as much as possible. Some people tell their linemen to "grab the grass." We have no weight on our hands. Because we move laterally, we do not want the weight on the hand. We must move laterally on that first step. If I have weight on my hand, I tend to fall forward instead of taking that lateral step first. I will talk about aiming points. I cannot move forward with that first step. I have to move laterally and get my helmet going toward the proper aiming point. We want the hand out in front, just brushing the ground.

On our splits, we go two feet. I have seen a lot of teams that split six inches and others that split more than two feet. Those splits do change depending on the type of blocks used. If we are working with another offensive player, we cut our splits down. When we are combo blocking, we want to get hip to hip with the other blocker. It does not make sense to be three feet away from someone if we are working with him on a block.

Our rule of thumb on our splits is the following. If the defense does not stunt a lot when we know we are going to combo block with someone, we will tighten down on our splits.

Next, I want to discuss the depth off the ball for our linemen. Our guard's helmet is on the hip of the center. We want to be back off the line as far as we can and still be legal. We want as much time as possible to get the head on the outside of the defender. It is difficult to block a man on your outside if you are up tight to the line of scrimmage. We back off the ball as much as we can to buy ourselves some space. We do not like the bucket step in our scheme.

On the first day of practice, I stress the fact we want to be loose in our stance. I ask them to shake their butts around so they will be nice and loose in their stance. Some times these kids get down in their stance and they are so tense they have snot bubbles. That is not good. When you are tense, you are slow. A boxer is never tense. You want to be nice and loose. We want to be loose in our stance where we can move smoothly and quickly. The tenser you are, the slower you are. We want the eyes up in the stance. We want to be able to see any linebackers moving, or any walk-up blitzes.

Coming from college to high school, I had to decide the kind of steps to take. A lot of college teams have a lot of steps on their offense. I try to use the KISS principle: Keep it simple, stupid. We have cut it down to two steps. Using these two steps, I feel we can accomplish everything in our offense.

The first step is a move-and-pop step. The move step is a lateral step. We do not set any distance for that first step. We stress that the aiming point determines the distance of that first step. If I am the guard and I have to block the 3 technique, he has to get his head outside. That lateral step is dependent upon the technique of the down defender.

If the defender is playing tight on the guard, does the guard need to take an eight-inch lateral step? No. The guard can reach that block and get his head outside on the man. If the defender is playing a little wider, he must take a larger move or lateral step. So, we do not tell the guard how long his step must be. It is strictly dependent on how far the down defender is removed from him.

The pop step is getting the second foot down after the move step. The move is a lateral one. The second foot pops and is down on the ground. It is very important to get the second foot down quickly. A lot of the time, we use the term "hot and heavy." I want the feet hot. When they hit the ground, they are up quickly and then they hit the ground. It is an up-and-down move. We try to get our feet moving on the hot-and-heavy theory before we get into our blocks. We are constantly calling out, "Move and pop. Move and pop." In their minds, they are getting the second step down quickly.

On the second step, we say, "Drop and pop." A lot of coaches refer to this as a bucket step. It is a step that loses ground vertically, while gaining ground horizontally. On move and pop, we have to get the head outside. We lose ground to gain ground because we cannot make a block on a defender that is split wide from us. We must work for the aiming point. We do that by losing ground at first, and then we make it up when we get outside to our aiming point. We have to push off horizontally and lose some ground vertically to get the head across the defender.

How do we know what steps to use? You must have the kids pick the steps that will work for them. Players are different and some kids are faster than others. You have to let them experiment to get the step where they can be successful.

In talking about what step to use, the first thing we must establish is the defender's technique. If the defender is lined up tight, we can move and pop. If he is wider, we may have to drop and pop. If you have a big tackle, he may not be able to take that first step laterally. He will have to drop and pop.

Our aiming point is the outside numbers of the defender. If I am the right guard and we are running to our right, I want to get my head on the outside of the number of the down lineman to my right. On the inside zone, it is more likely to be coming straight off the ball at the defender. Now, our aiming point is the outside number, but it is the inside part of the number.

Next, I want to talk about our hands. This may be the one area where we differ from other teams that run the zone plays. One of the big fads for the offensive linemen was to "put your hands in the holsters." A lot of teams still do that. They want to come out of the stance with their hands in their holsters. We do not do that. We shoot our hands directly out of our stance. "No hands in the holster!" As we come out of the stance, boom! I am shooting with my hands right now. We have our thumbs up and our elbows down as everyone else does. We want the elbows in tight. We are stronger with the elbows down.

We want the upper body loose and explosive. We are firing right out of our stance. A lot of people ask me why we do not put the hands in the holster. We do not put the hands in the holster for a couple of reasons. First, we all know the player that gets their hands inside first wins the battle. This is typical of offensive- and defensive-line play. I do not want to open myself up at all. I want to shoot my hands and be the first man to make the contact. I do not care how many pounds you can bench press. We all know that does not mean they are going to pancake anyone. The pancakes develop from the lower body. I want to get my hands on the defender first, and I am going to control the man.

The second is this. We want separation at all times. I never want my head buried. The reason for this is that, in the zone-blocking schemes, we are working down the line of defenders to the second level. It is not predetermined which person is going to the second level. If our center and guard are working the 3 technique to the second level, we cannot bury our heads. If we do and the linebacker comes on the blitz, we cannot see him if we have our heads buried. We want to shoot our hands out first, and we keep the elbows down for strength. We want to keep separation on the play so we can see the second level. We talk about having four hands on the down man and having four eyes on the linebacker. We cannot see the linebacker if our head is down.

Now I want to discus the scheme. The rules stay the same no matter what the defense is playing, or what the offensive play is. I think this is one of the big reasons teams are going to the zone-blocking scheme. The reason is for the simplicity of the blocking rules.

There are two points in this scheme. Either you are covered or you are uncovered. If you are covered, you have a defender head up, or shaded to one side or the other. If you are uncovered, there is no one on you and there is no one shading you to the called playside.

We worry about the down lineman first. We have no idea of who we may block on the second level. All I know is who I am blocking on the first level. It is a down defender. If you are covered, your aiming point is the outside number of the down defender to the side of the play called.

If we are uncovered, we push to the next down defender to the playside. If the zone play is going to our right and the center is not covered, he is going to reach to the right toward the 3 technique. We try to get hip to hip with our next linemen.

One misconception of this offense is that people think you must have big, monster-type linemen. This is not true. One reason Coach Botta went to this offense was because he was being out-manned up front. We usually have two blockers on the side the ball is going to be run. Ninety percent of the time, we get the two-on-one blocking advantage to the playside.

Just like all rules, sometimes things do not work out. However, 95 percent of the time, our rules hold up. If we are working with another linemen next to us, all we call out is, "Hip to hip." We do not want the defenders splitting the double-team block. We do not want any negative runs. We try not to turn our hips and we want our shoulders square, with our eyes up. Again, we stress four hands on the down defender and four eyes on the linebacker.

I want to run through a couple of our blocking schemes. I am not going to talk about the backs and receivers. I know nothing about them, and I do not really care about them. I teach all of my linemen to hate the "skinny kids." I am only going to show the fronts in these schemes.

The first defense we look at is the basic stack 4-4 defense. On the outside zone, the rules stay the same. We are covered or we are uncovered. Let us say the play is going to our right. As we look at the play, we see our tight end is covered (Diagram #1). He has someone shaded on his outside. His job is to get his head on the outside of the down defender. We want to create a lot of stress for the defense.

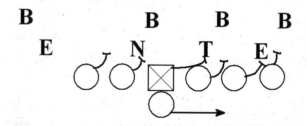

Diagram #1. Outside Zone Right versus 4-4 Stack

Defensive ends are gap control primarily. If we get our head on the outside of the defensive end, he is going to fight to try to maintain his gap. He widens the gap to keep the end from reaching him. We are creating a natural seam by trying to get our head on the outside numbers of that end. We are attacking their technique. They are trying to maintain their technique, and they are creating a lot of space.

Our tackle is uncovered. His rule is to push in the direction the play is going. He is pushing to the next down defender. He pushes to the defensive end. We should get a hip-to-hip relationship with the tackle and end. We should have four hands on him, with our eyes on the second level.

The only people we are worried about initially are the down defenders. As the tackle and end are blocking the down defender, their eyes are scanning the linebacker. They want to see what is coming into the double-team block. If someone comes in the area, they pick him up. The tight end is really blocking three-quarters of the defender. The offensive tackle is just trying to get to the defenders hip.

Here is where our rules break down. We do not want to screw our buddies so we must help the center at times. If we are running the play to our right, the right guard by our definition, is uncovered. However, he has a defensive lineman shaded to his inside (Diagram #2). I do not have a center that can reach the man inside the guard and get his head on the outside. If we face a 2i technique and the play is to that side, you are going to screw the center if you leave him to make that block.

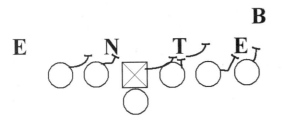

Diagram #2. Guard-Center Combo Block on 2i

We want the guard on the 2i to punch the man to buy some time for the center to come underneath on the play. We slow play it just as the center gets underneath the defender. This kind of goes against the rule.

As far as coaching these combo blocks, this is what we do. We start out blocking the 3 technique, the end, and a linebacker. There are a lot of blocking drills we use to teach the combo blocks, but I do not have time to go over them at this time. We break it down where our linemen work together in drills. We have three stations where the tight end and tackle are working together. The onside guard and center work together, and the backside guard and backside tackle work together. I would be glad to sit down with you and talk about the drills we use in teaching the combo blocks after the lecture is over.

We have a strongside and a quickside in our scheme. The reason we do that is because we do not have the personnel to do a lot of different things with our blocking scheme.

We do run the outside zone to the quickside. Our tackle has a man on his outside shade so he must reach the defensive end (Diagram #3). The onside guard must recognize the center cannot make the block on the defensive tackle in the gap. He must make contact with the defensive tackle and give the center time to get to his block. Then the guard slides off looking for the linebacker.

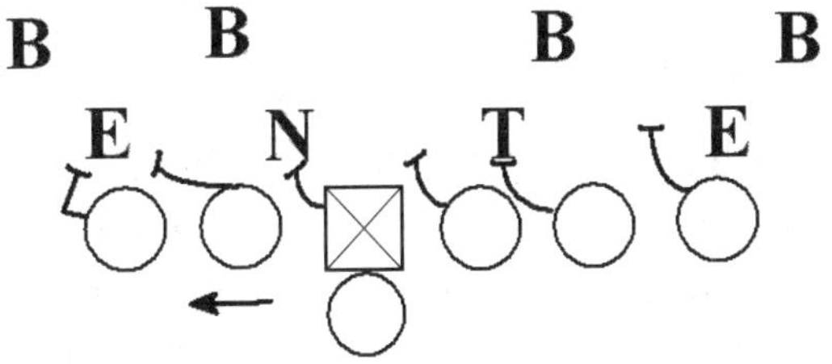

Diagram #3. Outside Zone Weak - Blocking theme

If you have any questions, we will be around all day. Thank you.

THE SHOOT WEST SPREAD OFFENSE

Lincoln High School, Oregon

First of all, I am honored to be here. It is a real honor to speak to this audience. I want to talk about the way we communicate and how we put things together. I will give you very little about our philosophy.

We call our offense the shoot west spread offense. It is a combination of the run-and-shoot and the West Coast offense. Our basic philosophy is this. "We will fight you anytime, and anywhere." That takes the pressure off of losing games. Our kids play with that mindset. We play like there is no tomorrow. "We will fight you anytime and anywhere." That is our basic football philosophy. That is going to lead into how we communicate.

Our basic offensive philosophy, and the one I believe in, is "a sense of urgency." If you are not coaching with a sense of urgency, you are not going to score a touchdown. If you are trying to be precise all of the time, you will find that doesn't work. We have a sense of urgency, and we have it in practice, in our individual drills, and in our groups. On Friday night, it shows up.

When we get the ball, we want to score as fast as we can. We want the bloodstream at a high level. A sense of urgency is a great tool to have for offensive football.

Our individual philosophy is to "invent yourself every day." I got this from my college coach. He was an awesome coach. He taught me to invent myself every day. There is nothing you can't do. Don't limit yourself on anything. That is how we come up with so many different formations. We do not want to limit ourselves in school, on the practice field, or in life.

Our receivers always have a passing tree. We number the passing-tree routes from 0 through 9.

We label our receivers from left to right: X-, Y-, and Z-receivers. We label our backs as well. We have our A-back and our S-back. Our A-back stands for all-around back, and the S-back is our speed back, stud back, super back, or whatever you want to call him. Basically, he is our tailback.

We give them a word to describe what we want them to do. When we communicate with our players, we do not stop with just one word. For example, let's talk about our 9 route. To most people, the 9 route is a fade route. For us it is also a go, see ya, touchdown, and it is also a hand signal that we give them. We can communicate at all levels.

Another example is our 6 route. It can be a dig, a cross, a post-dig, and an in route, plus the hand signal that we can give them. We go from 0 to 9 with those calls. When those words come out of the mouths of the coaches, the players know what we are talking about. If a player forgets the play as he breaks the huddle, we can yell out the play to him ("Give me a dig route!"). We use as many words on the practice field as we can. This narrows everything we do for Friday night.

An example would be our motion plays. We run a lot of motion plays. We always correlate Y with a word. "Y-O motion" is Y-over, all the way across the formation. "Y-O crack" looks like Y-O, but the ball is snapped at as he gets to the tackle. "Y-O out" means the goes toward the sideline. We have to be able to correlate all of these calls and all of the words.

Our communication with the quarterback is what it all comes down to. We call the plays and the protection. We signal this in to the quarterback or he runs over to the sideline for the play. I never send in a player with a play because we do not want any questions about what we want called. I eat lunch with our quarterbacks each day so we have the opportunity to talk with them. I want to know who he is and how his mind works.

Communication – Calling the Play and Protection

- Signal or quarterback runs to sideline
  - ✓ Play never goes in with another player
  - ✓ Breakdown in communication
- In Huddle
  - ✓ Run-run, pass-pass, party-party
  - ✓ Formation
  - ✓ Play
- Protection
  - ✓ Formation
    - ○ Signal motion at line to accommodate protection
  - ✓ Cadence
    - ○ Color
    - ○ Name
    - ○ Number
    - ○ Repeat

The best thing about our communication starts in the huddle. We call play, play-pass, pass-party, and party. The run is simply a running play, the pass is a pass, and party is play-action. We do not call our blocking scheme in the huddle. It is all called at the line of scrimmage by our quarterback. If the quarterback calls party-party in the huddle, the linemen know a color will be called at the line of scrimmage to let them know which blocking scheme to use. The backs know they are going to have some sort of action off the party-party call.

Next the quarterback calls the formation, and after that he calls the play signaled in or given to him on the sideline.

Our protection has been a big plus for our offense. We can keep both backs in for protection, send them in the middle, or check release them into patterns. It is all based in a color scheme we use.

The quarterback calls everything. He must protect himself first. He must call the protection he feels comfortable with in order to get rid of the football.

Our cadence is simple. The quarterback comes out and calls a color, a name, and a number. "Bill, red, 55. Bill, red, 55. Check corner. Check corner." He must have a demanding voice to call that out. You have to teach him how to project his voice on the cadence.

One of the interesting things we do with our quarterbacks is to give them a note card at lunchtime. It is a 6-by-9 card. We go through all of our plays. I start on Monday with about 15 plays. Here is the general format of our note cards. The called play is stack right, 969 wheel-check (Diagram #1). I draw the play up on the card. Below the play I give them the protection. I give them the best color, the second-best color, and a safe color.

Diagram #1. Stack Right, 969 Wheel-Check

Next, I go to our reads. We have a pre-snap read of the coverage. We have several reads: Q-fade, Q-out, Q-seam, and a Q-pivot read.

With trips, we have endless possibilities. Let your imagination work on this and see what you come up with.

In the pre-snap read, we want to make sure he is looking at the coverage. We want to make sure we do not get the bobble-head effect from the quarterback. The cards have helped us a great deal. When the quarterbacks get in the game, it is easy after going over it with me every day at lunchtime.

The Q read means the quarterback is going to throw the ball as fast as he can. I put up some routes, but this is how we do it. When our quarterback rolls out or sets up in the pocket, we do not have a set number of steps for him to take. We do not go 1, 2, 3, 4, 5, and throw the ball. I do not teach that method because the receivers are not open on the fifth step. They may just be in the middle of their fifth step. We throw the ball to the receiver when he is open. There are no rules for us that we want the quarterback to throw the ball on the fifth step.

People ask me why we do not have a play sheet. I do not need one because I have written these plays on the cards a thousand times in a course of a week. I know the type of play I want and the type of motion I want. On the backside of the card is written: "Run like hell if the play does not work."

If you put one of our plays on a wristband, it would look something like this. We start with the formation. It is always read from the left to the right: X, Y, Z. We call our strength to the Y-receiver. On trips right, the Y-receiver is going to be on the right side of the formation. The A-back gets the first word, and the S-back gets the second word called. If we want to switch the two backs, we call a special word and the S-back would be first, and the A-back would be second.

We call trips right and the play is 259 flat block. We would call trips right, yellow motion, 259 flat block. A lot of kids cannot remember all of that. So on the plays we use the most, we tag them with a name. Not only do we have numbers, we have names. I do not think you just have to do one or the other, I think you should do both. If we are in a hurry getting up to the line, I can call out a special word and the team knows what we want on the play.

Breakdown of Play* Insertion						
Formation	X	Y	Z	A	S	Name
Trips Right	2	5	9	Flat	Block	Flood Route
Stack Left	9	6	9	Wheel	Check	Alaska
Gun Shock	4	8	4	Corner	Swing	
*Not Real Plays!						

On our pass routes, they are only guideline numbers. They are not the exact routes. We want

to let the player know how to run a 9 route. If the defender is playing off the receiver, he may have to go get him. He may have to run inside a little to gain room to run the route. If the defender is pressing the receiver on his 9 route, he has to release inside and then run a go route. The routes are only guidelines where the receiver is going to be on the play. When we add routes to our offense, I give them this guideline. It is easy for a kid to relate to a number, 0 through 9. We want the receiver to run the route based on the coverage.

By numbering your pass routes 0 through 9 for the X-, Y-, and Z-receivers is a great way to start your program to get them organized as fast as possible. It will help with the youth programs that feed your school. The youth leagues are running the 0-through-9 routes. This helps us later on even though they are running them as basic routes. At least they have that in their systems. When they get to high school, they start learning what type of route each number is. It is a great way to organize your players and get them headed in the right direction. By the end of the season, you will have close to 20 plays that you like that you can run from different formations.

Different Formations

In looking at our trips set, we have several different looks but they are all called trips. We have about 55 trips formations I could write up. We have regular trips, trips medium, trips bunch, trips wide, trips spread, trips split, trips block, trips X tight, and trips X tight split (Diagrams #2 through #13). All of these words relate to the Y-receiver. The reason we want all of those formations is to have different players blocking and protecting at all times.

Q

Diagram #2. Trips Right

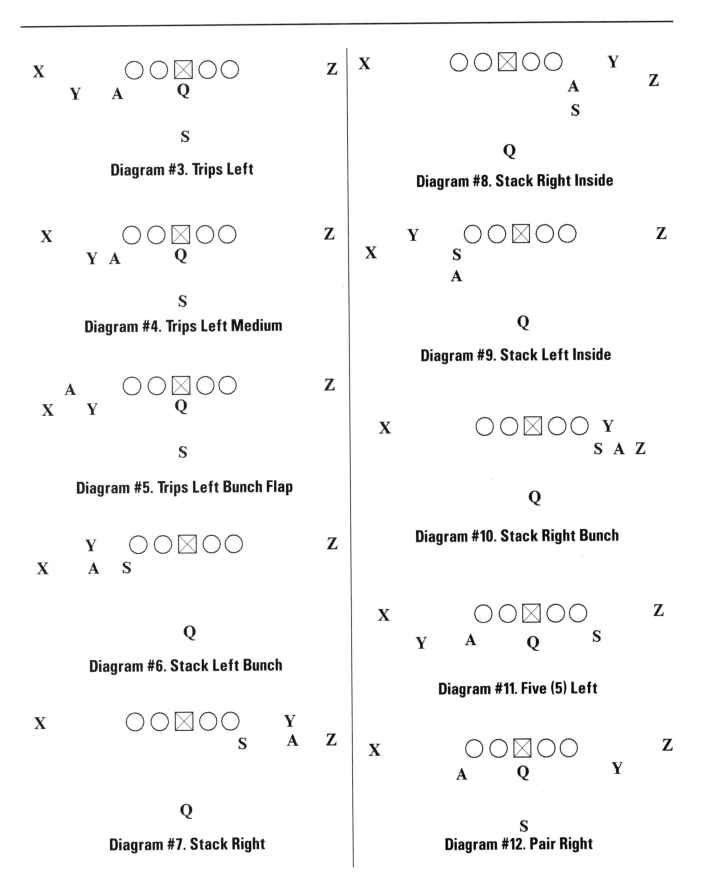

Diagram #3. Trips Left

Diagram #4. Trips Left Medium

Diagram #5. Trips Left Bunch Flap

Diagram #6. Stack Left Bunch

Diagram #7. Stack Right

Diagram #8. Stack Right Inside

Diagram #9. Stack Left Inside

Diagram #10. Stack Right Bunch

Diagram #11. Five (5) Left

Diagram #12. Pair Right

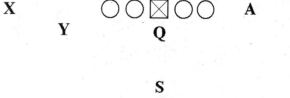

Diagram #13. Pair Left Flap

In our regular trips set, our X-receiver and Z-receiver are up on the ball. The Y-receiver is off the ball, and the A-back is one yard off the line and two yards outside the tackle. He can be a protector from this position, or he can block on a running play. The A-back is our best athlete. He is the type of player that can go out on the pass, and he is close enough to be a running threat from his position. The S-back is lined up behind the quarterback on a one-back set.

Once the players figure out the word that correlates to their position, we can come up with all kinds of different formations. You can move the Y-receiver up on the line and back the Z-receiver off the ball to come up with a different formation.

What are we trying to do on offense? We are trying to confuse the defense. You can run the same play over and over out of different formations. Just out of trips, we have 55 different-looking formations. We have found running a lot of different formations will cause problems for the secondary in high school.

If we call stack right, we still read the plays from our left to our right. It never changes. The X- and Z-receivers remain the same. Actually, the spot or location is the letter called. It may not be the same man. We have open substitution with our top six or seven receivers. We feel we are going to get more out of the players if they know they are going to be in the game. They are going in the game on their own. We never have to substitute them into the game. The receivers go in the game on their own. Trust me, your players will know who the best receivers are and they will be in the game when they need to be in the game.

The ratio works out about to 3-to-1, with the best receivers playing three plays to one play for the other receivers. If we want a particular match-up in the game, we will make sure we have the receiver in the game with whom we want to get the match-up. Other than that situation, the kids are in and out of the game on their own. They do a great job in handling the substitutions.

If you are going to throw the football, you must be able to protect. That is the key to offense. You must be able to switch players in and out of the game to protect the quarterback. Our quarterback is always going to feel good if he can get rid of the ball and make the play.

We do not play receivers that cannot block on running plays. This offense is more of a basketball-style offense. In our league, everyone that plays thinks they are a basketball player. The use of formations gives them an opportunity to run up and down the "court." I think they get a buzz from this because they are running up and down the field and stretching their legs.

We figure out the formations that will work against the defense. Once we find the formation that gives us an advantage, we run it over and over. We can move our receivers around by using basic words to change the formations. The kids feel comfortable with this system and we take it from that point on.

Do we have any questions?

The question from the audience is this: Do we have our youth leagues run our plays? No. They do use our numbering system, but I do not want them running our plays. That would take all the fun out of the game for their coaches if they had to run our plays. They have an imagination so we let them make up their own plays.

Thanks very much for your attention.

THE WINNING EDGE: OFFENSIVE FORMATIONS

Berwick High School, Pennsylvania

Men, we came a long way to talk some football with you. I just want to share this with you. For any of you who get tired of coaching this game of football, I want you to know I spent 35 years at Berwick High School. I retired in November, right before Thanksgiving. A month later, I took another coaching job. I will be 62 and I said, "I'm going back at it." So, I just wanted to tell you this. I can tell you that coaching football is in my blood. Sometimes we complain about our jobs, and if you are teaching, the kids drive you nuts.

School boards and principals are all full of it, but you know what guys? I found out one thing. I love the game. I will tell you one thing. I do not want to live without football. I will tell you how crazy I am. I took a job with one of our rivals. You must understand the background of Berwick High School. Also, you have to understand this town. I mean it is football. They postpone funerals if the football team is playing. I am not kidding you.

But, I took a job at the biggest rival Berwick has. The game is a sellout and you cannot get in the place. There will be 15,000 people there at a high school football game. I took a job with the rival school, okay? That is how crazy I am.

My topic is using formations to your advantage. There are two ways you can go on this topic. There are the basic running formations, and there are spread formations. I want to start with the running formations. Let me tell you, I was always a wide-open coach. We had 14 Division I quarterbacks. You guys might remember Ron Powlus and Jake Kelchner. We had some great quarterbacks in our program.

The big thing I got into is that Joe Gibb stuff. All right, how many guys remember Joe Gibb's team with the Redskins? I start utilizing those power sets. I used those unorthodox, unconventional power sets. I will tell you this. Is there anybody in here who is a defensive coach? Raise your hand. I will tell you what; I coached our defense. These offensive formations can drive the defensive coach nuts. They can talk all they want about spreads, but I am going to tell you what, guys. The stuff that I am going to go over, that I am going to show you, it gives the defense problems.

The big thing in using formations is this. I started out as a football coach when I was 21 years old. I was a head coach at 21 years old. I used to copy everything I could. I could never watch a football game without a clipboard in my hands. I would watch the college games and write down what they were doing. Later I started taping them. I would actually break those games down to see the formations they used. I would copy their formations. But, you know what, guys? The formations are not going to work because you have to know the philosophy behind the formations and why they are used. What are you trying to do with these teams? So, I put some notes down here that I just want to start you off with.

I think these points are important. What is the purpose of multiple running formations? Obviously, you want to give your kids an advantage blocking-wise. This is nothing new. You want to create mismatches. You want to create some poor defensive adjustments and maximize your count. That is one of the main reasons I went to multiple formations. I wanted to maximize our talent. I do not know about you guys, but we always get that small player. We get that kid who is not big enough to be a guard or a tackle, not fast enough to be a fullback or tight end, but he is a tough son-of-a-gun. I will show you some of the formations I run and you will see why I said that.

We can play a lot of kids. I have 12 power sets I am going to go over with you. We want to be able to play physical football, but we also want to play "plot" football. To me, football is one of two ways. If you've got the studs, you can run one formation, one play, and beat the shit out of everybody. If you do not have studs, you have to out-fox teams. You have to outplot those teams. The purpose of multiple formations, in my experience over the years, is that I want to out-fox you. I want to plot and try to outfox the defense. I want to try to give the defensive coordinators headaches in making adjustments. If you are coaching defense, I want you sitting at home at night thinking about what we are doing on offense. "That crazy son-of-a-gun, look what he is doing on offense now." This is the kind of thinking I want the defenses to do. If you get kids thinking too much, they are not going to be as aggressive.

Plot-defensive football teams have many defenses to jump all over your offense. I have been in the game a long time. I have seen the coming and passing away of the wishbone, the veer, and some of the wing-T. Football runs in cycles. Something will come out that is popular. A few years later, it goes away. Then it comes back for a few years and then goes away again.

Now we have the spread offense, with a running quarterback that Urban Meyer made popular. There is so much out there, guys. The things here that I am going to show you, maybe you have not see it in your area of the country. I tell you what, it boils down to this: "You either block the defense or you finesse your opponents on defense." If you have the studs, you can block them. If you do not have the players to block the defense, you must try to finesse them.

Continuing along this line, for years everybody ran conventional sets. They will run pro formations. Also, they are running the wing-T. They run a two-tight-end set with an I-back and with one flanker. Those are basic, vanilla sets. Defensive coordinators love that vanilla look. They know what you are coming out in; they know this.

I always say, "Do not practice to fail." What we are going to do with these sets is this. It is just like you heard the coach from Alabama say: "Coaches that run all of these plays and all these formations are crazy." We may get into a lot of formations, but we are only going to run maybe six to seven plays. Really, that is what we are all about. I will show you how we do this. We do not practice to fail. Here is what I am talking about.

We want our offense to understand what defenses do. Before we even put a play in, we want the offense to understand what the defenses try against the offense. They are going to be coming at you with blitzes, stems, and shifting. They are going to give you all kinds of looks. They want to disguise the coverage. But you know what, guys? If they are doing that to you, they are dictating to you. They are creating the tempo of the game. With my formations that I am going to go over here shortly, I want to dictate the tempo of the game. I want to keep the defense off balance. I think an offense that does some things that are a little different gives the defense more to think about.

Another thing we can do that is tough on a defense is this. We call the plays on the line of scrimmage. They are not called from the sideline. You send in a play to be called because you saw something on the down before that you think will work. They shift and then they are in a different defense. We try to eliminate that.

We package our running game. I will call the formations and we package our running game. I may give them two plays, and I will show you how we do this. Let us go over this. Do you practice to fail? Do not guess. We must be aware of the splits in the defensive line and we must recognize defensive fronts. We want to know if the defense is going from the 50 look, or if they are going from an even defensive look. Are they going from a 50 look to a split-4 look? Are they going from a 50 look to a bear look? Are they jumping into a 4-3 defense? Are they bringing corners?

We did not have one Division I kid in the last three years. But, we had a kid who rushed for 5,000 yards. We will have kids who will knock the crap out of you. They will hit you. They are not the brightest kids. My one guard, I asked him, "Joey, how tall are you? I do not think you are growing." He said, "Coach, I am 5'14"." He did not even know how many inches are in a foot. So, we do not have the smartest guys here, but they are tough kids and they love this stuff, and these formations.

We look at the little details. We must understand what defenses try to do to us. We must understand that every defense may change our splits. That is not practicing to fail. Look at your opponent, and at the people they put on the field. I do not know if you guys do this or not.

When I play a team, when I study them on film, we grade every kid on that team. How many guys do that here? Do you grade your opponents? We grade them. If I am playing you, I will watch your film with our whole staff. We will take the guards and the tackles, and we will grade them. We do the defense the same way. We grade them. We want to know who is the weak player on that team, if you have one. We want to know who the studs are. You must know their people. When we are done, we put that up on a wall—the kids' names and numbers—and we give them a grade. It is just like we grade our own kids.

We grade our own kids after every game. I have always graded our football team for two reasons. The first reason is to find out what we can do to make our situation better. The other reason I grade our players is for recruiting purposes. When a recruiter comes in to see me in January, or calls me to ask me to send them videos of our two best games on certain players, I go back and look for the grades on the films. I will select the two highest grades and send them those tapes. Sometimes you do not remember back September what the hell the kid did in the games. If he had a good game, then I will find it and send it to the colleges. When you have a lot of kids, it is hard to remember.

So again, I ask this question. How do you practice your offense? I think this is the key. This is all going to tie together, so hang in there with me on this. Let me show you these sets. I am going to show you a lot of formations right off the bat. Since I am pressed for time, I want to do it this way. I just want to show you the one set we have used this past year.

You have to understand how all of this evolves. Most people run a tight end here, and a tight end here. Now what we do is this. We will come out like this (Diagram #1). Look at that set. If you are a defensive coordinator, what do you think? Here is the ball. The whole theory behind what we do is to count the defense. I tell the guys if you can count, you can play for us. You can call the game.

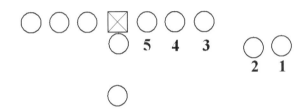

Diagram #1. Two-Tight-End Formation

If we are facing a split 4-4 team, we want to know how many guys they are going to put on the right side of the ball. In our set, I have 1, 2, 3, 4, 5 men on the right side of the ball (Diagram #2). We call that just a power twin set. We ask this question: how many guys do we have on the right side of the ball? We want to know if the defense is keeping four defenders on each side of the ball. The defense is a split-4-4 team, playing a three-deep secondary. We count on that.

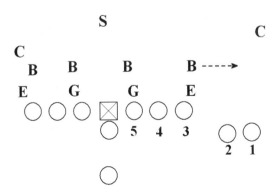

Diagram #2. Power Twin Set

Right now, we've got them outnumbered. Just to show you what we do off formation, we count the number of players they have on the strongside. We see most teams with 1, 2, 3, 4 on the strongside. If we have 1, 2, 3, 4, 5 and I pull a guard, we have six players on that strongside (Diagram #3). So we are playing a numbers game. We are trying to out-finesse you, to out-plot your defense. We are still going smack you in the face. Do not get me wrong on that fact. But we are putting more bodies at the point of attack than the defense is putting in that position.

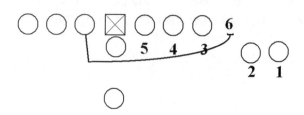

Diagram #3. Six on Strongside

We can also do this. I can walk this kid up at the snap of the ball. He walks up; he walks back. I put him in motion to the strongside. Now I run the stretch play to that side. I have 1, 2, 3, 4, 5, 6 out here on four. If they walk that defensive back up, you also have the play-action pass on the play (Diagram #4).

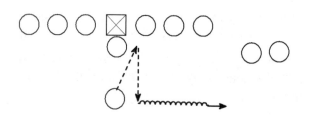

Diagram #4 - Twins-Right-Over

I am giving you one set that can drive defensive people crazy. That is called our twins set. When we put the back in motion, we call it twins-right-over. I am putting six on four. Now here is the best part of that: if the defense overloads on this play, what do we do?

If the defense kicks their front over one whole man to the slotside, and walks the corner up, this is

what we do. Now, I will really show you how to play games. These are unconventional sets. If they overload to the strongside and kick the tackle down, they are moving everything up a man, and they walk the corner up. Here is what I am going to do. The quarterback calls, "Down." Now, I am going to shift the back to the left side (Diagram #5). The back just moves to the left. All we have to do is to call "Down" and move to the backside. Now I am going to run the tailback counter to the backside. We block down, make a fake, lead block, and run the tailback counter away.

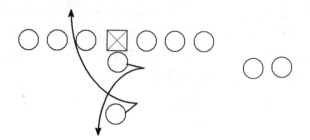

Diagram #5. Tailback Counter

So I can put them in here. If we put the slot and split end inside, we call it our brown formation. If we are split in the slot look, it is called our twins formation. We have taken just this one formation and we have given the defense a lot to work on.

I can show you how we drive people crazy. This is the best part of the deal. If you have a good receiver, you can take advantage of his ability. Here is how we are going to line this formation up. I call this our rover set. This really drove defensive people crazy.

I take a wide split with our best receiver. I am still going to use the two backs. Remember these two running backs? These are power-type backs. They are tight-end-type kids. They are what we call tight end between players. Remember I talked about between players? They are those 190-pound kids, or 180-pound players that will knock your head off. They are good, strong kids. I will use them on this set. I will use tight ends and fullbacks in this set. I still keep them in the backfield.

Here is what we do. This will be a tight end. This will be a guard or a tackle. This will be a split end.

Now, here is my tailback. Now, you are taking those two blocking backs, tight end, and fullback-type kids.

You can move him anywhere you want. We will start with this set. That is called a rover (Diagram #6). Now I've got 1, 2, 3, 4 with the fullback leading 5. I run to the right. We see a lot of the eight-man-front defenses. If they overload on one side, it gives us the advantage on one side.

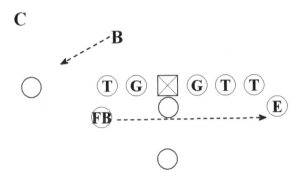

Diagram #6. Rover Formation

Now remember, I have a tight end so they have to respect him. They have to keep a defensive back to cover him. If they are loading up on the wide receiver's side, they will have inside help on that receiver. If they are taking the linebacker out underneath, you've got four on 1, 2, 3, and they are filling with the safety. You've got your fullback lead. So you've still got five-on-three or five-on-four. If you get the split end covered by the corner without any underneath help, you have your best athlete out there one-on-one. I am just trying to show you how we can outplot people.

We have been doing this for years. We will line up this way. What formation is this as you are looking at it on defense? That is a wing left, is it not? If you are playing defense on the other side, it would be a wing right. If you are on the defensive side of the ball looking at this, you are looking at a wing right. We come up to the ball on the line of scrimmage (Diagram #7). We wait until the defense gets set. We call "Down," we shift that end that is lined up in the backfield to the wing, and we have the fullback leading the play.

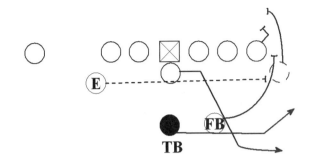

Diagram #7. Rover Shift

I shift this strong tight-end-type player and move him to the wing. Here comes the fullback, and here comes the tailback. We shift to that. What are we doing here, guys? We are taking numbers and trying to outnumber your defense. We are trying to out-fox you with numbers. That is our rover shift.

We take that same formation and line up this way: tight end, tackle, guard, center, guard, tackle, tackle, your best athlete is receiver, and your two power backs are set in there (Diagram #8).

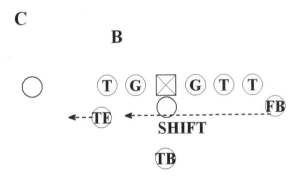

Diagram #8. Rover Twins Opposite

We shift these two guys to this and keep your tailback here. Now, that is a rover, twins, opposite. If I see you overload that way, I may shift it over to the other side, or I may line up in that rover look and shift to the rover twins. The defense does not have a chance to shift back. The defense is so screwed up after all that, that they are ready to call a time-out. They see five or six guys on one side of the formations they have worked on all week. Normally, they do not see these sets. Those defensive kids are all over each other. You want to get the defense into that type of situation. We are outnumbering you with the use of formations.

We shift to the sets and the defense cannot make the adjustments that fast. We may shift to another set and just run the quick pitch. We can pull the center or guard if we want.

Then we have done this all off the rover series. I went nuts with this set. We can call rover, twins, opposite. If I just said rover, twins, they would just line up to that side. This is the formation with a tight end always away from rover (Diagram #9). I may jet him out. When they overload this and then see this kid going in jet motion, now you've got three potential receivers there. You jet that kid outside, who is going out? Cover him. See my point? So here is what you have. If no one goes out with him, throw him the ball. We have started him on the jet sprinting one way, and then we bring him back on a little zippo reverse.

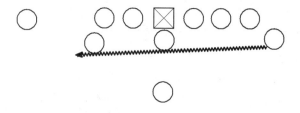

Diagram #9. Tight End Away from Rover

We can go rover, double wing. We put one of the guys on one side and another one on the opposite side of the formation. But here again, guys, everything we do is based on what the defense is doing up front. We have seen everything from overloads to you name it. They have tried that bear look on defense. They start putting defensive backs up on the line of scrimmage. You have to run the ball at those guys. They will play that seven-diamond look. We have seen it all. But the bottom line is: if we see that coming, we put the back in motion and run the stretch to our strength. If we see that there are less numbers on one side, and you can see that, we run the stretch that way.

We also run the quarterback counter. We drove the defenses nuts with that formation. You do not

have to have the best physical linemen to run that play. As I said, we did not have one Division I kid. But our kids knew what we were doing. We worked on everything in practice. Everything we did, we practiced with that set.

These are just some of the other sets I will run. When I put this back inside in the C gap, we call it Nebraska. If he is in the B gap, it is called Kansas. Then I can put the end in the backside out wide, which is our best split end, and keep a tight end in. That would be rover Nebraska. Opposite would be lobo. That is a set with four players on each set.

I know I am hitting you quick. I am just showing you the concept here. If you want to stay afterward and go over anything, I will talk to you. I am just trying to give you the numbers concept. I did this last year that drove the defense wacky. I came out with two tight ends. I do not know what you see, but in Pennsylvania everyone runs that split 4-4 look. That is about all we see. We see the 4-2, 4-4, and we see eight in the box. I love playing against the eight-man fronts. That is why I went to this.

I come out this way. We have twins to one side and a wing to the other side. We called this our falcon formation. Now, how do you defense that? There are five offensive men on one side and the defense only has four defenders. How do you defense that? Here is the best part. Five receivers can go out. So you defensive backfield coaches, we have five receivers showing. I may send four of them out, and if you start crowding us, I may keep one in for protection. We may only send three out and run our three-step drop. If you start crowding us too much, we will keep you honest.

But, here is what I did off of this. We looked at the numbers game. If that split-4 team stayed in place and never adjusted, and they still gave us four defenders to the opposite side, we are coming that way. I can run a jet sweep to get outside. That motion wingback is going full speed. We tell him to just take off with the darn ball. I can give him the ball in several areas on his motion. What is the difference if he lines up in one spot or the other? He is still going full speed when he touches the football. What am I talking about here today? I am talking about unconventional formations or sets to screw up the mentality of the defense. We want to take the aggressiveness away from them. We want to make them start thinking about adjustments. If you have to practice all week looking at that formation, and you do not see it all year, it will drive you crazy.

We have done this. This is my latest change. I go to trips on one side. Now, I've got six men on that side. How do you defense that? If you overload to that side, and start putting people outside of the trips, we start kicking out and run inside. We have two tight ends, and you have to bring a corner up. I do not know how they can handle this.

They can leave the outside backer outside. They can kick their linebackers over. Now, I will motion this wing across the formation and kick-out the end. The quarterback must take a step back so we can pull the guard, who leads the quarterback on the run. I have a running quarterback, too.

You are giving the defense an adjustment. I am going to our no-backs set. Motion the back out of the backfield and have him kick-out. The quarterback runs the ball. You could do this. You can motion the back and make it look like the quarterback keeper. Then the motion man comes back and runs the reverse off the play. In addition, we do run the keeper off this set.

I will put six out there and I will shift to look. We can block all six and just let the quarterback get behind them and run the ball. Again, everything we do is based on the numbers advantage we create with our formations. The quarterback comes up and he looks the defense over. He calls the play right on the line of scrimmage. I just tell the quarterback the plays we run. We run the perimeter, the stretch, the tailback counter, and we run the fullback trap. If you start flying to the perimeter, we run the trap. We will run hard dive plays. Then we can run the dive counter, and the dive keep. We are putting sets up there that will drive you crazy. Here is the bottom line. I give our kids sheets with alignments for our formations. They can write any formation down on paper. I give them sheets for every formation and I teach them how we number everything.

We look at the opponent's film and see how they are going to play us. The quarterback learns from this and this is how he can call the plays and run the game. We are looking for the offensive advantage. When you look at a 50 team, they usually put the strong safety to the tight-end side. We are going to motion or wing and run to the other side.

The offensive advantage is obviously the perimeter in that situation. It sets up the inside running game. We will run to the weakside if the numbers justify it. So, you count 1, 2, 3, 4, and if the strong safety is on that side, we know they only have 1, 2, and 3 to the other side.

These corners cannot be crowding up on the line of scrimmage. If they are, we send the wing in motion and run that way. If you do not want to motion him, we can fake to him with counter action and bring the quarterback outside. Our quarterback rushed for over 1000 yards last year. He is only a 4.8 or a 4.9 kid. He is not a 4.4. Most of my kids go to Division II schools in Pennsylvania.

We do this for every set. We shift, we count, and we run where the numbers dictate. That is my whole offensive philosophy. We are looking for the advantage. While those linemen are colliding and you have a quick running back, he is by the defense. I believe the hard dive is the best play in football. We make a living off that dive play.

I am trying to show you what we give our quarterback. He has to learn how to count the defense. If a man is cheating up from the secondary, we may count him as half a player. We do that with every formation.

I have so many formations that we start using in our junior high schools. They learn about five formations when they are in the eighth grade. In addition, they learn a couple more every year. By the time they are up with me, they already know everything. The nice part of this is that we can use so many kids in our system. I average 50 to 52 letter winners a year. That means that those are kids who earned a letter in our program. You can run a lot of formations and keep kids happy. It keeps the kids being a part of the offense and kids want to be a part of the team.

I just took a job at Wyoming Valley West High School. They are the big rivals of Berwick High School. They ended the season last year with 38 kids. I was hired last week and I had my first meeting with the kids this past Wednesday. We had 111 kids show up. Can I play that many? No! I will beat the shit out of them the first two weeks until we get that down to around 70 players. I will play 50 to 55 kids, because we can plug them into some of these sets.

When you sit down and you watch films, our kids can tell you what we are doing. If they had the clicker, they could say, "Look, coach. Look how they are playing the wing." The kids' wheels are turning. They are looking at that numbers game.

With that, I want to deviate and show you this. I might line up in a rover, twins, and shift into another formation. We are forcing defenses to use goal-line defenses against our formations. We practice against goal-line defense because we know we are asking you to run goal-line defense against us. The old theory today in football is a plot game. Today, everyone says that you have to run the football. You and I know, guys, if you do not have the kids, you cannot run the football. Some of the old-timers will say you have to run the ball even if you only get three yards. They say you have to pound the defense. Oh yeah? If I had the studs every year, I could pound them. But I will pound them from the formations that I am showing you. I have to get six guys on one side because I cannot run against the defense with only three blockers.

So again, guys, what I am trying to show you are the power sets and the numbering game. It is all about numbers, men. That is the bottom the line.

For variety, we run rover Nebraska and rover Kansas. If we run it to the left side, it is our lobo Nebraska or lobo Kansas.

Every offense has a philosophy. You just heard my philosophy. The wing-T teams are going to run their basic plays. They down trap, they run the gut trap, and they run the buck series. They belly their five or six basic plays. That is their philosophy. They may only run two or three sets. They might run a slot-T, wing-T, or double wing-T. It's no different from what I am doing. I am just doing it from a lot of unconventional, unorthodox sets you do not see in every game.

I did not even get into the passing game; I just showed you the running plays. I am telling you, guys. It has won a lot of football games for us over the years.

I hope you got something out of this lecture, men. Thanks.

SPREAD OFFENSE RUNNING GAME

Webster-Thomas High School, New York

Thank you very much for being here today. I appreciate the opportunity to speak with you. I hope you can pick up some techniques that will help your program down the road. Webster High School was a large public school. The school system split the school into two schools, and I had the opportunity to take over the program at Webster-Thomas. It has been an exciting experience.

When I got to the school, I did not know what I was getting into, but it worked out well. My hat is off to my staff sitting in the back of the room. They go beyond what I expect of an assistant coach.

We have had success over the last four years, but we have not gotten over the hump yet. We played in the state finals this year and the state semi-finals last year. In both cases, we lost to the team that won the New York state championship.

I am going to talk about the running game in the spread offense. We installed the spread offense, because in our early years we did not have the offensive linemen we needed to be successful in a conventional offense. We played our first season with sophomores and juniors.

We went to the spread initially to get all of our athletes on the field and it fit our personnel. It has worked out for us. I am a big proponent of running the football. I wanted to run the ball effectively from the spread offense. We use the ground game to set up our passing game. Most coaches think it is the other way around. This past year, we ran the ball 60 percent of the time.

We primarily ran out of the shotgun set. We had an athletic quarterback. With the quarterback as a run threat, it stretched defenses more.

Running the football is a mindset which we developed from day one in our program. We had four receivers on the field, and selling stalk blocking to them was difficult at first. Everyone in your program must be committed to the run for it to be successful.

I want to give you an overview and philosophy of our team before I get into the nuts and bolts of our running game. If you have any questions, just shout them out.

Our receivers are the key to our running game. They have to block, especially the slot receivers. We treat them as offensive linemen. They have an extensive period every day on takeoff and positioning in the stalk block. They come over into the seven-on-seven drills and our air raid drills. Sometimes they take a beating blocking in the running game.

We have to sell the takeoff, getting their hands inside on the chest of the defender. Every time we run the ball, our mindset is to break the play for a touchdown.

In the running game, you want to stretch the field vertically as well as horizontally. By using the spread formation and motion, we create a numbers advantage in the running game.

We use the no-huddle offense as part of the package to control the tempo of the game. If we get up on a team, we want to keep the tempo at a fast pace. We use the armband system of signaling our plays into the game.

We run the shotgun set to use the extra blocker. A large part of the offense is the quarterback reads on the 5 technique or defensive end.

As we break the huddle, the quarterback is reading the safety to see whether the middle of the field is open or closed. We played with a junior quarterback this year. We threw a lot of offense and reads at him and he did a great job. The next thing we read is the number of defenders in the box. If we have a free safety in the middle and six in the box, we can run the ball inside or on the perimeter.

If there are two safeties on the hash, more than likely there will be five in the box. We definitely want to run in that situation. If there is no safety in the middle, we see some kind of blitz. We have designed plays in the game plan that goes with that situation.

We consider the box to be an area two to three yards outside the offensive tackles with a six- to seven-yard depth. That of course depends on where we think the opponent might line up.

The backbone of the perimeter run game is the stalk block of the receivers. Watching the game films from two years ago to last year, we are going in the right direction. However, we are not there yet. I tell our wide receivers that stalk blocking is 80 percent effort and 20 percent technique.

An important part of the stalk block is knowledge. The receiver has to know who to block. We ran into those problems this year. Our slot receiver got confused in some of the defensive looks he faced.

We strive for no penalties in our stalk-blocking scheme. Since the position is so exposed to the referee, it is hard to block defenders in the open field without grabbing them. Holding is the big penalty usually called on offensive receivers. We do not want them to block behind the ball and we do not want them to clip. To avoid penalties it is important for the blocker to be in proper position that aids his techniques.

The wide receiver must have great takeoff. We want his chest over his knees and his knees over his toes. We must take off with a violent hand movement that causes the defensive back to bail out of his coverage. We have to sell the takeoff deep.

The receiver has to read the alignment of the defensive backs. If the defensive back is off the receiver by five yards or more, the receiver pushes the defensive back until the cushion becomes four yards. At that time the receiver breaks down and moves his body into the stalk block.

If the defensive back is less than five yards, the receiver uses a two-yard rule in the execution of the stalk block. If the defensive back plays press coverage, we run him off until he looks back.

Our inside zone play is 11-12 and 13-14. On 11-12, the aiming point of the running back is the inside hip of the offensive guard. The 13-14 play has an aiming point of the inside hip of the offensive tackle. In our play calling, we assign the even-numbered play as plays to the right. The odd-numbered plays go to the left side of the line.

Our offensive line this year was the best by far in the history of our school. They were all two- and three-year starters and made running the football somewhat easier.

The first play is the 12 play run to the right (Diagram #1). Our double-wide slot is our cat formation. Each offensive line player zone steps together with his right foot. We refer to the zone step as a bucket step. As they step, they lose ground slightly. That puts them on the proper angle with the defender. We work combo blocks for the linebackers in the front. The defense is a 4-2 look inside with all the wide receiver covered with a safety in the middle.

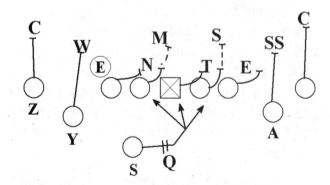

Diagram #1. Inside Zone at 12

The offensive line runs the inside zone-blocking scheme. We combination block the backside stack with the backside offensive guard and tackle. We block the playside stack with the center and playside guard. The playside offensive tackle zone steps to the outside of the defensive end. The backside defensive end is not blocked. The quarterback has to control him. The K-, A-, Y-, and Z-receivers stalk block the men covering them.

The quarterback in the shotgun set drops his back foot to the side of the running back. His eyes go directly to the 5-technique end on the backside. If the end crashes inside down the line, he pulls the ball and goes out the back door. If he gives the ball to the S-back, he carries out his fake to the outside.

The S-back takes an open and a crossover step before he hits downhill at the aiming point. The mesh occurs on the second step and the quarterback pulls the ball or gives it to him on the third step.

He has to be patient and not force the play. The longer the linemen stay on the combo blocks, the better the play works. He reads the defensive linemen. We tell him to cut back one hole for every defender that crosses his face. We want the linebackers to step up and fill the line of scrimmage. That is when the cut-back lanes occur.

We work on our shotgun snaps and steps every day. The quarterback and running back work on the mesh point and we have the quarterback read a defender on every play.

Let me go over the outside zone or stretch play (Diagram #2). The linemen run their zone-step scheme. The playside is right. The formation is a three-wide-receiver set. The twin receivers are to the backside of the run.

The aiming point for the S-back is the outside hip of the tight end or offensive tackle, depending on the formation. The offensive line has to take care of level one first with each member keeping his eyes up to look for linebacker blitzes. The running back stretches the play toward the boundary looking to get vertical. If the flow by the linebacker is over the top, the back cuts the play back.

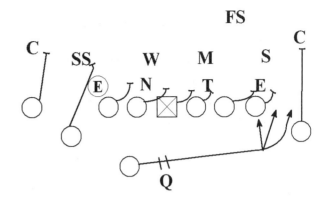

Diagram #2. Outside Zone Stretch

The quarterback from the shotgun has the same assignment on the 5-technique read. If he is under the center, he hands the ball off and fakes the bootleg.

We ran the option game with our quarterback as the alternative to get on the perimeter. We probably ran this play more than the stretch play.

There are a number of different ways to block this play. We can load the scheme and block the defensive end or read him. Game planning or alignment of the defense will make the decision. We like the option against an aggressive defensive end. We use a man-blocking scheme. In the past, we were fortunate to have fast athletic tackles. That gave us the opportunity to reach the defensive end and option the flat defender.

The option play is 18-19 (Diagram #3). We can run the play either way or from under the center. If you run the play under the center, the play hits quicker. When you run it from the shotgun, you have the

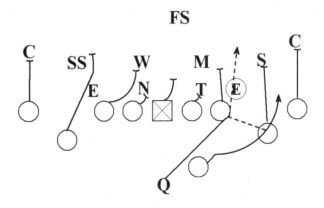

Diagram #3. Option 18-19

built-in space between the quarterback and the defensive end. When you run option, you hold your breath every time the quarterback runs the ball.

The quarterback secures the snap in the shotgun and gets his eyes on the defensive end. The quarterback has two hands on the ball and makes the defender make a decision. He has to take the quarterback or cover the pitch. The pitch relationship must be good so the defensive end cannot force the quarterback to pitch and tackle the pitchman before he turns the corner.

As the quarterback delivers the ball, he steps at the pitchman. He makes the pitch by extending his arm, rotating the palm of his hand out, and then turning the thumb down. He follows the flight of the ball with his back hip and knee. We want velocity on the ball at the same time. If the pitch is bad or the running back fumbles the ball, the quarterback's momentum is in the direction of the ball. It is possible for him to recover the fumble.

As a change-up, we put the S-back to the other side and ran the option away from his alignment. That kept the defense guessing. They cannot key the alignment of the back as to the flow of the option.

The off-tackle play is 35-36 (Diagram #4). On this play, we kick-out the defensive end with the backside guard. Defensive ends like to wrong arm on trap blocks. In that case, the guard logs the defensive end and the play goes outside. The backside tackle pulls and reads the block of the offensive guard. If the guard kicks out, he turns inside and blocks the first opposite jersey. If the guard logs, he takes it outside.

The playside guard, tackle, and center are sealing to the backside. They use combination blocking if there is a stack to that side. As I said before, our tackles were athletic types who pulled extremely well. We could run the play equally to both sides. In some occasions, we do not pull the tackle when we run the off-tackle play. If we got a hard inside charge by a defender aligned over the tackle, we left him in to block that technique.

The S-back takes a counter step away from the hole to let the tackle clear. He gets on the hip of the tackle and reads the block. If the tackle turns inside, he follows him into the hole. If the tackle goes outside, he stays on his hip. The quarterback keys the backside defensive end. If he runs flat down the line, he disconnects and runs out the backside.

We have a quarterback counter. We call the play 4-5 (Diagram #5). It comes off the inside zone fake to the S-back. It is a tackle trap. The tackle pulls and kicks out the defensive end. If the end attacks the pulling tackle with a wrong-arm technique, the tackle logs him inside and the quarterback takes the play outside.

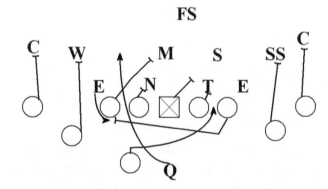

Diagram #5. Quarterback Counter 4-5

We run the play off the inside-zone play and we try to make it look that way with our backside blocking. The S-back runs the inside-zone fake aiming at the outside hip of the guard. If we are effective at running the inside zone, the linebackers will fly across the top with the S-back. If the defensive end closes inside with the offensive tackle pull, the S-back picks him off.

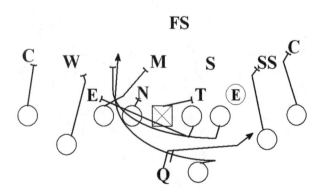

Diagram #4. 35-36 Off Tackle

We also run a quarterback draw called 21-22 (Diagram #6). The S-back is responsible for the playside linebacker. The right guard and tackle invite their blocking assignment to take an outside rush. If they go outside, we push them up the field. If we get an inside move, we take the defender inside and the backs adjust their path. The center and backside guard are responsible for the down lineman to the backside linebacker. The backside tackle kicks out and pass blocks the backside pass rusher.

Off the inside-zone play, we run a simple play-action pass to the slot receiver (Diagram #7). When we find the Mike linebacker flying over the top and trying to get upfield, we run the slot receiver behind him. We tell the receiver he has to get inside the flat defender and watch for the safety dropping down to the inside. He comes inside to a position over the Mike linebacker and looks for the ball. It is a short pass, but if you catch the free safety out of position, it can be a big play.

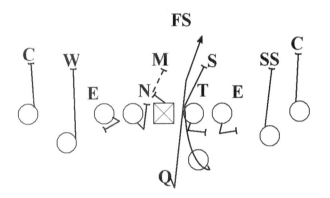

Diagram #6. Quarterback Draw 21-22

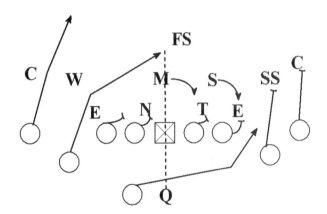

Diagram #7. Zone Play-Action Pass

We run this play because our quarterback is highly mobile. If we want to run the draw to the S-back, we call 23-24. It is basically the same blocking.

Gentlemen, that is all the time I have. If you have any question, I am going to the breakout room and I will answer them there. It was a pleasure for me to address this group. Thank you for the opportunity.

THE THREE- AND FIVE-STEP DROP PASSING GAME

Southlake Carroll High School, Texas

Thank you very much. It is great to be here. Hopefully you can get one or two things from our passing game that might help you. I am going to talk to you about our three- and five-step drop passing game.

We have been on a good run for the last four years in our program. We have played in the last four state championships. We have played 64 games over the last four years. Our season the past four years has gone right up to Christmas. We get out of school on a Friday, play our state championship game on a Saturday, and will not see our players again until our winter program starts.

During the first two days when we get back from the Christmas holidays in January, we conduct an exit interview. In this interview, we want our players to know where they stand in our program and the plans we have in the future. That is the start of our next football season.

We have an outstanding program. We have two freshmen teams and two JV teams. We have 300 kids in our program. We graduated 55 seniors this year. We have five freshmen coaches and 12 varsity coaches, including myself, who work with the varsity and JV. We also have eight middle school coaches. We have two middle schools that feed to our high school.

We practice about 70 players in our varsity practice. Our school is small for a 5A school in Texas. Our enrollment is around 2,300 students. There are schools in the 5A class that have 4,000 students in the school. Well, that is enough about the school; I want to get into the topic.

One of the keys to our success is that we spread the ball around to all of our receivers. It has

been that way in our program from the beginning. I will use the 2005 season as an example of what I mean. Our X-receiver position caught 100 passes this year. We have two players that rotate in and out of that position. Our A-receiver is our best athlete. He runs the jailbreak and tunnel screens, returns, punts, and kicks. He caught 99 passes this year.

The other slot position had receivers rotating into it and caught 55 balls. The Z-receiver position caught 57 passes. The running back catches screens, flares, and check-down patterns, and was the fifth wide receiver in our spread package. He caught another 42 balls.

The point I am trying to make is we have to spread the ball around to different players. I have someone on the sideline that keeps track of how many touches our receivers are getting. We cover that with our quarterback in between series.

We played 16 football games last year. In 13 games, we had seven receivers that caught passes. We want to spread the ball around and be difficult to defend.

From a passing standpoint, we want to average 22 completions per game. On our goal board, we asked our offense to be 50 percent effective on third down. The same statistic in the NFL is 33 percent. We achieved that goal 15 times this year. When I mention that to people, they think all we do is throw the ball. We had a tailback that rushed for over 1,500 yards and a quarterback that rushed for 1,200 yards.

The quick passing game is what allows us to be good on third down. The reason for that is we do not have many third-and-long situations. Everything in your offense is good on second-and-four. The quick passing game allows you to get into that situation all the time. We have a slant, stop, and a five-yard out route. The intent of these routes is to pick up six and seven yards on first down.

We have a no-huddle mode to our offense and we are a big numbers advantage team. If there are five defenders in the box, we run the ball. If there are six defenders in the box, we throw the ball.

I am going through these quickly. We break our pass into categories. We are a 99 percent shotgun team. We only align in three formations. We run two-by-two, three-by-one, and three-by-two. We do not use a tight end package and we do not motion. We get under the center to run a quarterback sneak or a dive in short-yardage or goal-line situations.

Our quarterback is in the shotgun 99 percent of the time. In the three-step game, he does not drop to throw. He catches the ball and throws it. We tell him to grip it and rip it. He is in the same stance as if he were under the center. He is five yards from the center. If he throws to the right, we call that "turntable." He pivots and throws the ball. The quarterback knows what footwork he is using before the ball gets into his hands. He has made a pre-snap decision on which way he is going with the ball.

Basically everything we do comes off a pre-snap decision of the quarterback. If he throws to his left, we use the term "coming across the bow." That term comes from baseball. Most of our quarterbacks have, at one time or another, played shortstop. His footwork is like the shortstop taking the throw from the second baseman and turning the double play. The quarterbacks understand that footwork because they have all played shortstop.

The first play we teach is 50 stop (Diagram #1). The 50 protection is a slide protection, but it looks like run blocking. The tailback gets a call from the tackle that tells him to block the C gap or the B gap. In the two-by-two slot set, all the receivers run a five-yard stop pattern.

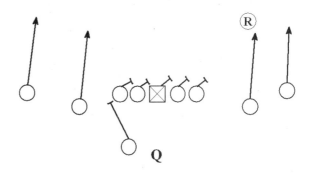

Diagram #1. 50 Stop

We never sight adjust our patterns. If we call the stop pattern, we run the stop pattern. The wide receiver comes off the line, posts up the defender, and becomes a "basketball player." The quarterback reads the defender on top of the number-two receiver. The quarterback can never be late throwing on the quick game.

If the defender crosses the slot receiver, we throw the ball to the slot receiver. If he stays on the slot receiver, we throw the ball outside. The quarterback throws most of our quick passes to the widest receiver. The quarterback works the shortest and softest throw. That is how Rich Rodriguez at West Virginia describes the throw. I like Coach Rodriguez's passing game. If we have a corner that aligns five yards off of one outside receiver and the other corner is seven yards off the other receiver, the throw goes to the receiver covered with the seven-yard cushion.

We coach our receiver on yardage and not steps. We talk in terms of a five-yard stop pattern and not a three-step stop pattern.

As a change up, we throw the 50 quick (Diagram #2). The outside receiver runs a quick out at five yards and the inside receivers run five-yard post cuts. The receiver can catch the five-yard out and step out of bounds for a six-yard gain.

In my mind, the beauty of the quick passing game is that we can take it anytime we want. I never was much of a slant runner. I did not like the pattern and did not like to coach it. Two years ago we started to throw the slant pattern and it has become one of our best patterns. It is not the same

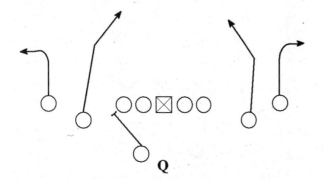

Diagram #2. 50 Quick

slant that we threw when I played. Today the pattern is a skinny slant. Our slants are flat patterns. They are like a three-step dig pattern or square in. We call the pattern 50 slant (Diagram #3). The receiver catches the ball at seven to eight yards, running the pattern under control.

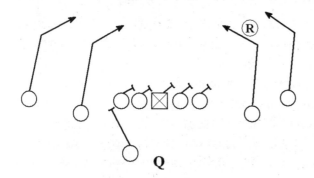

Diagram #3. 50 Slant

The inside receiver wants to run his pattern right through the toes of the flat defender. He wants to pick the flat defender. He wants the flat defender to engage him. On the snap of the ball, if the flat defender flies past the vertical stretch of the slot receiver, he sits down because he will get the ball.

We must have a plan in case that happens. We try to create the pick and let the outside receiver catch the ball at the midpoint of the original alignment of the receivers. This is not the old post-cut slant; it is another way to run the stop pattern, but stay on the move.

I want to clarify a point about the shortest and softest throw. On the stop-and-quick pattern, we throw the shortest and softest throw or the

cleanest side. The shortest throw is into the sideline or the shortside of the field. However, on the slant pattern, the cleanest side will be the wideside of the field. That rule applies to the wideside of the field because the receiver is running toward the quarterback.

The cleanside refers to the number of defenders under a pattern. If a side is clean, there are no defenders under the pattern. If the quarterback reads blitz, he throws the ball to the side of the blitz, because he knows that side will be clean.

The stop, quick, and slant work together and are very high percentage throws. If we get a flat defender tight on the slot receiver, we check to a dragon (Diagram #4). If the rover sets on the slot receiver and tries to work across his face and get underneath the outside receiver, we run 50 dragon.

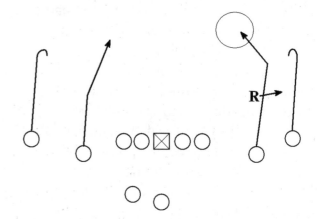

Diagram #4. 50 Dragon

The slot continues up the field and the outside receiver runs a stop route. On this pattern, as well as the other three patterns, we throw the ball off the defender over the slot receiver. We may not call dragon. The receiver understands what the defender is trying to do. He is trying to disrupt his vertical stem or get across his face and underneath the outside receiver. We may automatically run the dragon.

The next pattern is what I call crawfish (Diagram #5). I grew up in southeast Texas close to the Louisiana border. I grew up eating crawfish. If you have ever seen a crawfish, it looks like what I have drawn for the slot receivers. The slot receiver runs a bubble pattern. We do not consider this part of our screen game. Our offensive linemen are not getting out to the outside.

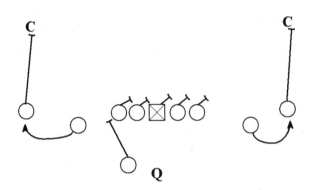

Diagram #5. Crawfish

The key to this pass is the accuracy of the quarterback and the blocking of the outside receivers. The outside receiver works the corners outside number and has to stay square on him. The advantage the corner has over the receiver is he sees the ball and the receiver does not. Therefore, as soon as the receiver turns his shoulders, he is dead. He has to stay square and ride the defender out of bounds and let the slot get inside of him.

When you run the no-huddle spread offense, the play you lose is the toss sweep. We are getting better with the stretch play, but crawfish is our answer to the sweep.

In practice, when we have our kicking-game drill, we drill our quarterbacks on this throw. The special-team period is 10 minutes. We round up every back, receiver, extra defensive back, or anybody not in the kicking drill, and run this route for 10 minutes. The quarterbacks throw this pattern repeatedly, until it becomes second nature. We tell the quarterback that it has to be an extended handoff.

When we first put the crawfish into the offense, we had a wide receiver that caught the ball and ran all over the place. He reversed his field and made all kinds of big plays. Every other receiver without his talent thought they could do the same thing. That is when we installed the seven-yard rule.

If the receiver does not get seven yards on the play, his grade is a minus. This play must gain seven yards. We want to catch the ball and explode upfield.

The last of the quick-game passes is HBO (Diagram #6). The outside receivers run the fade route. The slot receivers run a five-yard speed out. They cut the pattern at four yards and end up at six yards.

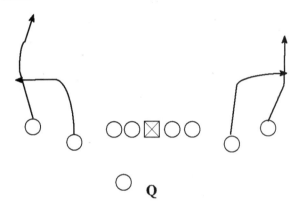

Diagram #6. HBO

Years ago we had a pattern we ran called HBO. Those letters stood for halfback option. We kept the name, but there is no option. They roll at four to six yards on the speed out. The quarterback reads from the inside out. We have a pattern we call fade. On paper, the patterns are exactly alike, but the reads on the fade are outside in.

We only have two pass protections. We have the 50 protection that goes with our quick game. We have 60 and 70 protections that go with our 60 and 70 passing games. If the back is on the right of the quarterback, it is a 60 protection. If he is on the left of the quarterback, it is 70 protection.

In the 60 protection, we block big-on-big with our offensive guards and tackles (Diagram #7). The center has the Mike linebacker and the tailback has the rover or support player to his side. The 70 protection is the same protection with the back on the left. If the defense brings the seventh rusher, the quarterback throws hot in the face of the blitz.

In the 60-70 game, we want to attack the defense with our inside-outside concept. We want to attack a team with a smash concept. We want to attack them with four verticals. We have a couple

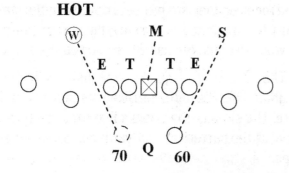

Diagram #7. 60-70 Protection

of ways to do that. We want to attack with at least one high-low concept. Those are patterns with shallow crosses and dig patterns with a post off the top. We want to attack the defense with our choice game, which is the tagged route for us.

When we game plan, we go into the game with all our quick passes. We have one pass from each of the inside-out, smash, and high-low schemes. We go into the game with our choice scheme where we tag all the patterns.

That is how we practice and go into the game. The first play in the 60 game is 62 all-sit (Diagram #8). This is the simplest play you can run, but it fits into my comfort zone. It is absolutely one of our most successful pass plays. All four receivers sell the vertical routes and sit at 10 yards. A 10-yard curl route in our terminology is a 10-yard sit. Many things carry over from the quick game to the 60-70 game. The quarterback picks out the cleanside before he snaps the ball.

He knows the side he wants to work and eliminates the other. He knows exactly what

defender he wants to read. For the lecture, he eliminates the right side of the pattern. He looks for the defender on top of the slot receiver on the left side. The only three coverages we talk about are 2, 3, and zero coverage.

The slot receiver releases on what looks like a vertical. The defender walls the slot receiver and the quarterback delivers the ball to the outside receiver. He knows he is facing a three-deep coverage with the seam defender carrying the vertical. There will be no one under the outside receiver.

If the defender over the slot crosses his vertical stem, the ball comes inside to the slot receiver. The slot receiver has a blitz rule. If the defender over the slot receiver blitzes, the slot cuts his route to eight yards. The quarterback reads the blitz and hit the slot receiver at eight yards.

The drop in the shotgun set is a three-step drop with one or two hitch steps. This pattern is a one-hitch pattern. If we are not careful, people will begin to read our passes happening at 10 yards. We must change up from time to time. We do that by taking a deep set and running everything to 15 yards.

The other change up we started running this year is 62 rail sit (Diagram #9). The outside receiver starts in at a 45-degree angle and get vertical up the seam. The slot crosses behind the outside receiver and runs a wheel route to a sit. We do the same thing to both sides.

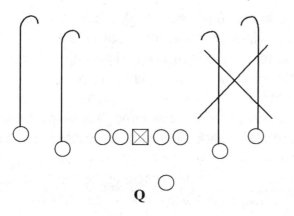

Diagram #8. 62 All Sit

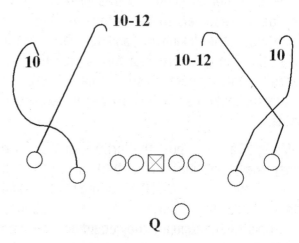

Diagram #9. 62 Rail Sit

The reads are the same for both patterns. It does not change his footwork at all. The rail concept is off our four-vertical scheme. In our world, when the receivers cross, corners and safeties for some reason get flustered and back off. It is the same play as the all-sit, except we switch assignments. That is an example of our inside-outside concept.

The next part of the attack is the smash concept. This play is 71 smash (Diagram #10). If you asked our quarterbacks what their favorite route was, they would say the smash route. They love to throw flag routes. Corners got so good at playing the route, we had to doctor up the routes.

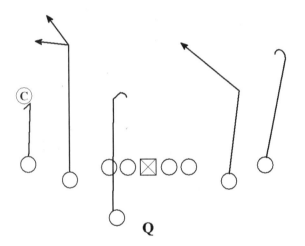

Diagram #10. 71 Smash

The left outside receiver runs a five-yard stop route. The slot receiver pushes and sticks his route at 25 yards. It does not matter what type of coverage the defense plays; the quarterback reads the coverage. If the coverage is a two-deep coverage, the quarterback brings the receiver down toward the sideline with his throw. If the coverage is three-deep, he throws the ball over the top.

The slot receiver to the backside reads the middle of the field. If it is open, he pops the pipe. The pipe is the middle of the field between the two deep safeties. The outside receiver runs a sit route at 10 yards. The running back checks his blitz read and run a check-down route at five yards.

We used to run this pattern and never looked at the backside. I now give the quarterback the freedom in the pre-snap decision to work the frontside or backside of the play. Whichever side he decides to work, he cannot be late throwing to either side.

If the safety is tight, we go to the playside. The quarterback reads the corner. He takes his three-step drop and one hitch. If the corner bails out, he takes the stop route right now. If the corner bites up on the stop, the quarterback hits the flag over the top.

If the quarterback decides to take the backside, his read is the safety. It is the receiver's job to beat the safety. If the seam defender jumps on the slot receiver and walls him out of the middle, the quarter goes to the sit pattern immediately. If the seam defender is dropping to a zone, the quarterback throws the pipe.

If we run the smash route into the three-by-one set, the outside receiver to the three-man side runs the five-yard stop. (Diagram #11) The outside slot runs the runs the flag route. The inside slot runs the pipe. We work a two-on-one scheme on the safety deep.

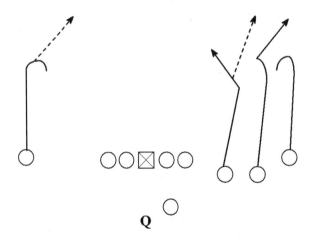

Diagram #11. 61 Smash

What we like to do is tag the single receiver with a glance call. The backside receiver instead of running a sit route takes the pipe route. When the inside slot hears the tagged call, he stays outside of the middle. We want the single receiver isolated in the middle of the football field.

The last thing I want to show you we got from Texas Tech. We call it slice. (Diagram #12) The play is a double smash. On a double smash, the outside receivers run stop routes at five yards. The slot receivers run flag routes. The outside receiver to the slice side runs the stop and slices to the middle of the field.

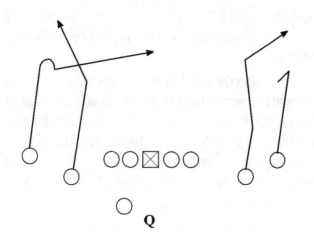

Diagram #12. Slice

I like this play against a two-deep coverage scheme. It is not good against a blitz. That is why we run it when we do not expect blitz. It is good against a team that rushes three or four and drops seven or eight into the coverage.

That is all the scheme material I have. I want to you to know that as simple as this may seem, it takes the entire year to make it work. When we finish football in December, we do not see our players again until we get ready to start our winter program. That starts the next drive for another state championship.

In January when we have our exit interviews with our team, the position coaches have interviews with the freshmen, sophomores, and juniors. I conduct the interviews with our seniors. I talk to our seniors because I do not want them to feel like we have abandoned them just because they are not returning to the team.

I do not want our players to think that we have used them for four years and now we are kicking them out the door. I want them to understand we will be there for them. That I am very interested in where they are going, and I want to help them in any way that I can. We want to encourage them to get their applications filled out and to do what they want to do. They have big dreams, but sometimes they need the extra push in that direction.

When our kids come back from Christmas break, we test them on bench press, squats, and the 200-meter race. The reason we test them on the 200 meters is to get them ready for track season. The month of January is spent working on the weights, speed development, and getting our kids ready for track season. At Southlake Carroll, if you play football, you run track. That is the way it is. They can play basketball or baseball, but they are going to run track. They might never run in a track meet, but they are going through the track workout. Players understand when they come into our program that dragon football and dragon track are the same thing.

As part of our weight program, we run gassers. That is an over-and-back run. We jog across the field and run back. Any time we do this, it is on the clock. Our linemen have to complete the circuit in 17 seconds. That is each of the linemen. If someone does not make it, everybody goes again. Everyone completing the circuit in the allotted time is the accountability factor we build into our team.

In February, we go into our quarterback school. I take all of the quarterbacks in our program, pull them out of the regular off-season program, put them into the school, and work with them exclusively. I have one junior, two sophomores, and three freshmen that will go into our quarterback training school.

We pull them out of the indoor program and they spend a month in the classroom and on the practice field. This is an intense quarterback-training session. The quarterback school has been a huge factor in the continuing success within our program.

We start to prepare our receivers for seven-on-seven passing camps. Those camps take place later in the year. We have four different teams that compete in the passing camps that happen all over the state of Texas. We compete in the seven-on-seven leagues for the reps it gives our team. I could care less whether we ever win a seven-on-seven game. If they keep score, our kids will compete. I tell our quarterbacks and receivers that I never want to come to watch them in a summer league and not know what they are running. I want them to run our patterns and our coverages. We can get a lot of good out of the league by running our offense and our coverages.

During the month of August, we run a dragon football camp for seventh-, eighth-, and ninth-grade players. We have 300 players in this camp. We have 28 coaches and a bunch of our football players that will work the camp. In our youth camps, I do not ask any of the teams that play in the third-, fourth-, fifth-, and sixth-grade leagues to run our offense. I would, however, like them to get in the huddle the way we do and stretch the way we do so they can get them ready for seventh- and eighth-grade football.

All of the teams in our youth program are called the dragons. They do not play against one another. They play against other teams in the area. It has been a unifying type of thing.

Our program is a year-round program which perpetuates itself. We never want to say we are rebuilding within our program. Our players want to be the next great dragon team to play in the state championship. They feel they can carry on in the tradition of what has made Lakeland Carroll High School great.

It was an honor to be here representing my school, state, and coaching staff. I appreciate the opportunity to come and speak to this group. I have enjoyed myself and I hope you got something you can use in your program. Thank you very much.

QUARTERBACK PASSING-GAME DEVELOPMENT

Cincinnati Hills Christian Academy, Ohio

A lot of things have to come together to have a season like we did this past year. We obviously had some good players, we had great team speed, we had great senior leadership, and our player's work ethic matched their goals. It is okay for your team to say they want to win a state championship if your work ethic matches that. If your work ethic does not match your goals, you have some things to talk about with your players. I am also surrounded by a very good coaching staff. Two of our coaches are with me today. John Robinson is our special teams' coordinator, defensive line coach, and technology guru. He put this PowerPoint presentation together for me. Reed Chacksfield is our defensive coordinator. Every year we have an excellent defense and it is because Reed knows how to get the best out of his personnel. We run a complex defense and every game we are very well prepared for the contest.

There are many coaches who have influenced me as a quarterback coach. I am always looking for camps for my quarterbacks and want to find places where I think they are teaching similar ideas that we are teaching our players. Mike Kapiche has a quarterback camp and certainly teaches outstanding techniques. I have spent some time with Hal Mumme, Mike Leach, and Chris Hatcher when they were at Kentucky. I learned a lot from them. I also have been able to sit down and talk to Jon Kitna. I was able to talk to him about the things that I teach. He was gracious enough to spend some time with me and give me some ideas on how to teach our quarterbacks.

In our offense, we are not just a passing offense, but we do like to throw the ball. I am going to talk about quarterback development in the passing game. I will go over the techniques and drills we use at Cincinnati Hills Christian Academy. I will also go over our audibles and automatics that have been very successful for us. Because we like to throw the ball, our quarterbacks only play offense. So when we are practicing defense, the quarterbacks will stay with me. We will work on individual quarterback drills. We will work on reading drills. We will work on their weaknesses. Sometimes we will watch our defense and I will ask our quarterbacks coverage questions. I will ask them who their read is if we are throwing a smash route. I like our quarterbacks to watch our defense because we use many different coverage schemes. It helps them understand defensive concepts.

I am going to begin by talking about quarterback characteristics. Our quarterback needs to be smart and decisive. He must be able to make quick reads and decisions. He has to take all of the information you have given him during the week and come out and understand who his read is on a particular play. He must be able to narrow things down and know who his read is so he can be decisive. The most important thing for the quarterback is to know what the defense is trying to do.

Next, I believe the quarterback has to be accurate. I do not care how strong a quarterback is, he must be able to put touch on the ball and put the ball where it needs to be. I think a quarterback must be physically and mentally tough. Our quarterback this season was a junior and we put a lot of pressure on him. He does a good job with processing all of this. The quarterback also needs to be able to forget his bad plays. He needs to understand why it happened, but he cannot be looking back. I think it is important that the quarterback be a competitor. If you watched Vince Young at Texas, you may not have thought he was that great of a technique quarterback, but there is no question about how he competes. If you watched the championship game, you saw him win that game because he is such a competitor. The demeanor of his team fed off of his leadership.

The quarterback also needs to be disciplined and team-oriented. He needs to be in the weight room. He needs to be encouraging other players. He needs to be disciplined in all the things that he does. Our quarterbacks also need to be technique conscious. He needs to be thinking about his technique all the time. We would like to not worry about technique during games. We can do that if our quarterbacks have understood the importance of proper technique. That allows us to concentrate on execution and reading the defense in game situations.

The last characteristic we expect of our quarterbacks is good arm strength. He has to have good enough arm strength to get the ball down the field and stretch the defense.

We also have some ideas on receiver characteristics. Obviously, they have to have great hands. I have never thought that if I had a freshman receiver that could not catch the ball that he would be able to develop that skill to become a productive receiver. Therefore, I tend to move those guys to other places quickly. We recently had a young man that proved me wrong in this area as he had 20 touchdowns and over 50 catches as a senior. I guess my attitude toward developing the hands of a receiver has changed because of this one player.

Our receivers have to be able to run good routes. He has to understand when to break down and when to run through. He has to understand the difference in defenses and what they are trying to do. Obviously, it is a position that requires decent speed. I think good receivers also have physical and mental toughness. Our receivers need to be good blockers, and without physical toughness they cannot do that job. He also has to be tough enough to knock balls down if the quarterback has thrown bad balls. I really think our receivers did a great job of exhibiting toughness this season.

Let me move into quarterback techniques. Let me start with how to grip the ball. I want to make sure the quarterbacks understand a couple of things about gripping the ball. I want the quarterback to grip the ball with one or two fingers on the laces. I would like to have two fingers on the laces. There should be air between the palm and the ball. If you palm the football, it will produce a throw that turns the nose down. There should be daylight between the palm and the ball as he grips the ball.

I want the quarterback to grip the ball with just enough tightness so that the ball does not fall out of his hands. Many quarterbacks get sore arms because they are gripping the ball too tightly. Even though we do a lot of throwing, our juniors and seniors rarely get sore arms because they understand how tight to grip the ball. If they are using proper techniques, they are not going to develop sore arms. One of the things that I picked up from Hal Mumme was that the thumb and the ring finger should make a perfect circle around the football. Coach Mumme believes that this helps create a more perfect spiral on the throw.

Next, I want to talk about our quarterback stance. In his stance, I am going to have his toes in slightly. This allows them to be in good balance and to keep from taking a false step. It also allows the quarterback to be able to go in either direction and to use the opposite foot to push off. The heels of the quarterback should be slightly off the ground. Our feet are parallel and we are bending slightly at the knees. Your hands should be set with the throwing hand over the non-throwing hand, with the left thumb under the right thumb. As the quarterback gets under the center, his middle fingers should be right in the crotch of the center. Elbows should be bent slightly, and the quarterback should give pressure with the bottom hand. Pressure with the bottom hand does not allow separation of the hands on the snap.

I would like to talk about the five points of release. I talk often about starting with the ball in the trigger position. This is something I got from Coach Curry. As soon as you get the ball from the center, you are going to get it into trigger position. I want the ball relaxed in the quarterback's hands. The landmark of the trigger position is in between the armpit and the earlobe. If the quarterback takes off running, we want the ball to stay in trigger position until he is ready to release the ball. In trigger position, the nose of the ball is turning down and the left hand is a bit under the ball. Next, we will push the ball back from elbow to shoulder height. We will push the ball back and get our elbow up to shoulder height. We do not want a sidearm thrower and we do not want a passer who is going to bring the ball behind his head. We feel that if the elbow is held low, then sore arms will develop. So we work hard on pushing the elbow back to shoulder height. As the elbow is brought to that height, the nose of the ball should point back.

Next, is our weight exchange. When we step, I would like a six-inch step. I think quarterbacks overstride a great deal, especially if they are throwing deep. If they take a six-inch step, the hips will be able to help in the throw. The quarterback also wants to point their lead toe at the receiver. If the aiming point of a throw is in front of the receiver, the toe needs to be pointed just in front of the receiver. You want to take your step on the whole foot. If you just step on your toe, your knee will lock out and produce a poor throw. We desire that we step with our knee bent. If a quarterback steps with a straight knee, two things could happen. If he releases the ball late with a straight knee, the ball will go into the ground. If he releases the ball early with a straight knee, the ball will sail.

The next point is our index-finger follow-through. As the ball is thrown, the pinky fingers are the first finger to come off the ball. If the ball is thrown correctly, the index finger is the last finger to come off the ball. That should lift the nose of the ball up a little bit. The follow through should be to the side pocket or to the groin area. I do not want the quarterback to end up across his body. I think that is hard on his arm. After the release of the ball, the palm is going to face down and out, the thumb is down, and the index finger is extended.

Finally, we want to finish with the opposite elbow breaking the plane of the back with our chin over the front foot. Our back heel should come off the ground and it may move forward just a bit. Jon Kitna said a great drill to emphasize this is to throw and step through so the hip helps the throw. If you get your hips into the throw, your heel may come off the ground and you will drag your toe to the opposite heel. We want all of these release thoughts to work together to get the shoulders and the hips into the throw.

I want to talk about our drops and then I will go over some of the drills that we work. The three-step drop will be worked on as the quarterbacks are on a line facing me. I will check their stance before we begin. I will say, "Big," and the quarterbacks will take a big step. The key on the first step is to gain separation from center. On the first step, the ball should be moved to a trigger position. As we step, I want to make sure we are heel to heel. I do not want to understride or overstride so that the quarterback ends up over a guard. I will then say, "Little." At that point, the quarterback takes his second step, which is a little step. We repeat that for our third step, and then I want each of them up on his front foot to simulate a throw. I want them to stop on the third step so I can see their finish position. I want to see that no one is overstriding and I want to see that their belly button is over their knee. After we have taken our steps, we repeat the drill at quarter speed. Before we begin, I am looking at their eyes to make certain they are looking up and checking their stances. We then will run the drill at half speed. We will finish our drop drill at full speed. I do not want to see the quarterbacks rush with a bigger second and third step. This will cause the ball to sail. If our footwork is not proper, I do not want the quarterbacks to rush. We will move back to slower speeds and work on our steps.

When we work on the three-step drop and throwing to the left, we work with his big, little, and cheat step, as well as his plant step. His foot is going to come around and turn so that the quarterback's hips can open and turn to the throw. This will get our front toe pointed at the receiver. We will go through the same processes of this drill as we did with our three-step drop to the right. If the quarterback follows proper technique, he will not have a problem throwing to the left.

The five-step drop goes through the same drill work that I have explained with the three-step drop. On our five-step drop, we want the first three steps all to be big steps as we work our way away from the center. The final two steps can be two short, shuffle steps with an emphasis on getting our hips down with a slight forward lean as we prepare to throw the ball. As we begin to work on throwing to the left, we will work on the same cheat step on the final step as we did with the three-step drop.

In our shotgun, our five-step drop is a three step and our three-step drop is a one step. With our three-step-drop routes in the shotgun, we work on just setting our feet with a small step and throwing.

On our spot and bubble passes, if I am throwing to the right side from under the center, I am going to step with my right leg to get my leg open. I am then going to take a gather step with my second step so that I can step into the throw. If I am throwing to the left, the technique is the same, but we really emphasize getting turned so the shoulder gets pointed at the receiver. The step needs to be in the direction of the target and will want to put the ball on the downhill shoulder of the receiver for the bubble. If the quarterback is struggling with throwing the bubble, there is a very good chance he is rushing his mechanics or not getting his shoulder turned. Out of the shotgun, our footwork is very similar, although we do not have to step back as far. We just catch the ball and take a small crow hop to get into proper position.

I will now cover some of the drills that we use. Every day we do our throwing drills. Our quarterbacks will face each other, 10 yards apart, standing with toes pointing toward each other. They will make their throws to each other with a shoulder turn. They do not step or use any lower-body technique in this drill. From time to time, I will walk in between the quarterbacks with my hands up so the quarterback has to learn to put the ball up and over me.

We turn the quarterbacks to the side with their toes straight and throw with a hip turn. We do this to both sides. Next, the quarterbacks will take a knee. This allows us to isolate the mechanics of the upper body. We want to get the ball to the trigger position and work their elbow up into proper height. I also look closely at their finish in this drill to make certain that the position of the arm is correct on the finish. I will also make the quarterbacks freeze their arms after they get it into a throwing position. This allows us to examine if the elbow is at shoulder height.

The last drill we use is to stand on one leg (left leg for right-hander). To throw, we must get a good shoulder and hip turn. The right hip should lead as you throw. This teaches the power you must use in your upper body to throw the ball.

We also work a great deal with our footwork drills. When I have our quarterbacks while the defense is practicing, these are some of the drills we will use. Obviously, we work on the drops that I have previously described. We also work on line jumps. We will be on a line working one-leg perpendicular jumps, parallel jumps, split jumps, and jumping to swivel our hips. We do all of these jumps with the ball in trigger position.

We work a great deal on line drops. We will put our quarterbacks on the sideline and drop to the hash mark. On my command, the quarterback will turn and drop, working on the ball and getting to trigger position in a relaxed fashion. We emphasize strides and speed in this drill. We want to get big strides and good speed in our drop. When the quarterback approaches the hash mark, I will put my hands up and he will set and throw me the ball. When you do these drills, you see what kind of feet each player has, and the mechanics of them setting up to throw the ball.

We also do a scramble drill. I will command to go, and the quarterback drops. I will point in a direction for the quarterback to scramble. If I point back, he will move back. I will also have indicators for the quarterback to throw the ball, or to run towards me. I may put my hands down for him to run toward me and when I put my hands up, he has to move to throw the ball. I will tell them that they can throw on the run or they can stop and throw. I want make sure they understand that they cannot be running away from a receiver and throw the ball to him. They have to stop their feet and step into the throw.

We also use the typical ladder drill with our quarterbacks. The only difference is that we will use the drills with a football being kept in the trigger position. We will do all of the ladder workouts: one foot in each hole, two feet in each hole, sideways, and the typewriter drill. We will then go to our dummy drops. I will align two dummies in seven lines. We will have the quarterback drop. When he gets to the top, he will slide forward, step with his back foot, come to the bottom of the dummies, then drop-step slide, and drop-step slide back around the top of the dummies. The quarterback will go through all seven sets of dummies in this fashion. We work this drill much like our scramble drill in that I will give the quarterback a sign to throw the ball as he is working through the pocket. He may not be able to take a large step to throw because of the dummies. I want the quarterbacks to keep their eyes up and not look down at the dummies.

I want to look at our automatics. If our Y-receiver in the slot is left uncovered, the quarterback will give him a signal and either throw him a spot or bubble route. The quarterback will tap the center before putting his hands underneath. This is a sign to the center that there will be no cadence. When his hands go underneath the center, the ball will be snapped without a call from the quarterback. The quarterback will turn and throw the spot pass without anyone else really knowing what is going on.

The next automatic is to our A-receiver, who would be the middle receiver in a trips set. If the outside receiver is the one left uncovered, we will audible to him and run a quick or fade route. These checks to uncovered receivers are something that has been very successful for us.

If the corner is playing up or well inside our wide receiver, we will signal for a one-step fade route. To practice all of these, we will come out at the end of our morning practice of two-a-days and run nothing but automatics and audibles. This is five minutes, very fast paced, working the quick and fade routes outside. The inside receivers will be working the spot and bubble routes. This allows everyone to get used to our signals. As we get into our scripts in practice, out of 15 plays, two of those will be designed for an audible. Out of the shotgun, we will use hand signals for an audible. We can call plays in our two-minute situation, but often we have situations that allow the quarterback to automatic to something else. This does not take a great deal of practice time, but does allow your players to take advantage of situations that are given to them. The players always have fun with it because they are doing a little of their own thing.

We check our weakside outside receiver often. We will audible his route and change the huddle call route based on the coverage shown. If the defense is giving us a slant, we can change to that. We can also change to several other routes as well. If we audible to the spot pass, we like for the corner to be at least six yards off the line. That would be seven yards if we were in shotgun.

I am out of time. I appreciate you having me at this clinic. I hope you got something out of this and if you have questions, give us a call.

THE LEGION OF DOOM BLITZ PACKAGE

Muskogee High School, Oklahoma

Today I am going to talk about our blitz package. Basically, we are going to get after the offense and apply the pressure. We call defense the "Legion of Doom" blitz defense. We are going to preach this concept, and we are going to sell it to our players. If you are going to be a blitz team, there are certain things you must do.

Every offensive coach will sit back and brag about their offense. "We love it when a team runs the blitz against us. When a teams runs the blitz, it opens up gaps for us on offense." I can assure you those coaches are not asking their quarterbacks if they like to see the blitz. I can bet that most quarterbacks are not going to tell you they love teams that blitz. He is sitting back in the pocket and getting his head torn off. We run the blitz with this in mind: we are going to punish your quarterback and we are going to make things happen. We want to create big plays on defense. Our offense is a big-play offense. We have the offense to do that, so our offense and defense meshes in this respect.

This is the most important statement I will make during this lecture: the goal of our blitz package is to limit the offense on big plays, but you must understand you are not going to eliminate all of them. With offenses the way they are nowadays, they are going to get some big plays on you. You must do the best you can against the offense, but you are not going to eliminate all of them. Your kids must know this and understand it to be successful in running the blitz. That is our goal each year. We want to cut down on the big plays. We know we are not going to totally eliminate them.

Our basic Legion of Doom philosophy is as follows. Coaches tell me they do not have the players to play the blitz defense. My deal is this: if

you can't cover the offense, you need to send more players on the blitz. If you sit back and play zone coverage, the offense is going to find holes in your defense. If you do not have the players that can make the tackles, it is difficult to play zone defense. If we have a hard time covering the receivers, we are going to send more on the blitz. There are two ways to skin a cat when it comes to the passing game. You can lock them down, cover the receivers, and play a tight zone coverage. The other way is to get after the quarterback and not let him be accurate. That is what we want to do in our blitz package.

Speed kills. We are going to blitz our fast players. We are not going to blitz our slow players. We blitz the players that can run. We do not want to blitz a man from the corner that runs a 5.2. By the time he gets to the quarterback, the ball will be gone. I am not a big inside blitz coach. I prefer the blitz from the perimeter. We do run the blitz inside, but the majority of our blitzes are from the outside with our outside linebackers and safeties. They are players that can run. It seems every time we run an inside blitz, the offense runs a draw play or a screen pass and they have us in a bind. You do not get hurt as bad if you run the perimeter blitzes. This is how we start teaching our defense.

- Play hard.
  - ✓ No loafing.
  - ✓ There is no reason why anyone in the state should play harder than us.
  - ✓ Execute every play at maximum speed.
- Be aggressive and physical.
  - ✓ No hit, no play.
  - ✓ Football is a collision sport; dancing is a contact sport.

- ✓ Make other teams scared to play the Legion of Doom.
- Be prepared.
  - ✓ Know your assignments.
  - ✓ Know your opponent's tendencies.
  - ✓ Five Ps: Proper preparation prevents poor performance.
- Execute.
  - ✓ Stop the run.
    - ○ Gap-control defense.
    - ○ No vertical creases with open-ended funnels.
    - ○ Have eleven "mad-hats" on the ball.
    - ○ Be a great tackling defense.
  - ✓ Control the pass.
    - ○ No bombs.
    - ○ Diversity.
    - ○ Disguise.
    - ○ Reroute receivers.
    - ○ Pressure the quarterback.
    - ○ Dominate on third down.
    - ○ Finish the play.

Legion of Doom Philosophy – Building Our Package

- K.I.L.L. Keep It Learnable and Likable (Not K.I.S.S.). Don't underestimate our players or our coaches. Be willing to learn it and teach it.
- Attack.
- Pressure the offense.
- Don't let the offense dictate the tempo.
- Attack and read.
- Employ diversity.
  - ✓ Be as diverse and flexible as the offense.
  - ✓ Not just front diversity, but also secondary.
- Use automatics.
  - ✓ Have an automatic versus every formation and a generic automatic versus bastard formations.
  - ✓ Use against ghosts and difficult formations.

Legion of Doom Alignment Calls

We play three types of defenses. First is our tight or regular defense. Second is our split look. The third defense we run is the bear look. I will show you a couple of stunts we run.

Tight (Diagram #1)

- Move to tight end.
- Double tight ends.
- Move to second receiver side.
- Auto: Loose away from call.
- Balanced set
- Middle of the field, move right.
- Hash, move to field.

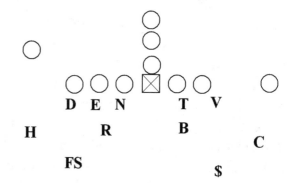

Diagram #1. Tight Defense

Split Defense (Diagram #2)

- Move away from tight end.
- No tight end, move to number-two receiver side.
- Balanced set
  - ✓ Middle of the field, move right.
  - ✓ Hash, move to boundary.

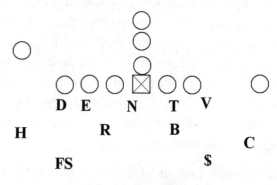

Diagram #2. Split Defense

Bear (Diagram #3)

- Move like tight.

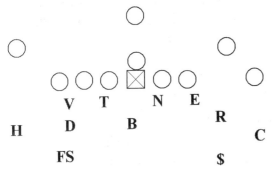

Diagram #3. Bear Defense

Griz

- Move like split.

Speed (Diagram #4)

- Move like split.

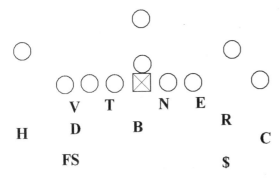

Diagram #4. Speed Defense

Bear Defense (Diagram #5)

- Philosophy: Pressure defense.
- Bring four to eight rushers.
- Use variety of twists, stunts, and blitzes to get into the quarterback's head.
- Linemen play pass and react to the run.
- Stem and bluff.
- Practice against all formations.
- Make something happen.

Split Defense (Diagram #6)

- Move like tight defense.

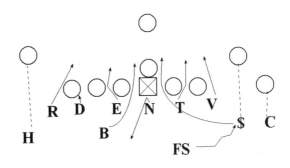

Diagram #5. Bear – Wish "O"

- Buck moves to strong A gap if strong walks out.
- Outside rushers must not let back cross their face and free release.
- Versus one-back: strong walks out and mans the number-two wideout (unless blitzing, then he stems to blitz).
- Free is responsible for blitzer's man.
- Corners man on number-one wide.
  - ✓ Do not count tight end in zero or cover 1.
- Four-wide = four defensive back's man (All defensive-back blitzes are off).
- Have a no-back rule (best match-up).
- $trong walks up in a 7 technique versus two tight ends. (Play technique like dog linebacker.)
- Viper and rock never get outflanked.

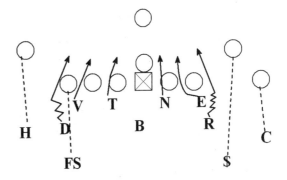

Diagram #6. Split Dog/Fire "O" versus One Back

Legion of Doom Coverage Numbering System

Cover zero = Match-up (Cat) Man

Cover 1 = Man-Free

Cover 2 = "Halves" Zone

Cover 3 = "Thirds" Zone

Cover 4 = "Quarters" Zone

Cover 5 = Man-Under-"Halves" Zone

Cover 6 = Three-on-Two Zone

Cover 7 = Man-Under / "1/3" (Used only in speed)

Cover 8 = Man Quarters (Read-Robber)

Cover 9 = Quarter, Quarter, One-Half, Zone

Legion of Doom Triple-Call Coverage System

- First Call ("Red") = Double width (Wide receivers on both sides) (Diagram #7)
- Second Call ("White") = Single width (Wide receivers on one side) (Diagram #8)
- Third Call ("Blue") = Three receivers on one side (Diagram #9)

    Example: Call = 8/3✓9

Diagram #7. Double Width – Red – Cover 8

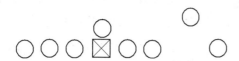

Diagram #8. Single Width – White – Cover 3

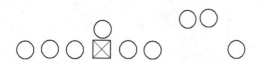

Diagram #9. Three Receivers on One Side – Blue – Cover 9

G.A.T.A (Get After Their Ass)

- Offensive coaches say they love it, but forgot to ask their quarterback.
- Create big plays.
    - ✓ Limiting "O" big plays will not *eliminate* them.

- ✓ "If you can't cover, send more guys!"
- ✓ Speed kills.
- ✓ Prefer perimeter blitzes.

Believe

If you are going to run this defense, you must believe in what you are doing. I see coaches that do not really believe in the blitz. They give the blitz away and you can tell when they are going to blitz and the defender that is going to blitz. All 11 of our players have the ability to blitz and all 11 have the ability to drop into the coverage with our zone blitz.

- Players and coaches get excited when a blitz is called.
- Never have doubt.
- Players must understand why the blitz is called (situation).
- Each players must know his role.
- Have fun.

It is important to treat the blitz as part of your *regular* package. You must teach the players how to gain leverage and what to do when they blitz.

Wednesday is our blitz-emphasis day. On the first day of the week, we make sure we have all of our base calls in our package for that week. We do a blitz period on Wednesday, and our individual practice is built around the blitz package. I coach the blitz aspects of our defense. The biggest point to make about the blitz is the aiming point. This is what we stress in that practice.

- Teach how to blitz.
- Aiming point: outside shoulder of deepest back.
- Play away, quarterback becomes deepest back.
- Always aim at quarterback's back hip.
- Teach where to blitz.

Blitz Period

Know Strengths and Weaknesses

- Dog/Fire weak versus power scheme is our perimeter blitz. Our strong safety and strong linebacker both are coming off the edge. They go through the D gap.

- Cat/Blaze is the stunt to the C gap. Blaze is for the strong safety going inside. That is the answer against the cloud coverage.

Have Run and Pass Blitz Packages.

- Make sure you know what blitzes you are going to use when you expect the run and the blitzes you want to use when you expect a pass. Have a plan for the use of the blitz against certain types of plays. We do not want to "grab-bag" on calling the blitzes.

Create Confusion for the Offense.

- Use multiple looks and blitzes out of every front.
- Make it easy for your players, but hard for offensive coaches and players.
- Must use zone blitz.
- Have "opposite look" out of same look (i.e., 'Bama 1 and Tide 7).
- Disguise the defense.
- Be unpredictable.

Game Plan your Blitzes.

- Determine offensive pass-blocking rules. All plays look good on paper. They must work in a game that is what counts.
- Use your offensive line coach to let you know the blitz that gives him the most trouble.
- Cut the number of plays the opponents use to the top five or 10, ideally five run and five pass.
- Give coaches and players ownership.
- Do recognition of all you think you might need.
- Understand their blocking rules.

Weekend Prep

Saturday

- Before 10 a.m.—Evaluate and grade film. We do not punch a clock. We are not working an 8:00 to 5:00 job. We tell each coach his job and what he has to get done. If a coach has a kid that plays Little League on Saturday afternoon, he can get his work done in the morning and go watch his son in the afternoon. If a coach wants to go to church on Sunday morning, he gets his work done on Saturday and goes to church on Sunday.
- From 9 to 10 a.m.—Players run and lift weights with freshman coaches.
- From 10 a.m. to 12 p.m.—Have a group film study. After this, our players are done and we do not see them until Monday. I say this because it is ideal. But we cannot get them to leave on Saturday. We have a new $1.5 million athletic facility with state-of-the-art equipment. We have TVs in just about every room in the building. We cannot get them to go home. On Sunday they come up to see if we have the weekly films graded.
- After 12 p.m.—We do all of our stats and opponent breakdown before leaving. One of the assistant coaches and I put the stats on the board.

I draw up all offenses by formation. I think this is more important than down-and-distance in high school. I think down-and-distance is important, but you can print that off the films. To me, using formations is first and foremost.

We draw all of the opponent's offensive plays on the board. Then we put all of that information on the scouting report. I use the scouting report to see how many times a team runs a particular play. That tells me how many times I am going to run a certain defense against that play in practice. If you run a multiple defense, you have to practice all of the calls. I am not knocking the multiple defense, but you must practice all of the different sets. That cuts down on the number of reps you are going to be able to see in practice.

You must determine what plays are important to look at from the opponents. We do it strictly by the percentages of the times they run a certain play. If the opponents run a play 30 percent of the time in their games, we are going to run our defense against that play 30 percent of the time in practice.

Sunday

- We must have the scouting report done by 3:00 p.m.
- Scouting report prep: each coach has responsibilities.
- We put weekly practice schedule and script assignments up on the boards.
- We sit down as a staff and pick out points of emphasis for the week. It may be tackling if we did not tackle very well the game before. Whatever we put on the board as the things we want to stress for the week and we do those things in practice. We cannot let the same mistakes hurt us week after week, so we write up our points of emphasis.
- Personnel discussions include who we are going to play, and what subs we expect to play.

Legion of Doom Grade Sheet

If the kids do a great job they get a plus. If they screw up they get a minus. We take the number of points and divide it by the number of plays to get the percentages for the players. Kids can understand percentages. This is a good deal for the players, but it is not what we really stress.

Individual Player's Grades

Player

Plays +

Plays 0

Plays -

Positive Plays

of Plays

Percentage

We are big on our points chart. Here are the points we give to our defense for making plays and the negative chart we keep when they make bad plays. It is each coach's job to grade the film and complete the chart for his position players.

Points for Making Defensive Plays

Positive Points

Tackles	+3
Assist	+1
Big Play	+3
Caused Fumble	+9
Recovered Fumble	+9
Oskie	+9
Break Up Pass	+2
Forced Pass	+2
Blocked Kick (Teams)	+6
Touchdown (Team)	+2
Sack	+4
Caused Oskie	+8
Tackle for Loss	+3
Quarterback Hit	+3
Extra Effort	+2

Negative Points

Mental Errors	-5
Missed Tackles	-5
Player Loafs	-5
Missed Oskie	-5
Missed Fumble Recovery	-3
Foolish Penalty	-6

Total Points

We take the negative points and subtract them from the total points the player scored on the defensive chart. If you end up with positive points for that game, you have helped us win the game. If you end up with negative points, you did not help us win the game. That is the way we approach the game. The players are either helping us or they are hurting us. I think this is a lot more effective than using the percentages. By using percentages, a player may grade out high in the 80s but never make a play the entire game. You can have a player that grades out at only 30 percent but makes 20 tackles in the game. I would prefer to have the player that makes the 20 tackles playing for me.

Practice Schedules

We have a Legion of Doom meeting every morning before school. We meet at 7:20 in my classroom. Our offense meets after practice each day.

We start every Legion of Doom practice with unity. It may be a celebration drill, and sometimes we may do team tackling. A lot of times it will depend on what we are emphasizing that week in practice.

Monday (35 minutes)

- Tackling circuit
- Recognition and installation of each blitz against every formation you expect to see

Tuesday (Heavy day – 65 minutes)

- Individual
- Group: Pass skeleton/inside drill, half-line drill, option period, etc.
- Team
- Goal line

Wednesday (45 Minutes)

- Individual
- Blitz drill
- Team

Thursday (Perfect Practice)

- Game script
- Recognition. Go against all defenses. We go against game situations.

When things are not perfect on Thursday, we may send the players back inside to get dressed in their street cloths, then dress out in their football gear, and then come back out on the field and start practice all over again. We want the practice on Thursday to be perfect.

The offense goes through the game script and reviews all of the plays. The defense then works on recognition of offensive formations, and finally we start running through our plays. I have all of the defensive stunts on a list. We may go through 60 calls in that session. We go through them as fast as I can call them. I call the defenses. On the snap of the ball, they take three steps across the line of scrimmage on their moves. It takes us 10 to 15 minutes to go through all of our calls. If the players can run those defensive calls at that rate, then they will be fine when we get into the game. The players will be able to figure out the defense called.

The hard part is on the coach calling the defenses. You must make sure you match up the blitzes with your secondary coverages. For example our strong safety must know he only blitzes fire, smoke, and blaze. That is all he has to know. He does not get involved with all of that other crap I am calling out. Each player has a few stunts that he must know. They must know their responsibility on each call. I have to know all of the calls and responsibilities on all of the blitzes. We can put a lot of different combinations with the calls. This is where the coach must do his homework and get the calls set up against the offense.

This is the way we do things at Muskogee High School. I am not saying it is the right way, but it is the way we do it on defense. You are welcome to see us anytime.

I want to show you some of our blitz calls used in games. If you have any questions, let me hear from you.

MULTIPLE PRESSURE DEFENSIVE FRONTS

Trigg County High School, Kentucky

I want to thank Nike and Clinic Director Larry Blackmon for having me at the Mid-South Nike clinic. I have been associated with the Nike clinics since 1985 by working at the Louisville Nike Clinic with Earl Browning. I think these clinics are by far the best clinics available in the country.

I am from a small 2A school in western Kentucky: Trigg County High School. Lake Barkley is in Trigg County, for all you fishermen out there. We were featured in the Bigger Faster Stronger magazine last month, and they recently honored us with a big surprise. One of my assistant coaches, Coby Lewis, somehow got us on the cover of the magazine and featured in an article in the magazine.

We have been very successful in power lifting for the past two decades. Just this decade we have become very successful in football, winning 56 games over the past six seasons. Trigg County has enjoyed some success in football by winning back-to-back Class A state championships in 1971 and 1972. We were state runner-up in 1989, but never have we had the kind of success that we have enjoyed over the past six seasons.

I am going to talk to you today about pressure defensive fronts. Coaches from Kentucky know me as a Bobby Redman protégée. Bobby is the head coach at Louisville Male High School. He has enjoyed many winning seasons over his 30-year head coaching career. Many call the defense we play the "confusion" defense. We refer to it as pressure defense.

Pressure Defensive Philosophy

- Apply pressure and the take opponent out of their normal rhythm.

- Stop the run. Most high school offenses run about 70 to 75 percent of the time.
- Pressure on the offense produces turnovers and points.
- Man-to-man coverage in the secondary allows us to play pressure defense.

By controlling the numbers on defense, and with great communication, we feel that we can disrupt the offense. We attempt to apply maximum pressure on the offensive unit's brain (the quarterback). When he feels pressure, the entire offense feels pressure. We outnumber our opponents at the point of attack and chase the ballcarrier down from the backside.

Numbers, Communication, Game Plans, and Players

- Defense is a numbers game.
- The objective of the defense is to disrupt communications. Quarterback pressure disrupts the source of all offensive communication.
- We can take away your best weapon and force you to beat us with something else.

This style of defense allows the quick, aggressive players to shine. Players are given only one responsibility and are expected to aid teammates when their job is done.

We will not allow you to beat us with your best weapon. You must be willing to beat us with something else. We are going to take your stud away. If you have more than one weapon, then we will make you use what we feel is not your best weapon, but your second best. Schools that have defeated us lately are schools that have multiple threats and have a coach who is willing to go to his number-three, number-four, or number-five threat in crunch time.

Absolute Musts for the Defense

- Take away anything quick across the middle: trap, slant routes, quarterback delays, or traps
- Every defensive player puts his eyes on his responsibility.
- First step: responsibility; second step: find the ball and pursue.
- Do not overrun the ball.
- Pursuit angles change every step on the go.
- Strongside, weakside, middle, and secondary of the defense must work as individual units. When combined, they form a very aggressive defense.

If you allow the offense to get in the middle of the field quickly, in this defense, then you are in trouble. Much of the time, we are in cover zero, which means that once the offense breaks the line of scrimmage, then we have no one in the secondary to make a touchdown-saving tackle. You play defense with your eyes. Your body cannot go where you want it to go if you do not have your eyes on your assignment. We key backs, we put our eyes on our back responsibility, and we play our responsibility first. If the ball is not going to our responsibility, then we find the ball on our second step and pursue relentlessly.

We teach that the first step should be responsibility, and the second step should be to find the ball and pursue. With such an aggressive style, we must prevent overpursuit. Many times our players overpursue and run past the ball or too deep into the backfield and take themselves out of the play. We must constantly be working on drills that keep us from overpursuing. We teach that pursuit angles change every step and at full speed.

We have four different units working on defense making up the entire defensive side of the ball. We have a strongside, weakside, middle, and secondary. Our strongside works as a unit. The strongside consists of the strong tackle (who normally lines up in a 5 technique), our strong end (who normally lines up in a 7 technique), and our strong corner (who normally lines up in a 9 technique).

Our weakside works as a unit. The weakside consists of the weakside end (who normally lines up in a 5 technique), our weak corner (who normally lines up in a 7 technique), and our monster (who lines up seven yards deep as a linebacker in a 2 technique). Our middle unit consists of our noseguard and middle linebacker and our secondary consists of two halfbacks and a safety. The halfbacks are locked up in man-to-man coverage on the widest receiver to their side of the ball. Our safety is locked up on the second receiver to the strongside of the formation. A member of both the weakside and the strongside have the following responsibilities:

- Dive (near back inside)
- Quarterback
- Pitch (near back outside)

Our middle unit is responsible for dive (near back inside) on both sides of the ball. As we cover our responsibilities on our first step, we step toward a gap, much like the gap-8 defense. Middle unit steps toward the A gaps. Dive from weakside and strongside step toward B gaps. Quarterback responsibility from both sides steps toward C gaps and pitch responsibility from both sides steps toward the D, or outside, gap.

This style of defense has provided us with many benefits over the years. I remember in 1993, Male High School won the regional championship and went on to win the state championship that year without scoring a single touchdown in the regional championship on offense. One of the most explosive offenses in Kentucky football history and they did not score a touchdown in the regional championship game on offense. They scored three touchdowns on defense. They intercepted a pass and ran it in from 35 yards out. They picked up a fumble, ran it back 80 yards, blocked a field-goal attempt, picked it up, and ran it in from about 50 yards out. This defensive style is capable of producing those types of nights.

Benefits of the Pressure Defense

- An exciting style of defensive play
  - ✓ Turnovers
    - ❍ Trigg County has had at least a +6 ratio in turnovers every year since 1999.
  - ✓ Scoring
    - ❍ Trigg County has scored an average of 46 points on defense since 1999, with a high of 72 points in 2004 and 2005.

Morale: This style of defense is fun to play.

Basic Principles of the Pressure Defense

- Gap-8 defense
- Strongside work as unit (ST, SE, SC)
- Weakside work as unit (WE, WC, M)
- Middle work as a unit (LB, NG)
- Secondary work as a unit (HB, S, HB) in man-to-man coverage
- Both strongside weakside have three basic responsibilities to share (dive, quarterback, and pitch)
- LB and NG have dive to both sides (weakside and strongside).

We can run many different defensive fronts with multiple stunts out of every front. We hope that the offensive linemen from the other team go to the sideline and start controversy with the offensive coaches about alignment, stunts, and so on.

Defensive Fronts

- Base-5 front
- 44 front
- 27 front
- 53 front
- Double free (if time permits)

I am going to show you each of these fronts and some stunts out of each front that we run. It is very important that you teach your players not to give away certain stunts based on their alignment. I hope I have some time for the double-free package, but if not, it is in the packet I gave each of you.

Base-5 Front

Strongside Stunts (Diagram #1)

- In call
- Out call
- Stack call
- Split call
- Swing call

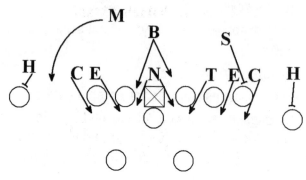

Diagram #1. 5 In-Red

Weakside Stunts (Diagram #2)

- Red call
- White call
- Stack call
- Split call
- Normal call

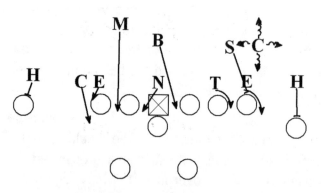

Diagram #2. 5 Out-White

The great thing about these stunts is they are separate on each side (strong and weak) and you can mix them up. Obviously, the in-red call is when you are expecting a tackle-to-tackle offensive play. The out-white call is when you are expecting a play to the outside. All of these are better for certain expectations of the offense.

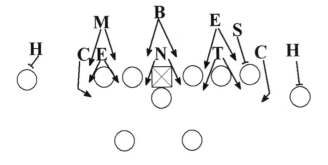

Diagram #3. 5 Double Stack

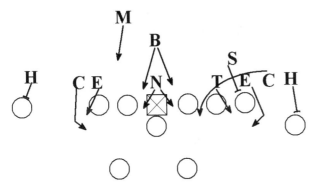

Diagram #4. Swing-Normal

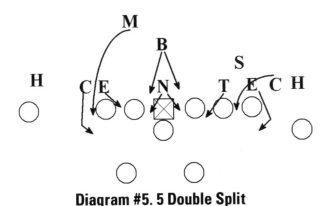

Diagram #5. 5 Double Split

When you are given a 4-wide formation, a basic adjustment is with the weakside monster locking up on the fourth receiver. We then slide to a 52 look by standing our strongside end up and sliding our middle linebacker to the weakside. Our middle linebacker is part of the weakside and our noseguard plays straight through the center and takes dive on both sides. Remember, eyes on responsibility and first step to responsibility, second step to the ball. Stunts only last one step. You do not continue your stunt if the backs are going away from you. You pursue relentlessly.

44 Front

- "M" stunt (Diagram #7)
- "W" stunt (Diagram #8)
- Stack (Diagram #9)
- Normal (Diagram #10)

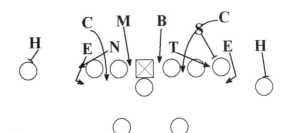

Diagram #7. 44 M Stunt

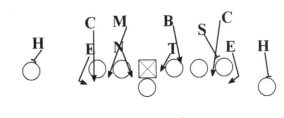

Diagram #8. 44 W Stunt

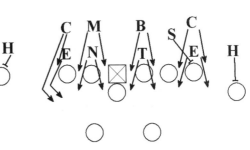

Diagram #9. 44 Stack

Diagram #6. Base-5 Adjustments to 4 Wideouts

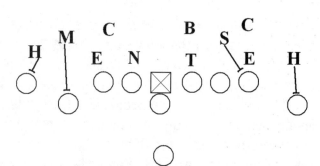

Diagram #10. 44 Adjustments to 4 Wide

Our normal call is exactly the same as our stack call except we play off at normal linebacker depth. Responsibilities are the same. In our 4-wide adjustments, we use the monster to lock up in man-to-man coverage and slide to a 43 look. Now our weakside consists of the noseguard, weakside end, and weakside corner, and our strongside unit stays the same. Now the middle linebacker has dive on both sides.

27 Front

- Normal (Used to take away trapping teams. 2 techniques usually move to 1 and 3 techniques. Monster is free and does not have a responsibility.)

We have some stunts in this alignment, but primarily we just want to cover the guards and take away the traps. We use this front against trapping teams like my friend Pat Gates back there from Caldwell County. He can trap you.

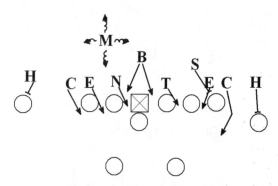

Diagram #11. 27 Normal

In our 27 package, our adjustment to a 4-wide set is easy because our monster is already free (Diagram #11). He just locks up on the fourth receiver (Diagram #12).

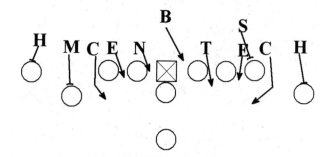

Diagram#12. 27 Adjustments to 4 Wide

Our last front is the 53 package and I do not think I am going to have time to cover the double-free package, which is our prevent package. (You have it in your packet and it is a man-under coverage with two-deep safeties. I will show you what it looks like.

53 Front

- Double red
- Double white
- Triple or double stack
- Double split

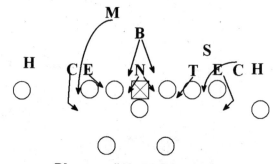

Diagram #13. 53 Double Red

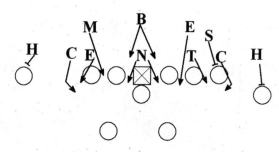

Diagram #14. 53 Double White

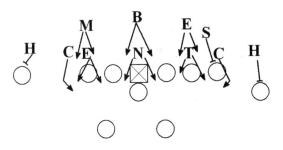

Diagram #15. 53 Triple Stack

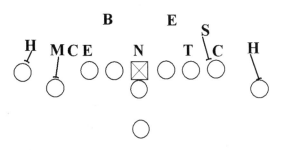

Diagram #17. 53 Adjustment to 4 Wide

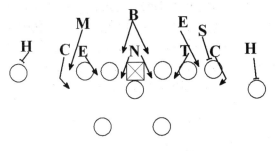

Diagram #16. 53 Double Split

For simplicity sake, we just use colors in 53 and we seldom flip our strongside and weakside (Diagram #17). This defense is balanced and not overloaded to the strongside. When we adjust to the 4-wide formation, we use the monster and go to a 52 look.

Double Free (Prevent Defense)

- Cover 2 with man-to-man under
- May have 6 front, 5 front, or 4 front based on the number of receivers.

Thanks again for your time, fellows, and I hope you got something out of our time together today. Thanks a lot.

ESTABLISHING THE SPREAD OFFENSE

Nease High School, Florida

First, I want to give you some information about my background. I have coached at the small single-A school, and I have coached in the PAC 10, and the Southwest Conference. To me, every stop along the way was the same. You are coaching kids, and loving them. It is having a passion and a love for coaching the game.

I could spend hours telling you about coaching jobs. The one thing I want to get across to you is perseverance. We were fortunate to win a state championship. All of our staff was involved; I just happened to be the head coach. I am 52 years old and have been in the game for a while. We had come close to winning it all in some other situations, but we did not win the state. In all of the jobs I took on, I never took over a school that was the perfect situation. As in most cases, in all of the jobs that are open, the person that gets the head coaching position must build a team up. Otherwise, those jobs would not be open.

Four years ago, I went back into coaching at the college level at Edgewater College in Jacksonville. They wanted to run our offense. After coaching there for one year, I applied for a junior college in California. I flew out to California in July and interviewed. I did not get the job. I told my wife that I was just going to take a year off from coaching. I had been coaching for 30 years and I decided to take a year off and go around to colleges and study high school programs, and watch football practice. That all sounded good after 30 years of coaching.

When August came around, I wanted to coach again. I looked on the FHSAA website and found there was only one head-coaching job open in the USA. That job was at Apalachicola, Florida. I went there at the age of 49 and took the job two days

after the practice season had started. Now, I had made a long journey, to say the least. I went from applying for a junior college job in California, to the head-coaching job at Apalachicola High School in Florida.

After I got the job, I drove up to the field and there were 12 players out on the field practicing with four dads. The grass on the field was as high as this table. I told the dads the first thing we had to do was to cut the grass. I told the fathers if they would cut the grass, I would take the 12 players and work with them. I told the fathers we had to get the grass cut to run the spread offense because the grass would slow us down. We did not have very many athletes in that group. However, it proved to be an interesting situation. When I took the job, I had made up my mind I would retire there. I was going to buy a house there, buy a boat, and I was going to eat oysters and shrimp, and drink Bud Light for the rest of my life.

Now, some of you that are in the big programs that have a big budget cannot imagine that situation with the grass that tall. The grass had not been cut all summer. The lawn mowers would not cut that grass. We had to go down to the prison and get some inmates to cut the grass with big mowers. The prison had the guards out on the field with their shotguns watching the prisoners. It was just like the scenes from *Cool Hand Luke*.

I told the team we were going to run the no-huddle spread offense. We only had 13 kids out for the team. I did not have an assistant coach. I was 50 years old and I was coaching the team by myself. I looked at the schedule and we were playing Ft. Walton Beach in our 10th game of the year. They were a 4A power in the state. We had to play some of the best teams in the area with those 13 players.

My wife and children were still living back in Jacksonville, Florida. After the games were over on Friday, I would drive back to Jacksonville to see my family over the weekend. Then I would go back to Apalachicola on Monday morning.

After that season, the Nease High School head-coaching job came open. I applied for that job. I drove up to Nease High School in my 1968 Volkswagen Beetle. All of the cars in the parking lot were Hummers and Mercedes. Those cars did not belong to the assistant coaches; they belonged to the players. I did not think I would get the job, but I did.

At the time of my arrival at Nease High School, we got a noseguard who transferred in from Trinity Christian School. He was a home-schooled kid by the name of Timmy Tebow. We made a quarterback out of him. He turned out to be the best quarterback I have worked with.

One day after practice, the coaches were in our staff meeting. I looked out on the field and saw a player throwing the football. He was working on his passing skills by himself. I took a closer look and saw it was Timmy Tebow. He had the greatest work ethic I had ever been around as a coach. Not only did he work his guts out, but also he had the ability to influence others with his work ethic. Tim has already gone to the University of Florida this semester and he has made an impression on the coaches in the weight room.

The one thing I was able to do at Nease, besides getting the opportunity to coach a player like Tim Tebow, was that I was able to surround myself with a great staff. I have a staff that loves the game of football. They have a passion for the game, and they have a passion for the kids. It is difficult to find great assistant coaches. We work as a staff in everything we do. We went to two-platoon football. At the time we went to Nease, we had 60 players out for the team. Now we have 160 kids out for the team.

In the time that I have for this lecture, I want to talk to you about our no-huddle spread offense. I want to talk about our strength program and how our kids started getting scholarships by becoming stronger. This past year we had 12 players that

signed scholarships. When I first arrived at Nease, the college recruiters would not even come by the school. Now our kids are much stronger and they are being looked at by most of the recruiters.

As a head coach it is difficult to find assistant coaches that are dedicated enough to develop the players in all phases of the game. The head coach wants to know if you are the type of assistant coach that is going to be there when needed. He must be loyal to the program, and he must love kids, love the game of football, and be willing to learn the game. It is difficult to find a staff with all of those qualities. On most staffs, you are lucky if you have two or three coaches like that.

We did a study of the teams that were similar to our situation to see what they were doing to make their programs better. Here are the things we looked at as we researched the available information.

The first question we want to know was how many players those teams have out for football. We wanted to know how many levels of teams they had in their program. How many teams did they have? What type of off-season program did they have? How much money do they have for their football budget? How do they have the booster clubs organized? How much money does the booster club give the football program? How many assistant coaches do they have?

By compiling all of this information, we came up with a formula. Here are the things those schools have that are similar to our program. When I went to Nease, the budge was $11,000 and we were $15,000 in the hole. When we looked at those benchmark schools, we found out the booster clubs were raising $100,000 for their programs. We played Hoover High School in Alabama on ESPN and their budget is over $500,000. It is like a college situation.

We looked at the number of coaches these schools had. Nease had five head coaches in seven years, but they had new assistant coaches every year. When that happens, the kids are learning new techniques every year.

So we decided we wanted to have a touchdown club that was separate from the booster club. We want to start raising money to elevate our program from an $11,000 budget to a $100,000 budget. We want 15 assistant coaches instead of three assistant coaches. Instead of 60 players on the JV and varsity, we wanted 160 players out for our frosh, JV, and varsity teams. We have been able to do most of the things we set up as our goals.

The big thing to me that I think has really made a difference in our program is getting those assistant coaches. One good assistant coach is worth five good players. We have 12 assistant coaches now and hope to add to that total. I am bringing in coaches with whom I want to be associated. I want coaches who want to talk football. We are going to run the spread offense. We are going to run a 4-4 package defense, and we are going to coach three levels of football. That is what we do. We do not have a freshman team that practices all by itself. All of our coaches work with freshman team, JV, and varsity levels. When we play a JV game, all of our coaches are on that sideline. I am the head varsity coach, but I am also the head JV coach. We have a year-round program. We have a great off-season program.

Our kids must dress in the parking lot. Even though we won the state, our kids still have to dress in the parking lot. Our fields are mowed, and it is not as it was at Apalachicola. The first thing we did with the money we raised was to put it into safety equipment for the kids. We got safety equipment such as helmets and shoulder pads. Then we started putting money into our weight room. We took over an old dance room that was not being used and made it our weight room. Our kids bought into our program. We work hard and we are going to compete. When we walk into our weight room, we coach in there just as we would in a game. We have the entire staff in the room and they all work. Our staff is dressed in coaching uniforms and works with the players they coach in the games. We compete in the weight room to make it more interesting.

Our kids come from nice homes and have many luxuries. The first thing have to do when we get them is to get after them to do what we want them to do on the field. That carries over into the weight room as well. We put them on the mats and have them compete against their teammates. Our kids learn to fight and they learn what it means to compete. The basis for our spread offense was to get our receivers to learn to fight and to compete on the field. Now, we were not throwing the football. We were working on the mats. Tim Tebow, who is 6'3" and weighs 245 pounds, would get in the group with the linebackers and he learned to compete on the mats. Now we will hear from Danny Cowgill on our strength and conditioning program and David San Juan will talk about our recruiting program.

Danny Cowgill – Strength and Conditioning Coach

(Highlights of the presentation on the goals of the Nease High School strength and conditioning program.)

- Build team unity through our strength and conditioning sessions.
- Develop functional strength.
- Teach the players the difference in strength and power. Football is a game of strength and speed.
- Build core strength.
- Develop flexibility, especially in the hips.

David San Juan – Recruiting Coordinator

Our recruiting program at Nease High School is related to the way we go about getting our players recruited to colleges. It is not about bringing in high school players from other schools to the Nease program. Our motto is, "If a kid wants to play college football, there is a place for him to play."

I want to go through a couple of basic points I think could help you in your program. I will give you a list of my contacts and a website that you can go to that will show you what we do in our recruiting program.

We educate our players and parents early in their high school program about the recruiting process. We give the parents a book that I will be glad to send you. We use the same basic approach with players such as Timmy Tebow. We put the players in our system and try to attract the colleges to our players. We do not wait for the colleges to find us.

Our website is: www.neaseprospects.com. That is the website I developed for our athletes. The cost to us was nothing. It only cost five dollars a month to host this site. We are up to 27,000 hits on the site. The site has my e-mail address on it.

I work with Derek Williams of Sunshine Preps. If you are interested in getting your kids recruited, it is a free service to your kids. He does a great job. You can reach him at: www.sunshinepreps.net.

Here is one quote I want to leave with you: "We coach for a loving and not for a living."

We had 30 seniors on our team this past fall. Five of them did not have a desire to go on to college to continue with football. Some 17 out of 25 of the other seniors are going to be playing football in college this coming fall at some level. We have 12 players that will be playing at Division IA programs. We figure we are gaining $300,000 per year in scholarship money using this system. Now I will turn it back over to Coach Howard.

Coach Craig Howard

After spending 15 years as a college coach, and then coming back to coach in high school, I thought having a recruiting coordinator would be worthwhile for our program. Our kids were smart, but they were not being recruited. We started the strength and conditioning program and that helped us a great deal. Our kids are being recruited because of the improvement we have made in our program in the last few years.

I think it is important for your best players to be your hardest workers in the program. You take the player you think is the best player in your program,

sit him down, and tell him you think he is the best player in the program and that you want him to be the hardest worker on the team. That will change everything in the program. The college coaches tell me we have the best website they have seen to promote the high school players.

We all know about some of the recruiting services that come into the school and want to charge the players parents $1,000 to get a player on their list. The question I ask those services is this: how many athletes have received scholarships using this service? I think the NFL should pay for this service. With our website, we can tell our kids they will have a chance to go on to play at the next level if they are good enough. We will see to it that they are exposed to the colleges through our website.

We all have the choice of the offense or defense to run in high school. We call our offense the spread offense now. I am going to give you a brief overview of why and how we have used the offense.

In 1978 and 1979 when I was running this offense, it was called the run-and-shoot offense. Today the basis of our offense is the run-and-shoot. We have averaged 45 points per game (three-year total). However, I want everyone to know the reason we won the state championship was our defense and not just our offense.

Items	Year	Year
Wins	11	13
Rush Offense	183	211
Pass Offense	347	250
Total Offense	**530**	**461**

We think we are balanced between the run and the pass. We are not just throwing the ball on every down.

We have combined our spread offense with the no-huddle offense. We use a lot of words to teach our system. We want the words to describe our plays as much as possible. Here are the features of our offense. Again, we are a no-huddle spread offense. We two-platoon on all three levels. We want to run as many plays as possible, as fast as we possibly can. We have not huddled in three years at Nease High School.

We run multiple formations. We use personnel groups to create adjustments, chaos, and confusion. We use code words or hand signals. We are not going to use cards. We like the short pass and the long run. We want to throw the ball short and make a long run on the play.

We want to find the flaw in the defense. We do not look at a script to call the play. We look at the defense to call the plays. The flaw may be a player. The flaw may be the way a team lines up. We do not want to find the flaw on defense on Saturday in the film. We want to find the flaw before the game so we can take advantage of the flaw.

Another thing we do very well is to "coach the game." If you play two-platoon football, what do you do with the players when they are not on the field? We meet with our offense when the defense is on the field. We meet by positions. Each player meets with his position coach. We can make any adjustments during the game. We set up the chairs on the sideline to allow us to meet in small groups.

Attack. What? We do not just call plays. We attack. We force the defense to show their hand. We do not use blind calls. We do not run all of our plays against every defense we face. We are only going to run certain plays against different defenses. Again, we do not call plays off a list. We call the plays off the look the defense gives us.

By running the no-huddle spread offense, conditioning becomes a factor earlier in the game by running a lot of plays. It allows the offense to control the tempo of the game. We can run our offense very slow or we can go very fast. We control the tempo. We want to score 50 points per game and we want to make the defense throw up. This offense is not complicated. We are using the same offense all the way down to the fourth grade.

By running this system, we see fewer defensive looks. Players enjoy it and it builds confidence with the team. We want to get max reps in practice. We see mostly a nickel and a cover-3 look. We may see a nickel and cover 4.

We can run plays in sequence. We call this stampede. That means we are going to call three plays and run them without saying a word. We come up with some kind of acronyms the week of practice to help our players remember the order of those three plays. We can run five plays in stampede if we choose to do so.

We have another deal where we call "El Paso." This means we are going to run our concepts passing game in sequence until we call the code word to get out of that phase of the offense. We may run 10 plays in a row without calling anything. All the linemen need to hear is a direction occasionally.

Another thing we use is called "rock and roll." This means we are going to run the zone read and then we will go back to El Paso. This is how we practice so we can do these things in the games. We never huddle in practice.

Here is what we are looking for in play calling. We are going to run with the numbers. These are our rules.

- Five or six players should be in the box.
- Check for the four-man side and run away.
- Run to the three-man side.
- Run to the bubble: Shade or 1 and 5 techniques.
- Angles—Down block and kick-out. Reach them and stretch them.
- Grass—Get the ball to athlete in most open space.

We throw with the numbers. If the defense has six in the box, we can run or pass against a single safety. If they have seven in the box, we throw the ball if they do not have safeties. If they have five in the box, we run the ball. We run the ball against a two-safeties, four-shell look.

I want to talk about our running game. Here is what we did in the running game in two years.

Play	Tries	Average Yards
Quarterback Wrap (Dart)	79	10.0
Isolation	66	6.8
Zone Read	51	6.6
Quarterback Isolation	39	9.7
Speed Option	39	6.4

We can run the dart several ways (Diagram #1). The way we run it against one team will be different from how we run it against another team.

Our next running play is our isolation play (Diagram #2). Our quarterback reads the defensive end.

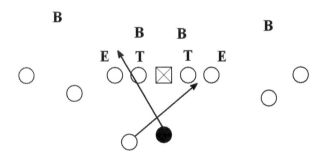

Diagram #1. Quarterback Wrap (Dart)

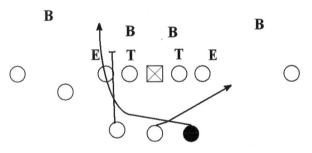

Diagram #2. Isolation Play

The third running play is our zone-read play (Diagram #3). Again, the quarterback must read the defensive end.

We also run the quarterback isolation play (Diagram #4). We have not used the play as much as some other plays, but we still average good yardage on the play.

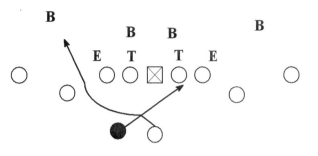

Diagram #3. Zone Read

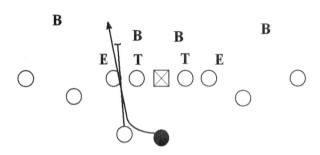

Diagram #4. Quarterback Isolation

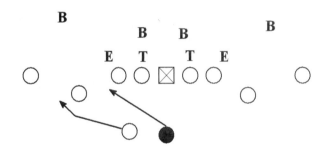

Diagram #5. Speed Option

Next is our speed option play (Diagram #5). The quarterback can keep the ball or pitch it to the halfback like most option teams do.

In our pass production, this is what we have accomplished in three years:

Years	2003	2004	2005
Yards	2566	4604	3528
Touchdowns	20	51	38
Interceptions	5	3	2

Our system comes fully equipped with the following types of plays. Different elements of this offense will show up with each quarterback. We adapt to our quarterback.

- Quick game
- Half roll
- Five step
- PAP
- Gun dash
- Screen game
- Running back
- Wide receivers

We want to throw one screen pass out of every four dropback passes we throw. If we throw the ball 40 times in a game, that means we are going to throw the screen pass eight times. We run the screen to the running backs and to the wide receivers. We will even screen the ball to the quarterback.

We feel that adapting the offense to the quarterback is important. Not every quarterback has the same abilities. You must run the offense that fits the quarterback who is in the game. We are still going to run the no-huddle spread offense, but we may not run those same plays.

The big question is why we move the pocket in high school. We do not want our quarterback sitting back in the pocket all of the time. We practice the scramble drill each week. If the defense has players that are better than the players we have, blocking them it is better to move the quarterback. We want the quarterback to have the ability to run out of the pocket to avoid that 6'8", 290-pound defensive lineman coming full speed at him in the pocket. By running away from that big dude, we accomplish several things. One, we are still running our no-huddle spread offense, and all of that running chasing the quarterback is hard on that defense man. We are not limited in our offense. We have versatility built into the system.

Another way to move the pocket is with the play-action passing game. If I had to eliminate some of our offense, I would go back to our run-and-shoot offense and roll the quarterback out on several plays. He can roll to his best receiver and he can roll to the side he throws the best from.

We have 10 basic concepts in our passing game. We are going to take shots at the deep ball in every game. Again, that is part of the game plan. The question we must decide is how many shots to take in each game. We do that in our staff discussions. When we take those shots is determined by several factors that relate to the game plan. We have a plan on the rationale of taking those shots. Our shots will be different each week.

I talked to you about our screen passes. We also use the flood routes and play-action concepts. We teach these concepts all year in our program.

Passing-Game Concepts

Concept	Number
Slot Option	0
Single Isolation	1
Screen	2
Play-Action	3
All Go	4
Smash	5
All Stop	6
Smash Bender	7
Bounce Scat	8
Deep Single Isolation	9

- First digit is the concept.
- Second digit is the protection.
- The "4" indicates the vertical concept.
- The "50s" are our dropback protection.
- The last digit tells our running back which side he lines up on.

For example, the call is 450. We are running four vertical routes, with dropback protection and the running back is on the right side. On even numbers he is on the right side, and on odd numbers he is on the left side. We spend a lot of time going over this with the players in the classroom. It is not that complicated once they understand the concepts.

If we can help you, we would be glad to share what we do in our program at Nease High School. Thank you.

SIMPLICITY OF THE ZONE OFFENSE

Douglas County High School, Colorado

It is a pleasure to be here today. Let me give you a quote before I get into the X's and O's. "The continuous quest for further knowledge and a deeper understanding of the dynamics of football are the mark of a good football coach. Ironically, it is the coach who knows more, but requires less of his players, who normally wins championships." In other words, a coach should achieve the status of the lifelong student, but only to the extent that he continually seeks new ways to make things simpler and easier for the athlete. That comes from Rex Ryan.

I got to thinking that as coaches we have to find things that let us teach in an easier and simpler way. If we do that, our players will perform at a higher level.

In our offense, the zone play allows us to do that. We get reps every day that allow us to become good at it. The inside-zone, outside-zone, and stretch plays have the players taking the same steps on each play. All of our players are taking the same steps. The running backs, offensive linemen, and tight ends are all taking the same steps.

We will get so many reps at those plays that we will get good at it. We will be good enough to handle variations we may see from defenses.

When you establish a program, you must have an identity to your program. We want to build our program around character and mental and physical toughness. We have a very simple approach to our program. We want to get after people and run the ball.

On our special teams, we got rid of many of the philosophical ideas. We want to do two things on special teams. We want to score and block kicks.

We do not have a punt return. We do not believe in it. We put ten guys up on the line of scrimmage and go after the punt. We blocked 12 punts and four field goals this year. That is what we work on in practice. We want to score and block kicks.

On defense, we want to create turnovers and stop drives. When we go through the things we do in the off-season, the only thing we want to know is: will this help us stop drives and create turnovers? Is the drill we do in practice going to help us stop drives and create turnovers? If it does not, do not use it.

Offensively, it is our job to score and control the tempo of the game. When we go into games, we want exploit weakness immediately. We script the first two series at the start of the game and the first two series coming out of halftime. We only have three running plays and a few passes. What we have on our scripts is the running play and the formation that will put the defense in a bind.

Our tailback set a 5A record in the state playoffs this year. He had 930 yards in four playoff games. He got a lot of credit, but our offensive line handled every little adjustment the defense presented to them. When we started the season, we saw many base defenses. As the season went on and people tried to stop us, we saw some of the most bastardized defenses you can imagine. Our offensive line was able to pick up nine defenders in the box because they knew where they had to end up.

In our offensive scheme, we want to use formations to create problems. If we play a 3-3-5 defense, it is not uncommon for us to go into an unbalanced formation. We play three and four tight ends at time in a game. We create running lanes. We want to get more people to the point of attack or spread the field within the box. If the defense has a 1 technique and the next defender aligns in a 7 technique, we will win that situation.

We are not going to check out of plays. We use the "orange call" and go opposite the call. The quarterback comes to the line of scrimmage and knows we want to run the bend play to the 1 technique. If the defense aligns in a 1, 3, and a 5 technique, with a linebacker over the top, the quarterback is going the other way. Our quarterback knows what we are looking for and runs to the bubble. We are going to make it simple on everyone involved.

We can dictate fronts and coverages by using formations. It is very difficult for teams to play cover 2 against us. It is difficult to play cover 1 against us. If defenses are matching up with us in man coverage, we put three or four tight ends into the game. They have trouble playing defensive backs against those types of personnel. We force defenses to play a lot of cover 3 against us. A big thing we do in our offensive scheme is to set up the play-action pass.

hen we run our off-tackle zone play, the aiming point for the running back is the crack of the butt of the offensive tackle. I will take you through all the techniques at the end of the lecture.

Our rule of thumb for our offensive line is to block right angles. We assign each lineman a gap and he blocks it. Our first step is a power step and not a bucket step. Old coaches have a problem with a lineman taking a six-inch power step back when we come off the ball. The technique is all about angles. We cannot come off the ball and get movement unless we improve the angle to the defender. If we take the short six-inch step back, we can come off at an angle to get to the defenders outside breastplate.

Everyone in the offense takes the same step. The running back aligns at seven yards deep and takes the lateral, gather, and go steps. Everybody is working together as one unit. The line uses the chip and combo blocks to get up to the next level of the defense and create those running seams.

The running back looks at the butt crack of the offensive tackle (Diagram #1). We talk about open and closed windows in relation to running lanes. The running back runs his path to the offensive tackle and stays on course as long as there is movement. If the window is closed, the running back gets into the line of scrimmage and bounces the play to the edge. If we have a big butt in the hole, we probably have the play sealed to the outside.

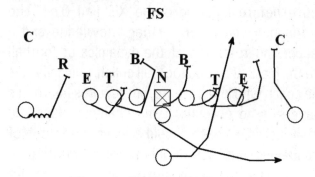

Diagram #1. Outside Zone 5-2

Against the 5-2, we re in a double-tight-end set. The right tackle is stepping to the 9-technique end. The right guard reaches to the C gap toward the 5-technique tackle. The center works the playside A gap looking to get up on the linebacker. The backside guard works to get on the noseguard. The backside tackle and tight end are stepping in to A gap and B gap to the backside.

We can experiment with motion to the backside to see how the secondary reacts to it. We tell the running back he has to be slow to exchange. We want to give the linemen time to be where they need to be and give him a three-and-a-half to four-yard cushion to visualize his path.

If we run the zone play against the 4-4 defense without a tight end to the backside, it becomes more difficult (Diagram #2). This play more than likely will bounce to the outside. The tight end gets on the rover back to the outside. The line takes their steps into their gaps and takes the defenders wherever they want to go. If we use motion by the backside slot to get on the backside defensive end, it allows the tackle to become more aggressive on the linebacker in the A gap.

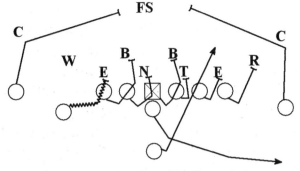

Diagram #2. Outside Zone 4-4

We are working our playside guard and tackle plus the center and backside guard on the three down linemen toward the playside.

This looks good at a clinic, but we averaged 7.1 yards per carry on this play. Over the last four years, we have averaged 6.7 yards per carry. It has been a very consistent play. Our inside-zone play complements this play.

We run the last example against the 4-3 defense (Diagram #3). The secret to the zone play is not to be in a hurry. We have to be patient and let the linebackers make the decision. They have to decide when to attack their gap. If the defenders continue to run to the outside, the defensive gaps get larger. This is where the discipline and repetition pays off. As long as the linebacker stays at linebacker depth, we do not chase him. We get on him when he attacks the line of scrimmage.

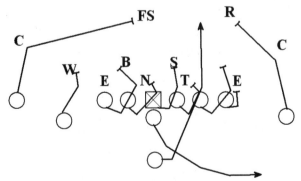

Diagram #3. Outside Zone 4-3

In the zone, we want to know how the linebackers are going to play us. They have to start scraping and hitting the gaps. That is especially true for the backside linebackers. They play a gap-responsibility defense. When the linebacker starts to fill, we start cutting the play back.

We set up everything we do with the zone play. We run that play until people are sick of it. When we feel comfortable that we can attack with the inside zone or play-action pass, we do it.

The other thing we do is use motion. That helps us get more people to the point of attack. We bring motion from one side of the formation to the other. If the defense trails the motion, we attack the side away from the motion, because they are one man short to that side.

The inside zone is bend. It gets its name because we bend the ball back on the run. People say if we run zone, we have to run the counter trey. We do not believe that. I think counter trey is difficult to teach and there are too many variables, so that you are bound to make mistakes. The way coaches teach that defenses today, it is too hard to run.

We look at the bend play as our misdirection. When you get the safeties coming down hard to stop the stretch and zone plays, is the time to run the bend. The back steps are the same, except his aiming point is the crack of the guard. If the guard's butt is in the hole, the back bends the play back.

In the 4-3 defense, we want to run the bend at the backside shade defense (Diagram #4). The 3 technique to the other side creates the crease we look for. The problem is we have to get the Mike linebacker to flow over the top into weakside B gap so we can combo up with our center.

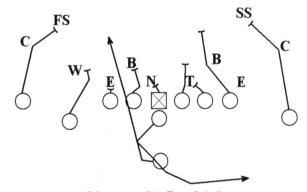

Diagram #4. Bend 4-3

The way we do that is to take the first level to the second level. We do not chase linebackers. We take the 1 technique and 3 technique and drive them back into the laps of the linebackers. The running back is not going to cut until he reaches the line of scrimmage. The guard and center drive the 1 technique back until the linebacker shows in the gap we are supposed to block. It works well. We use motion to solidify the over pursuit.

The important block to the backside is the double-team on the tackle. The backside guard and tackle have to take the tackle back with the guard getting off to seal the backside linebacker. The split end works hard to get to the free safety. His block will be important because we plan on the play getting into the secondary. The tight end can release and get downfield because the defender outside of him will not make the play.

Against the 4-4 defense, the angles work out somewhat differently on the linebackers (Diagram #5). The rules are the same. We double on the nose and drive him into the second level. We take the nose to the linebacker. He has to fill his gap at some point. When he does, the guard comes off for the block on the linebacker. We do the same thing to the backside. The double-team is the same as double on the playside. In the diagram, we show the running back working backside on his cut back.

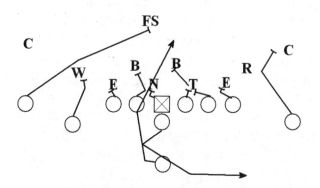

Diagram #5. Bend 4-4

This play averaged 7.8 yards, and in the last four years it averaged 6.9 yards per carry. In my opinion, you cannot do one without the other. If you run the outside zone, you have to run the inside zone. It is a hard thing to do because all of us grew up with man-blocking schemes. These two plays work well together. I truly do not believe you can be a zone team and have man principles on another play. If you are a zone team, that is what you must use.

For the offensive linemen, the two schemes are totally different in their concepts. The thing you have to teach your young linemen is to be patient on the double-team block. They feel like they have to get off the block to find the linebacker. We have to build confidence in them to understand if they stay on the double-team, the linebackers will eventually show in one gap or the other. If he does not show, we run right at him all day long.

The third play we run is the stretch play. We stretch one full man in our scheme. We still take the power step on the takeoff. We gather and stretch the power step and go to the next full man. If you watch the Denver Broncos, you see this play more often than not.

To get to the next full man, the angle is very acute. The step has to be a lateral step to get to the outside breastplate. That is hard to do sometimes. We do not expect them to get all the way outside and hook the defender. We expect them to get the inside hand in-between the numbers on the jersey and the outside hand on the outside shoulder pad. We want them to drive their pads right up into the defender's throat and run him. Let the defender go where he wants to go. If he wants to run outside, run him that way. If he wants to fight the blocker back inside, we bury him because we have the leverage.

Typically, the defender wants to stay on the line of scrimmage and work outside. The aiming point for the running back is the crack of the tight end or the H-back, who is the motion man. He has a three-way-go to run the ball. He can continue to run outside, which we discourage, get his shoulder square and go right down the middle, or cut the play all the way back.

In the NFL, the play looked nice. What we found out through trial and error, we had a lot of exchange problems. It really stretched the quarterback to reach the handoff because of the width of the play. It got so bad we decided to run speed option or the toss play. You get the same thing. We like the speed option, because we have a very athletic quarterback. We like the toss because the back receivers the ball at the same point without the exchange problem.

On the toss play, the back receives the ball, stomps his feet in the ground, and get the shoulders square. At that point, he runs the three-way-go. We do not use the play a lot as compared to the inside- or outside-zone play, but we do use it quite a bit. When we want the defense to flow hard, we use the toss. If the defense packs the box, we seal the edge with motion and get on the corner.

This play forces the defense to play the field. They cannot just pack the box and expect to stop us. If we can run six to seven of the toss or option plays per game, we are happy with those results.

From the bend play, we run two play-action schemes. We like to run the bootleg pass. The reason for that is the backside end. On the zone play, he thinks he can make the tackle coming down the line of scrimmage. Sometimes they do catch us from behind. We try to control the backside pressure with the bootleg pass or the second tight end to that side.

It also lets us judge pursuit angles of the defenders. The coaches in the box upstairs watch the safeties to see how they play in the run situation. If they come down hard, we run the bootleg in one of the first three or four plays. Teams are playing the safeties to fit into the C gap or B gap as part of the gap responsibility. Obviously, we expect the linebacker to step as we run the zone fakes.

We have a 300/400 package that comes off the bend play. It is a typical play-action pass. We use it to control the linebackers. We throw two types of passes. We throw option routes or select routes. We release two or three receivers to the playside in route combinations. In our two-receiver combination, we have two to three different passes. We always have a flat route and a deep pattern down the field.

We want people to suck up so we can hit the big play down the field. If they do not, we take the fake, and the tight end runs a shallow pattern somewhere.

If you are a running team, you have to threaten teams with the deep play-action pass. You need to do it early in the game. That makes the safeties worry about the deep ball for the touchdown. I was on the defensive side of the football for 13 of my 17 years of coaching. When you tell the secondary to help with the run, but do not get beat deep, it does not work that way. We want to make the defensive back nervous about the deep throw as quickly as we can. That allows us to stretch the field on the defense with the vertical stretch.

In the zone play, we sprint off that fake. It is a typical sprint-out pass and we have only two combinations off the play. The object of the sprint is to put pressure on the containment and the force on the edge. The players know if we call 500/600 zone, there are two combinations we use. We treat the pass as we do the run. We get good at doing a few things through repetition.

By using the pass package, we pressure the linebackers and secondary players. Are they going to play up and stop the run as their coach told them to do, or are they going to play pass? Any time we run the zone, the quarterback runs his play-action fake.

The fact that we have an athletic quarterback puts additional pressure on the defense. That has made a big difference for the team. That adds the third threat of the quarterback keeping the ball on the play-action schemes and running it. If the quarterback sees an edge, he takes it and runs the ball. If he thinks he can run for eight yards rather than throw for eight yards, he runs.

He does the same thing to the strong safety whether he runs the ball or throws it. When we get into a sudden change situation, we like to run sprint pass right at the edge defender. He does not have any help. He is out in a big area with a big responsibility. We take advantage of that.

In our quarterfinal game, we played a team that was very good and ranked number one in the state at that time. They geared up to stop the run and we ran bubble-screen pass five times in a row. We went 82 yards and scored. It is an automatic in our system. If the linebacker does not position to stop the bubble, we throw it every time. Our receivers have a five-yard window to his inside. If the linebacker is not in that five-yard area, he knows the play is bubble screen.

We have to take that play because we want to run the ball. It makes sense. If they pack the box, we have to throw the ball. The good thing about the pass is it is a high-percentage throw. If you screw up the play, you have an incomplete pass and it is no big deal.

We have five running plays. We run zone, bend, option, toss, and lead. We have four pass actions and a three-step game. We have 41 different formations and combinations. We run four types of motions with six different players. The motion tells us what the defense is doing. It forces the defenders to become simplified. They cannot do the gadgetry because they know they will not see the same formation two plays in a row. The defense has to dilute their package.

Teams are going to the 3-3-5 defenses more to defense the spread offenses. We played that type of defense in the semifinal game. We gave them a lot of unbalanced formation and motion. We created the unbalanced look and helped our situation.

We have three different personnel groupings. We have regular, jumbo, and spread. The formations do not change, the personnel groups do. The H-back in the regular grouping is wide slot, whereas in the jumbo set he is in the wing position. The difference from the wing position to the wide-slot position is a big difference to the defense.

The reason we run this offense is it is simple to learn. In our youth program with the little kids, they run the zone scheme. It took us some time to convince the youth league coaches that this was the simplest way to teach offensive-line blocking.

They believe it now. It does not matter whether he is a guard or a tackle; everyone takes the same steps.

People told us how good our offensive line was this year. It was but we had four new starters in the line. We had a senior that started this year that was 5'11" and 265 pounds. When he moved to tackle a year ago, he could not squat the bar. As he got stronger, he got so good at taking the zone step that his squatty body made him a natural with the leverage he got in the block. He was not a good athlete; he was a good technician.

By getting the number of reps they get in our practices, they cannot help but be good at the techniques. They are almost perfect in their execution of the techniques. We can get by with players that are not 300 pounds. We do not need them. We like the wiry players in the 210- to 215-pound range who are more athletic.

Using this offense prepares the offensive linemen for any type of defense they see. In our first game in the playoffs, we played a jailbird defense. We did not know what to call it. There were players all over the place. It did not matter to us what kind of defense they ran. We stepped into the gap and knew someone would show.

This offense fit into our personnel. It fits into our beliefs. By being good at the scheme, the players get confidence. It becomes a competition within a game of how well our linemen can execute the offense.

This type of offense teaches those three things that are important in our program. It teaches character, mental toughness, and physical toughness. All three of these things are incorporated into our zone scheme.

Gentlemen, if I can ever help you, feel free to call or e-mail me. Thank you.

PLAY-ACTION PASSES OUT OF THE WING-T

Calhoun High School, Georgia

Today my topic is play-action passes out of multiple wing-T sets. We are based out of the wing-T, but we are also very multiple. We will get into some two-back sets and some one-back sets. We feel like defenses are too good these days to stay in the base wing-T set. We are able to do a lot on offense because of smart, high-character kids.

Why Do We Run the Wing-T?

- We are able to adapt to our personnel easily.
- We get great blocking angles. Our offensive line is not very big.
- We can throw the ball and run it equally well.
- We feel we need misdirection plays.

Our Offensive Philosophy

- Give as many formations as possible, but run the same plays.
- Get the ball in playmakers' hands.
- Take what the defense gives us.
- Stay consistent. Believe in your system.
- Those who stay will be champions.

Our base offensive set is what we call red or blue (Diagrams #1 and #2).

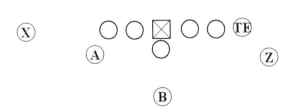

Diagram #1. Red Formation

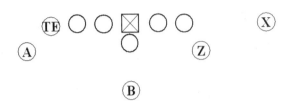

Diagram #2. Blue Formation

We do not flip sides with our backs because we feel it is easier to teach without changing. Other sets we use are unbalanced sets, which we call east or west (Diagrams #3 and #4). We also use double slot formations (Diagram #5). Also, we run a formation we call "nasty" where we have both wide receivers on the same side of the ball (Diagram #6).

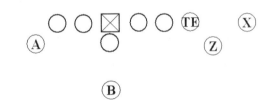

Diagram #3. East Formation

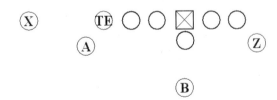

Diagram #4. West Formation

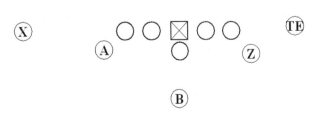

Diagram #5. Double Slot Formation

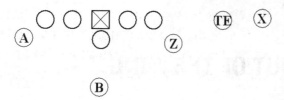

Diagram #6. Nasty Formation

The first play we want to talk about is our bootleg off the buck sweep. Some people call this play the waggle play, but we like the term bootleg (Diagram #7). If we bootleg strong to the tight end, our number-one read is the tight end on the corner route. Then we go to the B-back in the flat, and then to the crossing route by the A-back.

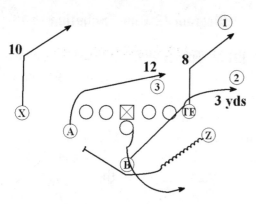

Diagram #7. Bootleg Play

If we want to throw the backside post route to the X-receiver, we call it in the huddle and it is an automatic call. Our bootleg weak changes the reads for the quarterback. He looks for the B-back in the flat first, and then he looks for the crossing route (Diagram #8). His third option is the run by the quarterback. Again, if we want to throw the backside post route, we call it in the huddle. Against cover 2, the quarterback looks for the post-corner first and then the crossing route.

We have some variations off our bootleg plays. One of our favorites is the switch route (Diagram #9). The A-back and the X-receiver switch routes. The X-receiver must cut his split down to about four yards. Our read changes a little and we still glance at the tight end. If he is open, we get him the ball. If he is not open, we look for the crossing route by our X-receiver. The next read is to the flat to the B-back.

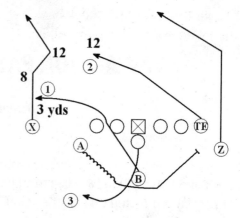

Diagram #8. Bootleg Weak

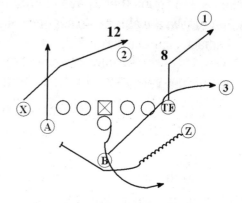

Diagram #9. Variation of Bootleg

We can also run the bench route off our bootleg (Diagram #10). The X-receiver runs a 14-yard route back to 12 yards. The B-back must hook up early to stay out of the passing lane.

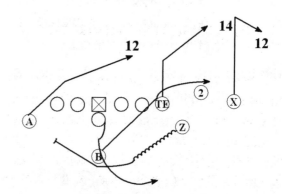

Diagram #10. Bench Route

Another variation we call is our Arkansas route (Diagram #11). It is a great route versus cover 2. Our first read is the A-back on the go route. Next we look for the X-receiver who is running a crossing route at 14 yards underneath the A-back. The cross is our second read on the play. Again, this is a throwback route.

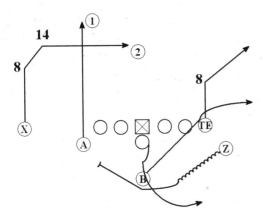

Diagram #11. Arkansas Throwback Play

Next I want to get to the play-action passes off our belly series (Diagram #12). The first route is a curl-flat route off the belly weak play. The quarterback must read the flat defender first.

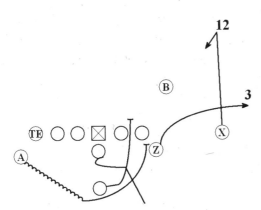

Diagram #12. Belly Curl-Flat Pass

The next play-action pass is our one-receiver route where we play games with the drop defender weak (Diagram #13), If the drop defender keys the slotback, we bring our slot inside as he does on the regular belly play. This will bring the drop player inside and open the passing lane for an eight-yard hitch route by our X-receiver. We can also run a go route with our X-receiver.

We also run what we call our roll pass (Diagram #14). This play is off our buck-sweep action. Also, this is a one-receiver route. We bring the X-receiver in like we are going to use a crack-back scheme. We do run a lot of crack schemes to set this play up.

The X-receiver fakes the crack block and then runs up the hash mark. The quarterback fakes the buck sweep and rolls with the sweep action. He sets his feet and throws to the deep pass to the X-receiver.

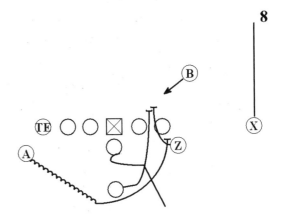

Diagram #13. One-Receiver Route

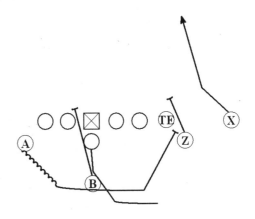

Diagram #14. Roll Pass

Also, we run the crack-and-up route off our quick-pitch action (Diagram #15). It is the same concept here. We are trying to get behind the free safety for the deep ball.

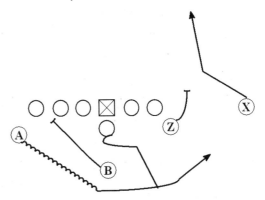

Diagram #15. Crack-and-Up Pass

We have one more play-action pass and it is off our jet-sweep package (Diagram #16). We call this play our flood route. We look for our jet back in the flat first. Next, the quarterback reads the corner route by our tight end.

I know I went over this fast. I hope I have given you some information that might help you with your program. If you have any questions, please feel free to call me at Calhoun High School in Calhoun, Georgia. Thanks very much for your attention.

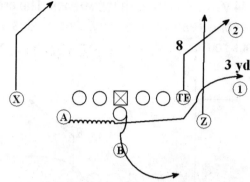

Diagram #16. Jet Sweep Pass

TWENTY KEYS TO A SUCCESSFUL PROGRAM

Natick High School, Massachusetts

It is exciting for me to be here today. I do not want to waste too much time. We are a two-platoon team. We will allow some of our players to play both ways, but they must earn their way onto both teams.

We dressed 84 players for our Super Bowl, and left another 40 freshmen at home. Our numbers are good, but I do not know which came first, the chicken or the egg. I do not know if our numbers increased because of the two-platoon system or the number caused us to go to two-platoon.

We had a great season. The varsity went 13-0, the JVs went 11-0, and the freshmen went 10-0. In my 27 years of coaching, I cannot remember that happening with our team or with another team. A football program with no losses in the total program is something to be proud of. That is the good thing. The problem is we graduate 26 seniors.

It will not be too bad, but we have serious quarterback problems. Our starting quarterback broke his ankle two days before the start of the season and missed the entire season. He came back and played a little in our Thanksgiving Day game. He played in the first playoff game and quite a bit in the second playoff game. We ended up playing a linebacker at quarterback and he was excellent. He will probably go to Springfield College and play quarterback there.

This is a system I developed to evaluate our program. We are doing these 20 things in our program. We won the championship this year, but that is not good enough. We want to continue to win it year after year. That is what you try to do in a program.

Building a Successful Program				
1	2	3	4	5
Poor	Fair	Good	Very Good	Great

Number	Ways to Build a Program	Score
1	Basic Philosophy Positive Regard, Confidence/Hard Guy, Few Good Men	
2	Staff	
3	X's and O's	
4	Game Plan and Adjustments	
5	Organization of Program Practice, Games Year Round	
6	Schedule	
7	Recruiting (hallways)	
8	Motivation	
9	Off-Season Workouts: Winter, Spring, Summer	
10	Summer Passing League (Linemen Challenger)	
11	Booster (Friends of Football Program Book)	
12	Paper Evaluations	
13	Media Day	
14	Pop Warner	
15	Parent Meeting	
16	Pre-Season Camp	
17	Scouting	
18	Website (Newsletter)	
19	Banquet and Awards	
20	College Recruiting	
Total Points (20 Items):		
Average Points:		

At the bottom of the sheet, you can give yourself a total mark. We rate the items one through five, with one being poor and five being great. In between, we have fair, good, and very good.

I am an athletic director now and just hired a new field hockey coach. I got some experience at Northeastern because the head football coach was also the athletic director. He let me do quite a bit of the interview process for positions within our program. I enjoyed that as part of my athletic director job.

This breakdown is something our assistant coaches can use in their interviews for jobs. This has worked out well for my young coaches who will be interviewing for a head coaching position. I think it is a thorough breakdown of the entire program.

The first item on the list is basic philosophy. What I do not want is a 50-page book that the applicant downloaded from the Internet. It has all kinds of philosophical junk from Joe Paterno to Woody Hayes. It has a beautiful cover and it looks fantastic, but he does not believe any of it. We throw that right in the trash. I have piles of that crap I got from my interviews for my field hockey coach.

If you are going to download all that stuff, you need to organize your philosophy and have something that you are passionate about. When you state your philosophy, the coach needs to tell me what he believes in and is passionate about.

I am going to tell you a couple of mine, and where we feel we start to build the successful program. The first thing we do in our practices is to create an atmosphere of intensity that allows the player to be the best he can be. We can compete and win five to seven games just hacking around. However, to win the next three or four games, we have to work our butts off.

If a player cannot see the importance of not coming to workouts a couple of minutes late, we relate to him that if you multiply that by 22 players, you have a big problem. That kind of discipline is vital to a program. We want to get that discipline and intensity to raise us to the three or four wins that makes your team a champion. I remind them of that point throughout the year, when we are cranked up on some kind of discipline issue.

The second point in my philosophy is what we expect of our players. The first thing is for them to be a great student. There is no reason they cannot be a great student. To some of our players, being a great student may be Cs. Whatever it is, be the best you can be.

The second thing is to be a great athlete. To us, that means playing three sports. I did it, and I believe in it. I think there is room for that within our program. Doug Flutie went to school here. He comes in a number of times during the year to talk to our players. He tells our players the same thing. He tells them to have fun. It is a grind at the pro level. If you want to be an NFL player, it is a grind to get there and stay there. Every one of those players looks back and wishes he had played more and just had fun.

We want our players to be great competitors. The greatest thing about football is taking a young man to the extremes in the human experience. You take him from kindness and feeling for his teammates, girlfriends, teachers, and his mother to the other end of the spectrum. On the other end is the nasty, nail-them-and-I-will-get-you-the-next-play type of mentality. You must have complete control of your emotions to be a kind man at one time and a nasty competitor at another time. You can do both. If you can control yourself emotionally, you will be a better man and grow into manhood. We work hard on teaching them how to be a great competitor.

We have some players that are too soft and cannot get cranked up. We have some that are too hard and are cranked up all the time. They are punching people during and after the whistle. It does not have to be on a field; it can be in the hallway at school. When I was growing up, the football coach controlled those people. On Monday, he punched them in the mouth and it lasted two or three days. Next Monday, they needed another one, but it straightened those people out.

It is not that easy anymore. That is not my style, for sure, but we have to find another way to control those crazy players. Those players are great in practice, but when they get in the hallways, they become a problem. It is a battle today to deal with those kinds of players. We are working from both sides to get them to be great competitors.

We want our players to have a positive regard for other players. That is my style to be positive with players. I am not a very good critic on the field. I do it, but I am a believer that football is the most difficult sport there is. You practice five or six days a week to play one game. Every other sport, including hockey, plays more than one game per week. This game is tough and it is work. That is why I want to be positive on the field.

One of the most important points comes from Bill Parcells. He said to make sure you say something positive to everyone every day. I talk to them every day. That is probably why we have 84 players on the varsity squad. We are not a program of a few good men. We have a program of a lot of good men.

Baseball is a good example. I can stand behind the batting cage and make a good hitter inept at hitting the ball in a matter of minutes. All I have to do is begin to offer advice on his swing in a critical way. By the time he tries to implement all the advice, he cannot hit the ball at all. If I stood behind the batting cage and said positive things, he would get better. I do not even have to watch what he is doing and he will get better. Try it sometime and see what happens.

It is human nature. When you hear good things, it builds your confidence. This game is too tough; we want to be positive with them. We try to tell them positive things, which is creative thinking. Try to find something they are doing well and compliment them on it. We almost had all of our players doing our warm-up right by the time of the last game. That is a challenge.

The second thing you want to rate is your staff. Sometimes you have to make changes. It is hard and I do not like to do it, but it is something you have to do. I had to let a coach go last year in our athletic staff and it was hard to do. I know you do not want to do it, but sometimes you have to do it for the good of the program. However, there may be a place you can move the coach, and he may perform better. You could move him up or down within the structure of the program and salvage something good for the program. My first year in this program I moved some coaches around within the levels of our program and they became better coaches. The ones we moved down to the freshmen level are better and happier coaches today. If you get your coaches in the right places, they can benefit the development of the program.

It is important to have someone you like and trust as your defensive coordinator. Your defensive back coach has to be a good coach. Players can get beat quicker in that position if they do not know what they are doing or if they do not like the coach. I believe the offensive line coach is a special coach. I will never take another position coach and tell him he has to coach the offensive line.

Offensive line coaches are a special breed of people. He is always sweating because he is always cranking with his big people in practice. If the players are having fun, I am not going close to that area of practice. The offensive linemen are a special group. They are not good athletes, hate to run, and probably did not sleep the night before worrying about what kind of conditioning we were going to do. The guys that weigh 175 pounds do not worry about conditioning. I have offensive linemen waiting in my office in the mornings wanting to know what the conditioning is going to be.

If you can find a coach who has a knack with those players or that position, you should hire him and hang onto him. If he has the knack for teaching toughness to offensive linemen, it is an unusual thing. It is difficult to teach detail and technique in this position. If you find a coach who can do all those things, you had better pay him more money because you will not have him long. The coaches that can teach toughness and technique move up very fast. On your staff, the offensive line is critical. I have a coach now who the players love. They all hang around his room at school.

We had a problem with one of our offensive linemen. I went to the coach and he wanted to handle the problem himself. He takes their behavior personally and feels like they are his boys.

The X's and O's are important in our game. Coaches must go to clinics, read articles, visit college programs, use the Internet, and study the game as part of being a good coach. You must stay abreast of the developments in the game to make the right X-and-O decisions. When I went into college coaching at Northeastern, it took me from one level of X's and O's to another level.

There are no miracles in the coaching game. At Northeastern, everyone in that league was good and it was hard to get an advantage over anyone. Even at the high school level, it is hard to get an advantage over anyone. The thing we do well is to not call too many bad plays. I see teams run plays into the wrong part of the defense all the time. They run pass plays that cannot work against particular coverages. If you run the right play, you have a chance of it being successful. That does not mean it will be successful. However, if you run the wrong play and execute it correctly, it probably will not be a success.

College coaches want high school coaches to come in to see them and watch film. They particularly like for them to come to practice. There are two reasons for that. First, they want to establish a relationship with the coaches in the area. Second, they want the coach see the talent level that their players are competing against. That way, the high school coach may begin to understand why his 5'11", 225-pound tackle did not get a scholarship offer. If they see the players at those practices, they understand what college coaches are recruiting.

I want to talk a little about game plan and adjustments. The defenses are getting so complicated that we are at the stage of having a general offense and it is multiple. We have a play to go in every hole and a pass to go every area. We want to keep it simple, but that is the best we can do. We go into the game, see what the defense is doing, and adjust accordingly.

This year, we had the most talented offensive team I have had in 27 years of coaching. Our right tackle was 340 pounds, the right guard was 300 pounds, the center was 225 pounds, the left guard was 195 pounds, and the left tackle was 275 pounds. We had three offensive players whose 40-yard times were under 4.5. Our wide receiver, who signed with Boston College, ran a 4.4. The tailback, who weighs 210 pounds, ran a 4.37. The slotback, who weighs 160 pounds, ran a 4.39. These times are not our times. Other people at camps timed them.

We probably operated at 70 percent, won 13 games, and won a championship. This was the most talented team, but not the best I have ever had. Even with the talent we had, you cannot put them up against a stacked deck on defense.

Having a good game plan and the ability to adjust because you are multiple enough gives you a chance to win. I do not go into games any more and say we are going to run off-tackle no matter what they do. We are going to run our off-tackle power plays, but we are quickly branching out from that thinking. In the fourth quarter, we are going back to the old power play, hammer it out, and eat up the clock.

In the organization of our program, we have a routine we use. Tuesday is our individual day, Wednesday is our group day, and Thursday is our team day. We keep each practice day the same each week. That helps our coaches who are not in the building know what to expect each day in practice. To have a consistent schedule helps us out quite a bit.

The big thing we did this year was our preparation for Saturday morning games. We are a Friday-night team. We play all of our home games, except for the Thanksgiving game, on Friday night. Friday night after the game, the locker room is alive with activity. It is high school football at its best. The problem we have is some of the teams in our league play their home games at 10:00 on Saturday morning. Our players were terrible in Saturday-morning games. We went back several years and looked at the record. We lost nine of eleven games on Saturday morning.

If you research Friday-night teams playing during the day, odds are they do not play well. When we went to our overnight camp this year, we got our players up at 6:15, took them to breakfast, and went to practice around 9:00. It dawned on me that this was about the same time schedule we go through for our Saturday morning games. Our players were doing well and energized during practice. So I adopted the routine we had in camp as a routine for Saturday-morning games.

I called one of our boosters who owned a restaurant. I told him we wanted to have our pre-game breakfast at his restaurant on Saturday game days at 6:30 in the morning. We followed the same routine we did at our camp and played well in the game. It worked well and we kept the routine going for all our Saturday games. The bus ride over and the locker room before the game was alive and our players were ready to play.

When you are building your program, you have to be careful of who you play. We have 12 teams in our league, 11 games, and no options of whom we play.

A big part of any program is to recruit your building. I think I am good at getting players out of the hallway. We get one or two seniors every year that has never played in our program. We get new players out every year that have not been in our program and they help us. I have a plan when I talk to kids in the hallway.

When I approach them, I make the suggestion they should think about playing football. I walk away after that and leave them with that thought. When I was younger, if a kid gave me a little positive feedback, I jumped on him with the hard sales pitch. I leave them alone for a couple of weeks before I approach them again. He has time to think about the possibility of playing.

If he wants to come out, I try to get him to go to our off-season program and mini-camps. I try to get him to go to the Boston College camp. It is right at the end of school, for three days, and is a helmet-only camp. That way, he gets to know the drills, how to line up, and there is no hitting. They get a feel for being an athlete.

The second step is to come to our base day camp. That is a three-day camp just before the team starts practice. This is a helmet-and-shoulder-pad camp, which takes him up another notch in his preparation. There is some hitting, but it is not full contact. When they come to our pre-season camp, they are ready to go.

I have found that, for the seniors who come out late, the only position they can play is defensive end or outside linebacker. If they are naturals, they might able to play tailback or wide receivers.

Motivation is a key concept, but I am not going to spend too much time on it. Motivation is a function of your personality. You are the only person in the world who can motivate the way you motivate, whatever that may be. Woody Hayes was the only person that could motivate like Woody Hayes. However, we take little pieces of the picture from those guys to imitate. Whatever you do has to come from you. It has to become your style, whatever that might be.

What is common among the great motivators in the world of sport? They are tremendous workers, love their players, are very intense, love to compete, have consistency in their beliefs, and are consistent from person to person. You are the only one who can motivate your way; you cannot be like someone else.

I want to tell you about a couple of things we have tried in our off-season programs. We do a winter/spring/summer workout program, like most of you do. We copied this from someone in our league. Our summer workout is called "tough camp now." We do this in the mornings three days per week. I do not believe we can follow the college style of lifting for four days. I do not believe high school players can push their bodies that hard for four days. We work Fridays, Mondays, and Wednesdays. I do not think high school kids can push themselves hard enough to get a complete leg workout in two days. We go three days. We have a great weight room. We can put a lot of players through there in a short amount of time.

We have a mini-camp we copied from the Patriots. The players buy into it because of that fact. In Massachusetts, between the winter season and the spring season, we have three weeks off without any contact. We take two of those weeks and have our mini-camp. We have to open all of our off-season training up to everyone. It cannot be a football-only activity. We have the mini-camp the first two weeks in March. We have the lifting program on Monday, Wednesday, and Friday after school.

We have six stations. We have three lifting stations along with a core-strength station, a plyometric agility station, and a lateral running station outside. We go ten minutes per station and it is not great for weightlifting. It is good for weightlifting, but great for everything else. It establishes tempo and gets everyone working.

No matter what we do, we always have a few kids that will not work. It always seems it is the ones you need the most who do not give it to you. They work hard in these sessions. We do the same mini-camp when school ends. With no sports going on during the last two weeks of school, we get another six sessions of mini-camp. It is good for the weightlifting, but great for team spirit, intensity, and enthusiasm. Our players go home feeling good about the upcoming season. We have about 90 kids in the program.

After July 4, we start up our summer camp. This is the tough camp I talked about earlier. All the players in those camps know the routine and we do not waste a lot of time.

We are in two summer passing leagues. We have one on Tuesday night and one on Thursday night at two different schools. That is working out really well. We are starting to get linemen camps in the state now. The linemen see the skilled players going to camps to improve their skills and they are taking advantage of it. The linemen challenges are based on the ESPN strongest man contests. They do some of the same events. It is starting up here now and the kids love it. It is not sports oriented as of yet.

I cannot coach the teams because of our state regulations prohibiting it. I cannot have anything to do with the passing camps in the summer. I cannot collect money for the camp or anything according to state rules.

Our booster club conducts a fundraiser in the summer called "Friends of Football/Program Book." They sell $10 a line in the program book. They sell them to the relatives, girlfriends, or simple friends of the program. They dedicate a line to the player. "Good luck with the season," or "Have a good year and do not get hurt" are some examples you might find in the book.

We have player evaluations. The difference between my staff and me is shown in player evaluation. Young coaches have a hard time with player evaluation. I do well because I am older and more experienced. I can look at a player and tell you he is going to be able to play. When I was younger, I could not do that. We have our big staff meeting between the winter and spring seasons and go over every player on our roster.

We want a good evaluation on a player before school ends. If we want him to change positions, he can go to camps in the summer at the new position. I do not want to come back in August and move someone. It is a great feeling if we change a player's position and he comes back smiling.

Evaluate your players with your eyes closed. Evaluate each player with what you know about him as a person and his character. Think about how big he plays. Do not look at his body. Small players can play big. Judge him on his qualities.

We do a good job with our media day. The Thursday before our last scrimmage, we have picture day. We put everyone in their game uniforms, and we give everyone a chance to take pictures. We invite all the mothers and fathers as well as the local papers and television stations. We send a schedule to the *Globe* and the *Herald*, but they do not come. I guess they are busy with the Patriots. It works out well and gets the pictures out of the way. I hate picture day. It is a wasted day. We do it before the last scrimmage because we are resting the players anyway.

One of my pet areas is Pop Warner football. If you are criticizing your Pop Warner program, you are criticizing the heart and soul of your team. Seventy to eighty percent of our team will play in the Pop Warner program.

I have to do two things if I do not believe in Pop Warner football. I either keep my mouth shut or get out and coach the coaches working with the teams.

We coach the coaches. Those kids are our future. Every Tuesday in February and the first Tuesday in March, we run clinics for the Pop Warner coaches at the high school. We run it from 6 to 7 o'clock. We do not want to keep them very long because they work all day and are tired.

When they have sign-ups for their program, make sure you attend the sign-ups. I walk around at the sign-ups and talk to people. I move around quickly because moving targets are harder to hit.

The third thing you need to do is attend the first week of practices. I am there to help any coach who might have a question or need help with a drill. I try to attend some of their games. I work with the Pop Warner league and it has worked out well. We do work together.

We have a mandatory parent meeting. I think it is good and I encourage you to have one. It saves you a lot of problems. Parents and players alike must understand that players can come to practice late if they have to stay after school for extra help with their academics. All they must do is bring a note from the teacher. That saves you 15 phone calls a season.

We do our overnight camp and try to be thorough and organized. We go to a former baseball campground. We tell our parents that the camp is open if they would like to come up for a visit. They never come. If we had said no parents were allowed, you know they would drive up. While we are there, we get them up earlier and start the day. We take the weight with us and lift at night. We do not get anything out of it, but it gives the players something to be proud of and talk about.

Our theme this year was: "Knock the Door Down." In years past, it was: "Knocking on the Door." We decided this was the year to break through and win a championship.

We want our players to be on time, to pay attention, to get everything given out, to be in condition, and to give 110 percent. To get your players to pay attention is a big step in high school. You are responsible for getting things done. You mother is not here to take care of you. One of the things I have to fight in overnight camp was hazing. That was an absolute nightmare for us. That can destroy a program quickly. I talk to the leaders of the team, the seniors, captains, and anyone I think can help us with this problem.

I think it all comes down to respect in the program. We work hard with the seniors to treat the sophomores in our program like a younger brother. We had one camp, when the seniors came to the coaches and told us the sophomores were hazing them because they knew we would not do anything to them. It never seems to end.

We do a good job with college recruiting. We had out a sheet with 11 questions to ask college coaches. When they are on a recruiting visit, they get nervous and do not know what to ask. I give them the questions. I have a sheet with our seniors on it. I have their names, addresses, phone numbers, SAT scores, interests in college major, height, weight, and 40-yard times. I hand that list out to every coach that comes into visit and recruit. That protects you from the parent who says you only push the stars to the college coaches.

All the seniors are on the list. When I give the list to the coach, I give the coach an indication of the players I think can play at their level.

We have 10 copies of our best player's films available immediately. I have transcript copies in the player's folder. When the recruiter comes in, we hand him the list of seniors, the transcripts of the players he is interested in, and a film. He thanks us and he is out the door.

I have run out of time. I hope you enjoyed the presentation and got something from it. Sorry I kept you too long. Have an enjoyable time at the clinic.

SHOTGUN OFFENSE: RUN AND PASS

Sacred Heart-Griffin High School, Illinois

Thank you. I appreciate you men coming out on a Friday morning to listen to some talk about football. My topic this morning is the shotgun offense, but I would like to give you a little background before we get started here.

I grew up in a town that does not even have a school anymore. I started coaching over at Chenoa. My first job came in 1977, and after serving as offensive coordinator, I went to Gridley High School, which also does not exist any more.

My last year at Gridley, we had 88 guys and girls in the whole school, and I had 18 players on the football team. I learned a very valuable lesson there and what I learned at that point, I have used all the way through. What we did was teach our young men how to coach themselves. We used our players as coaches.

The seniors were my assistants there. I know that Greg Townsend did the same thing with his defense at Aurora and they just ran the drills, the same things, over and over. That is a great lesson for all of us, but I do not believe in doing that offensively because we are always changing and fitting all of our schemes to the personnel that we have.

Today, I am going to go over all of that with you. We went from the run offense, we went to the run offense and defense, and from the run offense to the pass-run in 1999. We have just played with it ever since. That is where we came from.

We were an I team and we converted our I offense to the gun without making changes up front. I think you can do as many things as you want with the skill kids, but you cannot do a lot of things with your offensive linemen. I have a 75-year-old coach with the offensive linemen and he is a crusty old guy. He is a tough nut and a great offensive line coach. In the last four years, we have had one offensive lineman go to a Division III school to play college football from our high school—one guy!

So, you know, everybody says that our coaches are the worst, but we got all the talent and that is why they cannot beat us. You know, I have been at it for 29 years now and it just does not change. When they win, it is the great coaching job they do, and when we win it is because we have better people.

I learned when I was at Gridley High School with 18 guys on the team that I better not be worrying about what the other guy had. I made our kids believe they could win. The big thing we have to do as coaches is this. We have to make them believe that whatever we do is the best thing going, flat out. That is how it has to be.

We have to quit looking at everyone else, quit pointing the finger at everyone else, and focus on the things we can do. If we focus on the other guy, we are never going to be successful.

So, let us get back and focus on our shotgun offense. We converted from the I formation to the gun and it allowed us to be multiple while remaining simple up front. I will go through this real quick. We have gone from a run to a run-pass, from run-pass to pass, and that is our offense. I think you have to give multiple looks for the defense and not do a lot of different things. We have to slow and control the defense. We have the chalk last on offense so we can make the final move. That is the attitude you have to have on offense. We have the chalk last.

Our offense fits our personnel. You know what? It does because we adjust it with our personnel, and you will see, over the past four years, how we went from a run gun to a run-pass gun to a pass gun. What we are trying to do is get the ball to our best player.

Football coaching is not rocket science, but you do have in your hands the right to do anything you want. You go to these clinics and see where Bowling Green does this and Utah does that, but you have to look at what personnel you have and try to adjust to what they can do. You take the offense that you feel comfortable with and learn as much about it as you can, so you can fit your personnel.

So, get your best player the ball. That is what makes us good coaches. That is why I am wearing a ring today. I have learned that it is not about Ken Leonard and it is not about X's and O's—it is about Jimmys and Joes.

If you have one great player, get him the ball all the time. That is the best way to make big plays and that is the bottom line. Football is about the score. Outscore your opponent. It does not matter about the stats. The only stat that matters is my points against your points, and I am going to try to make sure that my points are more than your points, however I have to do it.

If you go to this gun offense, you have to make a commitment to practice it every day. The one thing that is overlooked more than anything else is the center. He is the most important player on your team offensively, because if you do not have a center, you "ain't got bullets in your gun." That is the key right there.

You always have to have a backup. We ran from shotgun 50-50 in 2000. In 2001 we got some guys hurt, went to the I again, did too stinking much, and in 2002 we started it back. But we always kept under center enough because if that center breaks his hand or you have a couple of injuries, you talk about the quarterback getting hurt, the center is the key—the snap in the gun. That is the key and you have to start working him right away. Whatever you do, you have to practice it every day—over and over.

I want to talk about our offense in these last four years to underscore the importance of getting the ball to your best players. In 2002, we had a tailback that broke the school rushing record. He is a great player who is at Indiana now. Guys, we ran him on trap, belly G, inside veer, the counter trey, the stretch play, or whatever we needed to do. We think of the trap in the I formation as a fullback play, but in the gun it does not matter. You can get your best player the ball. He touched the ball a lot.

Let us talk quarterback for a minute. In the third game of the 2002 season, I got smart. I put a sophomore quarterback in at that time and we went to the gun. From that point on, we have averaged 42 points per game. My quarterback became a great player, and he is at Northwestern now. He was the first quarterback in state history to run for 1,500 yards and to pass for 1,500 yards in the same season, which he did in 2003.

We set the offense up for him and we got him the ball. He scored 37 rushing touchdowns during his senior year, and he did not throw a pass in the second half until midway into the season. The point is, he was a great player and we got him the ball.

Now, compare that with this past season. The quarterback we had this year is a coach's son who broke all of the passing records. We know that he will have to run the ball more next year because of all the 3-5-3 stuff, and I will get into all of that in the next few minutes.

Okay, what does all of that say to you? You can see already how in 2002 we were 80 percent run, in 2003 we were 75 percent run, and in 2004 we were 60 percent run. We seemed to be getting a little more balanced each year, and then—boom! Last year, we were 71 percent pass. Now, you know that is not balanced offense, but you know what? At 14-0 and a state championship, I would say that is balanced enough.

You do what you have to do to win. That could be run or pass or whatever you have to do to win football games, because that is what we are paid for.

This is our outside counter, counter trey, GT, gap play. This is probably a little different look than what you normally see, but I think you have to do what is right for you, rather than what they are doing at the big schools. We do this thing a million different ways. We do counter trey full reaction, counter trey option; we do counter trey GH, GS, and everything else possible as far as our counter trey. It was our number-one running play. Now, we also run zone, the inside and outside zone, but with the counter trey that is it as far as running the ball.

Next is the alignment (Diagram #1). Our running back aligns with our guard. We have put him on the outside leg and we have put him on the inside leg, but we put him on the guard and not the tackle for one simple reason. We run veer, we run trap, and we want to have some flexibility there. I think that when you just have to take one step and you are right next to the quarterback, you can do a lot more things. For us on the outside counter, the running back is even with the guard, with his toes aligned with the heels of the quarterback. The quarterback is directly behind the center with his toes at five yards.

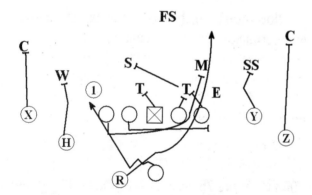

Diagram #1. Outside Counter Read

We do not have big linemen, but our offensive line coach takes them and goes through the blocking scheme over and over. They run the same drills over and over. The blocking on the play is all pretty much on angles, and they do a great job with it even though they are not very big.

What the gun does for you in the run game is this. Number one is option football, it is exciting football, and it cuts the defense in half. Everybody talks about slowing the defense. Well, these guys over here on our left side cannot run to the football.

That is what stymies your offense. You hand the ball off today and you get the 4-2 defense, or the safeties dropping down, and everybody playing smash mouth and running to the football. Well, I want to play the smash-mouth teams because they are flying to the football and we are going the other way.

We have to slow them down. We have the run game, and now we can put the pass game in to slow you down, and that is what it gets for you.

Are there any questions on the outside counter read? Our quarterback will read this defensive end on our left side, whether to give the ball and then, if we have a pitchman, we would option this outside linebacker on the pitch. In this diagram, it is just a give or a run.

That is our counter trey read. I can show you tapes where we option and do some other things off of it, but this is just what we call "counter trey read." This is our number-one play and I believe it is the best play in football.

Some defensive teams want to put six men in the box against the spread offense, but we do not see much of that. We are not going to see six guys in the box. If you put six in the box against us you are in trouble because we are just going to take advantage of everything underneath here and in the flat areas.

Now, here is our play against the 3-3 defense (Diagram #2). Because of the immediate threat to the outside, the inside backers have to be walked out a little. Our right tackle will just influence the

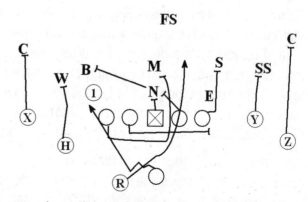

Diagram #2. Outside Counter Read versus 3-3

defensive end, and then he will block the outside linebacker, the Sam.

You know, some people just block right and left. We just went down to Memphis University to find out more about the 3-5-3 defense, and this is how we think we should block the play against it. The Sam is the tackle's man. We double the nose, trap the end, wrap the guard on the Mike, and the quarterback reads the defensive end away from the play. Actually, a better play against this defense, I believe, is the quarterback counter because now you have all the numbers.

I told you there are two things I want to be sure to cover today. The counter trey was the first one and the power is the second one, because when we get on the goal line, one of our great plays is power off tackle (Diagram #3). The combination of those two plays on the goal line is a great combination, although we will also run the stretch play down there, too.

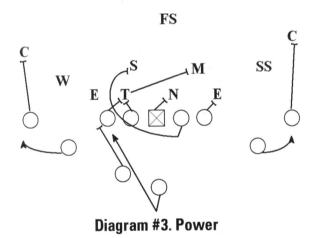

Diagram #3. Power

The quarterback alignment on power is the same as it is on the outside counter and the running back aligns anywhere to get an angle on his block. The quarterback shows pass first and then he hits his landmark. The running back blocks EMOL. His aiming point is the inside number.

Now, this is our "shovel" play (Diagram #4). Three or four years ago we put this play in, but I really did not know what I was trying to do with it then. Some of the colleges did a lot better with it. We called it "triple" back then.

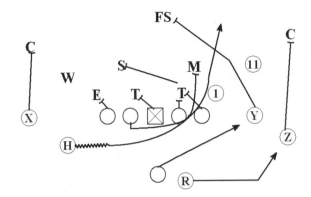

Diagram #4. Shovel

As you can see on the handout, it is based upon power blocking. Our H-back comes in motion and should be no closer than the outside leg of the backside offensive tackle at the snap. The quarterback opens flat or takes a slight arc, and he goes 75 percent on his first three steps. He reads the defensive end on his first option. He reads the defensive end for the inside pitch—which is a forward pass, men—and then he runs the speed option outside. This is a very popular play now.

You know, we completed 70 percent of our passes, and some of that was on this play. We throw the ball a lot of different ways. We threw 333 times this year, and that is pretty good. The key is to make sure we stay at this angle where the defensive end cannot defend both of them. You cannot let the defensive player dictate to you. Then, the quarterback cannot get there first because we cannot pitch the ball back at that angle.

We now run the shovel two different ways. We have the shovel option, which is actually a triple option, and we have the "run the ball" shovel, which is a pitch-or-keep play.

Now keep in mind that we want to spread the defense out and get the ball to our best player in space. We also know that we have to be able to run the football to be successful, and we ran successfully last year to set up our pass game. We averaged 9.8 yards per attempt, threw for 37 touchdowns, scored 41 points per game, and we won the state championship. We got the ball to our best players in space with our pass game, and let their talent take over.

I believe that defense wins games and the running game can always keep it close, but the passing game wins with less, and wins big. In the gun, we will pass about 70 percent of the time and run about 30 percent of the time. We are going to practice what we do, so practice time is rationed about the same in proportion, but we are going to keep it simple in the passing game. To do that, we will execute the same play out of multiple formations, and a big key is to match up with the running game in our formations and with backfield motion.

In addition to all of our play-action plays, we have a quick passing game, which includes the hitch-seam combinations and slant-bubble combinations out of our two-by-two sets. It includes the all-hitch combinations that we like out of the empty set and a double-out combination into trips (Diagram #5).

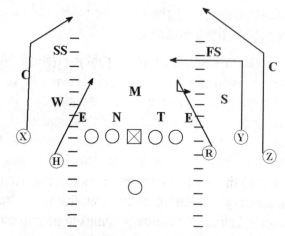

Diagram #6. Five-Step Short - Scat

We also have a five-step medium game that includes a three-level combination called shallow cross that allows us to throw the ball down the field (Diagram #7). We can also run 10-yard option routes with our inside receivers, and we can go to a trips formation and run flood routes to the trips side or individual routes back to the single-receiver side.

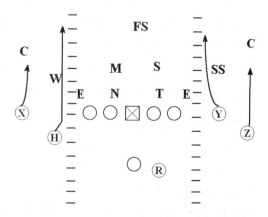

Diagram #5. Quick Game - Hitch Seam

We have a five-step short game (Diagram #6). We will clear out the deep coverage with our outside receivers and cross our inside receivers at five yards in a mesh combination, working them into open areas between the linebackers. We also run a three-level combination called scat into the middle of the defense, with our inside receivers running short option routes on the inside linebackers.

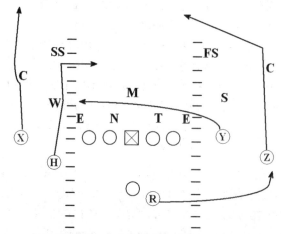

Diagram #7. Five-Step Medium - Shallow Cross

The threat of the run has helped to make our pass game explosive. I do not have the time today to get to the details of all of that, but I will be around here after this lecture and I will be happy to answer any questions you may have, and talk some more football with you. Thank you for your attention, and good luck in 2006.

Darrell Mayne

DEALING WITH ADVERSITY

Troy Athens High School, Michigan

I want to thank Don Lessner for inviting me to speak here today. I grew up in Trenton, Michigan. I was raised in Lincoln Park. I was always proud to be able to say I was from Lincoln Park.

I am going to be talking fast, so if you need to find out something that I went over too fast, see me after the lecture and I will go over anything you want me to cover. Hopefully, the things I am going to cover will help you.

I like to study successful people. It does not matter if they are doctors, lawyers, business people, or coaches. I am a great disciple of Coach John Wooden, the former UCLA basketball coach. I like to study how these people have been successful. There are common threads through all of these people. The one thing I find that we are not doing is this. I do not think we spend enough time with our young people to teach them to be successful in their lives.

An article just came out in the *American Football Monthly* magazine. The article is by a Ph.D. sports shrink. I am talking about those people that are paid all of that money to figure out what it takes to win. This guy makes this comment: "The vast number of coaches all know how to put a program together. They know how to do this and do that, but what separates coaches, and other professions, and every human being is this. It is their ability to deal with adversity." That is what I am going to talk about with you today. I am going to talk about a game plan for dealing with adversity.

I have been all the way to the top in this profession, and I have been at the bottom, and I have been everywhere in between. I have been there before. I took over a program down in Cleveland, Ohio, where the people told me we could never win.

So we had to have a plan to deal with all of the dynamics. What I am going to do today is touch on some of the points I used to turn that program around.

I am going to move fast on this subject because there is a lot of information I want to pass on to you. I am getting up in years in my coaching career, and I want to give back to the game some of the ideas I have used that helped me in my career.

Preface

It is not *if* you will face adversity in your career, it is only *when* and *what* type of adversity you will face. In what form will the adversity come?

- Budget cuts
- Athletic-code violation
- Player coachability
- Ineligible player
- Player injury
- Player relationships
- Staff relationships
- Loss in a very important game
- Media coverage
- Parental complaints
- Administrative concerns

And the list goes on, right?

I consider myself a survivor of the coaching profession. I take pride in this fact. I love the profession, but I will tell you one thing. It is not if you will face adversity, it is only when you will face adversity. The question is: do we as coaches have a plan to minimize the adversity? Do we have a plan to react positively to the adversity? Everyone talks about game plans and Xs and Os. Few coaches talk about how to manage adversity!

Questions

What defines the truly great programs? Think about it. Year in and year out, up or down, who are the toughest teams to beat, and why? In Ohio, it is St. Ignatius High School, Colerain, and Moeller of Cincinnati. It is Massillon High School and Canton McKinley High School. These are the high-powered programs in Ohio and you have to go against them if you are going to win the championship. Why are these teams so tough? The following list is from John Wooden. What determines who wins the tight games? Is it:

- Schemes or attitudes?
- Schemes or reactions?
- Talent or toughness?
- Talent or resilience?
- Talent or preparation?
- Athleticism or expectation of success?
- Them or us?

You get the point I am trying to get across. How many times have you been in a program where you figure you have a great offensive scheme and the best defensive scheme in the world, and the best kicking game? But the bottom line is this: when push comes to shove, you do not execute well enough to win. The reason you do not execute it well enough to win is for the same reason our kids do not execute it well enough. It is because mentally and spiritually in their hearts they were not good enough. That is the issue. In the society of today, we need more of that than ever before. What determines who wins the tight games?

The bottom line is this: it has more to do with the qualities of our hearts, than it does with the teams we play. We live in a media-consumed society. Players are looking at other athletes and are not concerned with "us." This is a big point and we are going to focus on who we are.

Think about these examples: Early 1990s, Colorado at Notre Dame. Notre Dame won the game, and after the Colorado team got back home, Coach Bill McCarthy and his staff locked the coaching room doors and tried to figure out why

Notre Dame was able to defeat the Buffalos. "Why is Notre Dame better than us?" The conclusion by the staff was this: Notre Dame was tougher mentally than Colorado. They could not come up with any reasonable answer other than the fact that Notre Dame was tougher mentally. Notre Dame had a greater expectation of success.

After that meeting, Colorado made some changes. Did they change their offense? No. Did they change the defense? No. They did not change any of that stuff. I will tell you what they changed. They changed their approach to the game of football. When they changed their approach to the game, they got the results they were looking for and they won the national championship.

In the year 2000, Ohio State was playing Miami for the national championship in the Fiesta Bowl. Miami was the big favorite in that game. *Sports Illustrated* did a 35-point analysis on the match up for the two teams. Miami was favored in 33 of those categories. Ohio State was ranked ahead of Miami in only two of the categories analyzed. Miami was the overwhelming favorite. The game looked like it would be a romp for Miami. Ohio State won the game in overtime and won the national championship. What made the difference?

When we won the state championship in 2000, we were not the most talented team in Ohio. Some people may think I am cutting our kids down with that statement. No. Let me tell you this: we were the best team in the state. Our kids did not care who received the credit. They were focused and they had the elements I am talking about today.

So, teach them:

- The elements of positive attitude.
- Not generalities—specifics.
- The proper "reaction ethic."
- To not assume they know how.
- The elements of mental toughness.
- That thoughts turned into words are powerful, both positively and negatively.
- That the small details of skills and schemes are vital to success.
- To focus on us, and the "power of us."

We talk to our kids about doing their best all of the time. It does not matter if they are up or down. We tell the kids if they are up by seven points, they should be thinking about going up 14 points. If we are up by 14 points, we want to get up by 21 points. What if we are behind by 21 points? We are going to cut it to 14 points. Then we are going to cut that to seven points. At the end of the game, we tell them to close their eyes. "What does the scoreboard show? We win." That is reaction ethic.

You can look at all kind of situations such as this, but the media is consumed with sending a message of violence to our teenagers today. They are consumed with sending that very destructive message. It is our job to give them a reaction ethic to this message.

I could talk about this material for hours. We cover all of the phases of the game in our practice schedule, but we program in time for discussions on the mental and attitude development. We have a plan for this.

We have found that whatever we talk about with our players is what we are going to get. If we talk to them negatively, that is what you are going to get from them. Words are powerful. We do not want our players talking to anyone—in school, at home, at a store, or a movie—in a negative fashion. Shame on them if they are doing that. That is something we have control over. Words are very powerful and we know someone is always listening. These things make a big difference.

There are three things I would like to encourage you to do. These things have helped me in my life. I feel there are three elements you need to deal with the adversity we face in the culture we live in today. I will cover those points in three parts.

- Part One: Being positively proactive – Plan your work.
- Part Two: Being positively reactive – Work your plan, plan your work.
- Part Three: Being at peace – Let faith play its part.

Back in the 1990s during Operation Desert Storm, I would rush home to watch the day's action in Iraq and in the Middle East. General Norman Schwarzkopf had these press conferences every day. I could relate to him because he reminded me of Bo Schembechler. Here was a guy fighting the war and running Operation Desert Storm. This is what he said. "Always plan for the worst-case scenario. By so doing, you are maximizing your chances for success. If worse does happen, you have demonstrated your leadership skill and foresight. If it is not too bad, you may well look like a smart leader." It may sound a little strange considering the seriousness of being in a war. There is so much truth to this statement.

Part One: Being Positively Proactive – Plan Your Work.

Know what you are attempting to build into each group of people you deal with. Do not leave it to chance.

Winning games does not come down to facilities, who has the largest weight room, or who has turf or grass. It comes down to you, your staff, and your administration, and that is all it boils down to in the end. When interviewing for the job, I am going to try to give the administration a very clear idea of what our vision is for our program. I do not lie to them and I do not try to con them. I do not tell them what I think they want to hear. I tell them who I am. I communicate with them in the interview, but also after I have been hired. Our administration gets a copy of everything we are doing in our program. I make sure they know what I am doing.

Administration

- Vision
- Attitude is everything
- No surprises
  ✓ Clear expectations
  ✓ Dates/Activities
  ✓ Player behavior
  ✓ Integration with total educational program

- ✓ Mental dynamics
- ✓ Parent groups
- ✓ Media
- ✓ Community
- Forewarned is forearmed
  - ✓ Keep advised in *advance*.
  - ✓ *Always* be truthful.

Coaches

- Vision
- Attitude is everything.
- No surprises
  - ✓ Clear expectations
  - ✓ Dates/Activities
  - ✓ Concern – approachable
  - ✓ Perspectives
    - ○ Administration
    - ○ Teachers
    - ○ Parents
    - ○ Support staff
    - ○ Community
    - ○ Media
    - ○ Officials
  - ✓ Communication
  - ✓ Goals/Objectives
  - ✓ Organization
  - ✓ Preparation ethic
  - ✓ Response ethic
  - ✓ Psych dynamics
  - ✓ We, not mine – ownership
  - ✓ Honoring wives and families
  - ✓ Honoring effort and achievement

Players

- Vision
- Attitude is everything.
- No surprises.
  - ✓ Clear expectations
  - ✓ Dates/activities
  - ✓ Concern – approachable

- ✓ Demeanor
  - ○ Administration
  - ○ Teachers
  - ○ Coaches
  - ○ Support staff
  - ○ Players
  - ○ Community
  - ○ Opponents
  - ○ Officials
  - ○ Media
- ✓ Goals/Objectives
- ✓ Playing time
- ✓ Battling a self-absorbed culture
- ✓ Big Eight
  - ○ Faith
  - ○ Work
  - ○ Discipline
  - ○ Intensity
  - ○ Team
  - ○ Improve
  - ○ Role
  - ○ Respect
- ✓ Sacrifice
- ✓ Positive programming of yourself

The Essence of Destiny

Watch your thoughts, for they become words. Choose your words, for they become actions. Understand your actions, for they become habits. Study your habits, for they will become your character. Develop your character, for it becomes your destiny.

- Faith — Belief that dreams are attainable.
- Work — Understanding that team and/or individual goals can only be accomplished through a sacrifice of time, energy, and sweat.
- Discipline — Trying to make proper choices, every time, in all situations. Whether feeling like it or not, even when no one is looking.
- Intensity — Investment of emotion, a driving

sense of purpose that propels one beyond the average.

- Team — "Together each accomplishes more."
- Improve — Continual improvement is crucial to ongoing success.
- Role — Willing to play a specific part, however big or small, in the overall goal of team success.
- Respect — For everyone, regardless of status or ability - "Respect all, fear none."

This information comes from Pat Riley of the Miami Heat in the NBA. "People automatically will operate within a certain code, even if the code is unstated, or unwritten. People will always operate in a certain code." He is absolutely right.

This is the core covenant. We talk to our kids about nuclear reactors, and about the core of an apple. If the core is defective in a nuclear reactor, in an apple, or whatever, it does not matter what else you do.

Does anyone ever see the core? No. However, if the core is defective, we have nothing going for us. This is our covenant for one year. This is what they wanted to be known for. We have the covenant on a big poster and we had all of the players sign their names around the poster. Now, I want you to know the kids came up with these points.

This Football Team Will Be Known by the Following:

- Walk with pride — Class on and off the field.
- Enthusiasm over fatigue.
- Relentless pursuit of perfection.
- Commitment to "special forces."
- Being willing to accept a role.
- Dedication to the family.
- Desire - Discipline - Determination.
- Leave everything on the field.
- Faith and trust in coaches and teammates.
- Evidence that intensity is faith set on fire.
- Confidence, not cockiness.
- Igniting the community.

Core Covenant:

- Have fun, but be disciplined.
- Respect everyone.
- Production, not prediction.
- Family
- We never want our heart, character, and pride to be questioned.
- Play every play like it is your last.
- Team over individual.
- Relentless pursuit of perfection.
- Class acts on and off the field.
- Appreciation of each teammate's role.
- Special forces.
- Leave a legacy of being the hardest working team ever.

Players Must Understand and Internalize the Following:

- "When adversity strikes, do exactly what your position coach tells you to do. Do it with great intensity, and then encourage someone else."
- "Your comfort zone must change for you to better yourself and your team."
- "If you will do anything to win, you will lose."
- "Play to perform." Do not play to win. This may sound strange, but that is what we must do.
- "It is not *who* you play, it is *how* you play." We do not want the players to form opinions before the game is played. If we could bring in a team and dress them in white helmets, white jerseys, white pants, and white shoes, our kids would not know who they were playing. That would be great if we did not tell them whom we were playing. We do not want them to form opinions before the game is played.
- "It is not who you are at 7:30 p.m. on Friday night, but it is who you are as of 9:30 p.m."
- "The only play that matters is the next one."
- "What's in the cup?"
- "We do *our* thing, we win." This is from John Wooden. At the end of practice every day, we bring all of the players up and have them in

unison blow out the "windows" with "Athens Troy *wins*!"

- "Better, not bitter."
- "Setback is a temporary inconvenience, but it does provide the spark for growth and the direction for change."
- "There is always bright sunshine above the clouds—*always*."
- "It is not what life brings to us; it is what we bring to life."

We have our own yearbook for the football team. From time to time, we put information in the update of materials we give the players with comments from them about attitude. We stress that attitude is everything and that attitude is a choice. The players write comments about attitude and we put those comments in the book with their photos. Here are some examples.

Player One – "The longer I live, the more I realize the impact of attitude on life. Attitude, to me, is more important than facts. It is more important than the past, than education, than money, than circumstances, than failures, than successes, than what other people think, say, or do. It is more important than appearance, giftedness, or skill."

Player Two – "The only thing we can do is play on the one string we have, and that is our attitude. I am convinced that life is 10 percent of what happens to me and 90 percent how I react to it. Therefore, it is with you. We are in charge of our attitudes."

Player Three – "It will make or break a company, a church, a home. The remarkable thing is we have a choice every day regarding the attitude we will embrace for that day. We cannot change our past; we cannot change the fact that people will act in a certain way. We cannot change the inevitable."

The next thing we talk about with the players is related to commitment.

Player Four – "Commitment is what transforms a promise into reality. The words speak boldly of your intentions. Actions speak louder than words."

Player Five – "It is making time when there is none. It is investing every fiber of your being every time."

Player Six – "Commitment is the stuff character is made of—the power to change the face of things. It is the daily triumph of integrity over skepticism." (Author unknown)

I have so much I would like to go over with you but I am running out of time. I am going to show the overhead material and if you want to see me after the lecture, I will be glad to talk with you.

How to Accomplish Your Goals?

- Establish what you want to teach.
  - ✓ Some of this comes from off-season interviews. (Get facts and feelings.)
- Establish when you are going to instill it.
  - ✓ Set apart time *in advance*, and
  - ✓ Discipline yourself to honor the time slots. (Sample practice plans for pre-season and in-season.)
- Establish how you are going to instill it. (Example: video cuts with discussion).

Parents

- Vision
- Attitude is everything.
- No surprises.
- Clear expectations
- Dates/Activities
- Approachable
- Playing time
- Understanding what their son has to gain regardless of playing time. "Everyone at the reunion did not start."
- Understanding their role
- Understanding that they determine the perception of their son. They determine the quality of the experience and the lessons learned.

Support Staff

- Vision
- Attitude is everything
- No surprises
- Communicate importance
- Express appreciation

Community

- Vision
- Attitude is everything
- Communicate importance
- Extend cooperation (media guides)
- What if it does not happen on Friday night?

Game Plan

- Psychological preparation of players
- Playing great team with great athletes ("They won that play.")
- Playing team with so-so record, but that is hungry and dangerous
- Playing poor team with few athletes
- Does it reflect preparation in all phases of the game? Includes kicking, defense, and offense.
- Overall, what risks are you willing to take?
- How do the risks change if the game became particularly more difficult?
- Clock management: ahead/behind. Who determines when the ball is snapped?
- Field department management: backed up
- Kicking
  - ✓ Key situations
  - ✓ Punting inside own 10-yard line
  - ✓ Onside kick
  - ✓ Onside kick return
  - ✓ Big kickoff return needed to regain field position
  - ✓ Field goal with no time-outs
  - ✓ Stop the clock with yards
  - ✓ Etc., etc. etc.

- Defense – Key situations
- Offense – Key situations

Are we fully prepared to confront all game situations successfully?

Most Important:

Program your mind and heart for the battle. Read the literature that enriches your heart and the hearts of those around you. Listen to tapes and CDs. Make it a part of your being. It is not, "What's in *your* wallet?" Rather, it is "What is in *your* cup?"

Part Two: Being Positively Reactive – Work Your Plan.

Know how you expect to react in each circumstance affecting your program. Do not leave it to chance.

- Administration
- Coaches
- Players
- Parents
- Media
- Support Staff

You have the plan in place. You have an anchor. It is in your head; it is in your heart. You have taught your team. You have programmed your staff. Now, focus on the elements of the plan.

When adversity strikes, if you have taught the plan successfully, then point out where and why the plan, the covenant, the objectives, and so forth, were not realized. Be *accountable*, and get back on track.

Part Three: Being at Peace – Let Faith Play Its Part.

Know that, at times, faith is all that you have left. It is at this exact moment that you, your staff, and your team have the greatest opportunity for the truly great "defining moment," which not only carries great value for the season, but for a lifetime.

Remember:

- Faith is only faith when there is reason to doubt. (Want to know who you really are? See how you react to adversity.)
- Faith is belief in spite of no tangible evidence to the contrary.
- Just as you have a plan for "fourth-and-inches," commit to holding to your plan.

Be steadfast! Hold on!

"Game plan it." – Commit:

- That you will always find the positive in any set of circumstances.
- That you will look to teach positive lessons in moments of personal pain.
- To enrich the lives of kids who look to you for hope, for encouragement, and for direction. ("Stability in the storm.")

"When your face is in the dust, all you can do is trust. But trust you must." (The Reverend Dr. David Schuler).

There is always sunshine above the clouds. "Attitude is everything."

Your role as a coach is one of the most important missions in the world today. Your life is on display every day, and in every circumstance it will clearly demonstrate to generations ahead that faith, character, and work ethic are the true building blocks of a successful life. Show your kids your purpose, your passion, and your poise so that they may grow up to become men who are good husbands, good fathers, and good citizens.

Remember, your greatest chance to make a difference in the life of a teenager is when the storms hit. Think of the crises in your life and the person that helped you through them. The greatest chance you have is when things are not going well. Be that rock. Be the beacon that shows the way.

God bless for staying true to your mission. Thank you very much.

COACHING THE DEFENSIVE FRONTS

Opelika High School, Alabama

Thank you. It gives me great pleasure to be here in the state of Indiana. My dad was from Washington, Indiana. He passed away while I was in college. He was an All-American basketball player and played for the state championship in the Butler Field House. I wish he had been alive to see Hoosiers. That was the real deal. He scored four points in the state championship. I think French Lick is about 30 miles from Washington. Larry Bird is one of my heroes.

I am from Alabama and I know everyone will make fun of my accent. But I have been a head football coach for a long time. Even though I am a head coach, I dabble around in this defensive-line stuff because it is what I have always coached and it is what I know better than any other position. I want to share a few things about what I believe about running a program before I get into defensive-line play.

My first job was at Montgomery Academy and I coached Bear Bryant's grandson. I was a young coach and it was a thrill to be around an icon like Coach Bryant. He called me in his office at the University of Alabama one day and I was thrilled thinking that I was going to get to talk football with one of the greats. As I sat down, Coach Bryant asked how I was doing and proceeded to tell me that if I let anything happen to his grandson, he was going to kick my butt.

Before I left his office, he did give me something about coaching that I have found useful. Coach Bryant told me that winning coaches took mediocre players on a team and made them think they were good. They would take good players and make them think that they were great. He said, "You may never get a great player, but if you do, control him." At the time, I walked out of that office very disappointed,

thinking that I did not get anything out of my time with Coach Bryant. Thirty-three years later, I view it as one of the best pieces of coaching advice that I have ever heard.

Pat Dye may not have been an easy coach to get along with, but he was a great football coach. I also have been lucky to hear Coach Dye speak. He likely turned me into a defensive-minded coach by convincing me that the most important thing needed to win is a great defense. Next, you need an offense that is able to run the football. Third, you need a quarterback that makes no mistakes. You can take those three basic ideas and I believe you will have a winning football team.

Finally, I want to share a story about Joe Kines, the defensive coordinator at Alabama. Even though I am the head coach, one of my jobs is to run the scout-team offense during the week. I have been doing that for 20 years. Since I think defense is the most important phase of the game, I run the scout team offense. I have the other team well-scouted and we do everything exactly like our opponent.

It does frustrate me when we are playing a team that runs about 20 million plays out of all kinds of formations. Coach Kines told me those are the teams that are not very good. He said the ones you have to worry about are the ones who run about six plays out of all of those formations. What I took from Coach Kines was this. Find something that you are good at, and work it to perfection on both sides of the ball.

In Alabama, we are no different than everyone else in modern football. Everywhere you look, there is a spread offense. I think the day is gone when you collision receivers with outside linebackers. We still try to do it, but it looks like a covey of quail coming out at the snap of the ball. I wish teams would just go back to running the ball. In my mind, you are ruining the game. We ran the spread for a couple of years, but the game lasted past my bedtime, so we had to go back to running the football. I like to run the football and I like to stop the run, which is why I am here to talk to you today.

I want to give you my theory on football. As a head coach, you are going to have several things happen to you in your career. I want to share some things that I think are important. Sometime, these things will happen to you.

Don't Put Your Rocks on a Prima Donna

You may have a stud football player who you let do things that you do not let other people do. You think that is okay. Your belief is that he will win you some games. If you do not treat that player the way you treat your team —it may not be equally, but it must be fair—I will guarantee you that he will get you beat in a pressure situation. He will not win any big games; he will get you beat. Do not go soft on a talented player or a returning starter. You will be creating some problems by going soft.

I have 15 seniors coming back next year. We made it to the semifinals last year and it would be easy for me to take it easy on those seniors. I am doing just the opposite and probably doing it too much. Do not take it easy on those players and they will thank you for it.

Off-Season Is the Key to Development

Every head coach needs to be the person running the off-season program. In our off-season, we are in the weight room four days per week, being out of the weight room on Wednesday. We run and do footwork on Wednesday.

Cleans, squats, and benches are the major lifts for us. We do add some supplemental lifts as well. We have players coming in before school all the way to four o'clock in the afternoon. It wears me out even more so than football practice. The hardest part of the season for the head coach is the off-season.

This is where your football team is made. This is when you find the players that are going to quit. This is when you find the players that will play for you in the fourth quarter. I tell them every day that football is a tough sport. This is a tough sport for tough people. I think wrestling is the toughest sport and football is number two in toughness. I think your off-season develops toughness.

I think cleaning is the best lift you can do for football. We spend one day on clean lifts. We do 164 reps in 37 minutes. It is the greatest workout I have ever seen in my life. I want to go through this with you. Everything we do in the weight room is on the whistle. Makes it just like football, blow the whistle, run the play.

These are our varsity players who can handle more weight then the younger players. We have three players per rack. We do power shrugs with 135 pounds for three sets of 10. We have one player going after the other. The player does 30 reps during that part of the workout.

We then do high-pulls with 95 pounds. We want their feet in and their elbows above the bar. We want a wide grip. We want him to keep his shoulders in front of the bar, and the bar against the chin. We do 10 as fast as you can. We do those three sets of 10. That makes 60 reps.

We then do three sets of 10 of shrug flips with 95 pounds. They shrug the bar and flip into the clean position. That makes 90 reps so far.

We then hang clean in sets of six, four, and two. We start with a percentage of our max and add 20 pounds when we go to four reps. We add 10 pounds when doing two reps. That is 12 more reps for a total of 102 in the workout.

After that, we do two sets of 10 of flip, dip, and drives. We flip the bar to the clean position while dipping into a front squat. We drive up from the squat position to a standing position with the weight in the clean position. That is a killer after doing the hang cleans. That adds 20 more reps to the regiment for 122 reps.

We finish with power cleans with the same weight and reps that we used in the hang clean. We do the six, four, two routine again. That brings us to 134 reps.

The last thing we do is three sets of 10 with five seconds of rest between each set of quick flips with 95 pounds. After that, we do three sets of 20 push-ups and three sets of 20 sit-ups. That gives you 164 reps in 37 minutes.

I have seen that best weight room lift in 33 years. We are doing this year-round. The only thing that bothers me in the weight room is a player who skips reps. Instead of doing 10 reps, he does eight. If that happens, I blow the whistle and everyone in the room does 30 up-downs. We do not have that problem again. People that skip reps are cowards.

Sell Out or Get Out, But Let Them Be Kids

Some coaches practice seven days per week and want to keep the kids all the time. You bombard them with football the entire year and make everything important. These are 16- and 17-year-old kids. You need to understand that your players need time to be kids and that football is not the most important thing in all of their lives. I have seen programs that keep their kids occupied all summer and throughout the off-season. I think you need to remember that they are kids and they have other things to do.

You'll Know if You've Burned Them Out on the First Day of Basketball Practice

I am really kidding about this point, but it is true. If your players are hanging around watching the first basketball practice when it starts in October, you know you have burned them out. If they come to the locker room, get dressed, and go to weight training, you know everything is all right. I have been at schools where the day basketball starts, there is a different attitude among the players that play football and basketball. We have solved that problem at our school because everyone has bought into what we do.

Lose the Same Way You Win

These last two things are the most important things in this lecture. Your players need to remain humble in victory and prideful in defeat. You must be able to shake your opponent's hand whether you win or lose. When you beat someone, the last thing you need to do is to attempt to show him up.

You do not need to run out on the field and do cartwheels and all the other crap I have seen go on. You must send your kids onto the field to shake their hands, look them in the eye, and tell them it was a great game. You can have a victory celebration, but do not do it in front of the other team. It took me a long time to realize that. I want to hear people tell me that our team has a lot of class. Shake his hand and go because if he has worked as hard as you have, he commands that respect.

If we lose, we are going to stay on the field and shake hands as well. All this crap with players laying on the field or running off without shaking hands is not what we teach. Nobody likes to lose and we do keep score to see who wins, but the coaching staff has to teach the players how to win and lose. If you can teach your players to win and lose the same way, you have a football team. Winning and losing is not what it is all about. We are teaching kids how to become men.

Don't Let Your Priorities Change You

My whole life was changed last year when Dennis Parker came to our school and talked about character education. He was from Minnesota. We have a five-minute period before practice every day where we talk about morals, character, and things of that nature. He shared with us a way to take 15 minutes a day to talk to kids about their life and character.

He gave us ideas on the kids keeping a notebook. One of the things they had to do was to write a letter to their mother on why they appreciated her. Not e-mail, not typed, not faxed, but a handwritten letter to their moms. We gave our team some time to write these and we mailed them to their mothers. We did the same thing with our players writing a letter to teachers in the building.

The response was amazing. Our teachers were so moved. I had a teacher moved to tears about the letter one of our players had written to her. She told me she was going to put it on her dresser and leave it there until the day she retired. She could not believe he wrote a letter like that to her.

Character education is a lot better than the X's and O's. Everyone has to set their own priorities. My priorities start with my Lord and then my family. I hope none of you young coaches let the time slip by without spending time with your children. They will be gone before you realize it. If you get your priorities messed up, it will mess you up.

If there is one thing that I learned from our season, it is that you need to work on two-minute offense and two-minute defense more than what you are working. I think I am a good defensive coach and I try to cover everything. When we practiced two-minute this year, we practiced it against each other. The problem with that is that our two-minute offense is under center. We made the mistake of never practicing it against what the other team might do. The game we got beat, our opponent had the ball at the 30-yard line. They never went under the center or huddled the entire drive. They drove it and beat us in less than a minute. That cost us a trip to the state championship. We are the 46th-smallest school in 6A. We have 700 kids in our school and the biggest school has 1,800. The odds are stacked against us, but it was our two-minute work that let us down. It is hard to simulate in practice, but we will do it next year.

I am going to go over our defensive-line alignments. We are very simple. We line up in two defenses. We have been running the Shade 50 for years (Diagram #1). I think it is the best run defense and the spread offenses have not been able to run us out of the defense.

E S N T E
WIDE TIGHT WIDE TIGHT WIDE

Diagram #1. Under Defense

In our under look, the nose is shaded on the center to the tight end and can never be reached.

We can play him three ways. Tight sets the nose just shaded off the crotch of the center. Wide puts the inside foot of the nose on the outside foot of the center. Jet places the nose in the A gap. Those same looks move the entire interior across the line of scrimmage. The noseguard in this alignment is in a wide alignment and the Sam is in a tight alignment.

It is important that your weakside end never get reached. When we reduce him down, everyone wants to run back to the weakside. We always play the weakside end in the wide 5-technique alignment. That helps him to not be reached.

The defensive tackle aligns in a 3 technique to the weakside and gets into a tight alignment. The Sam is aligned in a zero technique to the strongside and the outside linebacker aligns in a wide 9 technique.

The other front is shade (Diagram #2). Shade is just the under look flipped over to the other side. The responsibility does not change from the under to the shade defense. The tackle playing the backside shade of the center cannot be reached by the center. The noseguard moves to the 3 technique and plays in a wide alignment. The Sam defensive end moves into a tight 9 technique on the tight end.

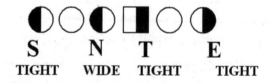

S N T E
TIGHT WIDE TIGHT TIGHT

Diagram #2. Shade

We can give a bear look by putting our Sam into a jet alignment outside the tight end (Diagram #3). This is a good defense to stop the run. The nose moves to a wide 3 technique and cannot be reached. The tackle bumps down to a zero technique head up

S N T E J
JET   JET
R

Diagram #3. Bear

the center and the end comes down to a wide 3 technique. The nose and end are in a position where they should never be reached.

We move the Jack or Will linebacker to the weakside edge in a jet alignment and bring him off the edge. We run these major alignments. We do not have any inside-shade alignments. All of our shade alignments are on the outside. We have moved away from inside shades the past couple of years. The defensive coordinator got me out of inside shades. It is an entirely different animal to practice against. The inside shade has to play different in his reads. It is easier to coach one technique then it is to coach two.

Our defensive line is taught to crowd the ball. We have two line coaches. One of the coaches does nothing in the take-off drills, but works on getting up on the ball. We crowd the ball with everyone on the line scrimmage. We work hard on ball-snap recognition so that we do not get offside. We will get as close to the line of scrimmage as we can.

On our calls, the nose and the Sam always go to the call, while the tackle and the end go away. If you trade with us, we will trade with you. I am not sure why anyone thinks that is so hard to do. The linebackers will make those calls for that movement. Our defensive coordinator spends 10 minutes per day on alignment.

We use the Bear Bryant numbering system in terms of the technique calls that we make (Diagram #4). The offensive guard has the 3 technique on the outside shoulder, 2 techniuqe is head up, and 2i technique is the inside shoulder. On the offensive tackle, we align in 5, 4, and 4i techniques. The 4i alignment is a slight movement off the head-up position on the tackle to the inside. The techniques on the tight end are 9, 6, and 7 techniques. Those techniques represent outside-shoulder, head-up, and inside-shoulder alignments.

The numbers are the same going to the other side. The center has a zero technique in the head-up position, and strongside and weakside shade,

The last thing on alignment is stemming. We think we are creating problems for offensive-line rules when we are stemming. If we are playing against a team that likes to use wristbands and call the play at the line of scrimmage, we may not even line up until we stem after the quarterback has made his call.

Usually, we will stem once about every three plays. I like to do things within the rules but I do teach our defensive linemen to yell the word "move" when we stem. To the offensive linemen, that sounds like the rhythm of their cadence and they may jump. Our linebackers will make the initial stem call and the defensive linemen will call move, very quickly and very loudly. Our stems are called from the sideline and we have had good success in drawing our opponents.

I think stemming makes the offense think. It makes them tentative. You are giving them an advantage if you sit there and they know where you are. Our kids really enjoy stemming and I think it has really helped us.

I want to show some video of our defensive line. I do not want to run out of time, but I think this video is important. We meet with our kids at the beginning of the season and we use this tape. I got this tape from a coach from Tulsa University. The tape is called *Code Red* and gives you some things you should look for in the game of football.

We meet with our defense at the beginning of the season. The players we coach are not rocket scientists. You cannot show them football all the time. You have to show them something different to get them fired up.

Imagine if you would, you are my defensive players. This is the first day of practice. I would tell them, "Guys, we are going to have a heck of a defense this year. I am going to show you the kinds

9 6 7	5 4 4i	3 2 2i	S O S	2i 2 3	4i 4 5
			H H		
			A A		
			D D		
			E E		

Diagram #4. Technique Numbering System

of things we are going to do. I am going to show you this film called *Code Red*, and this is basically the way we are going to play defense."

[Editor's Note: *Coach McCracken showed a videotape that had nature clips of African lions hunting their prey. The first clip shows four lions running out of the bush. In his dialog of the film, he likened the lions to defensive linemen, chasing down a water buffalo. He followed that chase with a football game clip, showing a defensive lineman in almost the same attacking action sacking a quarterback. Next came two female lions attacking out of the brush and chasing a gnu, which he described as a quarterback. The female lions represented the linebackers. He followed that with a game clip of a linebacker blitzing and unloading a tremendous hit on the quarterback. Finally, he had a clip of four cheetahs, who represented defensive backs running down an antelope.*]

This tape gives you a number of odd things and plays that occur in football and the theme that we hit with our defense is that from day one, we have to be prepared for anything we might see. Then, there are plays where the defense makes great plays by playing hard. I always tell our defensive ends to trail the ball. You show your players how effort and running to the football will allow you to make plays.

What you get to see are a number of plays made from the backside and they are made because of effort. That is nothing more than playing hard. The next concept that we get from this tape is to finish. There are a number of proper tackles and hits that allow you to understand how to finish. This gets our group all fired up to start the season.

I want to move back into some of the fundamentals of what we do. Here is what we look for when we are looking for players to play in the defensive line. In the off-season, we do mat drills and we wrestle. We do not wrestle like normal wrestles. We lock up and they have to fight to get

on top for 30 seconds. It is an emotional, intense drill. We have wrestling records. Those with the best records are the ones that will play in the defensive line for me.

When you work on stances, you know you have found a good defensive lineman if he has a flat back and his weight forward in his stance. Some guys cannot play defense because of their stance. If they do not have a flat back, they need to move on over to offense. We use a three-point stance with our inside foot back no further than the heel of the other foot. Our inside hand to the ball is always the hand down.

The width of our stance is shoulder-width. We always use a six-inch power step with the inside foot. We are a little different in where we are stepping. I do not think we can move on the ball and read on the run at the same time. We move on the reaction of the V of the neck of the offensive lineman. On pass downs, we may call ball and we are all looking at the ball.

We throw hands on our first step. It is an unnatural movement to take a six-inch step and throw your hands at the same time. We have an old sled in the weight room and we work on this movement year round. We do all kinds of drills to improve on throwing our hands. After you throw your hands, you have to teach your players to bring their feet with them. This is the only way they can develop leverage.

Next, you have to teach how to get off the block. We do a push-pull drill from a six-point stance to teach our players how to disengage. We will do this drill to both our right and left. They are telling me that I am out of time, so I am going to finish with this. I am big on three-on-three drills. I think you can begin to recognize the entire offensive blocking schemes in this drill.

If you ever get to Alabama, come down to see us. I hope I have helped you today. Good luck to all of you, and God bless you.

Ivan McGlone

HANG YOUR HAT ON THE WING-T SWEEP SERIES

Russell High School, Kentucky

Before we start, I would like to tell this quick story. My first real coaching job—that is, one for which you are paid—was as an assistant to Tom Perdue. For those here that might be from Ohio, you may remember Tom was the captain of the 1960 Ohio State undefeated team.

A few weeks later, I was asked to call about tickets to a college game. I knew when I called they would ask me to spell my name. This time I fooled them. I told them my name was Perdue. The reply was, "Could you spell that, please." "P-E-R-D-U-E." Some of you may be wondering why I have mentioned this story. Today when I arrive at the clinic registration desk, I picked up the clinic schedule. On the list of speakers, someone by the name of M-c-G-L-O-A-N was listed as speaking today at 2 p.m.. Well, I am here to tell you he could not make it today. I am filling in for him this afternoon, and my name is Ivan M-c-G-L-O-N-E. My name is Ivan McGlone: spelled M-c-G-L-O-N-E.

I coach football at Russell High School. We are the Kentucky AA champions for 2005. One of our coaches, Steve Hicks, played for Ashland High School when they won the championship in 1994. We often kid him about being a Tomcat. He even wore his ring for luck. At an assembly that night after the game, he spoke. He said that he would not downplay the fact that he was on a championship team at Ashland. He emphasized it was a great moment. I do not intend to downplay the fact that we are the AA champions for 2005. Our team is excited, our fans and community are excited, the coaching staff is excited, and I can tell you I am excited. It was a great moment. Because of the fact that we won, I am here to chat with you.

Earl Browning called to ask if I would speak. With the same breath, he asked what the title of my speech would be. I really had no idea what my topic would be, but I did give him a title. I said something about having "something to hang your hat on." Then I spent the next two months trying to fit something into that title. I hope part of what I say today falls within that context. If it doesn't, then it doesn't. However, my intention is really to just chat with you about our team.

I can comment on some conflicts that came up during our season, the emotion that surround our trip to the championship game, and as well the emotion following the game. At some point, we might get into some X's and O's from the offensive side.

I have two claims to fame. The first is that I am a first cousin to Ellis Johnson. For the young people here, or for those who are not familiar with Kentucky sports, Ellis Johnson was a great athlete at Ashland High School between 1924 and 1928. He played basketball at UK and was there when Adolph Rupp came to Kentucky. Ellis was Rupp's first All-American at the University of Kentucky in 1932.

The thing with being his cousin was that he was 28 years older than I was at that time. You see, I was the youngest son of the youngest. I think you get the drift. Anyway, as I was growing up I would visit Aunt Eva and on a couple of occasions, Coach Johnson would be there. I think I finally learned what I looked like. Anyway, he became the head coach at Morehead State in both football and basketball. I would brag to my friends that he was a cousin of mine. They would snicker when I told them that story.

When Morehead would come up to play Marshall in football or basketball, some of my posse and I would go if we could find a ride to Huntington. On one occasion at a basketball game I was able to work my way close enough to him to say hello. He spoke to me as he turned his head. He said, "Well hello, cousin." He may have addressed everybody by cousin as far as I know. I do not know and it did not really matter at that time. At that moment, I was the one. I was on cloud nine. My friends were in awe. I strutted around very proud. Here was a coach, the greatest profession in the world, acknowledging me. I was in awe, too. The word spread that I indeed was the cousin to a head coach in college.

Needless to say, my stock rose. Today I am still in awe of outstanding coaches. I don't know exactly what the moral to this story is, but after winning the state championship our community has gone berserk. We have had parades, fire trucks blasting their horns, assemblies, and many more activities. Also, we were even invited by our state representative and state senator to visit the state legislature.

Then on the Tuesday after the game, the coaches, team and cheerleaders board buses and visit the elementary schools in our system. We would go into the schools, these little tykes would form a gauntlet, and we went through it. They yelled, screamed, and touched everyone's hand. They were excited. You travel the gauntlet beginning with kids about shoulder high touching hands as you go by, and at the end of the lines, they seem to be a foot and a half tall. We had to bend over to get down to their level. By the end, we were praying that some taller kids would be at the end of the lines that would allow us to straighten up.

When we got to the end of that line, a few of our coaches are sitting on the floor with those young people. Naturally, they make you bend down as well. All this time you can hear the names of players being called out, as well as the names of the coaches being repeated. Each player wanted to be acknowledged, and we did that as best we could.

We went into the gym at one school that was filled with future Red Devils. They were lined up along the walls screaming and yelling. The players sat in the middle of the gym. The student body and the faculty began to sing "We Are the Champions." Our team caught the spirit and began singing as well. The young people wanted autographs. They wanted to touch the players and coaches. They wanted to know if I was the coach. They told us they loved us. One kid wanted to know if I knew Drew Mell. He said he was his cousin. That made my mind drift back to Ellis Johnson, my cousin. At that moment, as if I did not suspect it before, I realized that we, as coaches, have the most prestigious job in the world. We have the best job in the world.

I have been invited to Kiwanis Clubs, Rotary Clubs, and other business meetings. The people at those clubs are CEOs, executives, and business owners. Some of them make a lot of money. They look at me with envy and somewhat in awe. I make it a point to tell them that each one of them would love to have my job. It is the greatest job in the world. But I also tell them they do not want my pay. So there is the balance.

The second claim to fame is that I have the dubious honor of having the longest interval between coaching a state championship team in the state of Kentucky. It has been 27 years since we won our last championship. The time period stretched from 1978 to 2005. Believe me, we have talked about winning another state championship every day for 27 years.

One of the big differences between that year and the present was that in 1978 we simply boarded a bus, went to the game, played, got back on the bus, and came home. There was no media bombardment, and I was not asked to speak at any clinics. They did not rush us off the field for a press conference. In fact, we did not have a press conference then. When the Kentucky High School Athletic Association sent us the small football medals, they sent them to Russell County High School in Russell Springs, Kentucky, and not Russell High School in Russell, Kentucky. They knew very little about us then.

This year we had a team picture taken in front of the scoreboard. Today, that picture is on our video. I am not in the picture because I was inside doing a press conference. Some of our key players missed the pictures.

The amazing thing about not winning a state championship for 27 years was how I kept my job. If you go 27 years without winning the state, you could lose a job. You could easily be fired.

Let me discuss the trip from Russell to Louisville to the state finals. The big question is this: how do you keep the players focused? We had a "good" plan. Our athletic director, Sam Sparks, did a great job of organizing the trip. It is great to have a traveling secretary. We were able to leave the school on Friday around 10:30 a.m. We traveled throughout the town in order to recognize the fans in our community. We traveled to Lexington, Kentucky, where we have one hour of practice. We leave Lexington around 2:30 to go to Frankfort. We spent an hour and a half eating. We got into Louisville close to 5:30 p.m. when we registered.

At 6:30 p.m., we left for Papa John's Stadium to watch the 4A championship game. We left there at halftime. We got back to hotel around 9:45 p.m. We ate supper and had a team meeting until around 11:00 p.m., then we sent the players to their rooms. The next morning we had a meeting at 10:00 a.m. Then we had breakfast, which ended around 11:30 a.m. From 11:30 a.m., the players had free time in order to get packed, relax, and then load the bus. We boarded the buses at approximately 1:45 p.m. and arrived at Papa John's Stadium a little after 2:00 p.m. By controlling almost every minute, we kept the focus strong.

What else can we talk about that would be of interest? How about the coin toss? Everything about the title game is choreographed. The state association tells you when you can go on the field, when you come off the field, where you stand on the field. They cover everything. They have everything planned out. They even have how long you can celebrate after the game. Speaking of celebrating, the state playoff rules called for 10 minutes on the scoreboard clock and they run this for celebration time. Officials even ran one team off the field for coming out too early and they were the more experienced team.

As I said, I actually missed the team picture on the field as I was being kidnapped to the news conference room. Anyway, back to the coin toss. We all go out to get our instructions from the officials. We are ready. The official turns to Micah Johnson of Fort Campbell High School, the Mr. Football for 2005 in the state of Kentucky, who was the honorary designee to toss the coin. He did not have the coin. They look to the assistant commissioner, Julian Tackett, for the commemorative coin. At least I was under that impression that there would be a commemorative one. He pats his pants. He does not have one. He turns to the official. He does not have one. The referee turns to the other officials and they did not have a coin. Even the guy blowing the bugle for the "call to the post" did not have a coin. I reached in my pocket and there was a nickel and a penny. Now, I have this on film. I take out the nickel and hand it to the official to toss. The commemorative coin was my nickel. They gave it back to me. It was a plain old nickel.

After the game I told Mike Jones, one of our assistant coaches, that I would like to give him the coin. He did not want to take it. He said that I should keep it. When I handed the nickel to him, I think he was a little mad. He is an eBay kind of guy. If you see that nickel on eBay, you will know it probably was what we used for the coin toss.

The game was built up as old school versus new school. Also, it was publicized as a ball control offense versus the spread offense. This build up became media hype. This was never my intent. You do what you do, and I do what I do. To me this was a game against Owensboro Catholic High School and Russell High School and nothing else invaded that thought. It is merely a matter of execution and luck.

In that game, many things went our way. We played with intensity and purpose, and we played well for only one reason and that was to win the game. It was not to say that one offense was better than another was. We played many teams with spread offenses. Sometimes, we win and sometimes we lose. It usually depends upon how well we execute or how well they execute. For everyone's information, we have practiced the spread offense. However, it has taken me eight to ten years of practice to put into play.

Let me talk about "hanging your hat on to something." You have to have something to you hang your hat on in any walk of life. Football is no different. Your situation often dictates what that thing might be. Factors that might influence these decisions would be school size, number of athletes that normally come out, or the interest of the community. All of these factors and pressures will sway the coach in his decisions

I love small schools. I coached at one before coming to Russell High School. If you could get 30 kids out for football, you were on cloud nine, especially if five or six of them could play the game. In that situation, you could get excited over a first down or a completed pass. And when you score, oh my goodness, what a feeling. I was lucky back then. We had four or five of the best players the school had seen for the last 40 years. We were able to win a few games. I was told by an experienced coach, "If you go into coaching, go somewhere that you have half a chance to win." I did not know it when I took the job, but I did have half a chance to win at Huntington Vinson High School. That small school was good to me.

Another small school in our area, Raceland High School, has hung their hat on a spread offense. While we are mentioning Raceland High School, I need to set the record straight about a rumor. Owensboro ran the spread offense. They received some help from a former college coach that ran the spread offense. The rumor flew around that the Raceland High School staff conferred with us about how to defense Owensboro Catholic's offense. That did not happen. They did help us with our headsets. But Raceland High School has elected to switch to a spread and have been very successful when their execution is "good."

Sometimes hanging your hat on something does not take a long-range approach. Sometimes the need for short-term survival is important. We went to play Estill County who was struggling at the time. In order to survive, Coach Jones installed the old single wing against us. His kids seemed to be enthused during the game. I know one thing, our players remained focused trying to figure out what to do on defense. Coach Edwards wanted me to tell them how to defense it since I was familiar with the old spinner series in high school. I told him the only thing I could do was to tell him what was called after they ran the play.

Let us look at other small schools that have struggled. Lewis County has always fought to maintain a program. It is coaches like Corky Prater who was able to keep his teams going. If it were not for people like Corky, many of our school's football programs would fail. We should be thankful for these coaches. I have great respect for those that put their effort into keeping those small programs afloat. We will miss you Corky.

For us, we hang our hat on the running game and it is mostly from the wing-T. The reason for doing this is that it is what I understand. We practice other types of formations, but once we get into a game we seem to go back to this basic formation. I do want to point out one other thing. We have always used the power-I play as a supplemental running offense. Some years we run it more than other years. In 2004, we were such a "good" wing-T team that we ran very little of anything else. This year I did not feel we were quite as effective in the wing-T so we ran more I formation than usual. In the championship game, 24 of the 60 running plays we ran were from the power-I. I told someone that I love the wing-T, but I am not stupid.

We will do what ever it takes. Before we start with X's and O's, I want to state that our offense is very guard-oriented. That is probably an understatement. In our system, the pulling guard is the celebrity position—of course, next to the running backs. We put a lot of emphasis on them. Sometimes they are big and sometimes the guards are small. We have no stereotype. But they must be able to run. Because they run so much, we need to have four guards ready if possible so we can alternate them. This is especially true if they also play defense, and they usually do. This year we were a little thin at this spot as we really only had two guards. That created a lot of wear and tear on them. This may have been one reason we were just a little less consistent with our basic wing-T this year, and actually ran a little more power-I than in the past as we did in the championship game.

This is our basic wing-T formation (Diagram #1). We have five basic running plays on this formation.

- Sweep
- Short Trap
- Dive
- Bootleg Run
- Reverse or Counter

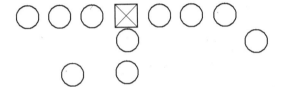

Diagram #1. Basic Wing-T Formation

Why do we like our wing-T formations? We feel these formations are better for the sweep and dive plays (Diagrams #2, #3, and #4).

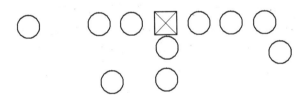

Diagram #2. Wing Right with Split End Left

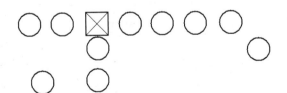

Diagram #3. Unbalanced Right Wing Right

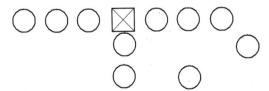

Diagram #4. Wing Right – Tailback Strong Right

I want to go over the sweep to the left and to the right. This is against the 5-4 defense (Diagram #5). Following are the coaching points:

- Outside
- End and tackle talk
- Both guards pull when possible
- Running back finds the second guard
- Fullback fill – varies

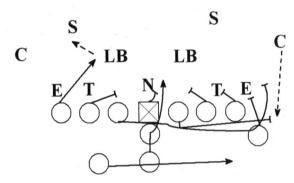

Diagram #5. Wing Right - Sweep Right

If we face a 6-2 defensive alignment, we all block down and we do not pull the onside guard (Diagram #6).

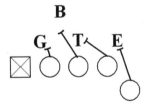

Diagram #6. Wing Right Sweep Right versus 6-2 Defense

If we face a team that plays soft and backs off the line, we run the play with both pulling guards (Diagram #7).

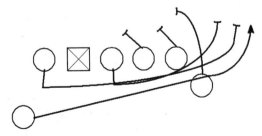

Diagram #7. Sweep Right versus Soft Defense

On the bootleg run, we can run it right or left. This is how we run the play with the quarterback keeping the ball (Diagram #8).

The coaching points include the following:

- You do not always have to make a great fake. (However, this year we did make the good fake.)
- The block for the fullback varies.
- The fullback and pulling guard work together.
- The quarterback must find the pulling guard and get behind him.

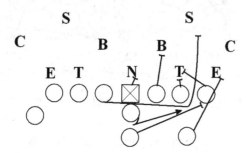

Diagram #8. Wing Left - Bootleg Run Right

Next is our short trap play (Diagram #9). This is against the 5-4 defense.

Here are the coaching points:

- Have an imaginary line through the center and the quarterback.
- We do not want the fullback to be in a hurry. We do not want him reaching for the ball.
- His steps are 1, 2, cut.
- He must read the pulling guard.
- He must keep his feet moving.
- He must be able to move left or right laterally.

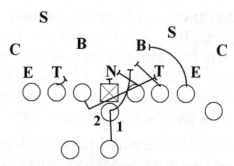

Diagram #9. Wing Right – Short Trap Right

Against the teams that play the TNT look in the middle of the defense, we block down and put the backside guard for the trap (Diagram #10).

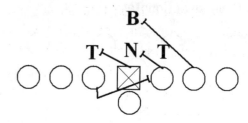

Diagram #10. Wing Right – Short Trap versus TNT

Against the stack-six defense we still block down, pull the guard, and trap the first down lineman past the center. We call this GUTS (Diagram #11).

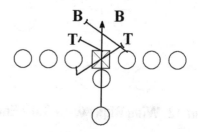

Diagram #11. Wing Right – Short Trap versus GUTS

Thank you for your attention, and good luck next fall.

THE 4-4 DEFENSIVE PACKAGE

Weir High School, West Virginia

Thank you. I appreciate everyone being here. I have attended the Coach-of-the-Year Clinics a number of times and I am honored to be asked to speak here. When I was called in December to speak, they told me they wanted a defensive lecture. I said I do not coach any defense at all. On defensive days at Weir High School, I kind of walk around, blow the whistle once in a while, observe, and try to help out. In view of that, our outstanding defensive coaching staff, led by our defensive coordinator, Dan Rovira, will conduct a big part of this clinic session.

I want to start by discussing some of our philosophies, which I am sure are very similar to the philosophies that you have at your high school or college. These are things that we have posted in our locker room for our defense, but also for our offense, for special teams, and even for our general football family. They are important things that we continue to just pound into our kids' heads on a daily basis, beginning in January when we start our weightlifting program. I want to discuss our defensive objectives with you to begin with.

Defensive Objectives

- Seven or less points
- Defensive score
- No plays over 15 yards
- Create three turnovers – win turnover margin

As long as it is sufficient for a Weir High victory, we want to hold our opponents to seven points or less. Now obviously, if we lose a game 7-6, that is not good enough, but if we win 28-6 then we feel that our defense has done an outstanding job.

Also, we like to get a defensive score. Throughout the season, besides the great job that the assistant coaches did this year in preparing our kids, we were very fortunate that we had outstanding team speed. It was just one of those years where we were very blessed. As we all know, having great players makes all of our jobs a lot easier as far as wins and losses go.

Another objective, and this one is tough to get, but we try to stress to our players that we want to allow no plays over 15 yards. That is a pretty tough objective, especially the way teams are throwing the ball in this day and age.

And then, the last objective that we list for our defense is huge. We want to create three or more turnovers per game. If you follow the Ohio State Buckeyes, you know Jim Tressel's post-game statements and pregame statements are always the same. He always talks about the turnover margin and he has made believers out of us. This past season our coaching staff really stressed the value of taking care of the ball on offense and being aggressive on defense. We ended up with a plus-18-turnover margin, which I believe was a major factor in our winning the state championship.

It was obviously a very special year for us. Our defense held our opponents to an unbelievable two yards per play, and we outscored our opponents 532-102 over the season. We had a 1600-yard rusher, a 1500-yard rusher, and a quarterback who passed for 1300 yards and rushed for another 500 yards. Our team went 14-0 and won the state championship, so it was very special.

The last thing I would like to do is show you our typical weekly practice schedule once school starts. After that, I am going to introduce my assistant coaches and let them talk to you about our schemes on defense.

Monday

3:00 p.m. Varsity lift, run JV walk-through

3:45 p.m. Team meeting, Helmet awards

4:00 p.m. Varsity Friday video, JV game

5:00 p.m. Scouting report and opponent video

5:30 p.m. Kids out

This schedule has been adjusted from year to year and will probably be adjusted several more times, because you kind of get ideas when you talk to other coaches and hear what they are doing.

On Monday, we do not take our players outside. It is strictly a mental day and a hard weightlifting day.

Dan Rovira, who is going to be speaking in a few minutes, does an unbelievable job in the weight room during the off-season, and we continue to lift throughout the season. We max our guys in July and we max them around Thanksgiving during the playoffs. Not only did our guys maintain their strength, they got stronger and you could see it in the physical style they played throughout the playoffs.

On Mondays, the varsity usually will lift weights and then maybe go out on the track and run a little bit just to get loosened up. During that time, our JVs will have a walk-through. Then, at 3:45 we will take our kids into the school theatre for a team meeting. We will wrap up our previous opponent, give our helmet awards, review our objectives, and set the tone for the next week.

At 4:00, we show the video of Friday night's game and then the JVs take off if they have a game. That takes about an hour, so at 5:00 we have the scouting report and video of our upcoming opponent. After that, the offensive line gets their blocking sheets for the week, and I meet with the skill guys to go over the passing game and any adjustments we are making to the running game. Our kids are out of there at 5:30, and our staff will finalize the game plan.

We do not meet with our kids on Saturdays or Sundays. All of the varsity players are required to report to the facility and see the trainer on Saturday mornings at 10 o'clock, and after that we have a "varsity check" that requires every varsity player to check with me before he leaves. It may be just a minute or two, but it gives me a chance to tie up any loose ends from the night before and make sure his health status is good for the coming week.

Tuesday

3:00 p.m. Varsity lift, JV walk-through

3:55 p.m. On field, team walk-through and flex

4:15 p.m. Specialties

4:20 p.m. KO, KOR, XP

4:35 p.m. Conditioning

4:45 p.m. Individual group

5:10 p.m. Team run

5:40 p.m. Perimeter pass protection

5:55 p.m. Team pass

6:25 p.m. Off field

6:35–7:20 p.m. JV lift (Tuesday/Wednesday)

Tuesday is an offensive day for us. We begin with a varsity lift at 3:00. It is not a casual thing. We have coaches at stations, we do not allow music, and everything is structured as part of our practice schedule. Guys who miss any part of it must come in after practice and make it up. We lift from about 3:00 to 3:40 really hard, on Mondays, Tuesdays and Wednesdays. Obviously, we are working different body parts each day.

We are on the field for a team walk-through at precisely 3:55. We go over any new fronts, talk personnel, review blitz pickups, and anything else that we can cover offensively in 10 minutes. At the end of 10 minutes, we break up and do our flex routine.

We have a specialty period at 4:15 for kickers, snappers, holders, and return men, followed by special-teams work at 4:20 on kickoff, kickoff return, and extra point. At 4:35 we are going to do conditioning work, which I know is a little different, but we condition them hard because we want them practicing tired. We want them physically tired and mentally tired to get them in the right frame of mind like they will be playing on Friday night.

After a water break, we go to offensive individual group work at 4:45, followed by team run at 5:10 where everything is scripted, including any trick plays and all of our play-action passes. We follow that with 15 minutes of perimeter pass protection, and then finish with 30 minutes of team pass, including all of our draw plays. We are off the field at 6:25.

At 6:35, we take our JV guys to the weight room and lift them hard for 45 minutes. They will lift two days a week on a little different program, but it is still intense. I know that makes their day a little bit extended, but when they get to varsity they get to go home a little earlier. That is just part of the deal.

Wednesday

3:00 p.m. Varsity lift, JV walk-through

3:55 p.m. On field, team walk-through and flex

4:15 p.m. Specialties

4:20 p.m. P, PR, XP

4:35 p.m. Conditioning

4:45 p.m. Individual

4:55 p.m. Group

5:15 p.m. Team run

5:55 p.m. Skelly pass rush

6:25 p.m. Off field

6:35–7:20 p.m. JV lift

Wednesday is our defensive day. It is very similar to the Tuesday schedule. At 3:00 they are in the weight room ready to go at their stations. We will be on the field at 3:55 for a team defensive walk-through, followed by specialties, punt, punt return, extra point, and then conditioning.

After that we break up into defensive individual groups, and then team run. We will go through all of

the opponent's run plays and we will really, really preach technique during the team-run period. From there we go to skeleton pass rush at 5:55, and we are off the field at 6:25. You might notice that there is no defensive-team period. We find out that when we do the team-run session, and then we do the pass rush and the skeleton, we do not need to do much defensive team on Wednesday. We will pick that up on Thursday.

Thursday

3:00 p.m. Offensive and defensive meetings

3:30–4:30 p.m. Review game plan

Thursday is a light day for us. We may have some meetings to tie anything up that we may have switched at the last second on our game plan. We have a one-hour practice, and we have a study table after practice—which is mandatory for guys who need it.

Friday is game day. Saturday we have varsity check-ins and staff meetings, and if we do not meet on Sunday, the staff is off and can do individual work at home.

At this time, I want to introduce the architect of our defense, our assistant head coach and defensive coordinator, Dan Rovira, and hand this session over to him.

Coach Dan Rovira

Thank you, Coach Meek. I came to Weir High School right out of college and I have been here for 13 years. I am originally from Anaheim, California, but I played college ball in Iowa, got married, had two kids, and came to West Virginia to coach.

Our philosophy at Weir High School is speed. If you cannot run, you cannot be on defense. A small kid who can run will play ahead of a big kid who cannot. We are a AA team, but we play a AAA schedule, so we play the big teams.

Principles of the 4-4 Defense

- Swarm and penetrate, pursuit drill every day, four-corners turnover drill, fumble drill, strip drill, tip drill, pass-rush sack-quarterback drill

- Outphysical our opponent, weight training, play another sport, must lift two times per week (mandatory)
- Assignment execution, know what you are doing
- No long run
- Confidence in what you are doing

We swarm and penetrate. A lot of guys just penetrate and get up the field, but we actually have a read concept to the penetration and I will cover that when we go over the fronts.

We do a pursuit drill every day in practice after we stretch. We do a pass pursuit, a run pursuit, and we mix it up. We make our kids get to the ball and show their speed. When we do sweep in team run, everybody needs to get to the ball. If they do not, it is a punishment and we do up-downs. Every coach is around, kind of like a bubble, watching every guy get to the ball, so we teach that swarm in practice.

We also teach our kids to create turnovers. We set up a four-corners turnover drill, which has four turnover stations. We have a "strip" thing with a partner coming over the top stripping the ball. We have a tip drill at a corner and a fumble drill at another, where the first guy tries to scoop the ball instead of falling on it. If we miss it the first time, then we would fall on it the second time. We do lose fumbles like that, but when we do pick it up our speed takes over and we do not get caught. It is a touchdown then, so we live with the other.

We also do a little quarterback thing in that drill where we do a pass rush and strip the ball from behind. That is the fourth corner of the drill. We do those four drills all at once and then rotate stations.

We want to outphysical our opponents. The first six years I was here our weight room was not very big and not very good, but our boosters took over, raised some money, and improved it so that it is now comparable to some college weight rooms. That has been a major factor in our success and in our ability to out-physical our opponents.

We have 30 to 35 kids lifting at any one time in the off-season. We lift three days per week, and if a guy plays another sport we still require him to lift two days per week. I am sure that some of the other coaches do not like that, and sometimes we have conflicts, but everything works out. They must lift twice a week if they play another sport. That is mandatory.

As everybody knows, we have to line up first. When we line up and we know what we are doing we are great—just like any other team. Because of that, we will always keep things simple. I will go over some of our stuff and you will see that, although it has a lot of words in it, it is really simple. We do a lot of movement up front because we are not real big there. Our front guys are speed guys so we do a lot of angles, slants, and things, which I will go over with you.

We try to limit our opponents' success of course, and we try not to allow any long runs or passes, but we know our opponents will have some big plays. We play man-to-man coverage. We go to the seven-on-seven at Pitt, and we will play cover zero in seven-on-seven when we cannot blitz anybody. We want to do that, and then when we get into our season, obviously we will blitz and that helps our man coverage.

We know we will give up long passes and we live with it. We also get hurt on screens. It is tough on our inside backers to pick up screens, but we do not think opponents will make a living off of screens. You might hit us once but then we are going to come back and hit you.

Our kids have confidence, perhaps almost too much. Our staff is also very confident. I am very confident when we go to our football games and we try to preach that to our kids. We do not want to be overconfident, but we want to go into every game as a team believing in ourselves, and confident in everything we know.

I am sure that each of you has a system of game planning, and ours looks like this:

Defensive Game Plan
- Recognize all formations

- Five favorite running plays
- Five favorite pass plays
- Play percentages
- Coordinate coverage with the front
- Goal-line "D," bear front with stud on tight end
- Two-minute "D"
- No-huddle "D"

We break down every opponent formation but we do not punch it all into computers. I am a board guy, so we draw up every formation we see on this big board and any time the team runs that formation we mark one time. We do the old system, on the board, writing everything. I think things stick in your mind and you learn them better when you write everything on the board.

We pick our opponents' five favorite run plays and five favorite pass plays, and we figure percentages on each one. Every Monday we have a walk-through and we go over how many times they are going to run the power G, how many times they are going to run the trap, what formations they run them from, the percentages for first-and-10, second-and-long, second-and-short, and so on. That is how we do that.

Now we do not have too much time in practice, so we try to make our goal-line defense out of our 4-4. Basically, we will jump into a bear alignment and it makes it easier for us. We can do it with less teaching. We do not get into a 6-2 and make our outside backers play that tough 'cause they are speed guys and not real big. We can get into a bear where most of our linemen are covered and our Mike linebacker becomes the bear guy.

We are always going to be prepared for the two-minute situation with our defense, and I will go over that. Sometimes we see a team that runs the no-huddle offense and that only helps us because we are in zero coverage and you are not really going to confuse us. We do play three-deep. If we are confused, or if you are hurting us with drag routes and we cannot adjust to it right there, then we jump into cover 3 for maybe two plays just until we adjust to it.

I believe you can play cover zero if you teach it in the off-season and teach it during the season. It helps our blitz and it helps my guys move. I am not a zone guy. I like maximum pressure. We are always blitzing somebody and we rarely play base unless we are really killing you and our four guys are getting pressure. We usually send one of those backers and sometimes two backers. One inside and one outside are coming.

We have a rule that on the single receiver side we are always going to send our outside backer. I do not care who you are. You should know that. It could even be trips to one side and split end to the other side and we are sending that outside backer every time and aiming him for the hip of the tailback. If the tailback swings he is good enough to come off, but we are going to send him.

Here are our alignments (Diagram #1). We go by numbers. We used to go by words, but there were a lot of words and our kids got confused, so we went by numbers to kind of help us out.

Diagram #1. Alignments

Our zero technique is our shade technique now. We changed that to shade. Our 1 technique is on the inside eye of the guard, our 2 technique is head up on the guard, and our 3 technique is on the outside eye of the guard.

Our 4 technique is on the inside eye of the tackle, our 5 technique—which we call tough now— is head up on the tackle, and our 6 technique is on the outside eye of the tackle. Our 7, 8, and 9 techniques are similarly aligned on the tight end.

When we call our front, the first call I make is to our strongside tackle. If I call a 3 shade, we know that our strongside tackle is in a 3 technique and our nose on the weakside is in a shade technique. To us, the strongside is always to the tight end. We do not do it by the receivers or by formation. If there is no tight end, we might go to the wideside of the field, or then we could go to the receiver side depending on scouting report, but otherwise we go strength to the tight end all of the time.

This is our base front (Diagram #2). This is our 33 front. We used to have our outside backers off of the line of scrimmage three-by-three, but we had a problem there. I do not care how you teach it. Unless you have a stud there, there will always be a wide gap there when the fullback kicks out the outside backer. The tailback is always cutting it up into that alley. No matter how much you tell the guy to squeeze it, his reaction time still is too slow for him to squeeze that.

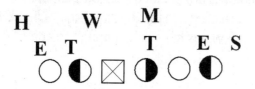

Diagram #2. 33 Front

We put our Sam on the line of scrimmage in a 9 technique and it worked out very good. We put our end on the inside eye of the tight end and their two jobs were to not let that tight end off of the line of scrimmage. They are jamming him every time. If I am the defensive end, I am jamming the tight end with my left hand while Sam is splitting the other half of the tight end and jamming him with his right hand. We are keeping him on the line of scrimmage and he is not going to get a free release. He will not get to our backer, so our middle backer can scrape better.

The only thing we teach is if the tight end blocks out or tries to hook our Sam, our defensive end is on an automatic pinch for trap or anything else. He will not feather with the tight end, widen, and leave the off-tackle hole open. He will automatically pinch, looking for anything pulling or the fullback trying to kick him out on the power play. That is one of the rules we have.

Our tackles are both in 3 techniques and the backside defensive end is in a 5 technique. Our middle linebackers will split our tackles at five yards with the outside foot splitting the tackle's butt and the inside foot in the A gap. We believe that

splitting the tackle gives the linebacker a better read and gets him to the off-tackle area better. That is our base front. We teach it during two-a-days, but we do not use it too much in the games.

This is one of our favorite fronts here, our 31 front (Diagram #3). We can slant out of this or angle out of it, which I will show later. The only difference here is the backside tackle and Will linebacker. The backside tackle is in a 1 technique on the inside eye of the guard. His job is to blow that guard up, rip through his shoulder, and get at least two yards of penetration to cause problems. We know we are giving up the down block. His eyes are also on the center. If the center scoops playside, he is down the line of scrimmage right now. He cannot be scooped by the guard.

Diagram #3. 31 Front

Our Will linebacker moves to the B gap weak. We do that a lot because we send our outside backer, so our Will replaces the outside backer on his stunt to the single-receiver side. Right here, our hero will be coming. Now, our Will is a little bit outside more so he will cover the back out, or read for screen. Will replaces hero on that, so we like the front.

In our 22 front, our tackles are head up on the guards (Diagram #4). We have had some success with this front and we think it hurts the isolation play. You cannot block us out and you cannot Bob us, or block us "big-on-big."

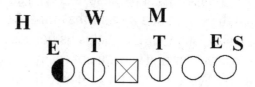

Diagram #4. 22 Front

We move out of this front a lot, just as we do in 31. We slant and we run our "dog scrapes" and "dog goes," which I am going to show. Our linebackers are stacked, which protects them and prevents the center from getting to them. The tackles' job is straight ahead, and we are reading on the run. They are charging straight ahead and trying to get penetration like they were in a chute.

If we get doubled by the strongside tackle, we teach getting hips in the hole. That will prevent the combo block off to the linebacker, or if they do, our tackle is here in the hole. We do not teach falling to the knee so they must double us, and our linebacker is responsible for cutback.

Ideally, if we go 22, I would call 22 tough. The tough call is to the strongside end, moving him to head up on the tackle. That covers the off-tackle hole, but I do not like the spacing there.

We have an 11 defense in our playbook, but I am not a big fan of this front (Diagram #5). If I did call 11, it would most likely be against a spread formation with no tight end. It gives us penetration in the A gaps and puts our inside backers more to the outside to help with screens and swing routes. If we are in 11 against the run, I would make a tough call and move the strongside end head up on the tackle, which helps with the bubble.

Diagram #5. 11 Front

The last front I will show you is the 3 shade (Diagram #6). The strongside is the same as base, but the weakside tackle, or noseguard, is in a tilted position on the center. We teach a quick swim or rip move to backdoor the center. That is his goal—to backdoor the center. His butt wants to get behind the center's butt and sit there. People try to scoop him

Diagram #6. 3 Shade

with the backside guard, but it never happens. When the center tries to block back, we are swimming or ripping him, so we are pushing him back and squeezing everything. It is really hard to trap that.

Now I want to show you some of our stunts. Our guys are not real big, so we like to "angle" (Diagram #7). When we make an angle call, it just affects the two tackles—angle strong or angle weak.

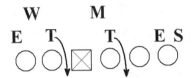
Diagram #7. 31 Angle Strong

When we angle, it is a little different, as I told you earlier. We are not just running upfield; we are going to read on the angles and slants. If our 3 technique tackle angles strong and the offensive guard's helmet comes inside, then right now he will redirect himself. We back our tackles off of the ball maybe a yard or two on this stunt, and when the guard blocks down we will reroute ourselves, turn our shoulders, and look inside.

The next stunt I want to show you is the "in" call (Diagram #8). Ideally, we run this stunt from a 22 front, but to keep the offense honest we will also run it from 31 or 33. The tackles are now going A gap hard like an angle and it helps us to be off of the ball two and a half yards. If we were in a normal 3 technique, we would be tighter, and we may not be able to get there.

Diagram #8. 31 In

It really helps us against the zone teams. When the guard takes that big step, we are coming inside and we reroute ourselves, come right down the line, and make the tackle. It really helps us when we get a lot of teams reaching. We will rip right through the center's shoulder. Obviously, the linebackers know they have B-gap responsibility.

When we call 31 crash, it involves everybody (Diagram #9). We run this from our base alignment and everybody is crashing down. The strong end will be angling to the C gap.

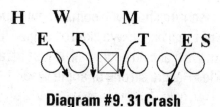

Diagram #9. 31 Crash

We like to run this to the single-receiver side because our backer is also coming. We have a lot of guys squeezing everything.

I like to run this stunt out of 31 tough (Diagram #10). That moves the strong end to head up on the offensive tackle, so he would crash the B gap. We like this in short yardage. Once again, we are angling and we are reading. It takes away the trap play, and it protects our linebackers. Mike knows he scrapes to C gap.

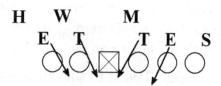

Diagram #10. 31 Tough Crash

We also have our free safety over on the tight end when we are in cover zero, so he is just like another linebacker in the off-tackle area and he is very, very active. We can also run a cover 1 where he is free and he roams. Everyone else is in man and we let him spy inside out, so there is no bad read for him.

On the 22 out call, we are just angling our tackles to the outside (Diagram #11). They are ripping or swimming to their regular 33. We just use this to get our guys going and use their speed.

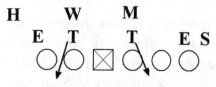

Diagram #11. 22 Out

The next stunt we like is the 22 tough slant strong (Diagram #12). We can run this from any of our fronts, and we like to run a "Mike go" with it. Mike would blitz A gap strong, which really confuses the offense. If we call tough, our end will slant to the playside, but if he is in his regular alignment he will just play base.

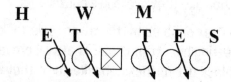

Diagram #12. 22 Tough Slant Strong

We run several individual blitzes and I will review them quickly, but I want to get on to our combo blitzes. Dog strong puts our Mike in the A gap, and we can dog both linebackers, or we can show late and dog both backers. We can run an X stunt with our inside backers and cross them on their dog stunts. Mike would go first and Will would go right behind him. That just mixes up the show dog.

Scrape strong is a stunt between Mike and the tackle. The tackle goes A gap and Mike scrapes to B gap. Fire game involves our outside backers coming off the edge. Fire strong involves Sam, and fire weak involves our hero.

We run a loop stunt involving the defensive end and outside linebacker. The end gets upfield to replace the outside backer and the outside backer comes inside. If we call squeeze, the end just pinches and the outside backer aims at the outside hip of the deepest back. They are both crashing down.

We put the individual blitzes together to give us our combo blitzes and I want to show you a couple of them quickly. We like to run 31 squeeze strong/scrape weak (Diagram #13). I know that it sounds long, but our kids do not have trouble with the call. On the strongside we run the squeeze stunt with the end aiming at the offensive tackle's hip. On

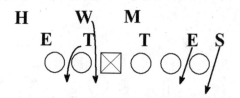

Diagram #13. 31 Squeeze Strong/Scrape Weak

the weakside, Will and the nose run a scrape stunt, and we can change that up on the backside by running a dog weak with Will.

Another really good combo blitz is 3 shade, scrape strong/loop weak (Diagram #14). Mike runs a scrape strong with his tackle, while the hero runs a loop stunt on the backside with the defensive end. Our hero is our best athlete, and probably the fastest, so he can run the play down sometimes when it goes to the strongside.

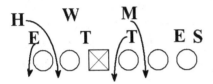

Diagram #14. 3 Shade Scrape Strong/Loop Weak

There is always some risk of getting caught in a blitz, but that is our style. We believe we are going to get you somewhere in those three downs for a loss. If not, it will probably be a long night anyway. We think that giving you a loss on first or second down and putting you behind the down-and-distance will give our speed a chance to take over. That is when we will jump into our 4-3 blitz package.

I think this is a great package. If you take any one thing from me today, I think you should take this 4-3 blitz package (Diagram #15). If we just call 4-3 and nothing else, then Will aligns in a stack behind our strongside end, but we are usually never in it. We just start out teaching it from there. Our tackles know that they are in twos, tight on the line of scrimmage, taking away the trap. Their main job is to keep the guards off of Mike.

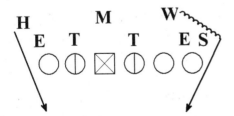

Diagram #15. 4-3 Thunder Strong

If we call 4-3 thunder strong, Will creeps to the outside and blitzes off the edge, while hero is also

coming to the single-receiver side. The only thing that hurts us on this is trap, but on third-and-long we will live with that.

We can also call 4-3 thunder weak, which really causes problems (Diagram #16). We will run this to whatever we get. If we get twins, our outside backer will go away, and in cover zero the free safety is right behind the hero backer. We call it thunder lightning. The Will wrong arms everything and blows up everything inside, while our hero aims at the deepest hip, tailback or quarterback, whoever that becomes.

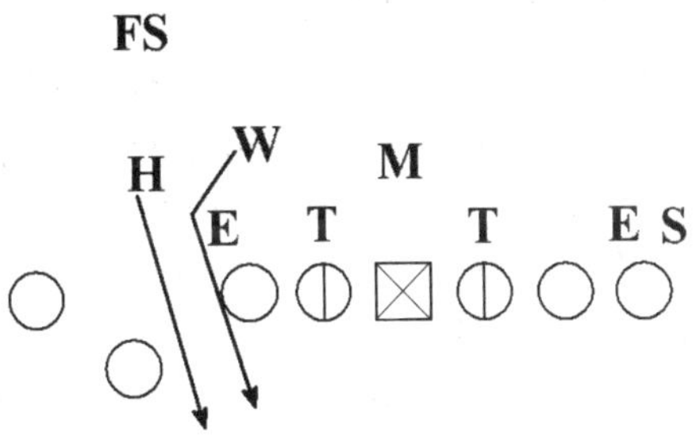

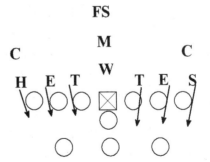

Diagram #16. 4-3 Thunder Lightning

The last front I want to show you is 5-3 attack (Diagram #17). Now Mike is usually bigger, so we would probably put him down on the center and stack Will behind him. We are attacking everybody's outside shoulder and jamming everything inside. Our outside backers no longer have pass responsibility on this defense. They are strictly run players. We will also "hard roll" the secondary any time we see three backs in the backfield. Our middle linebacker reads the fullback.

Diagram #17. 5-3 Attack and Roll

I would like to thank you for listening. If there are questions, I will be around here for another hour. Thank you.

Jamie Mitchell

THE 50 SHADE DEFENSE

Olive Branch High School, Mississippi

I appreciate Nike giving us an opportunity to share some ideas. Make no mistake about it; I am a guy that believes that defense wins football games. I am an offensive coach but we have been very blessed to have nine coaches. I realize most of you don't have that, but we have five offensive coaches and four defensive coaches. I can't take credit for anything you are going to see here today, other than the plan that is there. While everyone today talks about a 4-3, we believe in the 50 front. While it has some issues in the weak flat, we believe we have ways of handling that.

There are numbers here that are staggering when considering what we have been able to do on defense. We want personnel that can move their feet. We are a one-gap, slant-pinch scheme team. Our nose and 4 techniques are slant-pinch players on every single snap. We do not ask them to be a two-gap player, nor do we ask them to read and react. There are many things that coaches talk about in the 4-3 defensive front that fit into what we are talking about in our defense. We want guys up front that have great feet and can get up the field.

We tell our players that on defense we want to teach from the eyes down. On offense, we like to teach from the feet up. On defense, if our eyes are in the wrong place, we have problems. It takes discipline to have your eyes in the right place. You are going to have players that want to look into the backfield, that want to find the football. They must learn to put their eyes in the right places to succeed. We coach our defense from behind the offense because we want to see where their eyes are.

I want to throw some numbers up here for you and I want you to understand that this has not come easy. We were not a very good football team when I got to Olive Branch. We were a team that had not scored an offensive touchdown in league play in two years. We have been able to get some things going with great players. Look at what we did in 2002. We gave up 1,600 yards rushing, 920 yards passing, for a total of 2,520 yards with a 6-5 football team. We started to play good defense at that point. In 2003, we gave up 1,528 yards rushing, 906 yards passing, for 2,434 total. I am a fanatic about average per rush. We will find a way to stop the run.

In 2003, our average per rush defense was 3.9 per-carry. During the winter, I told our defensive coaches that 3.9 yards-per-carry was not going to get it. Giving up four yards-per-carry was why we were getting beat. We had to find a way to defend the run. We did not change our scheme, but made some changes in what we were doing defensively. In 2004, in one more game, we gave up only 994 yards rushing, 852 yards passing, for a total of 1,856 total yards in 12 games. Our average per rush had dropped to 2.5 yards-per-carry. As that number dropped, our win total began to go up as we won 10 games. In the off-season, I challenged our defensive staff to cut the average per carry down even further. In 2005, we played 14 games and gave up only 871 yards rushing and a little over 1,000 yards passing. But, look at the average per carry. We allowed only 1.79 yards-per-carry. We lost two games to South Panola High School, and if you take those two games out, we gave up only 35.2 yards rushing per game. That is how we went 12-2 this season. We were able to stop the run and force our opponents to put the ball in the air. Inside of those numbers is the story of our success. When you can hold someone to less than two yards every time they turn and hand it off, you are going to win a ton of ballgames. I believe that you do whatever it takes to stop the run.

Our base alignment is a straight 50 defense. We play most of the time with 4 technique tackles and a zero technique nose. We have one coach who coaches those players. Their job is to penetrate their one-gap responsibility. I played center and there was nothing worse than having to block a nose that I did not know where he was going. We don't want the offensive player to have any idea where we are going.

The nose will be an A-gap player, the tackles will be either B- or C-gap players. We want those offensive linemen guessing when they come to the line of scrimmage as to where we are going. Our Sam linebacker is aligned over the guard and his eyes are burned right there. Our Mike linebacker is in a 30 alignment and his eyes are burned on the guard. The hardest thing to teach those linebackers is to get their eyes in the right place. We are a read linebacker scheme. We check the eyes of every player other than our TNT's. Our eyes have to be in the right place. The hardest thing to do in coaching our defense is to get our players to understand how important our eyes are to how it all fits.

Our anchor end, we generally align in a 9 technique. His eyes are burned on the tight end. He is going to put his hat where the tight end's hat goes. If it is a down block, I squeeze. If it is a reach block, I do not get reached. Our Will end must be an athlete. Our guy that played there last year signed with the University of Memphis. He was 6'3", 210 pounds, and could run. He was the perfect guy to play that position. We replaced him with a bit smaller guy, but someone who could run. This position is one of the most important to what we do. He must be an athlete that can play.

The Will end and the strong safety are going to work to take away some things in balanced formations. They must be athletes. Our corners alignment depends on whether we are playing man or zone (Diagram #1). We want our eyes in the right place depending on our coverage. The free safety is more of a middle-of-the-field player. That is our base alignment.

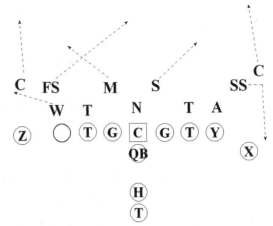

Diagram #1. 50 Cover-3 Strong

We do have adjustments in our fronts. None of these changes are going to shock you. The first is our eagle-weak alignment (Diagram #2). We are still going to be a slant-pinch front from an eagle-weak alignment. All we have done is reduced the front on the weakside so that we will be playing a zero, 2, and 4 technique with our nose, tackle, and Will end. We will actually widen the Mike linebacker alignment in this look. We will put him in more of a B-gap alignment. It is a great blitz alignment. We can go slant strong or slant weak out of this look. We can go pinch with a nose strong call. We have some weakness to the weakside. We do have a call that will roll our free safety to the weak flat and the strong safety back into the middle of the field. I promise you, we have ways to protect ourselves on the weakside so we are not as naked as it looks.

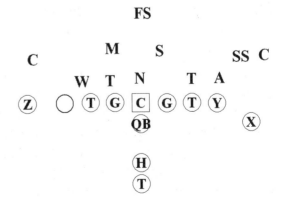

Diagram #2. Eagle Weak

We are also a team that is going to take the strongside of the formation away from you. If we can force you back to the weakside, we are going to do that. We have the ability to rotate our safeties if that is what we need. In eagle strong, we reduce our strong tackle from a 4 technique to a 2 technique (Diagram #3). We like to stem this move in a pre-snap move. It is an easy thing to do, sliding him down to a 2 technique just before the snap. It creates confusion for the guard and the tackle. We also feel it creates an alignment that is difficult to zone. If you are trying to man block, stemming creates tremendous havoc.

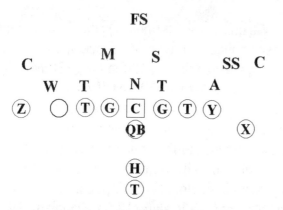

Diagram #3. Eagle Strong

Our double eagle is used for a great blitz alignment (Diagram #4). It does take our linebackers back to B gap. The hardest thing to teach for our tackles is to not cross their feet when they are pinching from a 4 technique to the inside. If we step with our inside foot, we end up in great shape. This is a great alignment for us to bring pressure.

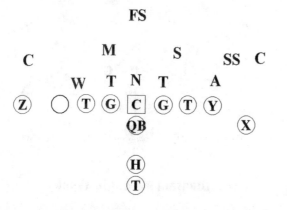

Diagram #4. Double Eagle

Next, is our 50-stack look. We can play games with our Will end. We can walk him into the weak flat or we can stack him. This look helps us get more people in the box (Diagram #5). It gets the Will off the edge and gives us another person who can help us in the A or B gap against the run. The Will reads through the guard to the fullback. Even though the Mike linebacker now stacks over the nose, he is still keying the guard. The Sam will stack over the tackle, but key the guard as well. The strong safety will key the tight end.

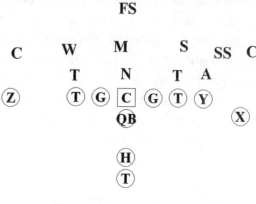

Diagram #5. 50 Stack

Let me put up our walk alignment. If you are going to hurt us with the hitch, we will walk our Will end out in the flat, in a similar alignment as the strong safety (Diagram #6). That gives us quick coverage to both flats. While most 50 teams walk the Will out most of the time, we don't do it that often. We want him on the line of scrimmage most of the time. He can put a lot more pressure on the offense from the line of scrimmage than if he is

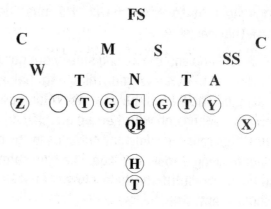

Diagram #6. 50 Walk

removed and walked out into the flat. As long as we can get away with it, we are going to leave him on the line of scrimmage.

We have to have a way to take care of one-back alignments. We use two different calls to deal with one-back offenses. The first thing we will hear is an ace call (Diagram #7). This is an indicator from our defensive backs that we have a one-back set. Our call will either be an ace monster or an ace Will. We will keep our front intact, but on ace monster, we will move our Mike linebacker into the weak-flat area and stack our Sam linebacker over the nose.

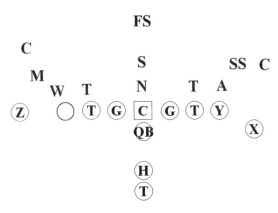

Diagram #7. 50 Monster

On ace Will, we are going to lose our Will end. We will keep our two-linebacker look inside and walk the Will end out to the weak flat. This forces a bit of a change to our front as one of the tackles has to become a contain player. The Will and strong safety will have similar coverage responsibilities and should be very similar athletes. We have two different packages of blitzes for the ace monster and ace Will looks. We do like to blitz and we will come after you some. We do not start with teaching our defense through blitzes because we want to teach our players to read and react.

I want to take a look at some things we do to get our players to do the things we want them to do. We are notorious for getting our players to chase the football. If you can't run to the football, you don't need to be on the field. We will condition our defense with these two pursuit drills. We will set these drills up at the end of practice and we will condition by chasing the football. We are not going to line up and run a bunch of 40s when we can do things like this. I think it teaches a lost art in the sport of football—pursuit angles.

Pursuit Drill

- Huddle call: Swarm pursuit front and coverage call.
- Quarterback will give a strength call with the tight end. Then the defense breaks the huddle.
- Players run by the cone and break down on the sideline stripe.
- At the whistle, everyone sprints up to the first cone and breaks down and calls out, "Swarm."
- Coaches will indicate with thumbs up or thumbs down to determine any repeats.

Our strong safety has won two ballgames for us because of this drill. He was able to reverse his field on a reverse play and knock the runner out at the three-yard line. I don't think that was a reaction thing. He was able to understand pursuit lanes because we had practiced it. Even though he was in the wrong place at the point of attack, he was able to get in the right angle to get to the ballcarrier before he scored. We were able to make a great goal-line stand because he made a great pursuit-angle play (Diagram #8).

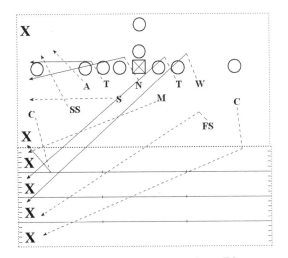

Diagram #8. "Swarm" Perfect Play Pursuit Strong

We tell our guys that they must run to the football if they expect to play (Diagram #9). We must coach and teach those things. I think you can turn average players into good players if you teach them to be relentless in their attack of the football.

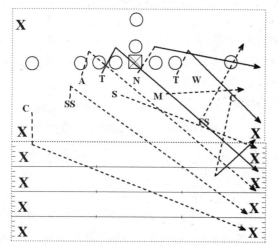

Diagram #9. "Swarm" Perfect Play Pursuit Weak

I want to talk to you about some coverages. I will start with our cover-3-weak alignment (Diagram #10). We work a lot on rotating our secondary. We don't want to just sit in a cover-3-strong alignment. We can help ourselves in the weak flat by rotating our secondary and dropping our anchor end into the flat. We can give the anchor an arrow call. An arrow call locks him up on the tight end rather than running him to the flat. We are playing cover 3 except for the anchor. We roll our secondary to the weakside of the offense. If the tight end protects, then the anchor will rush. It gives us an opportunity to not lose a rush player. A tight-end delay hurts us sometimes with this call. If we play man coverage with the arrow call, it allows the free safety to come on a blitz.

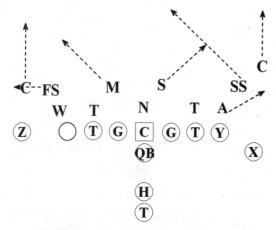

Diagram #10. 50 Cover-3 Weak

Cover-3 strong is the common coverage for 50 teams. We will line up in a balanced look with our two safeties so you will not know which way we are rotating. We can either pre-snap roll, or roll the coverage at the time of the snap. On the snap of the ball, our strong safety will become a flat defender in cover-3 strong, while the free safety will rotate to the deep middle. Both corners will play deep outside thirds. We like to have a cover-3 strong and a cover-3 weak. We have a lot of opponents that attempt to attack the weak-flat area. You cannot defend the hitch unless you put someone underneath it. This gives us two different ways to roll our secondary.

We play a great deal of cover 4 in our defensive scheme. If someone is hurting us a great deal throwing the football, we will play quarters coverage with our corners and safeties and play four under (Diagram #11). Two of those will be flat players and the two inside players will play hook-to-curl. That leaves us with just three guys to get after the quarterback. We have to make a decision as to defend and cover or come after the quarterback. Many times in a cover-4 look, we will bring one of the linebackers, giving up the hook to curl zone on that side. We can rob the curl with the safety on the blitz side and play the other safety to a cover-3 look behind it.

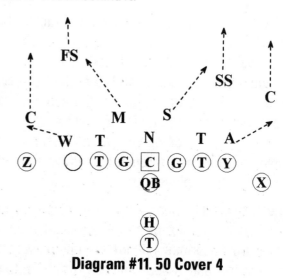

Diagram #11. 50 Cover 4

We also play nickel coverage a good deal of the time. I never want to give up an easy long pass on a third-and-long situation. We like our nickel-dog package (Diagram #12). It does get us out of our 50 alignment. We will take away the short underneath routes by playing man with our five under defenders. We will have deep protections by playing deep halves with our free safety and nickelback. We will play some straight zone, but I like the man-under look. Down-and-distance will determine how we decide to cover in this look. We can take the Mike and strong safety and play flat coverage and play cover 3 behind it. We can also end up in a four-deep look as well.

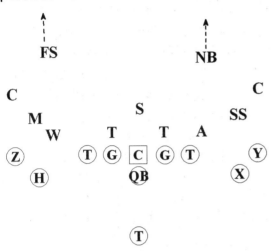

Diagram #12. Nickel Dog

We will play some dime coverage. We don't play this very often, but I have seen too many times where a pass is completed on the last play of the half or the game when the defense is sitting in their base alignment. I don't want to give up a Hail-Mary pass on the last play and be in my base defense (Diagram #13). As a coach, you must give your kids a chance. That is why we put this package in. If they want to hand it off, great. We will tackle them and win the game.

Diagram #13. Dime Dog

That is most of what we do with our defensive front and defensive coverage. I want to go to some film and talk you through some of our looks and blitz packages.

Tim Murphy

COACHING THE OFFENSIVE LINE: "HERE'S THE BEEF"

Clovis East High School, California

Thank you very much. It is a pleasure to be here today. When you think about football, there are a lot of star positions and notoriety in the game. The bottom line is the offensive line is what makes everything go. I love coaching the offensive line. They are the greatest kids and they're so excited to be on the field. They are out for the team for the right reasons. They are a pleasure to coach.

I coach the offensive line, but I have never played a play at that position. I tell our players that I never played in the line, but I always respected what they did. The offensive linemen do not get the rewards that the running backs and quarterbacks get in the newspapers. They work day in and out, put in some serious hours, and get very little credit for it.

I am glad to get to speak about them. The success we have had in the last year or so is because of them. I have had only one Division I lineman in eight years. Our offensive linemen are rarely over 220 pounds. They are smaller-type, tough players, but very easy to coach.

I did a lot of film work, talked to many good line coaches, and tried to formulate what a perfect block looked like. I came up with something that I feel is the number-one thing we do with our offensive line. Every year we rush for at least 3,000 yards. The rushing totals are generally around 4,000 yards. One year we rushed for 5,000 yards. With the exception of last the couple of years, we have not had any major running backs. The last two seasons, we had a big-time back who is going to California on scholarship next year.

Our success is not necessary our scheme, but what our offensive line does. I am going to share it with you today and I hope you get something out of it. I believe the content of my topic will be better than the presentation.

We run the double wing as our base offense, but we are really a double-tight-end offense. What I am going to talk about, we will start doing on Saturday when I get back. Our offensive line comes out for about an hour and a half on Saturday to work on offensive-line development. It is a volunteer program.

Let me tell you a quick story. I was in southern California last week helping a coach put in our offense at his high school. While I was there, my wife and I took a little trip to see Long Beach Poly. I have never seen a nicer inner-city high school.

There was a little cocker spaniel running down Atlantic Avenue, which is a huge street in Los Angeles. My wife told me to get out and catch the dog because it was wearing a collar. I got out of the car in the pouring rain, running down Atlantic Avenue trying to catch this dog. I ended up slipping and falling on my tailbone trying to catch the dog. The funny thing was what she said to me. She said, "Why didn't you do that thing you are always yelling for your players to do when you watch the film. You should have balanced up on the dog and you would have caught him." Therefore, I will not be able to demonstrate anything today.

We start in a two-point stance when we get to the line. We have stiff elbows, hands on the knees, and the eyes are up. We are in this stance before every play in the game. We do that for a couple of reasons. We want to see what the defense is doing and where they are aligning. We want to see if someone is tipping the blitz, or who is not going to blitz.

The quarterback comes to the line and calls ready. The linemen get into a three-point and make their calls. In the three-point, I am very particular about their stance.

In the three-point stance, I like the feet at armpit width. I like the feet at armpit width, but I will let them get in a shoulder-width stance. One of our line techniques is the get-off. I believe the offensive lineman can get off better if he has a narrower stance. When they put their down hand on the ground I want at the width of their ear.

They put the hand down an inch or two in front of their eyes and form a tent with their fingers on the ground. I want all five fingers on the ground with no knuckles. I want the weight balanced between the feet and hands. We pull a lot and must have balance in our stance. I think a player can get off just as well in a parallel stance as he can with a stagger.

I want the toes pointed slightly out. You cannot get off as well with the toes pointed inside. That lets us push off the inside of the feet. We teach a flat back a different way. We tell them to get their chest out and their butt out. The last thing is to get the eyes up, looking through your eyebrows.

The off hand in the stance goes almost to the ground next to the ground hand. Your pinkie knuckle should be in line with the wrist of the down hand. Once you get positioned, make a relaxed fist with the hand. It is almost like a four-point stance.

The off-hand position helps us load our arms in the get-off. We get so much out of loading the arm that I believe it is a mistake not to do it. When we load our arm, we keep the chest at the exact level as in the stance. We take the hands and place them just outside of each of the butt cheeks. I want the arms going back as far as the shoulder girdle will allow. The arms should be at a 90-degree angle. When you work in the weight room on power cleans and snatches, the arms are in a load position. We load our arms on the first step.

We make contact on the second step. The lineman has to make two steps with his feet and two steps with the arms into the contact stage of the block.

Within our program we have established an adage about the offensive line. We have t-shirt, which comes from the TV commercial about "Where's the Beef?" Our tee shirts read: "Here's the B.E.E.F."

If you study the history of football at any level, you will find that running the football is essential for having a successful offense. At the core of every successful running attack are sound and aggressive blockers. It does not matter how talented the ballcarrier; if the men blocking are doing their job, the offense will move the ball. Within each run block, there are some basic principles that each blocker must perfect. We use the acronym B.E.E.F. to remind our blockers of the four critical points in carrying out a successful and dominating block. When this is mastered through practice and repetition, the blocker becomes more confident and aggressive, thus producing a dominant football player.

We have an off-season program that takes place on Saturdays. We conduct it for 11 Saturdays. If they make 10 of the 11, we give them a t-shirt. Any time you can reward an offensive lineman and make him feel good about what he is doing, you have to do it.

The first principle is blastoff. This is the first step in the block progression. In the blastoff, quickly take a three-inch step with the playside foot. We simultaneously load the arms and hands until they are in line with the bottom of each butt cheek. It is imperative that your upper body stays at the same level as it was in the three-point stance. If the body lifts as much as an inch, you will lose significant potential power. When you make this move, you keep the chest over the knees.

The point is you are in a three-point stance for several reasons. It allows you to direct in any direction. When the arms are loaded, the transfer of weight occurs and we gain momentum. There is absolutely no reason to rise up with the body. When they raise four to five inches out of their stance, they lose potential power in the block.

I align my players in a three-point stance and place my hand one-inch over their shoulder blade. If any of them hit my hand, they have to repeat the drill three more times. The hand acts like a chute but more adjustable to the height of the players.

When you power clean, the techniques used to lift the weight are essential. If they lift their butts, they lose all their power in the lift. That is the same thing on the offensive line.

Each player on our offensive line this year averaged about 200 pounds. We played some big teams. Because we spend so much time on this drill, we are able to compete with larger teams.

When we explode, it occurs in the second step when contact is made. The blocker must quickly and violently get the second step on the ground and explode into the defender with his eyes aiming for the playside armpit. He unloads his forearm into the defender's numbers with a powerful lifting action. At the same time, he punches the other hand into the armpit on the same side as his head.

We try to get our second step on the ground before the defender gets his first step on the ground. It may not happen, but that is the goal.

If the target is the hip of the defender, good contact is not made. That target is too low. They cannot lift the defender because he is so low. The armpit is much more achievable for the offensive blocker. If the head is in the armpit, it is below the head of the defender and we win the leverage battle.

If we can get the weight of the defender going up, he becomes easier to move. That is the reason for the lifting action, which leads us to the next step.

Elevate is not a step, but an action that needs to take place in the second step. At the same time that you are exploding, you are also violently elevating the defender. The blocker arches his back and rolls his hips forward, as the forearms and hands punch the torso of the defender, in an attempt to get him vertical. By getting the defender vertical, the blocker takes away all of the defenders forward lean. When that happens, the defender's body

weight and momentum is irrelevant. From that point forward, the offensive blocker is in total control.

The final blocking principle of the B. E. E. F. is the finish. The finish begins by getting the third step down immediately. The third step is like a fistfight in a phone booth. Every step after this is effort and good foot position and technique. The blocker drives with short, choppy continuous steps. When he drives, the feet push off the inside part of the foot, with the toes pointed out.

He pounds the ground with each step and keeps the feet wider than the defender's torso. He keeps his butt pointed at the ballcarrier. When the defender tries to escape or the blocker gets him elevated, he locks him out with both hands on the top of his numbers. He runs on the balls of his feet and goes full speed until the whistle blows or he takes him to the ground.

When we make contact with the defender, I want the forearm, upper arm, hand, front shoulder, and the facemask to hit at the same time. It does not always happen.

As the offensive blocker comes off in his first step, I want his butt and shoulder at the same level as when he was in the stance. If the butt lifts up, the blocker loses the potential power in his legs. The legs are extremely important in power blocking. If the torso lifts, the blocker loses the potential power in his butt muscles and lower back.

When the blocker comes off for a linebacker, he has to elevate somewhat to maintain his balance. However, I do not want him coming up more than halfway. Although we are blocking a linebacker, who is not as big as a down lineman, you still have to generate a significant amount of power. You cannot do that if you are too high up.

Many wing-T teams like to get the offensive line as far off the ball as the referee will allow. We are just the opposite. We want to crowd the ball. Our toes are generally on the center's heels. We want to get into the defender as quickly as we can. We feel like we can get into the defender before he is ready to take on the block.

Some defenders like to get on the ground to hold off the double-team. We feel we can get into them before they can execute that technique.

The length of the second step will vary from lineman to lineman. We want the second step as long as we can take and still maintain the proper power angles. We do not want to take a step so long that it is slow or out in front of the blocker. We must have the body weight forward and the chest over the knees. Getting the foot in front of the torso is like trying to lunge forward when you are leaning back.

The drill we do is a first-step takeoff. The linemen get in a three-point stance. They go from a three-point stance to the loaded position as fast as they can. They take the three-inch step and reset. I put my hand one inch above their shoulder blade and call the cadence. They have to go three times without hitting my hand. We step them straight ahead with the toe pointed straight like a base block. We do the same thing with a 45-degree first set with the toe pointed straight as a reach block. We also make them step at a 45-degree angle with the toe pointed at 45 degrees as they would in a down block. In each situation they do three reps and reset each time. They go to the right three times and to the left three times.

The 45-degree step with the toe pointed forward is a reach-block step. I do not want the defender to know we are trying to reach him, although we are going for the cut-off angle. When we execute this block, the facemask goes into the outside armpit of the defender.

We are big on vertical push. I do not care about horizontal push; I want the defender moving backward. It usually does not happen unless you double-team a defender, but that is the goal. We never try to reach and wheel the butt around to the outside. That is a position block and we do not gain ground or create a new line of scrimmage.

In the same drill, we work on the first steps of the trap block. We have to open the hips and get a good angle. When we run our power play, we pull differently. We pull our backside guard and tackle

with a crossover step. That idea comes from baseball. If a player is trying to steal a base, he steps with a crossover step instead of an open step. He gains more ground and it is quicker. We applied that to the power pull. We feel we can get there quicker.

When we pull, we run a square pull technique. We do not turn the shoulder to the sideline. We keep the shoulders square to the line of scrimmage and cross over with our feet. That allows the guard and tackle to turn up and be square. When they do the drill, they have to pull using the crossover step and stay low. That is difficult to do. If the offensive lineman pulls and is hit by a run-through blitz, it knocks him into the backfield. If he is low and has his pads square to the line of scrimmage, he handles those types of plays and is not collapsed. He can attack the run-through because his shoulders are square and he is low.

When we do our sweep pull, we open two feet into the backfield. They have to execute that pull without raising up. We make them go three times to the left and to the right without hitting my hand over their shoulder blades. They have to execute every block we have in the one-step drill without getting high coming out of the stance.

They have to do this drill repeatedly to get to the point that they must stay down. It gives them the mindset as to what they have to do to be successful. The players began to think if the coach spends all this time doing this drill, it must be important. I told them I would not do any drill if it was not going to help them.

I want to talk about our line-of-scrimmage run blocks. The offensive lineman needs to execute these blocks when blocking a defender on the line of scrimmage.

We use the down block more than any other block in our offense. It provides a great angle with the defender we are blocking and by alignment places our butt where it is supposed to be. We use the down block on a defender on an inside shade to the next offensive lineman.

The offensive lineman on his first step points his foot in the direction of the defender and executes his B.E.E.F. technique. This aiming point is the near armpit if the defender is a playing a read technique. If the defender is a penetrator, we aim at the far armpit.

The combo block is an advanced version of a double-team in which one of the two blockers will come off the double-team and block the nearest inside linebacker. As the two blockers are making contact with the defender on the second step, they should both get their eyes on the nearest inside linebacker. If the linebacker fills inside of the post man, he comes off the double-team and picks up the linebacker. The double man needs to see this happening and takes over the block himself.

When the linebacker scrapes over the top of the double-team, the double man comes off the block and blocks the linebacker. The post man pushes the double man off the double-team and takes over the block simultaneously as the double man leaves. When the double man leaves, he comes off straight and not inside or the inside linebacker will run past him.

The chip block is similar to the combo block, except the double man is blocking the linebacker every time. The post blocker will block the defender on the line of scrimmage. The chip block is to assist the post blocker with his block and does not take it over.

The on block is a base block. The defender aligns on the blocker and the blocker drives him away from the point of attack of the play. The blocker blocks a defender within the framework of his body. He always makes contact with the forearm away from where the ball is going. The aiming point is the armpit to the side of the play.

On the first step, the blocker steps outside the playside foot of the defender with his toe pointed straight down the field. He aims his eyes at the point-of-attack armpit. The second step splits the crotch of the defender and he should elevate his torso with his inside forearm. When he gets his third step on the ground, he wheels his butt toward the

sideline. He never lets the defender cross his face. If the defender beats the blocker, it must be from underneath and never across the face.

The reach block is an on block. The blocker is blocking a defender outside the framework of his body. His first step is a 45-degree angle outside with the toe pointed straight up the field. The wider the defender, the flatter and wider the step has to be. He aims his eyes for the outside armpit and carries out the block using the on-block techniques.

The trap block is like an elongated down block with two exceptions. The blocker blocks a defender that is further away and his goal is to make the defender penetrate. On the pull, the blocker scrapes the butt of the offensive lineman next to him and pulls into the line of scrimmage. On the trap block, the blocker must not elevate until he gets to the defender. Once he gets to the defender, he executes the techniques covered in the B.E.E.F. technique aiming for the near-backside armpit.

I am going to show you our Saturday workouts with our offensive line. We start the workout with a warm-up and go from there to sled and dummy blocking. We start the workout with a sled drill. We have a seven-man sled outfitted with five pads. When we line up on sled, we have a mixed group of players. You can see the more experienced players in the back of the line coaching the younger players on the mistakes they are making and giving them tips on the correct technique.

This is not a high-pressure drill filled with intensity. We do not drive the sled until we are finished with the steps and technique teaching. We only take three steps on the sled. It is nothing more than a reinforcement of the teaching of the first three steps in the get-off. We go for an hour on nothing but the first three steps. If you do anymore than that in the first 15 minutes, you have your players so tired that they will not learn anything. Their techniques will be bad and the entire drill is a waste.

If you want to condition by using a sled, you should do that at the end. But, this is a teaching period and we want the players to pay attention to the details of the techniques. The first group starts the drill and does their three-step drill. They go five times in a row and go to the back of the line and get a break while the rest of the players go.

The first thing we do when we start the session is a warm-up drill. We do some random warm-up exercises to loosen up and get ready for the rest of the workout. We do some backward runs, ins and outs, and forward runs to loosen the legs.

In the warm-up drill, we work a one-on-one drill with form blocking. They are using short, choppy steps. I want to hear the ground being pounded with their feet as they push in the warm-up. The pressure is on the inside of the feet and they are pounding the ground in a rhythmic thump as they work their man back. We want them to use technique, although it is a warm-up. We want the feet in the ground and off the toes. We want a wide base and pushing with a short, choppy pattern.

The first thing we do is the one-step drill, like I talked about in the lecture. After the first step, we add the second step and drill that with the hand, shoulder, and face placement. We listen for the rhythm of the feet in the first two steps. It should be a rapid placement of the feet on the ground. We do not explode on the sled while we are working on the footwork. They lean into the sled rather than explode.

On the second step, they bring the forearm up into the armpit area. We watch their feet to make sure they do not step underneath their bodies. He must maintain his base in the first two steps.

The second step is where the offensive linemen shift their momentum and begin to roll the hips and arch the back to get maximum lift on the torso of the defender. A point you should look for as the lineman gets into the dummy is the position of the knee and ankle. If the knee is in front of the ankle, that means he is on his toes and has no push. The knee has to be over the ankle to get maximum push from that power angle.

Another coaching point that has to be emphasized all the time is the eyes. The eyes have to be looking up. If the head is down, the butt will come up. If the hands get too high on the dummies, they can get no push. They must have their hands at the level of the armpits to achieve the type of push we look for.

When we work the entire progression, on the first step we shift the weight. On the second step the explosion occurs, and on the third step they push the dummies as far away as they can. That last step is the lock-out move.

A player who throws the shot put in track should understand what we are doing. On the shot-put throw, the players slide across the ring and get total explosion, full extension, and maximum unloading of all the force in their bodies. That is what we are trying to get in our second and third steps.

We do the same type of drill teaching the down-block technique. We make them down block to the left and right, stepping at the 45-degree angle. They have an aiming point on the dummy to represent the armpit of a defender.

We have a linebacker drill, where the dummy is placed three yards in front of them. Most of the players will pop up a bit out of the stance. We do not expect them to stay as low as they do on a down lineman, but we want the same techniques.

Finally, we work on our trap techniques and our fullback kickoff block. The fullback block is essentially a trap block. In every block we do, the basic fundamentals are the same and all the elements of the B.E.E.F. are emphasized.

The last thing we do is have a competition in driving the sled. We have the right side against the left side. The side that pushes the hardest will turn the sled in the other direction. We want to see if their techniques break down once they start competing.

Before I stop, I want to show you three plays we run in our offense. These are our bread-and-butter plays. We have to run this play so that it gains five yards per carry. We call the play 24 power (Diagram #1).

24 Power

- RTE down to backer
- RT down to backer
- RG down to backer
- C down to backer
- LG pull and wall off PS LB
- LT pull and wall off BS LB
- LTE cut B gap to cut off
- RW backer to safety
- FB aim for inside hip of 4-man (RT) kick-out first man past RT with right shoulder
- LW big open step motion, catch ball, run hard, get five-yard minimum
- QB reverse pivot, soft pitch, second level kick-out

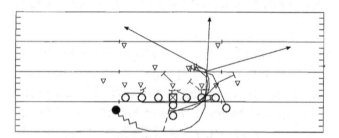

Diagram #1. 24 Power

This is a variation of 26 power (Diagram #2). Since it is a 6 call, the double-team shifts to the RTE. The fullback now aims for the inside hip of the

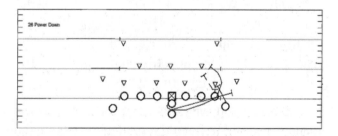

Diagram #2. 26 Power

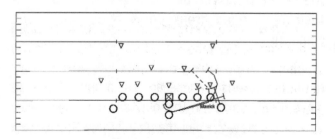

Diagram #3. 26 Mavrick

RTE and kicks out the first man past the RTE. Everyone else's rules are the same except the ball will be taken one hole wider. The quarterback blocks inside.

The next play is the 28 striker sweep (Diagram #4). It is a good sideline play.

28 Striker Sweep

- RTE on
- RT pull flat with crossover step, wall off playside inside LB
- RG same as RT, but wall off safety
- C man on RG cut or reach him, man on RT cut or reach him
- LG #2 backer
- LT #3 LB, if their is no #3 LB, wall rotating OLB
- LTE safety
- RW reach first man past RTE assignment
- FB aim at center's left foot, give great fake, and get tackled
- LW striker motion, take ball with left arm up, get wide in a hurry. Attempt to get to sideline unless contain defender is being kicked out. If he is, cut up early
- QB open left with big step at 5:00. Get your back to defense, give forearm length hand-off, three-step drop, and fake throw.

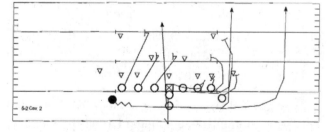

Diagram #4. 28 Striker Sweep

Football is a game that is all about teamwork and effort. If you have an offensive line, you have players that want to block downfield and they know how to do it. You must have a terminology that lets you communicate with your players. It is a lot of fun when you have a progression like this and you are all on the same page. I feel like I can tell a player why he is not making his block consistently. I hope it helped you guys out. Thank you.

STRENGTH AND CONDITIONING PROGRAM

Bellevue High School, Ohio

Thank you very much. It is a pleasure to be here. I have been coming to this clinic for 15 years. I appreciate having the opportunity to speak here today. When I go to clinics, I try to pick up one or two things to take back to my program. I hope you guys can pick up a few things today to take back to your program.

The coaching profession is a great profession. When you look at the youngsters that come through a program and see how the coach affects their lives, makes it noble. In this day and age, there are a lot of things a football coach has to put up with, but we have to remember why we coach. We coach for the players.

The relationships you make in coaching will last a lifetime. I want to recognize my coaching staff and tell you they are a strong and dedicated group of coaches. I want to give them credit because we would not have the success at Bellevue if it were not for those coaches.

Bellevue High School is about 15 miles off Lake Erie between Cleveland and Toledo. The city of Bellevue is about 8,000 in population. Our high school has about 300 boys in the school. In my 15 years at Bellevue, we have had as many as 80 players out for the team and as few as 45. I want you to get an understanding of what type of program we run. In the 15 years I have been the head coach, we have had five Division I football players.

The players we have are successful because they work hard. We work extremely hard in the weight room. We have to do a good job in the weight room because we play many of our players both ways. We feel like we need 10 good players per class to be successful. If we can get 10 kids per class who are legitimate high school players, we can be successful.

Our players, for the most part, have a blue-collar mentality. We have an important job and we have to do it. We have a core of players that really work hard in the weight room. Then we have some that duck you in the hallway to keep from coming to the weight room. I do not think any of us have won a game with a player who was not sure why he was playing.

We are into our weight program and are lifting four days a week. We work Monday, Tuesday, Thursday, and Friday. We work Monday and Thursday on our legs and lower body. On Tuesday and Friday, we work on the upper body. In the summer, we go three days a week. During the summer workouts, we go on Monday, Tuesday, and Thursday.

On Monday, we do legs and lower-body exercises. On Tuesday, it is an arms and upper-body day. Thursday is a combined lifting day, which gives the players the weekend off. Our football players are two- and three-sport athletes at our school. With 300 boys in our school, we encourage our players to play as many sports as they can. That being the case, you have to deal with that in the summertime and off-season workouts. We would like to have the players all the time, but it does not work out that way.

We have a weeklong period in the summer when no program in the school can have contact with the students. It is usually over the July 4th holiday. However, the state of Ohio gives the schools 10 days per program in the summer to work with your kids. If we have a three-sport athlete, that means

30 days of his summer is involved with a sports team in practice.

We set up our weight room to get the players in and get them out. We do not have our players standing in line waiting to get on a machine. When we have young players come into the weight room, I want them to be able to get on a rack, feel good about it, and not be intimidated.

When I buy a machine for our weight room, I do not buy just one. If I am buying a neck machine, I buy five or six of them. We have 10 squat racks in our room. We have a good weight room. There are probably many weight rooms that are better than ours, but there are many that are worse. We have the mentality that we need to get a workout. If it is a garage with bricks in it, we need to get a workout.

I know schools that have million-dollar weight rooms and the players never sweat in there. They do not work at it. We want to know the mentality of our players. We want to know if they are going to work and be dedicated. One of the most important pieces of equipment in our weight room is our stereo. I know this is a point with some coaches.

It is my job to be in the weight room four days a week. I like to listen to the music myself. I do not like everything that comes out of the stereo, but I like most of it. We do not allow any songs with profanity or other types of disruptions.

I listened to the strength coach at Ohio State, Al Johnson, and he said he thinks that is part of the program. The deal is: on Friday they have to listen to my music. I am an old Motown guy. I like Marvin Gaye, Al Green, any artist in that category. I enjoy Fridays and the players like it, too. They call it "Funky Friday." We try to create an atmosphere where they are having fun.

If I go too fast or you have a question, just raise your hand. I do not have all the answers, but I have a good plan that works for us. Whatever system you have, you have to teach your players to buy into it. You have to sell it to your players and they have to believe in what you are doing.

The thing you have to do is earn the title of coach. We want the coaches to be visual in the weight room. I need to be in that room. I want my assistant coaches to be in there. I do not tell the assistants they have to be in the room, but the players like to see them in there. How can I have a weight program if I am not in the room and the assistant coaches are not in the room? Are the players going to buy into that type of program?

We have a basketball coach in our school who believes that lifting weights screws up the player's shot. He does not come in the weight room and his players do not buy into that theory. When he gets pushed around on Friday night, he wonders why. If I were the golf coach, my players would be in the weight room. You may not be able to hit the ball further, but you will intimidate the crap out of the other golfer on the first tee.

Three years ago I had a band wall set against one wall in our weight room (Diagram #1). I had a player whose father owned a welding company. We had steel girders in the room and he welded three-inch tubing with a grid pattern. On the grid, it had a low rung, a low-middle rung, a high-middle rung, and higher rung. This grid is 27 feet wide. We use this wall for our rubber-band workouts. We can hook the bands on at the height we need and do our workout. I can get as may as eight players on the wall working with band exercises.

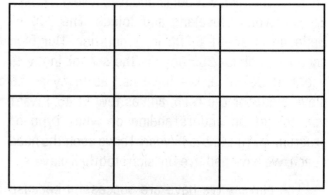

Diagram #1. Band Wall

We get our players in the weight room and get them out in an hour and they have a good workout. I got rid of all the cable machines. They constantly had to be maintained and broke down at the wrong times.

The first thing we put in our weightlifting packet is the quote:

"If you keep doing what you're doing, you will keep getting what you get."

If your players come to the weight room every day and they do not get any stronger, they are not pushing.

Seek knowledge because knowledge translates into authority. If you want to have authority, get the knowledge. It is out there. You coaches in the room obviously want to pick something up from this lecture. That is why you are here. Utilize the resources. Coaches love to talk about their programs. I can be the biggest pain in the butt because I will keep bugging you until I get what I want. Pick your fellow coaches brains about what they are doing.

I am 47 years old and I did not come up in a weight-training program. What I know, I have researched. Find a program and adapt it to fit your program. What I will talk about may not apply to what you want to do, but maybe it does.

When we start our weight training, I work the room. We finish our season in late November and we do not have much contact with the players until January. Our program starts and I am ready to go. I talk them up and coach them every minute they are in the room. I want to challenge them and motivate them. I use the time in the weight room to connect with some players, especially young players who may be intimidated by me and the room. Make your upperclassmen help the young players whenever possible. Learn the name of everyone who comes into the weight room and call them by their first name.

This is a chance for the coach to talk to the players and make them feel comfortable. I couple of years ago we had a couple of young players come into the program. After the workout, my coaches would shake their hands and tell them, "Good workout." Now they wait in line to shake your hand when they leave. That happens every day; that is what you need to do. Get to know your players

personally. These players have to be stroked and encouraged.

Make sure your standards as a coach are higher than those the athlete sets for himself. We set goal weekly with our players. On Monday and Tuesday, we check their last set and bump them up when needed.

I played at the University of Toledo from 1977 to 1981. Flexibility was the big thing at that stage. Now, the people I have talked to would rather the player run for five minutes instead of coming in and stretching. They want to get the heart rate up and the body warm.

What we do is a dynamic warm-up. If it is an upper-body day, we do something to get the upper body going. We do the same things on lower-body day. It is a two- to three-minute warm-up (Diagrams #2 and #3).

Group Warm-Up (Two to Three Minutes)
- Four corners
- Side-shuffle down-hurdle bounce
- Shuffle punch
- Ladder
- Hurdle routine
- Medicine-ball throw shuffle

Diagram #2. Shuffle Drill

Diagram #3. Hurdle Routine

After we do the group warm-up, we go to individual stations. At the individual station, we do another warm-up for the body group we work that day.

Leg Day

Crunches	30
Leg swings	30
Superman/Aquaman	10
Partner calves	25
Three weighted and three unweighted jumps	
Jump rope	100 cuts

Upper-Body Day

Tri-plate raise	10
Medicine-ball drops	25
Skywalkers	40
Jump rope	100 cuts
Superman/Aquaman	10
Three weighted and three unweighted jumps	

We have six groups with six players in each group. They go to the individual stations. When I blow a whistle, they move to the next station. The items that are italicized in the list are done every day we lift. I do something for the abs and back every day. The weighted jumps are done with 10-pound plates in each hand. The exercises you do not recognize will be talked about later.

The weighted and unweighted jumps come from the New England Patriots' strength coach. You can do this every day. It will increase your vertical jump, and it is not hard on the legs. I do not care how the players jump the rope, but I want them to do 100 cuts with the rope. We had a big, good-looking kid come to our program. He could not jump rope, got embarrassed, and never came back.

The medicine-ball drops is an exercise in which a player stands over another player laying on the ground. He drops the medicine ball and the player on the ground catches it and punches it back to him.

I go through these six stations and it takes 10 minutes. I did not have to do any flexibility. We did group and individual dynamic and it took us 15 minutes. Now we are ready to lift.

When you go to the weight room, have a plan. If you fail to plan, you plan to fail. Know what you plan to do and why you do it. Set goals for your players.

Make a decision on which way you want to run the program. The biggest mistake coaches make is they make no decision. Make a decision, even if it is wrong.

In your program, you have to do some things consistently and very well. If you are in our program, you work the neck, back, and abs every day. On leg day, we hit the hamstrings hard. Speed is in the hamstrings. If you want to improve your speed, the players must strengthen the hamstrings.

You have to plan for variety in your program. We want to change things up with the different squats and bench presses. On Friday, I have a schedule with exercises they like to do. In the spring of the year, they will cut out on you when the weather starts to get warm. I do the beach muscle exercises on Fridays. If they bail out on me, I do not feel too bad because I got the heavy lifting done the other days.

I am going to show some tape about our program. The first thing you see is what we call the Apache plate circuit. The first thing we do is a chest press for 10 reps. He follows that with bent-over rowing, military press, curls, triceps, and upright rowing. He does all these exercise for 10 reps each. He continues this group for five minutes. The players come in on Friday, and see Apache plate circuit on the board. They know they will get out of the workout early and bust their asses to get finished.

The next circuit is the warrior circuit 144. In this circuit, the player does 12 reps each of the following exercises. They do bench press, at the cold strip, bent-over rows, upright rows, shrugs, and curls. They go through the circuit two times for a total of 144 reps.

We have a maximus leg circuit. In this circuit, we do the exercises on a timed basis. We do the following exercises for 40 seconds. We do speed squat, lunges, split jumps, and squat jumps. I give them two minutes to rest and they come back and repeat the exercises again. That is a tough circuit to go through. On the quad blaster, we must do additional hamstring exercises before and after the circuit.

We have a variety of squats and press variations to change up the exercises we do. We use a safety-squat bar. I bought two of them. The players really like them. When they do their squats, I like to get them in the chair position at the bottom of the squat. We want to keep the back straight through the squat. We want the players to get a little below parallel in their squat. If they get a little below parallel, it puts less stress on their knees. I do not like them to lock the knees out in the up position. We have a bungee cord attached to the steel standards. If they do not get low enough, the rep does not count.

Squat Variety

- Back
- Front (hang cleans)
- Speed (deep every 10)
- Single leg
- Box
- Band
- Pause

The press variations are for the upper body. We alternate the different bench presses to keep the players fresh so they do not get bored doing the same exercises all the time.

Press Variations

- Bench (DB)
- Incline (lowest rung)
- Close grip
- Coil bench (four positions)
- Band press (standing)
- Standing military
- Band press (standard)

When we do the incline bench, I like the bar on the lowest rung. The players handle the weight better then they do if the start is higher. We like to do the bench press with a close grip. When they bring the weight down, the elbows come down close to their sides. I do not want the elbows to go out.

I like to do exercises that make the players stand on their feet. We do the band press on the bank rack. When we use tight grips, that is generally the way we want our players to play with their hands. If you keep the hands tight, you do not risk injury. The wider the grip, the more susceptible you are to injury because you overextend the joint.

The older I get, the less I care about the bench press. I remember being focused on that, and the players like to do them. We use external motivation to increase the interest and levels of success in our weight program. We have a bench and squat clubs. We give them incentive t-shirts. In the weight room, we have a top-10 board. We have a conditioning-champion board in the room that displays the name of the winner.

We have a gridiron club. To get into the club you have to amass 155 points from the set criteria to get into the club. If they qualify for the gridiron club, we put their name in the club and give them a bronze football. To get into the gridiron club, the players have to meet the criterion in the following categories:

- Bench max
- Squat max
- Pro agility
- Pull-ups
- Dips
- Sprint test
- Bench reps
- Four corners
- Vertical leap

To get into the gridiron club, you make your points by doing the following items in your testing program. Points are awarded for:

- Bench or squat goal — 40 points (1 point for every 10 pounds over goal, -point for every 10 pounds under goal)
- Reps — 1/3 point for every dip
- Pull-ups — 2/3 point for every pull-up
- Sprint test — four points for every sprint within 0.5 of the fastest time on your three sprints

Excellent = 155 points or more
Good   = 140 to 154 points
Average = 125 to 139 points
Poor   = Less than 124 points

If you are not getting better, we are getting worse. Nothing in life stays the same.

We do not test for one max lift. We use a calculation chart to compute the max. The chart goes up to 10 reps. When we test our players, I do not want to test anything lower than eight reps. If they go off the chart, we use the three-percent rule. I got this from Al Johnson in 1997. If a player can bench 200 for 15 reps, we calculate his max this way:

200 pounds for 15 reps

Three percent of 200 is six pounds

6 pounds x 15 reps = 90 pounds

90 pounds + 200 pounds = 290 max

In the weight room, we must practice safety. I look at every position we use and evaluate it. I do not want anyone hurting themselves in the weight room. We use a safety-squat bar to prevent the weight from dropping off the shoulders. We use the solid-chair position because it is easier to teach the younger players.

We avoid lifts that may overextend a joint. When we do bench and military types of presses, we use closed grip and keep the weight in front of us. We want to keep the lat pulls in front of the body. We never do an exercise that puts the weight behind the head. When we incline press, we use the lowest rung on the on the rack to keep control of the weights.

Agility and Foot-Speed Drills

- Jump rope
- Dot drill
- Speed ladder
- Hoop run (jump ball circle 37.5' circumference)
- Hexes
- Pro agility
- Line drills

In the weight room, we have rules. I make sure everyone knows the rules and I enforce them. I do not want players wearing earrings in the weight room. I am an old-school guy. I do not want them to wear their hats backward. I've been coaching for 25 years and the one thing that has constantly peeved me off is players walking around with their hats on backward and their pants hanging off their butts. I do not like it. I treat the weight room as my house and I do not want anyone disrespecting it. This is the copy of the weight-room rules, I send home to the parents for them to review. I have the athlete sign the sheet.

Bellevue Weight-Room Rules

- No one is allowed in the facility without qualified staff present.
- No jewelry is to be worn in room.
- The on-duty supervisor should direct overall room conduct and use of the equipment—including sound system and heating system.
- Collars are mandatory at all times.
- Supervisors are not responsible for personal belongings, lost or stolen items.
- Misuse of equipment and facilities may result in immediate expulsion.
- Spotters must be used when necessary.
- Weights are to be moved from the racks to the bar only. They are never to be set on the floor or on a bench. All rubber bands should be removed from machine and put away.
- Respect the equipment and facilities (weights must not be dropped or thrown).
- Horseplay and offensive language are not permitted.
- Shirts are to be worn at all times. No jeans are allowed and athletic shoes are to be worn.
- No gum, glass bottles, or food allowed in facility.
- Direction by any coach must be followed.

Bellevue Weight-Room Pact

I, _____, have read all the Bellevue High School strength and conditioning facility rules and hereby agree to follow them as written. I also acknowledge that my failure to comply with these rules may result in the loss of the weight-room privileges for a given period of time and/or disciplinary action from the team coach.

Athlete's signature _____

As part of our conditioning, we use what is called the dynamic lap. There are 15 items the players have to execute. They continue moving while changing from one exercise to the next.

- 25-yard jog, arm circle forward
- 25-yard jog, arm circle backward
- 25-yard skip for height
- 25-yard skip for quickness
- 25-yard heel ups
- 25-yard heel kicks

- 5-yard shuffle walk
- 5-yard walk shuffle, walk opposite way
- 20-yard lunge walk
- 25-yard backpedal walk, reach back
- 25-yard backward run
- 10-yard shuffle slide
- 15-yard open and run
- 10-yard shuffle slide opposite way
- 15-yard open and run

The last two or three things I want to show are the charts we use to keep track of our development during the week (Diagrams #4 through #8). There are also some explanations of the warm up exercises I talked about earlier.

Thank you very much. I have enjoyed being here. I hope you got something out of this presentation.

Diagram #4. Chart #1 — Inch Work

Diagram #5. Chart #2 — Tri-Plate Raise

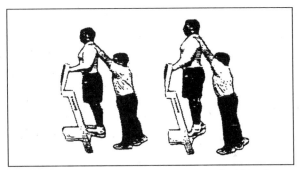

Diagram #6. Chart #3 — Partner Calf Raises

MONDAY   JUNE 5, 2006

Warm-up: 10 Superman/20 DB Calf Raises each leg/Hurdle Routine/30 Crunches/10 Leg swings/ 3 WEIGHTED JUMPS/ 3 UNWEIGHTED JUMPS

	SET 1		SET 2		SET 3		SET 4		SET 5	
	WT	REP	WT	REP	WT	REP	WT	REP	WT	REP
Squats		12		12		12				
Band Rocks		FATI	GUE							
Bands		SIDE	STEP							
Jammer Pow Walk		1 x 5								
Jammer Ext.		5		5		5				
1 Leg Squat		8		8		8				
Ham & Glute		10		10						
Neck		10		10		10		10		
Stiff Leg Dead Lift		8		8						

Cool-down: ladder 1 foot down & back, 2 foot down & back, modified inch worm

---

TUESDAY   JUNE 6, 2006

Warm-up: 10 Ball Roll Outs/Jump Rope 100 cuts/Tri Plate Raises 10 each/4-way Neck 10 each way/ 20 Sky walkers/ 3 WEIGHTED JUMPS/ 3 UNWEIGHTED JUMPS

	SET 1		SET 2		SET 3		SET 4		SET 5	
	WT	REP	WT	REP	WT	REP	WT	REP	WT	REP
Bench		12		12		12				
DB Bench		8		8		8		8		
DB Military		10		10		10		10		
LAT Pull Front		10		10		10		10		
Jammer Rotation		5		5		5				
Reverse Hyper		8		8		8				

Cool-down: ladder-zig zag down & back, side step down & back, slolum down & back, mod.

THURSDAY   JUNE 8, 2006

Warm-up: Partner Calf Raises 20 /4-way Neck x 10/ 10 Crossovers ea. leg/10 Leg Swings/ 20 Med Ball throws/ 3 WEIGHTED JUMPS/ 3 UNWEIGHTED JUMPS

	SET 1		SET 2		SET 3		SET 4		SET 5	
	WT	REP	WT	REP	WT	REP	WT	REP	WT	REP
Pause Squats		6		6		6		6		
Hang Cleans		6		6		6		6		
Coil Bench		3		3		3		3		
Reverse Hyper		8		8		8				
Biceps		15		15		15		15		
Triceps		15		15		15		15		
1 Arm Rows		8		8		8		8		
Dips		5		5						
Row Press		8		8		8				

Cool-down: dots-2 sets 10 sec. Both feet. hex jumps-2 sets 10 sec. Each. modified inch

Diagram #7. Chart #4 — Workout Week

Diagram #8. Chart #5 — Dynamic Lap

FROM SPREAD SETS TO THE FULLHOUSE-T

Haslett High School, Michigan

Thank you very much. I want to thank Don Lessner and Nike for the opportunity to speak today. I think the spread offense is a hot-button issue for fullhouse-T coaches. There is a bit of dissension in our ranks right now. We have veer coaches, spread coaches, and T formation coaches confused about where to turn with their offense.

In the last three or four years, there has been discussion among T formation coaches about how to make the fullhouse better. To go into that, you need to understand my background with the T.

In the mid-1970s, Elmer Engle, the coach at Bay City Central, had two sons, Jim and John, who were both assistant coaches under Irv Sigler at Cheboygan High School. They implemented the fullhouse-T in 1978 with Coach Sigler.

I was playing peewee football at that time, but from grades 6 through 8, we ran the fullhouse-T. I played high school football at Cheboygan from 1980 to 1984 and we ran the fullhouse-T. I was in the fullhouse-T from the sixth grade until I graduated from high school.

I went on to Adrian College and ran the Delaware wing-T. I was there from 1984 to 1988. There is considerable difference between the fullhouse-T and the wing-T.

After graduation, I worked two years at Central Michigan as graduate assistant. We ran the multiple I formation. That gave me an opportunity to see what else was out there in the offensive world. I did not think about adopting the I formation as an offense, but it influenced what I wanted to do.

Playing in the wing-T, I found out I could not throw the ball. I could not execute the three- and five-step dropback game. I could throw the play-action passes. There are some things in the Delaware wing-T that I liked and some things I did not like.

When we threw the ball, we had a spread and pro set. After playing in this offense, I wondered when I got into coaching what the fullhouse-T would look like.

I was the head coach at St. Ignace High School from 1990 to 1994. I installed the fullhouse-T. I installed the Iowa wing-T blocking scheme in 1991 from Barry Pierson. I implemented a multiple play-action-pass scheme. We took the various motion packages for the Iowa wing-T that Forrest Evasheski ran in the '50s and '60s.

The package I put in had more motion than anything that I had ever done. From there, I adopted Irv Sigler's blocking scheme. To adopt some of the ideas I was considering, I had to add formations or plays. I implemented a multiple play-action-pass scheme and various motion packages. I was more liberal at St. Ignace than I had been at Haslett until 2004.

At St. Ignace we had success and were able to get into the playoffs in the 1992–93 season. We ran into a hell of an Iron-Mountain team in 1992 and St. Francis in 1993. We were doing many different things. We used motion, wings, and double wings as part of our offense. I liked our blocking system, but our faking that we got from the fullhouse-T was suffering.

One of the things I decided to do when I came to Haslett in 1994 was to become more conservative. One thing that we experienced was the base package in the fullhouse-T had grown considerably. In 1990, the offense had been around for 20 years.

One of the challenges we had was how to run the offense and still be effective.

The northern Michigan and Upper Peninsula area had seen the T since 1978 and we were facing teams that had some confidence defending it. Mentally, it became more difficult to run the fullhouse-T. In addition, our archrival was still running the fullhouse-T.

In 1994, when I got to Haslett High School, I wanted to get a fresh start. I wanted to look at what was going to constitute the base package. I became extremely conservative in 1994. I kept the eight basic plays and cut down the play-action-pass package to something that was more workable. I wanted to be more efficient in that part of the game. I did keep a sprint-out series.

As 1995 went along, we tried to teach our players how to win because they had not been to the playoffs since 1981. We added an option, because that was a natural progression with the fullhouse-T. We added the wing and double wing to our formations. If you do not adapt, people will become comfortable in defending what you do offensively.

We felt that if we changed too much, we would lose our identity as a fullhouse-T team. We decided to add blocking schemes. We may run the fullback trap 25 times per game, but now we block it five different ways. That was our school of thinking for a long time.

In 1997, we added a power series. That helped a lot to help us move the ball. We made the finals in 1998, with our quarterback out for the majority of the season. With him out, we had to stay base in our offense. For 12 games, the offense worked very well.

In this offense up to 1990, we rushed 2,800 yards. Since then we have rushed for 4,400 yards. All the additions and adaptations we had made to offense had payed off.

However, if you run the fullhouse-T long enough, your opponents will get better at defending you. That is what we have experienced. We have been fortunate enough to make the playoffs every year since 1998, but people have gotten better at defending us.

We have another problem. We are stubborn as hell. We are going to run the fullhouse-T regardless of what everyone does. As T coaches, we can either be stubborn or give our opponents a package that fits the T concept and personnel and gain an advantage. The best advice I have to give is: do not let your pride get in the way.

It is a fact that players like to run the passing game. Passing the ball from the gun is fun. Players love it, fans love it, and it gains an advantage for us. It is difficult to recruit players from your building to be a tight end. However, you can find wide receivers.

I got to be friends with Jim McElwain from Michigan State. We talked about personnel and decided I could run a two-by-two formation and line up in the same personnel that I use in the fullhouse-T. That is how we evolved into a spread team. I spent four or five meetings in East Lansing talking to Coach McElwain.

The first thing he wanted to look at was the type of passes we had in our offense. He only wanted to consider passes that were not out of the two-tight-end set. He kept asking questions about our reads and patterns and I did not have any answers. We sat down in the winter of 1994 and put together a package that we felt could be effective.

The first thing we had to consider was our quarterbacks and wide receivers. We had to work on running better routes. The second thing we had to do was develop a quarterback, which is an ongoing process. We had to develop the quarterbacks at a younger age.

To put the protection scheme together, I went to Michigan State for help. The offensive line coach at Michigan State recommended we use the quick and slide protection. The next problem is our players do not know how to pass block. They have never done it to any extent. He told me that was probably an advantage because they do not have any bad habits.

During the off-season, we took three players before and after school and started working with them on the spread offense. All we wanted to do was teach them the basic concepts of the offense. We were scheduled to go to Michigan State in July. They invited teams into their second series of camps. Steve Stripling who coached Michigan State before he went to Michigan has two sons go on the Haslett High School team. Most of our players could commute to practice at Michigan State. We had the entire team on campus and all we worked on was the spread offense. We went back to Michigan State's team camp in 2004 and again in 2005.

We had to be careful trying to implement the spread along with the fullhouse-T. You must have a plan to give the time to both offenses. I could envision myself getting sidetracked and locked into one facet of the T and having no time to practice the spread. We grouped our team and flipped the practice schedule. We told our players they had to give great concentration when we went from the T to spread offense.

We separate with two different groups and two different teams. In 2004, we lined up in the fullhouse and shifted into the spread set. We did that for six or seven weeks in the season. After that, teams knew what we were doing and they had no trouble shifting their defense from one offensive set to another.

I had to find a way to merge the spread with the T offense. We could not be in fullhouse for one series and spread for the next. We had to mix the two offenses into a game plan, which ran spread and T plays in the same series.

We took our bubble screens in the spread offense out in 2005. The package was not a big package, but it was too much to run. We knew if we added anything to the offense we had to take something out. The things we took out of the offense were things we did not do well or did not run at all.

On of the things that helped was that all of our plays were on cards. It was like a beefed up scout team. Our players struggled a bit in 2004 with the plays. We came up with a new terminology to run the offense. They were short, one-syllable words. We called our two-by-two formation "state" and the three-by-one formation "sky."

I want to talk about our pass concepts in the spread offense. I had to determine how to teach the quarterback where to throw and what the checkdowns were. We cut down our base play-action series. The thing I realized about the spread offense was the ability to run the football. Our running game from the spread offense has been more effective and more important than our passing game.

The thing that really helped us was scripting the plays so we could be unpredictable. That is the secret to scripting plays. When you script the plays, you have to stay with the script and not let your heart take over the play calling. That way, you can call the play that keeps you unpredictable and not call the play that establishes your tendencies.

In 2004, we were in the spread offense 20.1 percent of the time. Our goal was to be in the spread 30 percent of the time, but I felt that was too much. In our fullhouse-T, we rushed for 2,000 yards and threw for 188 yards. In the spread offense, we rushed for 626 yards and threw for 426 yards.

We thought that was a solid, but not a great, start in the spread offense. We needed to change some things in the offense. In 2005, we ran the spread 24.5 percent of the time. We gained 3,214 yards rushing the football from the fullhouse. We threw it for 218 yards from the T. In the spread offense, we ran the ball for 1,196 yards and threw it for 829 yards.

We told our players when we went to the T passing game that we had to be effective and run great routes. We had to make it look like the running game. Our T package has been more effective. We have fewer incompletions and interceptions. Defenders are looking at the fullhouse and the spread game, but they tend to forget the play-action pass from the fullhouse.

Opposing defenses have to spend time defending the spread. If we are running the fullhouse 75 percent of the time, the defense should allocate 75 percent of their practice time to defending the fullhouse. Our mindset is spending 75 percent of our time practicing the fullhouse package will be more efficient than the opponent's 75 percent spent preparing to defend it.

We played Stevensville Lakeshore in the playoffs. I read the comments of their head coach in the paper the next day. They play two-platoon football and the coach said, "We could not allocate enough time to be comfortable with the fullhouse and spread sets." That is why we needed to implement the spread.

Our faking in the fullhouse-T got considerably better in 2005. When we went to T group, we told our players they had to maintain focus. If we are going to be in the spread offense, we have to be good at it. If the fullhouse offense is suffering, I will not stick with the spread formation. When we are in the T formation we have to be unbelievably efficient.

All the coaches thought something would suffer. That has not happened. We run better routes in the T formation. Our tight ends run better pass routes because of the spread. They are used to being split out wide and they are used to running crossing patterns and hitch routes. The wide receivers run better routes and have developed their confidence in catching the ball.

Our offense now is a tractor-and-Corvette mentality. We are still going to be T people and that will not change as long as I am here. We are going to be tractors and we will keep that identity. If we lose that identity, we are in trouble because all we have is a Corvette in the barn that we bring out at certain times.

The Corvette is supposed to help the tractor. It is not going to replace it. We are not going to come out and run the spread offense all the time. The spread offense will make our fullhouse-T better.

The one thing it did was to spoil the hell out of my fans. When we go to the spread offense, our

fans can see the ball. Inherently it is not their fault; they are just ignorant. They cannot follow the ball in the fullhouse-T. They like the scoreboard lighting up, but in between that, the offense is not something they can relate to. They do not see this offense on Saturday in the college game. The fans interest all boils down to winning games.

One of our base formations is "state." That is the two-by-two set. We call the receivers to the right of the formation, Y and Z. The receivers to the left are A and B. If we call "right-state" (Diagram #1), the receivers to the right side are Y and Z. The A and B receivers align to the backside. The back in the backfield is to the left of the quarterback, who is in the shotgun set. We call him the fullback.

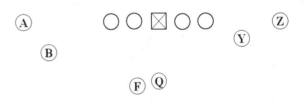

Diagram #1. Right State

The other formation I will focus on is the tight formation. We did not install this last year until late. I was worried about adding too much. Because we play fullhouse-T, we have tight ends to fit this role. If I call "tight left" (Diagram #2), the tight end aligns on the left side of the formation. The Y and Z align right and the A-receiver aligns left off the line of scrimmage. All we did was replace the B-receiver.

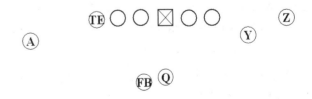

Diagram #2. Tight Left

The first concept we put in was "state-right fly-seam" (Diagram #3). We run four verticals out of the double formation. The quarterback has to read one or two high in the middle of the field. If there is one safety in the middle, the quarterback reads him and throws accordingly. We do not inundate our quarterback with a thousand different checks. If the quarterback reads a blitz by the strong safety or outside linebacker, he throws to the seam receiver to that side ASAP or he scrambles.

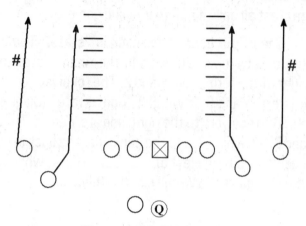

Diagram #3. Fly Seam

The next concept is the curl-dig pattern. We call "state-right curl-dig" (Diagram #4). If the coverage is a cover 3, the quarterback reads the strong safety. If the strong safety goes to the flat, he throws the deep curl. If he backs up or sits, he throws the flat pattern.

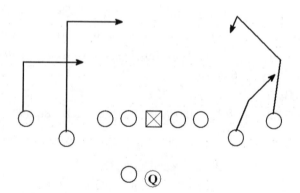

Diagram #4. Curl Dig

If the defense is cover 2, the quarterback looks to the dig concept on the backside. They run a short and deep dig. The B- and Y-receivers are the pressure beaters. If the quarterback does not like what he sees on the curl concept, he can come back to the dig patterns on the backside. However, if the quarterback does not like what he sees, he pulls the ball down and runs it. Since we have a good running

quarterback, that is a good choice for us. It goes back to the idea of blending the two offenses together. One of the things that scares the defense in the spread formation is the quarterback running the ball.

The linemen are in a slide-protection scheme. Once the quarterback decides to run, we ask the linemen to stay on a defender. Deciding to run the ball is an afterthought for the quarterback. He pre-snap reads the coverage as to the throw, but not the scramble.

If the quarterback reads a cover 2, he reads the outside linebacker. He looks for the open window. If the linebacker drops, he throws the short dig to the A-receiver. If he sits, the quarterback throws the long dig to the B-receiver. The B-receiver has to take an outside release.

The next concept is "state right Zulu" (Diagram #5). The quarterback reads the middle for one or two high safeties. This is a great red-zone play. We run mirror route to each side. The inside receivers run flags unless they see cover 2. In that case, they break their routes to deep outs. The outside receivers run hitches. The quarterback reads the corner. If the corner bails or plays off the wide receiver, he throws the hitch. If he sits or presses, he throws the flag. If the quarterback reads cover 2, the flag routes become deep outs.

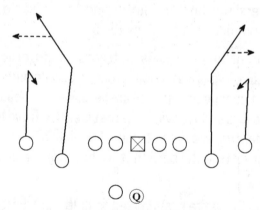

Diagram #5. Zulu

We thought we would be efficient with the fullback trap from the spread formation. We run the fullback trap in the T a lot. We were not very good at running the fullback trap from the spread. We looked at the trap Northwestern was running and it hit a little wider. The timing was never there. We did not want to pull the tackle. We stuck with pulling the guard and adjusted the alignment of the fullback. In 2004, the play did not seem right and I did not run the play.

On the fullback trap, we adjusted the back to a half-yard from the quarterback and a half-yard back (Diagram #6). He is close to the quarterback. The timing has come along and the play is effective now. With the trap scheme, we run the fullback trap, quarterback option, quarterback draw, cutback, and quarterback cutback.

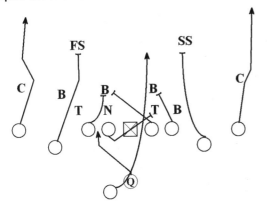

Diagram #6. Fullback Trap

We ran the option from the tight-left formation. We called "option left" (Diagram #7). The talent of the quarterback will determine what we do with the blocking scheme. We wanted our quarterback to keep the football as long as he could. We loaded the blocking and had the tight end reach the defender over him. Beyond the normal techniques to run the play, we did not get too technical.

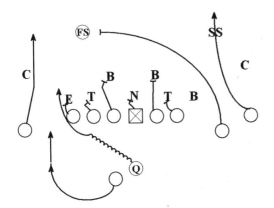

Diagram #7. Option Left

The passing concept does not change in the tight formation. The tight end runs the B-receiver routes. He runs the seam on the four verticals and the dig on the curl-dig.

We can run the fly seam with the tight formation. We tell our inside receivers that if they read a two-deep scheme with the safeties bailing deep, pull up in front of them. The outside receivers continue to run to pull the safeties deep.

I want to show you the 10-11 play off the fullback trap (Diagram #8). That is the quarterback-trap play. The fullback has to remember which side to align. We do not tag a call to move the fullback around. He has to know.

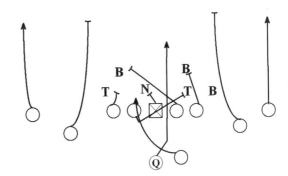

Diagram #8. Quarterback Trap

The last play is the option run from a raven set (Diagram #9). The raven set reverses the alignment of the inside and outside receivers. On raven, the Y- and B-receivers are on the line. The Z- and A-receivers back off the line of scrimmage. On this option, we do not load the play. The quarterback will probably have to pitch quickly on this play.

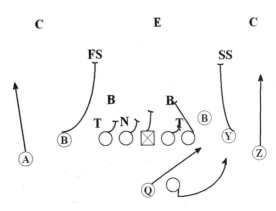

Diagram #9. Raven Option Right

I am going to show you a little film of the plays I just showed you on the overhead. I picked out 10 and we can rewind them as many times as you would like. At the end, I have a highlight film to show you. This next tape is for the love of football. This is a highlight tape, but if you love high school football, this will put goose bumps on you.

This comes from *Any Given Sunday* with Al Pacino as a professional football coach:

I don't know what to say. We have three minutes to the biggest battle of our professional lives. It all comes down to today. Either we heal as a team or we're going to crumble—inch-by-inch, play-by-play or we're finished. We are in hell right now, gentlemen. Believe me. We can stay here and get the crap kicked out of us, or we can fight our way back into the light and climb out of hell, one inch at a time.

You know, when you get old in life, things get taken from you. That's just part of life. But you only learn that when you start losing stuff. You find out life is a game of inches. So is football. But in either game, life or football, the margin for error is so small. I mean, one half step too late or too early and you don't quite make it. One half second too slow or too fast, you don't quite catch it. The inches we need are everywhere around us.

They're in every break of the game, every minute, every second. On this team, we fight for that inch. On this team, we tear ourselves and everyone around us to pieces for that inch. We claw with our fingernails for that inch. Because we know, when we add up all those inches, that's going to make the difference between winning and losing—between living and dying. I tell you this: in any fight, it's the guy who's willing to die that will win that inch.

I know if I am going to have any life any more, it is because I am still willing to fight and die for that inch. 'Cause, that's what living is. I can't make you do it. You have to look at the guy next to you and look into his eyes. Now, I think you will see a guy who will go that inch with you. You will see a guy who will sacrifice himself for this team because he knows, when it comes down to it, you will do the same for him. That is a team, gentlemen. And either we heal as a team now, as a team, or we will die as individuals. That's football, guys. That's all it is. Now, what are you goin' to do?

If that does not put goose bumps on your arms, I do not know what will. I have seen this at least 50 times and it still almost brings me to tears. That is why we do what we do with kids. It is nice that we have had success at Haslett. When you play at Ford's Field in the finals of the state playoffs, it is tremendously fulfilling.

Any questions I can answer? Thank you very much.

CONCEPTS OF THE VEER OFFENSE

Rochester Adams High School, Michigan

Let me start by saying it is a great pleasure to be here. For a coach, being asked to share what you do is the greatest compliment you can get. The unfortunate thing is our program is successful because of a lot more things than what I am going to talk about today.

We have a great defense and special teams that put the offense in the short field all the time. That makes it easier for the offense to be successful. The problem we encountered when we got to Rochester Adams High School was that they were a traditional wing-T school. It was a big ordeal to come in and sell the concept of the option game to the staff and players.

I really believe in what we are doing. The problem is that we are in the middle of an arms race. Defensive coordinators are smart. They are smarter than most of us offensive guys. They have done a nice job over the years at taking away the traditional split-back veer offensive philosophy.

We used to be a double-team down on the tackle, read the end, and away we go. Now we see many 7 techniques, eight defenders in the box, and disguise in the secondary—things had to change for us to be successful. Most of what I am going to say today, I learned from someone else.

A number of coaches have shared their ideas to make this offense what it is today. Ultimately, each coach has come up with a hybrid offense. They come up with their own version that works for them within their offensive philosophy.

I have talked to many coaches who run the wing-T. They are running the midline series out of the wing-T set, and it is very effective. We have seen it this season. There are teams lining up in the shotgun formation and running the midline blocking schemes and doing a great job of it. As we go through this today, if it fits and you like it, do it. The bottom line is not to be afraid of the option.

Some coaches think forward passes and options are nothing more than fumbles in the air. Bad things happen when you throw the ball or run option. The bottom line is that it takes repetition and practice. If you commit to the option, it is not risky. It is sound, fundamental football.

This is our playbook that we give to our kids. It is the blueprint for what we like to do against different kinds of fronts. We see all kinds of different fronts in our schedule.

We are not going to add more offense until I am confident we have mastered what we have installed up to now. If it takes two weeks for us to become comfortable with the inside veer, I am not adding anything else until we master that play. If we are not good at the inside veer, nothing will work. This play drives the whole offense.

We try to limit our audibles to an either-or system. I am not a good play caller, but our staff has coached our quarterback to make good checks at the line of scrimmage. If the system is too complicated, quarterbacks get lost under the center. Things go too fast. Every check we have for the most part is a check-with-me, which changes the play from one side to the other, or a this-or-that, which is a two-play package. The quarterback runs the first play or the second play.

The quarterback who played last year was a two-year starter. He got to the point where he could look at the linebacker level and secondary level and make a secondary check.

That was something he did on his own. He did not learn it from me.

We will use formations when necessary to manipulate defenses. We have to be flexible. If you do not have the right personnel to do everything we do, do what fits. You have to be flexible.

Some veer philosophies have not changed since day one. We want a double-team at the point of attack. Our offensive line last year averaged 183 pounds per man. We got decent movement on the line of scrimmage because it was a two-on-one block. There are some important points we like to tell our offensive linemen. We do not want to see any daylight in their double-team block. If there is a crack in the block, a good defensive lineman will split the double-team every time. That is one of our points of repetition.

The other thing that drives what we do philosophically is concept that offense is not as aggressive or mean as defense. Somewhere along the line, there was a divergence in our culture in football. The tough, mean guys played defense and the pretty boys played offense. We coach the philosophy on offense that we are going to try to push the defense around. Although our kids are smaller and slower, we are going to push the defense around. We are going to come off the ball and win every single snap. It does not happen, but we ask for it.

We want to be aggressive and it starts when you come out of the huddle. We get to the line of scrimmage and get down. We do not have the accordion style of alignment. That is when you have five guys aligning at five different times. We are coming out of the huddle, get white in our knuckles, get the weight forward, and come off the ball. That is an important mindset for offensive players.

I do not mean to sound cocky, but I coach that anything short of a touchdown is a failure. A punt is the consummate failure. That is a dirty word in our football practice. If you ask my players about dirty words, they will tell you punt is one of them. I do not want to punt; it is like saying it is okay for our defense to give up first downs. No defensive

coordinator would ever say that and that is the type of approach we want on offense.

Everything you see in this playbook is out of our double-slot look. We accordion our slot a bunch but it is a balanced look. It is a two-by-two set that everyone in the world runs. That has done one great thing for option coaches. In the old days when we were in a double-tight flanker set, it was not hard to play a five-man front with a cover-3 rotation and take things away.

If you go double-slot formation, there is no strength in the middle of the field. That makes defenses get out of things that they are comfortable with because of the offense set. Now we have a chance.

In our playbook, we have all our plays drawn up against four different looks. The one we do not have is the West Virginia 3-5 front. Our base set is the double slot with two split ends and one back. For the clinic purpose, we will put up the 4-3 defense.

When we run the inside veer, I want to run at the narrow aligned tackle (Diagram #1). That gives us the angle for the center and guard to scoop his butt out of there. We must have 12 to 18 inches of movement off the line of scrimmage. If the defensive tackle is in a 3 technique on the guard, it is hard to get him out with a double-team or single block. That is why people started going to the midline veer. We want to run the inside veer at the shade-technique tackle or the 2i tackle.

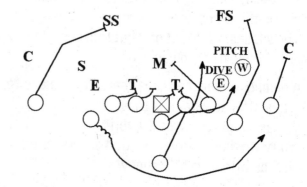

Diagram #1. Inside Veer

The dive key is the 5-technique defensive end. The pitch key is the Will linebacker. We do not block either one of those players. On the backside, we scoop the 3-technique tackle up to the Sam linebacker.

There was a funny quote from one of our quarterbacks from a couple of years ago. He now plays linebacker at Wayne State. They asked him what was different in running the offense at Adams versus the wing-T. He told the reporters, "At Adams we do not block anybody." That is how the quote appeared in the paper. He was saying we did not block anybody on the playside.

The key to the entire play is the dive and the read of the quarterback. If the fullback hits the seam fast and the quarterback reads the play correctly, this is a dynamite play.

The splits for the offensive linemen have to be the same every time. They cannot vary one iota. There must be two feet between the center and guard and three feet between the guard and tackle. It cannot vary because everything else is built around the aiming points on the offensive linemen.

The fullback's hand is at four yards from the line of scrimmage, unless he is slow. If that is the case, we move him up. We have never had a back we had to move back, but we hope that will happen eventually. The aiming point of the fullback is the inside ankle of the playside guard. He explodes into the mesh point with the quarterback.

The center steps with his playside foot and the guard steps with his inside foot. The center and guard get hip to hip with not daylight showing in their double-team and take the 2i tackle inside. The rule we apply to our blocking is: "When in doubt, block down." The toughest block is the tackle's block on the Mike linebacker. He is probably the defense's best football player. Every team in our league has a stud playing at Mike linebacker.

The offensive tackle will be yelled at as many times as the quarterback is yelled at on the play. If the tackle goes to where the Mike linebacker aligns, he will be there waiting for his mother. He has to anticipate the quick movement of the Mike linebacker into the B gap. When quarterback steps

to that side, the Mike linebacker fills the gap looking for the tackle to block him. The first step of the playside tackle is almost flat to the line of scrimmage and the collision point will be about the heels of the defensive tackle. It's almost like an inverted arc release by the tackle. He has to step hard, stay low, and collision the Mike linebacker. Everyone else in the offensive line reaches to the playside.

We do not tag motion to our slotback, who becomes the pitchback for the option. That is unique to what we do. The players must memorize the situation they need to come in motion. Anybody who plays in our backfield has to know all three back positions.

There are a couple of coaching points about pitch position. The quarterback reaches back with the ball to ride the fullback. He makes his decision to pull the ball or leave it by the time the ball reaches his front hip. He pressures the ball up into the fullback belly if he wants to give him the ball.

If he decides to pull the ball, he lightens the pressure and the fullback continues to run hard into the crease. The quarterback cannot bubble back on his path. He has to stay down the line of scrimmage. We call the sequence: "reach, second to the first, and step with the ride." He reaches and the fullback runs over the ball. The quarterback reaches, steps forward, and shifts his weight to the inside foot. If he pulls the ball, his inside shoulder and hip drive downhill. I never want the quarterback to lose ground.

If we are parallel to the line of scrimmage or backward, the defenses we play against will catch us from the backside. We cannot run east and west; we must attack the defense downfield. When the quarterback pitches the ball, he pitches at the front armpit of the pitchback. The pitchback wants his hips and shoulders headed downfield. To be a great pitchback, you do not have to be fast. If he takes off at the appropriate time and gets his hip and shoulders going downhill, he will make yards. If the wideouts do a good job of blocking the tunnel, the pitchback has a great vertical track. You may only get to the pitch key four or five times a game. When we do get to it, the pitchman has to be in position and going downhill.

When we come out in a balanced set, the defense cannot preset their coverage and rotate. We see many teams running four across the board in the secondary. They are rotating on the motion by the slotback.

If the defense is an odd-front defense, we can run the inside veer (Diagram #2). If the defensive tackle is outside our offensive tackle, we run the inside veer. We cannot run the outside veer from this formation against this defense. We double the nose guard and run the inside veer at the widest defensive tackle.

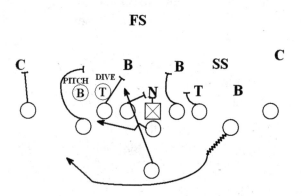

Diagram #2. Inside Veer versus Odd

If the defense is an odd front with two 5-technique tackles, the quarterback looks for a roll by the strong safety. If he reads the strong safety down to one side, he runs the play the other way. We want to force the defense to play four across in the secondary and come late to contain our play.

If the defense brings both safeties down into run support, we throw the ball and look for the big play. We use the run to set up the big play opportunities in the passing game. We have thrown the ball for over 3,000 yards the last two years. In 2003, 49 percent of our offense came from the passing game.

The defense must commit more than six defenders to the run in every situation or we will run the ball and have the defense severely outnumbered.

We let our quarterback decide what we run. We play more 4-3 and 4-4 defenses than any other defenses. The quarterback reads the defensive tackles. If they align in a 2i alignment, we run inside veer. If the tackles get wider, we run the midline. You have to be careful when talking to your players. You assume they know what you are talking about, but you may be surprised.

I made a mistake in the weight room the other day. I asked one of our good JV linebackers where he lined up in the 50 front. He told me, but he had no idea what the technique was. We said it a thousand times and assumed he knew it.

The next option is the midline veer. This has been the greatest thing about option football in the last 10 years. When the back moved behind the quarterback, splitback people did not know what to do. The smarter coaches tuned into Syracuse and their midline and Air Force under Fisher DeBerry. If you watched Navy play this year, half of their downs were the midline veer. They beat some good football teams doing it.

The midline means the fullback replaces the crack of the center's butt. He gets to that position as quick as he can. The quarterback recesses to the opposite side. His eyes read the 3-technique tackle the entire time. It is awfully temping for the 3 technique not to tackle the fullback. He wants to drill the fullback in the worst way. That is normally what happens.

If the 3-technique tackle closes, the quarterback pulls the ball. We have some strong indicators to help the quarterback. If the quarterback is able to see the strip on the opponent's pants, give the ball. If the quarterback cannot read the 3 technique's number, give the ball. If he cannot get a look at the 3 technique's face, give the ball. He is not looking for all those indicators, but any of those things probably means the tackle is not closing.

If he can see the number, cannot see the strip on his pants, or looks him right in the face, pull the ball. On the midline, the quarterback has to make a fast read (Diagram #3). That means the ball has to get back to the fullback. In this particular version of the midline, we have a double insert. We bring the playside slot down on the Mike linebacker. The playside guard can move up on the Mike linebacker. I like the idea of double-teaming the Mike linebacker. He is the player in the defense that will kick our butts.

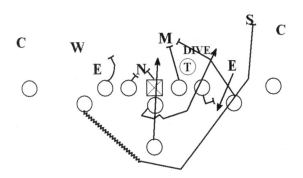

Diagram #3. Midline

We motion the opposite slot to the top of the I set. It is tough because he has to get to the back of the fullback and be in balance, because he has a tough block on the Sam linebacker. We want him to kick out the Sam linebacker, but he blocks him wherever he can. When the Sam linebacker sees the motion, he knows what is coming and will probably be coming at the slotback.

An important block is the block of the onside tackle. It is a pass block for him. He posts his inside foot and protects the inside area. He gets his inside hand up and turns the defender outside.

If the quarterback is fast enough, he pauses for a hair and lets the blocking develop. Movement on the backside is essential. If the shade nose gets penetration and slows the quarterback down or causes the fullback to spill either way, we have no play.

I am one of the few coaches left in Michigan that runs the outside veer. We still like to do it, especially on the goal line. The quarterback calls "inside/outside check with me" and keys the tackle. I am going to show this on the goal line against a standard 6-2 goal line (Diagram #4). I like to run it down there because everyone generally slants inside. The alignments are 2i, 5, and 9 techniques for the down linemen, with the linebackers over the guards.

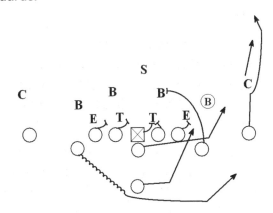

Diagram #4. Outside Veer

If the defensive end aligns in a 5 technique, we check to outside. We normally would have a double-team on the defensive end, but he more than likely will pinch. That means my 190-pound tackle can wash him to the inside because that is the way his momentum will take him. The wingback seals the Mike linebacker. The wide receiver runs off the corner, who is in man coverage.

We double-team on the playside 2i because we cannot have any penetration. That one thing causes problems. The quarterback cannot give ground. If the quarterback were to get to the pitch key, there is no one left to play the pitch.

The steps for the quarterback on the outside veer are big, little, little, and ride. He takes a big step, drops his hips, and takes two little steps. If the quarterback is going to his right, that puts his left foot inside the alignment of the front hand of the playside offensive tackle. He extends the ball and rides the fullback. This is a tough play for the quarterback. The fullback is flying to get to the mesh area. In the old days when we ran the splitback veer, it was harder.

If the quarterback looks at the diveback, he cannot see his handoff key. His eyes have to focus on the handoff key from the moment the quarterback gets the ball until he makes his decision. The 9-technique linebacker is in a bind. He sees the wingback go inside and he closes. When the quarterback sees that, he pulls the ball. There is no one left to play the quarterback and he can walk into the end zone.

The wingback in this offense is a hard position to play. He is a vertical threat as a receiver. He has to block down on a 5 technique in his blocking scheme. He has pass-protection responsibility on some plays, he has to block on the second level, and arc block on a safety. We felt the best stance for this position was a stand-up alignment. He puts more weight on his front foot than on his back foot. We placed the hands slightly below his belt line. That allows him to step with either foot in any direction with equal balance and have no problem.

If the defense puts the handoff key in a 7 technique, pinches him inside, and rolls the coverage to that side, that stops the outside veer. When that happens, we run a new sequence of plays and load everything. Instead of having a triple option, we have a double option.

When teams play us, their linebackers play fast flow tempo. They fly off the movement of the quarterback. One thing we use to slow these linebackers is the trap-counter series. The key to our trap is it has to be fast. The window for the trap is not very big. The play opens quickly and closes as quickly. We use the "check with me" to identify the tackle to be trapped. We want to trap the 3-technique tackle. That is a classic trap scheme that everyone and their brother runs. What is different is what we do with our quarterback and what we are trying to set up.

If we are going to run the trap to the right, the quarterback steps to the right at five o'clock just as he does on the inside veer (Diagram #5). Instead

of taking the second step to the first step, he makes a complete spin and gets his hips pointing downhill. He has to face the opposite tackle. If you go to veer camp, the quarterbacks literally rip holes in the grass from spinning on this play. The fullback comes over the center's outside heel looking to get north and south as quickly as he can.

The fullback should anticipate the defender to close and try to spill the trap block. The fullback wants to get north and south as quickly as he can. If he stays tight, he can run past the unblocked Sam linebacker. The quarterback gives the ball to the fullback and carries out his trap-option fake down the line.

We take the play one more step and run the counter-T (Diagram #6). That is the quarterback-trap play. The backfield action is the fullback-trap play. The line is blocking a trap on the 5-technique defender. The playside guard blocks down on the shade nose. The playside tackle comes down on the Mike linebacker. He gets help because the Mike linebacker is reading inside zone and then traps. The right guards and traps the 5-technique defensive end. The quarterback rides the fullback, pulls the ball, and gets downhill immediately.

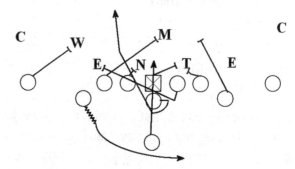

Diagram #6. Counter-T

If the defense decides to come inside to stop the quarterback, we load with the pulling guard and put the quarterback on the edge (Diagram #7). The play becomes quarterback counter-sweep, for lack of a better expression.

The trap play and quarterback keep off the trap have the same rules for the odd-front defense. The secret is the 18 inches of movement on the noseguard.

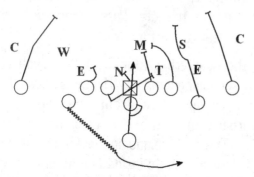

Diagram #5. Fullback Trap

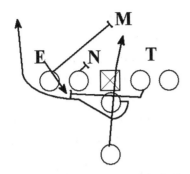

Diagram #7. Quarterback Sweep

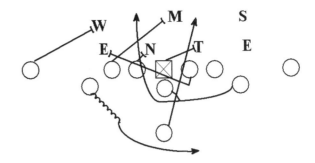

Diagram #8. Slot Counter-Trap

Most of the defensive coaches think that I am simple. They may be right. I am simple. Their thinking is to stem their defensive tackles to keep the quarterback from making the checks. There is some truth to that. However, when we play a team that moves their down front with stem movements, we quick-snap them. If we come to the line and catch the defensive line in a stem, the offensive linemen can move them and we will have some success.

I like to keep things as simple as I can for the offensive linemen. Anytime we can give the defense a multiple look in the backfield but not change anything for the offensive line, the better we will be. You do not have to be a detective to know this next play is the same play as the counter sweep. The only difference is there is a different backfield action. The linemen get to work on the same techniques but the play looks different. We can run a completely new series of plays without teaching the offensive line anything new. Our quarterback hurt his knee in the third play of the Harrison game and we had to stop running the option. He could not run. We went to this type of play. We got the ball to our fullback and slotbacks, and threw the ball. We had to protect the quarterback.

We ran the slot-counter play off the inside-veer fake (Diagram #8). The quarterback and the fullback run the inside-veer fake. It is not a long ride. The slot cross the mesh area and the quarterback gives the ball back on the slot counter-trap. The fullback has to sell the play and the slot has to work to get downhill on the play.

The slot has a tough job because I do not want him to stop and turn into the hole. I do not want him

to drop his shoulder to get into the hole. I want him downhill as fast as possible. It takes a lot of repetitions in practice to get the play right. If the slot is too flat, he misses the hole because he is too wide. He has to be able to get all the way back to the center outside heel and be square heading downhill.

If we could cut people in the secondary, it would be easier to create a level-two tunnel for the slotback. We cannot cut, and it makes blocks on the linebacker harder. The backs have to be where they are supposed to be and at the right time or they will get their heads knocked off. The blocking rules for the line are the same as the quarterback counter-trap. If the tackle is narrow, the trap is outside. If the tackle is wide, the trap is narrow. When we check the play on the line of scrimmage, we want to run it to the tight tackle. It gives everyone great angles on their blocks. The playside guard blocks the tight tackle down and we trap wide. The playside tackle has a better angle at the Mike linebacker. It is a very difficult block, but he has to get a piece of him. The wingback has to block on the Will linebacker.

A staple for many teams that do not run the option is the lead option. The shotgun teams have speed options from that formation. Speed option is an opportunity to set up a play-action pass or get the ball to the edge. We see an awful lot of inside-shade techniques. That causes us problems in our blocking scheme.

When we find teams playing a shade technique or that have a big blitz package, we run the lead option to get the ball to the edge (Diagram #9). It is hard because you cannot cut block. We want to crack with the wide receiver and lead on the corner with the fullback. The quarterback hops straight back from the center, plants, and takes off down the line of scrimmage. The hop is almost like a short three-step drop.

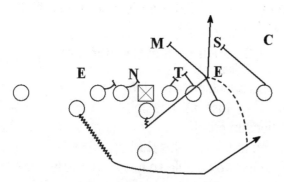

Diagram #9. Lead Option

The quarterback attacks the inside shoulder of the defensive end. By attacking the inside shoulder, it prevents the hang-and-break technique by the defensive end. If the quarterback goes to the outside shoulder of the defensive end, he can play games with the quarterback. In the hang-and-break, the defensive end hangs with the quarterback until he pitches the ball. After the pitch, he breaks down the line of scrimmage and makes the play on the running back. He plays both the quarterback and the pitch.

If the defensive end is a good athlete, he can create turnovers and cause all kinds of problems. I want my quarterback to make a decision and I want him to make it now. When he attacks the inside shoulder, he is telling the defensive end if he does not make a play on him, he is going to run the ball inside of him. When the defensive end sees the down block and the path of the quarterback, he more than likely will play the quarterback.

When the defensive end plays the quarterback, we can get to the pitch key. Our quarterback under the center is extremely low in his stance. He has good knee bend and has no trouble executing the lead option. He has to have strong hands on the ball. The hop makes the play-action pass more effective. It disguises the play-action because it looks the same. If the safety misreads, we run past him.

Fortunately, I had some coaches who were wing-T coaches before they came to work for me. We had an issue. Everyone was closing the line of scrimmage on us and crowding us down inside. We needed to get the ball to the edge. Unless you get the ball to the pitch, you are not getting to the outside. In Michigan, it is rare that you see a team that does not have some form of the jet sweep in their offense. The jet sweep is a way to get the ball outside the box against teams that are crowding the box.

We run the standard jet sweep like everyone else (Diagram #10). It is easier to run the play if the defensive tackle is head up or an inside shade on the guard. Because we run the midline, they do not like to commit one way or the other and line the defender head up. That makes it easier for the guard to get out. If the tackle is on his outside shoulder, we have trouble getting the guard out. He has to get out because he has seal block on the Mike linebacker.

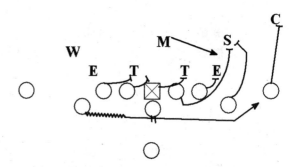

Diagram #10. Jet Sweep

We also run a fullback trap off the jet sweep. We run the trap in the same direction of the jet sweep. The Mike linebacker has to fly over the top if he wants to get to the jet sweep (Diagram #11). If

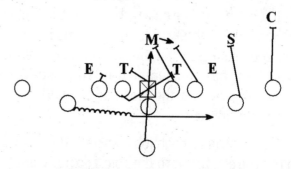

Diagram #11. Jet-Sweep Trap

he goes too fast, we run the fullback trap behind him. It is the same blocking as the other trap, but a different look for the defense.

If you run the veer package with the midline, you must have an effective play-action series out of your running game. If you have no play-action passing game, you will have safeties playing three yards off the line of scrimmage. We cannot block them all. We established a couple of play-action passes to help us out.

The first pass is off the jet sweep. It is a simple pass (Diagram #12). We take the playside slot and slip him up the field. The safeties get anxious when they see the flat motion by the slotback and want to stop the play. They commit to the sweep, and the slot slips up the seam behind the safety.

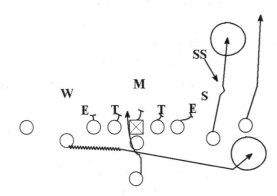

Diagram #12. Jet-Sweep Pass

In man coverage, if the quarterback fakes the ball to the jet motion and drops to throw, he has another option. The slot running the jet motion gets lost almost every time. If the safety picks up the playside slot, generally the jet motion is open.

The next pass is the inside veer pass (Diagram #13). For the pass to be effective, it must look like the run. The quarterback steps at five o'clock, steps second to first, and plants. He shifts his weight and has to clear. He has to create separation from the line of scrimmage. It is tough to do but the quarterback has to give the run pursuit time to clear. The wide receiver has to get wide and close to the sideline to pull the corner wide in his third.

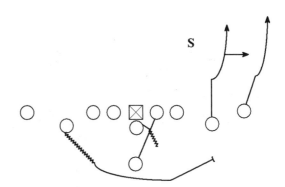

Diagram #13. Inside-Veer Pass

The slotback works off the strong safety. If he gets flat and sits down, the slot finds the window and looks back. If the strong safety overcommits, the slot goes up the seam. He has to stay out of the middle and stay wide in the seam. It is important for the split receiver to occupy the corner and not let him fall back on the slot.

What makes me mad is the corner coming off the split receiver and making a play on a receiver that should be open. If they have good spacing on their patterns, it is the quarterback's decision where to go with the ball.

It is easier to throw against three defenders. Having an option that works allows you to throw the football more.

Thank you. That was awesome. I got through it.

SCREENS AND THE QUICK PASSING GAME

Fayetteville High School, Arkansas

Thank you. I feel there are 10 keys to being a successful head coach. Football is a game of numbers. To be successful you must get into your school and:

- Get the players out for the team. You cannot rely on players simply coming out for the team. You must recruit them.
- Teach the fundamentals of the game. The success of any program depends on the teaching that goes on within your practices. Everything starts with fundamentals. When things go wrong, you must return to the fundamentals of the game.
- Get good assistant coaches and let them coach. Trust your coaches and let them contribute to your program.
- Get your players to believe in your system.
- Have a positive attitude with your staff and players.
- Give and demand effort and concentration.
- Make and enforce rules to govern your team. Every successful program has strong disciplinary structure.
- Study film of your opponent and make sure you respect every opponent. Upsets occur when a team takes the opponent for granted.
- Evaluate your players daily and weekly.
- Coach and teach every drill in practice and every play in the game.

Each day before we go to practice we make sure our players understand the importance of respecting every opponent we play. We want them to play hard each day. They have to play hard every play. When we play a game, we never look at the scoreboard. We want to play as hard as we can and the scoreboard will take care of itself.

Offensive Goals
- Win.
- Score 24 points.
- Gain 400 total yards.
- Allow no turnovers.
- Allow no sacks.
- Have no unforced penalties.
- Have no drive-ending penalties.
- Make two passes over 30 yards.
- Make three runs over 20 yards.
- Make five or more big plays or cockroach blocks.

We have an offensive philosophy that is important to the success of our offense. Our offense at Fayetteville High School is designed to spread the defense, control the number of defenders in the box, and limit what coverage the defense can run. We want that ability whether we align in an empty, one-back, or two-back set. The no-huddle aspect of our offense gives us the ability to see how the defense aligns. It allows us to get the proper play signaled that has the best chance to succeed. We take what the defense gives us.

Controlling the tempo is another big advantage of running the no-huddle attack. Having the ability to speed the game up or slow the game down allows us to play at the speed we desire and makes the defense have to adjust. There are a number of reasons and advantages for running the no-huddle scheme.

The offense is fun for the players as well as the coaches. When you run this type of offense, you are never out of the game. We have the ability to score quickly. There is no need to change the offense in "must-score situations." The scheme gives us the ability to get more snaps per game. We averaged 62 snaps per game last year. When you play this type of offense, it increases the number of players participating in the game. We play about 19 players each game in our offensive scheme.

Because the offense allows us to change plays at the line of scrimmage, we are always in a good play. This scheme makes it hard for opponents to simulate in practice. Because of that fact, it takes more time for the opponent to prepare for us. It gets the defensive coordinator out of his comfort zone.

Because we do not huddle, the defense cannot regroup after plays and communicate. We have the ability to get all of our skilled players involved with the game.

We are a no-huddle offense about 90 percent of the time. We have three ways to communicate with our players. The first and most common way is a simple verbal call from the sidelines. The quarterback comes to the line and verbally calls the play. We change all our terms and vocabulary each year to keep teams from reading what we do.

The second way is physically signaling the play into the game. The receivers, backs, and quarterback know our hand signals. The quarterback calls the blocking assignment for the linemen when he comes to the line. When you use signals, they must be simple, efficient, and easy to understand and comprehend.

The third system we use is the wristbands. We have used this system for the past five years. I think it is the best system for us. We have 120 plays on our wristbands. There are 60 to the right and 60 to the left. It works for us and allows us to use the check-with-me automatics.

With this type of offense, you can control the tempo of the game. When we run our regular offense, we snap the ball with 5 to 10 seconds left on the clock. When we add the word "dog" to our call, we get into check-with-me calls at the line of scrimmage. The next thing we can do is add the

word "peso" to our call. Everyone on our team knows the call given at the line of scrimmage is a dummy call. The quarterback comes to the line and barks a cadence. If no one on the defense jumps, he steps back and recalls the play.

If we need to speed up the tempo, we give a hurry-hurry call and snap the ball on the first sound. The last thing we do is called "swarm." We use this call to slow the game down. We get in a huddle five yards from the line of scrimmage. The quarterback calls the play, breaks the huddle, and runs the play. Any time we huddle, almost 99 percent of the time, it is a check-with-me call.

We want a balance in our offense. It may not necessarily be 50/50 run/pass, but we want to be able to run and pass with equal effectiveness so we can take what the defense gives us.

We cannot install our passing game in one week. We work on our passing game starting in January. We commit the time and the players give their time to develop what we do in the passing game. We rep this offense so much by August we can run it with a great deal of efficiency. We do not put the offense in during August practice; we rep it. We average 28 passes per game. Twenty of the 28 passes are safe passes. They are of the quick-pass variety. We do not put ourselves in a position to drop back in a five-step passing game. We are a man-protection team, which is hard to execute in a five-step game. We get rid of the ball quickly and into the hands of the playmakers.

In our formations, we give letters to the receivers and backs in the set. The ends are X and Y, with the Y into the strongside and X to the weakside. The A-back is a slotback and the C-receiver is the flanker. The A and C are the slot receivers with A going to the X-receiver side and C going to the Y-receiver side. The B-back is the tailback. If we go to the three-by-one set, the X-end is to the one-receiver side. The A-receiver, C-receiver, and Y-end are to the other side.

We adjust the formations to suit the need of our offense. In our formation, the C and Y go together.

The C-receiver is the slot receiver and the Y-end is the split end. If we want the C-receiver on the line of scrimmage and the Y-end off the line, we say flop. That way we can use all four of our wide receivers in motion if we want. That gives us the flexibility to throw to any one of the receivers on any screen play.

We call our passes using a passing tree. We have two types of trees. We have a number tree and a word tree. On the number tree, the odd numbers are the inside routes and the even numbers are the outside routes (Diagram #1). The zero is the speed-out cut. The 1 route is the stop-curl route at six yards. The 2 route is a 10-yard comeback. The 3 route is a four-step slant. The 4 route is a 15-yard out pattern. The 5 route is a 12- to 15-yard dig pattern. The 6 cut is a 12- to 22-yard flag. The 7 route is a 8- to 10-yard post pattern. The 8 pattern is a six-yard arrow route. The 9 pattern is a fade-seam pattern.

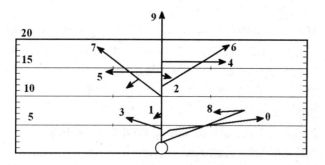

Diagram #1. Number Passing Tree

In addition to the number tree, we use a word tree (Diagram #2). We use the word tree to tag number routes. The under route is a two- to six-yard crossing route. When we run the Whip, the receiver works off the linebacker. A space route is a 6- to 10-yard crossing route used to find holes in the coverage. The cross pattern is a 10- to 16-yard

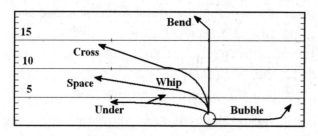

Diagram #2. Word Tree

crossing route. The bend is a two-deep seam route, bent away from the safety. The bubble route is the slot-flare pattern used in the bubble screen.

Our passing game starts with our quick passes. We start with the hitches. We run that pattern at three yards. On our wristband, we add the word quick plus a letter. This may be play 30 on the wristband. On the linemen's band it says "quick" and nothing else. They know it is a quick pass and their rule is to cut the defenders at the line of scrimmage. The letter added to the call is the receiver that gets the ball. If the quarterback calls quick A, the pass is a hitch thrown to the A-receiver.

An example of the hitch pattern is gun left flop, B lucky, quick C. The left formation is our trips set left with the Y as the outside receiver and the C-receiver and A-receiver in the slot. The C-receiver is the outside slot and the A-receiver is the inside slot. However, the word flop means the Y-end in his alignment is inside the C-receiver (Diagram #3). The B lucky is motion left into the set by the tailback. The widest receiver not catching the ball blocks the corner. The inside receiver blocks the nearest second-level player. The quarterback catches the ball and throws to the C-receiver. If the called letter is off the line of scrimmage, he takes two steps up and one back to catch the ball. If the called number is on the line of scrimmage, he takes one step up and two steps back. He catches the ball and reads the blocks.

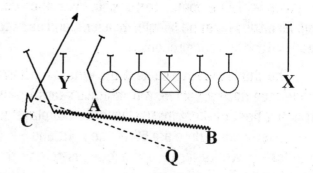

Diagram #3. Hitch

To call the bubble pass, we use rio/lobo and a letter. The linemen run a zone protection scheme toward the direction called. Rio is to the right and lobo is to the left. We throw the ball to the lettered receiver. An example of the bubble screen is doubles gun, C lucky, lobo C (Diagram #4). The formation is a double slot. The C lucky call brings the C-receiver in motion left. The outside receiver blocks the corner. The inside receiver blocks the most dangerous man. It will be the outside linebacker or the safety.

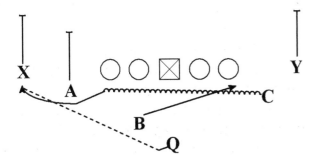

Diagram #4. Bubble

The B-back runs a token fake to the opposite side of the bubble. The quarterback catches the ball and throws the pass. He does not worry about the fake to the B-back. The aiming point is a foot in front of the chest of the receiver. The receiver bellies back and starts forward aiming for the inside leg of the outside receiver. We want six yards out of this play. The receiver gets six yards on the sideline before he makes his cut.

Along with the bubble screen, we run the snag routes (Diagram #5). We run the B-back in motion to the three-receiver side. The outside receiver runs a snag. The snag pattern is a hairpin out route. The inside slot runs a stick or choice route on the inside linebacker. The outside slot sits down in the first open space he can find. The B-back runs the bubble pattern.

The quarterback reads the linebacker. If he comes up on the bubble, the quarterback throws the snag pattern. If the linebacker stays back on the

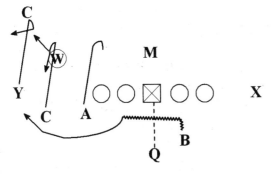

Diagram #5. Snag

snag pattern, the quarterback throws the bubble to the B-back.

We call the three-step pass Ray. If we call Ray 93 (Diagram #6), Ray means three-step pass and 93 designates the routes. The term designates the protection scheme. It is a slide protection toward the 3 technique. Our left blocking scheme is Larry. To the backside, we block man-to-man protection with the back blocking the backside B gap.

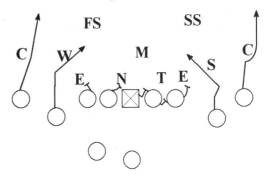

Diagram #6. Ray 93

The five-step drop is the next pattern. On the wristband, the term is "blast" with numbers or names. Our pass patterns have both numbers and words to designate the patterns we run.

We have a sprint-out scheme in our passing game. We call the patterns with numbers or names and a direction call for the sprint. We use the terms rocket or laser to designate the sprint-out and the direction. The line protection is a zone protection toward the direction call. If we have a back in the backfield, he blocks away from the flow. He does not aggressively go to the backside and block the end. He filters to the backside and picks up anything that seeps through. If we add the word boss to the play, the back goes to the frontside and helps the tackle with his block.

When we run our sprint-out, we can call numbers or pro names. This call comes from a left formation. We call rocket (Diagram #7), which is the sprint-out pass right. The play is razor boss 10. The formation is a trips set to the left. The razor call brings the A-receiver in motion to the right. The boss call tells the B-back to help the tackle on his block. The 10 pattern is a curl route by the outside receiver and a flat route by the inside receiver. The

X-end runs a curl to the inside at about 12 yards. The A-receiver runs the flat route at five yards. The backside receivers always run a drag by the inside receiver and a post by the outside receiver. This is a full sprint-out for the quarterback. The boss call tells the quarterback there is no protection from the backside if he pulls up.

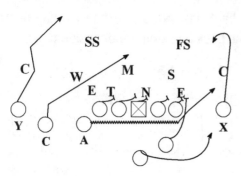

Diagram #7. Rocket

The second way to call the sprint-out is using pro football names. When we use the pro name, we flood a zone with receivers. This cuts down on the verbiage for the quarterback. This particular play is right rocket boss Charger (Diagram #8). It is our base play and my favorite. The outside receiver runs a stop route at eight yards. The outside slot receiver blows the top off the coverage. He is our best and fastest receiver. The third receiver runs a corner route at 12 to 22 yards.

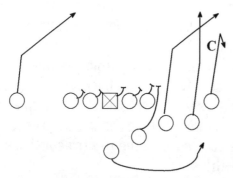

Diagram #8. Charger

The quarterback reads the corner. If the corner drops, the quarterback throws immediately to the stop route. If the corner bites on the stop route, we throw the corner route.

The next play is Cardinal (Diagram #9). People call this a pick play, but we do not run picks. We like this play on the goal line. This formation is a double slot. We run rocket with "rock" motion. Rock sends

the A-receiver into motion to the playside. The play is rocket boss Cardinal. The outside receiver runs a crack-flag pattern. The inside receiver runs a Whip route and the A-receiver runs a flat route. The quarterback reads high/low from flag to flat route.

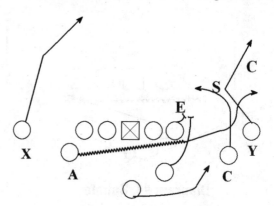

Diagram #9. Cardinal

The Chief route is also on of our favorite routes to throw. The call is laser boss Chief (Diagram #10). The outside receiver runs a curl or post depending on the coverage. If he sees two-deep coverage, he runs a post at the safety's inside shoulder. If he sees three-deep coverage, he runs the curl. The number-two receiver runs an out-and-up pattern. The third receiver runs the speed out.

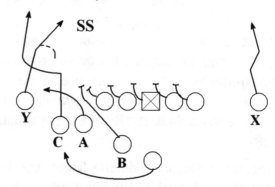

Diagram #10. Chief

The last thing is a Packers game. We run this out of our bunch set. This particular call is rocket boss Packer (Diagram #11). The outside receiver runs a shallow route across the field. The second receiver runs a flag-curl. The inside receiver runs the flat route. The quarterback sprints right and looks for the curl or flat routes.

If we add the letter "O" to the call, that designates a play-action pass. The example is red

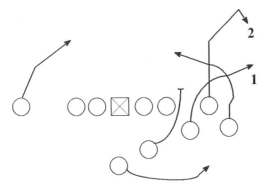

Diagram #11. Packers

Bama O-77 (Diagram #12). Red designates right, Bama is the isolation play, O is the play-action pass, and 77 is the pattern. We fake the isolation play to the right and throw a double-post pass. We can use any running play we have in our play-action scheme.

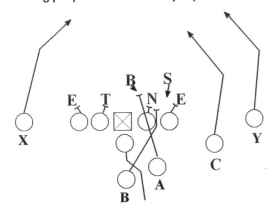

Diagram #12. Play-Action

The R series is something that I picked up from Mac Brown of the University of Texas. This is probably one of the best things we do. This gives us a chance to get five receivers into the pattern. We are sound in the protection scheme and the quarterback gets a chance to do a bit of running in this series. In the R series, all the receivers run the same route. If the pattern is R-9, all the receivers run a takeoff and the linemen use a man-protection scheme. We can use a tag in this series to get an individual route. We call "R-9, C shallow." All receivers run the vertical route, except the C-receiver, who runs the shallow.

We used this in one of our games this year. Our best receiver matched up on a linebacker. The receiver was a 4.4 40-yard dash player, and the linebacker was about 5.0 for the 40. That was a total mismatch and we took advantage of it. We ran everyone deep and threw underneath to the mismatch. By calling the tag pass, it takes the pressure off the quarterback to find a receiver. We throw to the tagged receiver and there is no read.

We throw the bootleg off any of our running plays. To run the bootleg we add a certain word such as boot to tell the line and receivers what to do. An example is red Bama boot (Diagram #13). That tells our receivers opposite the call they have to beat somebody. The number-one receiver runs a 25-yard comeback pattern. The number-two receiver runs a shallow into the flat area. The number-three receiver runs the drag or Whip route and the number-four receiver runs the post. The number-three receiver could be the fullback or tight end coming from the callside. Those are the rules for the bootleg pass. The formations and the personnel groupings change, but the rules remain the same.

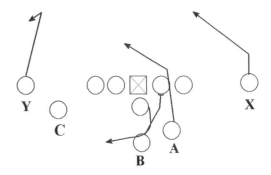

Diagram #13. Bootleg

We run the shovel pass two or three times per game (Diagram #14). We like to run it off our speed sweep look with the flanker coming in motion. We run the shovel underneath to our slot with the counter-blocking scheme. We usually send the playside tackle up on the linebacker and kick out with the pulling guard. If we call red spade set, the tackle pass sets on the defensive end and blocks him upfield. The pulling guard turns up on the linebacker.

In our screen package, we have every screen possible. We run the sideline, tunnel, middle, double, and the tunnel screen with a hook and lateral. We run every screen known to man. When we call the screen play, we call the type and letter of the screen receiver. We practice our screen package every day for about 10 minutes.

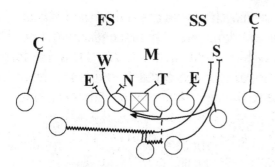

Diagram #14. Shovel

If we run the sideline screen, we add the word "smoke" and the letter B. We like to run the sideline screen from the two-by-two set. The call is red double gun, B smoke (Diagram #15). We are in a double-wide slot with the fullback sitting to the right of the quarterback. The playside outside receiver runs a square-in at five yards and cracks the inside linebacker. The playside inside receiver runs a post at eight yards and blocks the safety. The playside tackle blocks two counts and pulls down the line of scrimmage and blocks the corner. The playside guard blocks two counts and pulls down the line of scrimmage and blocks the strong safety.

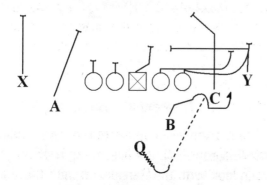

Diagram #15. Sideline Screen

The center blocks two counts, pulls, and picks up the backside linebacker. The backside linemen block their pass responsibilities. The backside receivers stalk the defensive backs to their side. The B-back sets up for two counts, gives a little ground, catches the ball, and follows the guard and tackle's block. His blocking assignment is the defensive end. He makes a poor block on him and releases behind him. The quarterback takes a drop looking through the goal post. He fades to the playside and delivers the ball.

If we want to throw the middle screen, we use the term mud to designate the middle screen. The call is double gun, C mud (Diagram #16). The outside receiver to the playside stalk blocks on the corner. The playside tackle invites the defensive end upfield and blocks him.

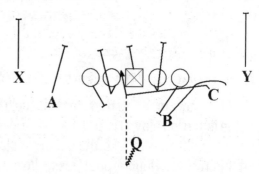

Diagram #16. Middle Screen

The playside guard holds for two counts and blocks the number-two defender from the sideline. When we designate defender from the sideline, we start the count from the playside and work across the field. This applies to all counts and defenses (Diagram #17). The center holds for two counts and blocks the number-three defender from the sideline. The backside guard holds for two counts and blocks the number-four defender from the sideline. The backside tackle blocks the defensive end to the outside. The backside inside receiver blocks the force defender. The outside receiver stalks the corner and blocks him.

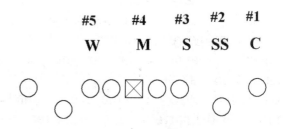

Diagram #17. Blocking Count

The C-receiver holds for one count and goes to set up behind the center. He catches the ball and turns upfield. The B-back fakes the smoke screen. The quarterback shows the smoke screen and drifts back and throws to the receiver behind the center.

We start working with our receivers in February. We work them hard each month and teach them how to catch. We will do countless number of reps on catching. Every one of our receivers will be able to catch. Right now, we have 18 players that are decent receivers. They can all run routes, catch, and have good speed.

In March, we start teaching our receivers the route tree. We go through all our number routes and then go to the word tree. Each player learns the route and word tree in the month of March.

In April, we do our inter-squad seven-on-seven practice. Right now, we are working hard on how to run routes and read secondary coverage. We do a tremendous amount of teaching during the months of April and May.

We have good receivers, and on any given night, any of them can be the receiver of the night. When we find mismatches in the defense, we take advantage of them.

In our sprint protection, we had some trouble with pressure on our quarterback from the backside. To solve our problem, we put the B-back to the backside to block any pressure seeping through the line. He faked the counter and cut off the backside. We added a screen off this action called banjo (Diagram #18). The guard and tackle to the backside hold for two counts and get out on the screen. They block it like the sideline screen. We told the backside receiver to run off the coverage. When we run this play, we maximum protect the quarterback.

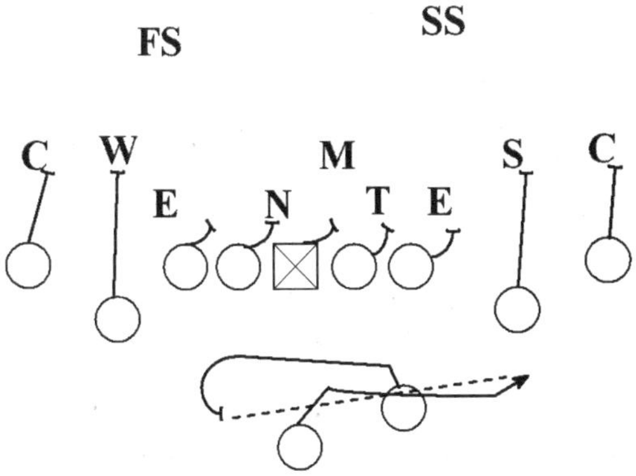

Diagram #18. Banjo

We can throw the ball to any receiver, as I have said previously. We can put the A-receiver in motion to the backside, keep the B-back to the sprintside, and let him help block on the outside force. We throw the banjo screen to the A-receiver.

The next screen we use is the tunnel screen. The call is gun right red, C Tommy (Diagram #19). The formation is a right trips set. We throw the tunnel screen to one of the widest receivers in the set. In this case, we could throw the ball to Y or C. When we call C Tommy, the C-receiver is the screen receiver. The Y-receiver stalks the corner and blocks him. The A-receiver blocks the man over the C-receiver.

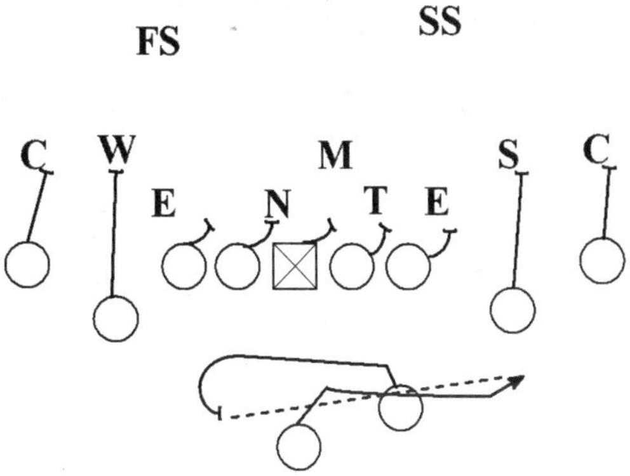

Diagram #19. Tommy

The playside tackle invites the defensive end upfield and blocks him. The playside guard holds for two counts and blocks the third defender from the sideline. The center holds for two counts and blocks the forth defender from the sideline. The backside guard holds for two counts and blocks the fifth defender from the sideline. The backside tackle invites the defender upfield and blocks him. The backside receiver stalks the corner aligned on him.

The B-back fakes opposite the screen and goes to block the safety. The first thing he looks for is a blitz by a linebacker. The quarterback fakes to the B-back, drops three steps, and delivers the call to the receiver.

The tunnel screen was a big play for us in past years. This past season, for whatever reason, it was not a good play and we did not throw it more than five or six times all year.

The next screen is our double screen (Diagram #20). Two years ago we only ran this play to the left. This year we ran it both ways. We run this play from our deuce right. That formation puts the A-receiver and the B-back on either side of the quarterback in the backfield. The Y-end and C-receiver are to the right and the X-end splits left. The Y-end runs off the coverage and stalks blocks when he recognizes screen. The number-two receiver to the right runs a six-yard pattern over the ball and sits down.

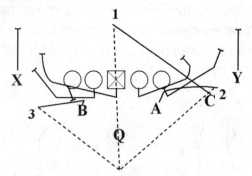

Diagram #20. Double Screen

The right tackle blocks two counts and pulls down the line of scrimmage and leads upfield. The right guard blocks for two counts and pulls behind the right tackle. The center blocks for three counts and pulls behind the left guard. The left guard blocks for three counts and pulls down the line of scrimmage and leads upfield. The left tackle invites the rush upfield and blocks him. The A-receiver sets up to the right, holds for two counts, and gets to the outside for the two-count screen. The B-back sets up behind the left guard, holds for three counts, and gets to the outside for the three-count screen.

The quarterback is in the shotgun. He takes the snap and drops three steps. He looks for the number-two receiver over the center as his first option. If the defense covers the six-yard pattern, the quarterback goes to the two-count screen first and the three-count screen next. We have never thrown the three-count screen. We never get that far in our progression.

The next play is our tunnel screen with a hook-and-lateral scheme in the play (Diagram #21). We align in a right formation or trips formation to the right. The coaching point when running this play is not to get in a hurry. We flop the set to put the C-receiver on the line of scrimmage and the Y-end off the line of scrimmage. We run the tunnel screen to the Y-end. The C-receiver invites the corner to get under his block and hooks him to the inside. The A-receiver does the same thing.

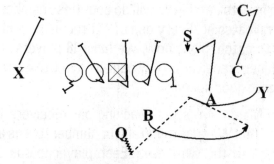

Diagram #21. Hook and Lateral

The B-back has to time his move. He sets up to block and releases on a flare route to the outside. The Y-end catches the tunnel screen and laterals the ball to the B-back going to the outside. We ran the play four times this year and scored on it twice.

We have a 40-play script we use in our practice session during the week. We have 20 running plays and 20 passing plays on this script. From that list, we pick the plays that go into our game plan for Friday night. We have two quarterbacks, two running backs, and two A-receivers we play. They have different abilities and strengths and the plays reflected on the call sheet are for their respective skills. On the sheet, we list the package, play, wristband number, quarterback, B-back, A-receiver, and number of touches by each player.

The important column for me is the number of touches each player receives. I want certain players to get at least 10 touches on the football. That keeps everyone involved and makes sure the ball gets into the hands of your playmakers.

The three-step route is a Ray call. That means slide protection for the line. If we need to slide left, the center calls Larry. The B-back blocks opposite the line slide in the B gap. This particular set is a jumbo strong (Diagram #22), which is a power I set

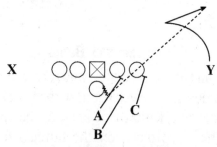

Diagram #22. Ray Whip

to the strongside. We call this play Ray Whip. It is a one-receiver route by the outside receiver.

The next formation is a double formation. The call is Ray 9 space (Diagram #23). We did not make a color call with the play selection. Therefore, the frontside and backside receivers run mirror routes. The outside receivers run the 9 route and the inside receivers run the space route. This is a goal-line play. The outside receivers both run a fade route into the corners of the end zone. The inside receivers run a space route. Space routes do what the name says they do. The receiver runs inside looking for an open space to sit down between linebackers.

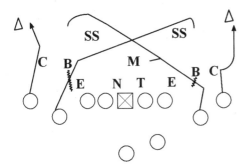

Diagram #23. 9 Space

If we put a color call into the play, it changes the patterns of the front and backsides. If the call is red Ray, the receiver to the right runs the first two calls and the receivers to the left run the last two. The call is 9 space Whip 7 (Diagram #24). The outside receiver to the right runs the 9 route and the inside receiver runs the space route. To the backside, the outside receiver runs the 7 route, and the inside receiver runs the Whip route. The sequences of the calls run from the outside of the callside to the outside of the backside.

I have tried to give you everything we run. We sprint-out with numbers and pro names. We can do the same thing with our five-step game. We can use the numbers or the pro names. An example of a five-step pass is right blast Chief.

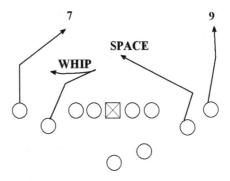

Diagram #24. Color Call

We have a choice route that we run (Diagram #25). We can do it from the bunch set. The outside receiver runs the clear out. The number-two receiver works off the inside linebacker and the third receiver runs the flat route. We tell our number-two receiver, as he comes inside to work on the linebacker, to stay calm.

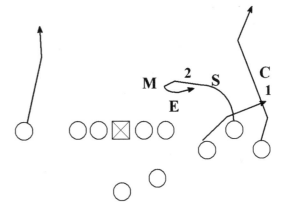

Diagram #25. Choice

The quarterback looks to the flat pattern first. There is no need for the number-two receiver to get separation from the linebacker until the quarterback looks his way. If he gains separation and the quarterback is looking to the flat, he wastes a move. He wants to escape from the linebacker, when the quarterback looks his way.

Thank you. I hope you have good luck next season.

WING-T BLOCKING TECHNIQUES

Allegany High School, Maryland

Thank you very much. It is good to be here today. Allegany High School is a small AAA high school in Maryland. When the enrollment qualifications change from time to time, we are an AA school. We decided our best chance for success came in the form of the wing-T offense. The problem we faced each year was finding offense linemen with the skills to play in the wing-T.

It is a great offense, but you must have linemen with the skill to play in the offense. Our base formation is a wing formation with a split end opposite the wing (Diagram #1). We set the halfback to the side of the split end. At the split end position, we can take a small player or a tall player and isolate the corner.

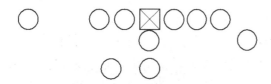

Diagram #1. Base Formation

When I came to Allegany, they were running a two-tight-end formation. I had enough trouble finding one tight end, let alone two. I could not find a second quality tight end, so I replaced him with a wide receiver. The second reason we went to the split-end set was the plays we could run from that set.

For the linemen, we wanted to keep the offense as simple as possible. We ran the base plays from the wing-T. We ran the 100 and 900 series plays. The combinations of plays are plays run to the right and left of the formation. The base plays are 121/929 buck sweep, 124/926 guard trap, 187/983 belly, 981/189 belly pitch, 149/941 quick pitch, 182/988 down, and 929/121 waggle. The 121 play is the buck

sweep run to the right outside the tight end. The holes are numbered from right to left in sequential order from 1 to 9. The off-tackle hole to the right is the 2 hole. Sixteen plays in the offense are all the linemen have to learn.

We wanted to make it simpler. If we flipped the strongside and weakside of our offensive line, the linemen would only have eight plays to learn. The only question we had was: would we be too predictable? We simplified the learning process for the linemen. However, they had to increase their techniques if they were going to play left and right.

We had one guard who was quick, but did not have great size. We had another lineman with a lot of heart, but we have a hard time getting him on the field. We had to play him somewhere and hide him. We had two good athletes playing in the offensive line. We play them together on the weakside of the line and they do most of the pulling and cutoff work.

We break our offensive line down into five positions. We have a strongside guard and tackle and a weakside guard and tackle. Of course, the center is the fifth position in the offensive line.

Before we talk about our personnel, let me draw up the buck sweep (Diagram #2). We align with the tight end to the right side of the offense.

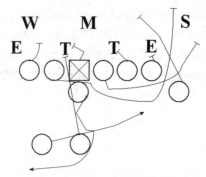

Diagram #2. Buck Sweep

The defense is a standard 4-3 defense. The tight end blocks the man on him. The strong tackle blocks down on the 3-technique defensive tackle. The strong guard pulls and kicks out the first thing to show off the edge.

The weakside guard pulls flat past the center and bubbles back past the strong-guard position. He turns up outside the tight end and seals inside.

Our strong tackle on the buck sweep blocks down 90 percent of the time. He does not have to learn to pull or trap anyone. The player you play in this position can be big player who does not have good feet. When you are one lineman short, this is the position where you can put that questionable lineman. On our power play, he will double-team with the guard or tight end depending on the alignment of the defensive tackle. We can play a questionable player in this position because he is always blocking down or getting help.

The strong guard can be the bigger, but slower, of the two guards. His job on the buck sweep is to pull and kick out the first thing that shows off the edge. He is closer to the hole and does not have to worry about the fullback. He does not have to worry about getting in front of the back.

The weakside guard has to be quick and agile. He has to be quick enough to beat the back to the hole, and agile enough to seal back inside. He has to pull past the center flat, bubble back, and seal the inside. He does not have to be big because he will not kick out anybody. I like to steal fullbacks from the running back coach and make guards out of them.

The second play is the quick pitch (Diagram #3). We motion the wingback or trade the tight end to the weakside to seal the defensive end. The weakside tackle pulls and kicks out the support player. The weakside guard pulls and executes the same technique as he did on the buck sweep. He seals the inside scrape by the linebacker. The quarterback reverses out and pitches the ball to the halfback. The halfback on his first step works for depth before he gets width.

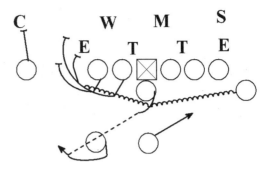

Diagram #3. Quick Pitch

The problem we have seen with the tackle pull is the way the defense plays his pull. The defensive coaches have taught the defender as he reads the pull of the tackle, to follow him. Therefore, the weakside guard may not get off the first level with his block. He may have to block the defender following the pulling tackle.

Coach Jeff Kinderson

The first series you will see is the buck sweep. The strongside guard looks for the player to kick out. The weakside guard pulls and keeps his head to the inside of the strong guard looking to turn up on the kick-out block. He looks for the first linebacker to show from the inside.

Most people try to attack the buck sweep before it gets started. The weakside tackle has to do a good job of not allowing any penetration from the backside as the guard pulls. The fullback and the weakside tackle have to protect the edge from the backside.

The tight end rule tells him to down block. If he has a defender on his inside eye, he down blocks on him. If the defender aligns outside, he lets him go. If the defender aligns inside and jumps to the outside, the tight end stays with him and blocks him outside.

The strong guard has to get depth on his pull to clear the down block of the strongside tackle. The center steps playside on his first step and checks to the backside. We step the center to the playside and let the fullback fill for the backside pulling guard.

The blocking techniques for the quick pitch are important. The weakside tackle opens at a 90-

degree angle. That gives him a better angle as he turns upfield. His job is to kick out the first opposite-colored jersey that shows. The scouting report will give him an idea, but most likely it will be the outside linebacker. If the corner gets off the split end's block, the tackle blocks him.

The weakside guard opens parallel to the line of scrimmage and looks to get underneath. We call the technique by the tackle and guard "jab and uppercut." The tackle does the jab and the guard does the uppercut. The guard's job is to seal any penetration. That may occur quickly if a defender has followed the pull of the weakside tackle. The guard cannot allow anyone to cross his face. He may not get to the linebacker.

The tackle always has the kick-out block on the outside. However, if the defender does not come outside, the tackle can seal him to the inside. Having the tackle open so wide in his first step gives him wide vision of what is on the field. We stress those things in our individual drills.

The wingback comes in motion and his job is to seal the last man on the line of scrimmage. That is generally the defensive end. The fullback takes a step away from the playside.

Everyone thinks the motion is the key to direction of the ball. We run the motion toward the split end and quick pitch the ball to the tight-end side. The tight end takes the place of the wingback's seal on the end man and everything else is the same. If we do not bring the wingback in motion, and instead quick pitch toward the wing, the wingback and tight end block like the buck sweep.

Coach Tom Preaskorn

The diagrams are great, but if you do not block the play, it will not work. When we teach the plays to the offensive line, we break the teaching down into three phases.

In the army, they say every soldier has to be a foot soldier first. Before he does other things, he has to learn how to carry the rifle. We feel the same thing holds true of football. Every player has to be a blocker first. The first phase in teaching the block is shoulder skills. We take five to ten minutes every day in doing these skills.

The next phase is small-group drill, to perfect the plays we want to run. We work on their footwork and depth from their stance. We want the head in the hole. We spend 15 to 20 minutes each day in the small-group drills. In many of our blocking schemes, we do not incorporate the tight end right away. We use the center, two guards, and two tackles; we work within these offensive drills.

I am going to start out talking about the short trap. We work against both the odd and even front. In the drill, we work with the center and two guards (Diagram #4). Everyone's first step is a 45-degree angle. The playside guard pulls at a 45-degree angle at the center. The center steps at a 45-degree angle to the backside for the cutoff block. The pulling guard comes off the hip of the center and stays low throughout his block. If the trap is wider, we make a call to the lineman to let him know he has a longer pull, but his steps never change from the first step.

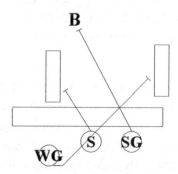

Diagram #4. Trap Drill

When we work the waggle and buck sweep, we work both guards at the same time. On the waggle, the steps for the guards have to be the same, done at the same time. On the buck sweep, the weakside guard stays flatter until he passes the center. After that moment, their steps become similar.

If the guard has to block the corner, we do not attack him. We make the corner make the decision as to what he has to do. If you have two cars going 55 miles per hour at each other, they get there sooner. We get in an area five yards outside the tight end. He gets on this track upfield. He lets the corner make the decision to attack.

The buck sweep and waggle drills are primarily the same drills (Diagram #5). The steps of the guards are the same. They step with a 45-degree angle. We emphasize staying low at all times. We want the knee to the chest as they pull. The guard crossing the center has to get a 90-degree bubble step as he passes the center. The onside guard takes a 90-degree step as he pulls. It is the jab and uppercut using the guards.

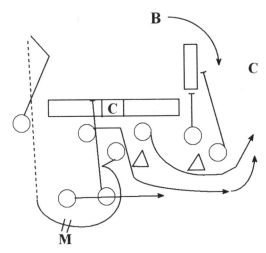

Diagram #5. Waggle / Back-Sweep Drill

Before we do the drill, we take our striper machine and paint an area on the ground to mark our offensive line. The center is marked on the line and the guards align on the center. We bring the backs down along with the tight end and wingback. We have a stand-up dummy or player outside the tight end. In this drill, we set a cone in the playside center and guard gap parallel with the line of scrimmage and slightly behind the center. We set a second cone in position behind the offensive tackle off the line of scrimmage. This path is the route run by the guards as they pull.

The frontside guard is the jab and the backside guard is the uppercut. We can add a corner and linebacker to this drill. We want the linebacker to come hard into the C gap and scrape hard on the pulling guard. The buck sweep breaks down when you get penetration from the linebackers. The

backside pulling guard has to drop his shoulder, come back, and seal the linebacker scrapping from the inside.

We can bring the split end into the drill and let him run his waggle route. The quarterback fakes the buck, hands the ball to the halfback, and throws the ball to the split end on a waggle route. The quarterback hands the ball to the halfback and a manager give him another ball as he rolls in his waggle to throw to the split end.

That lets us incorporate the waggle and buck sweep into the same play. We work on the blocking of the buck sweep and the passing of the waggle. The tackles are not involved in the drill and can work on some other aspect of the game. I take them and let them work on their down-block and post-block techniques.

We do the same type of drill on the quick pitch (Diagram #6). We line the field with the striper. In the drill, we have the wingback, weakside guard, and tackle. We have the quarterback and the halfback. We have a dummy outside the offensive tackle and two dummy holders representing the inside linebacker and corner.

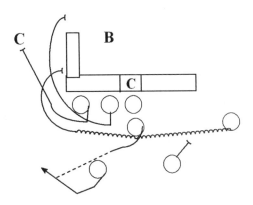

Diagram #6. Quick Pitch Drill

The wingback comes in motion and hooks the dummy inside. The weak tackle pulls and looks for the first thing to show outside. The guard does the same thing and starts to work upfield, hugging the block of the wingback. He is blocking anything scraping to the outside. As the guard pulls, he cannot let anything cross his face. If the linebacker comes through the B or the C gap, he seals on the linebacker. His overall responsible in the scheme of things is to control the linebacker.

We do these drills every day. We work the same drill with our strong tackle (Diagram #7). We align the tackle on the line of scrimmage with a cone on the line to represent the outside foot of the guard. The defender aligns on the cone. The tackle has to block down and prevent penetration by the defender. The defender tries to penetrate the gap and the tackle has to step, get his head across the defender, and prevent penetration.

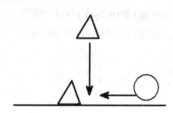

Diagram #7. Down Block

He is not a gifted athlete, but we work on it and work it hard. The thing that hurts the wing-T is penetration. If the defender gets penetration, all the timing of the play is thrown off. If the defender is a reader, the tackle steps at a 45-degree angle. However, if the defender is a penetrator, the tackle steps flat to the line of scrimmage. We do not care about a great block; we want to stop penetration. We work on that every day. We work on turning the hips and getting the chest on the thigh.

On the trap play, we had trouble with a defender in the A gap. If a defender aligned in the A gap or slanted into the A gap, our angle from the pulling guard was bad. For the guard to get an angle on an A-gap defender, he has to pull tight to the center. He has to put his head into the hip of the center. If the center does not get out of the way, it screws the trap up.

We want the trap blocker's hips to the sideline. We do not want to block downfield on a trap block. The first day you get your linemen in pulling drills, they probably look like ours. They pull with their chest up and the helmet out. We work hard to get the guards to rotate the hips and get the chest over the thigh. We work on the pull step every day, with

the chest over the thigh and exaggerating the arm movement.

Teams try to take the trap away. They do that by moving into the inside shoulder alignment of the playside guard (Diagram #8). It prevents the guard from getting across to the backside linebacker. In addition, it makes it hard on the trapper, because the angle is tight and close. We made a rule and called it Idaho. Instead of a 124 trap, it becomes a 123 trap, which is one hole wider.

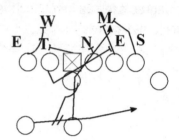

Diagram #8. Idaho

The guard blocks down on the inside shade, the tackle blocks across on the linebacker, and we trap outside the guard. We teach the fullback to read the pulling guard. The fullback comes down the midline and it does not matter which way he breaks. To combat that problem we can run the trap the other way with a backdoor trap. Instead of a 124, we run it in the 6 hole to the backside.

We run a lot of power plays. We run 32/38 power plays. Depending on what teams do, we run a 33/37 power play. That is moving in one gap. We had success this year even when we moved inside one hole. There will always be a double-team block on the 32/38 power. The strong tackle is always going to double-team with someone. It will be the guard or the tight end, depending on the alignment of the defense.

His rule is simple. If he is covered, his double-team is with the tight end. If he is uncovered, he double-teams down with the guard. If the tackle has a man in front of him, his first step is straight ahead. He steps straight ahead and slides his head to the inside. That allows the tight end to come down low on the hip, and ride the defender down inside.

If the tackle is uncovered, he has the down block and the guard steps straight ahead and gets his head inside. Since the number-one block for the strongside tackle is the down block, he should be able to execute that block.

On the 32 power, the tight end blocks inside on the linebacker (Diagram #9). The wingback turns out on the corner. In this case, the tackle double-teams with the guard on the 3-technique tackle. The center blocks back on the shade tackle to the weakside. The weakside guard pulls and turns up in the 2 gap. He is looking for the linebacker as he goes. The fullback kicks out at the off-tackle hole on the defensive end.

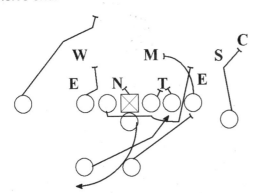

Diagram #9. 32 Power

We put the halfback in one-step motion toward the fullback, which allows him to get downhill on his path to the hole. We could put him in motion from the slot into a position of the back in an I formation and really get him going downhill. He takes the ball and follows the pulling guard.

We can run many passes, but this one we run off the power play. This is the 132 power pass (Diagram #10). When the defense sees the one-step motion by the halfback, they think power play. The fullback blocks the defensive end and the halfback fakes the running play. The wingback releases inside at the defensive end and back out to the flat. He tries to make the play look like the buck sweep or the power play.

The tight end releases inside and back out to the flag. The split end runs a post cut through the middle safety. The quarterback fakes the ball to the halfback, goes to his drop, and reads the corner. If

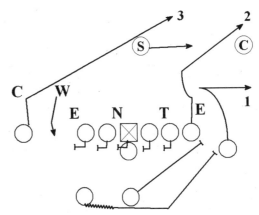

Diagram #10. 132 Power Pass

the corner bites on the flat route by the wingback, the quarterback hits the flag over the corner's head.

If the corner drops into the third, the quarterback takes the wingback in the flat. If the safety takes the tight end going to the flag, the split end who is running down the middle of the field is open. This is a good play against a cover 3.

The offensive line protects away from the playside of the play. The weakside tackle has the important block because he is responsible for anything coming off the edge. He kicks out and takes the widest rusher. The guard takes the next defender and so forth down the line. To the callside, we have the fullback and halfback blocking on the outside.

If the weakside tackle has a man over him and no one outside of him, he blocks the man on him. However, if there is someone outside of him, he has to block outside. The guard will block the man over him.

We run other formations, but still run the plays using the same philosophy. The weak guard knows that on the waggle play he never pulls across the center. He has to pull away from the center on the waggle play. That is an advantage of playing weak and strong positions in the offensive line.

We can shift the backs from one position to another. We have formations that align our backs at different positions. Whatever the defense wants to take away by alignment in one formation, we can get to it in another formation or a shift. The wing-T is versatile and has the ability to adjust.

Thank you very much.

ORGANIZATION AND MOTIVATION

Executive Director, Texas Coaches Association

It is a pleasure for me to be here. I am not going to be talking on X's and O's today. I am going to be talking about things that I consider very important. I have strong beliefs in our profession. I believe in what coaches do around the nation. I appreciate Dave Johnson inviting me to speak here. I have had some great days here and I have had time to get around this beautiful state. What a magnificent state. I even had good weather in my visit the last few days. My wife has been with me and we have really enjoyed this visit.

I am going to talk about some things that I believe to be extremely important to you as a coach, to our profession, and to our athletes. I am convinced there is no activity in our schools today that has any more carryover values for adult life than competitive athletics. Athletics are the last stronghold of discipline that we have on our campuses today. The leadership of the coaches has never been more important. I have always been proud to say I am a high school coach because of the people that make up the coaching profession. I have been fortunate to get to know a lot of quality people in this profession. I believe the majority of coaches whom I have met over the years are coaching for the right reasons. Those coaches have made our profession strong, and we appreciate them.

Over the years, we have heard comments like, "He coaches for the right reason." We hear this a lot about coaching. However, we need to ask this question. What is the right reason to coach? I have been the executive director of the Texas High School Coaches Association for the last five years. I left coaching to go with the THSCA. I have had the opportunity in the past several springs to talk with a group of college seniors each year from UTSA in San Antonio who have chosen to enter the coaching profession. One of the questions I ask those students is a question I believe every coach should answer for himself.

I ask the students these questions: why do you want to coach? What is your purpose of coaching? What is going to motivate you to get up every morning to go to work? I believe you must have a purpose and a passion for what you do to be successful in any profession. If a coach is getting up to go to work just to try to win football games, then I think his job is with a shallow purpose. If we are getting up and going to work because we feel we can change the lives of the young people we work with, I can see the purpose of the work. If I am going to work in the morning to try to turn the lives of young people in the right direction, then it is something I can feel proud about. It is something I can have a passion for.

I do not know of a profession that has a greater purpose than that of being a strong influence in a positive direction for young people. It is important that we believe in our kids. Many people say the kids of today are no good. Strange enough, people were saying the same thing about kids years ago. Kids are like all of us. They have a force within them to do good, and they have a force within them to do bad. What they need is positive leadership. They need someone who supports them, someone who disciplines them, and someone who encourages them.

In a society where there are so many broken homes, it is important that our young people have someone they can look up to, someone who sees the good in them, and someone who can bring out the good in them.

I believe we are in one of the greatest professions in the world. I believe coaches can be some of the most important people in our society. Think about it. We have been given the unique opportunity to work closely with hundreds of young people on almost a daily basis at a very teachable time in their lives. We have the opportunity to develop worthy values, knowledge of physical skills, and attitude traits. What a great purpose. What a great responsibility our profession carries with it.

Several years ago, I read an article in the *American Football Quarterly* by Sam Rutigliano. He was the former head coach for the Cleveland Browns, and later he coached at Liberty University in Virginia. He pointed out some statistics that really jumped out at me. I want to share those stats with you today:

> There are approximately 139,000 junior high, high school, and college coaches in America today. In a lifetime, each of us has an opportunity to impact 20,000 young men and women. The potential influential power in the coaching profession is unmatched.

I believe we have a great opportunity and a great responsibility to have a positive impact on our schools, our communities, and our society. I believe our young people of today, more than any other time in history, are begging for discipline. They are looking for love and direction. What we are doing with the hearts and souls of those young individuals is a lot more important than any physical skills we could teach them, or any physical development we can give them.

I believe the coach has two tasks. One of those tasks is major and the other task is minor. A minor task is in teaching the youth the techniques and skills of the game. Our major task is in the positive attitudes and character traits that we have an opportunity to teach. All too often, we get the relative importance two tasks mixed up.

I have no doubt that the proper attitude is the key to success. I believe the most important thing I can do as a coach, or a teacher can do for their students, or a parent can do for their children, is to teach them the importance of a proper mental attitude.

Let me share some things I have heard about attitude over the years. We use to try to teach these things in our classrooms. We tried to make sure we were getting some of these messages across to our kids. Here are some of the things I have heard about attitude over the years.

In America today, there are over 50,000 different types of schools that teach how to do anything and everything. They will teach us how to trim toenails and fingernails, how to operate heavy machinery, how to become a doctor, and how to become a lawyer. But there is not a single school in existence today that will teach how to be any better than mediocre unless we have the proper mental attitude.

I have also heard it said that as we undertake a project, our attitude is the most dominant factor of the success of that project. In short, our attitude is more important than our aptitude.

Several years ago there was a study done by Harvard University. That study revealed the fact that 85 percent of the reasons for success, accomplishments, and promotions out in the business world are because of our attitudes. Less than 15 percent of the reasons for success are related to our technical expertise.

My favorite approach to attitude is by Charles Swindoll. I think he hit the nail on the head when he talked about attitudes. Let me share it with you today.

Attitude
By Charles Swindoll

The longer I live, the more I realize the impact of attitude on life. Attitude, to me, is more important than facts. It is more important than the past, than education, than money, than circumstances, than failures, than successes, than what other people think, say, or do. It is more important than appearance, giftedness, or skill. It will make or break a company, a church, a home, a team. The remarkable thing is we have a choice every day regarding the attitude we embrace for that day. We cannot change our past. We cannot change the fact that people will act in a certain way. We cannot change the inevitable. The only thing we can do is play on the one string we have, and that is our attitude. I am convinced that life is 10 percent of what happens to me, and 90 percent how I react to it. And so it is with you. We are all in charge of our attitudes.

I have one additional thing that I want to share with you related to attitude. I saw this at a football clinic in Texas several years ago. The person that was giving the lecture was not talking about X's and O's. He was a motivational speaker and he was talking about being successful. He showed the details about a study from Stanford University. This is what he said.

If we want to move toward success, if we want to move toward our goals, we must have some of each ingredient on this chart of success goals (Diagram #1). He went on to say the key to success was to understanding the percentages needed for each of the following four areas:

- Knowledge
- Skills/Habits
- Innate ability
- Attitude

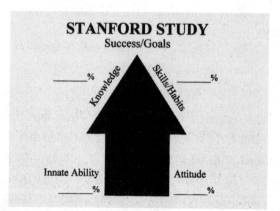

Diagram #1. Stanford Study – Success Goals

If you compare knowledge with skills and habits, innate ability with attitudes, you get an interesting result. What percentage of knowledge would you need, compared with skills and habits, to be successful (Diagram #2)? When the question was presented, I was thinking that one would need about 40 percent knowledge compared with about 60 percent skills and habits. I was way off on the numbers.

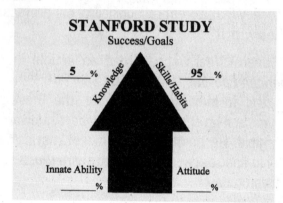

Diagram #2. Knowledge versus Skills and Habits

This was his explanation of the numbers. He said one only required 5 percent knowledge and 95 percent skills and habits. When he said that, it did not make sense to me. My feeling was this. Before you do something, you must know what to do. This is necessary before you can develop skills and habits. As he explained it more, I started to understand what he was saying. He said, "Knowing what to do is one thing. We can know the Ten Commandments, but it is how we apply them to our life, that makes a difference. Knowledge is knowing what to do, and skills and habits is knowing how you do something."

As a football team, we can have the knowledge that using the running ropes will help us have better feet. That is having the knowledge. The key is how do you do the running ropes. What emphasizes do you bring to the running ropes? What type of intensity do you bring with the running ropes? That is going to make a difference whether you are successful or not. Knowing how to run the zone as opposed to running the zone makes the difference in how good you are. That is important for our kids to understand this concept.

The next area the speaker compared was the innate ability to attitude (Diagram #3). By innate

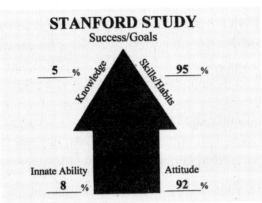

Diagram #3. Innate Ability versus Attitude

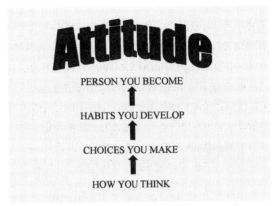

Diagram #4. Attitude

ability, we are talking about God-given ability. How big are you, how fast are you, how intelligent are you, and how good looking are you? How much does this have to do with having success as compared with your attitude?

This is what he said. The innate ability was eight percent compared to 92 percent of attitude. We all have had kids that fit this description. How many of you have said, "I wish I had that guy's attitude in this guy's body." I have had several players who could run a 4.6 40 yards, but they were not near the football players as those who could run a 4.8 who had the best attitude. That was because of their attitudes and the way they approached things. Do you think it is important for the players to know this type of information? I promise you it is. It is understanding how those attitudes control everything.

I used to ask our players this question. If attitude is so important, then what exactly is it? If you look it up in the dictionary, we find that it is the habits of the mind, which one displays. However, my favorite definition came from one my players. One of my players said, "Coach, I believe your attitude is how you think." I believe he was exactly right. Another player said, "Coach, I think it is the choices you make." I believe he was right as well.

Here is how I think your attitude works (Diagram #4). How I think determines the choices I make. The choices I make determine the habits I develop. The habits I develop determine the person I become. When I chose a habit, I chose the end result of that habit.

It is critical for our kids to know and understand this about attitude. They need to know that what

they allow to go into their mind, the people they hang with, and the people they allow to influence their thinking is going to make a difference in the choices they are going to make in their life. Those choices are going to make a difference because of the habits they are going to make in their life. Those habits determine who they are, what they are going to become, and what they are going to have in years down the road.

Every morning when they get up, they are making those choices a mile a minute. When we got up this morning, we were making those choices. Here are choices of attitudes we make every day.

- I can choose to be enthusiastic about the day.
- I can choose to have a sour disposition.
- I can choose to be a hard worker.
- I can choose to be lazy.
- I can choose to be committed.
- I can choose to go along with the crowd.
- I can choose to have a persistence of effort about me.
- I can choose to quit when it gets tough.
- I can choose to love.
- I can choose to hate.
- I can choose to be disciplined.
- I can choose to take the easy way out.

It is those little yes-and-no decisions that we choose every day that determine who we are, what we are going to become, and what we are going to have 10 years down the road. The difference between accomplishment and failure is having the right mental attitude. It is thinking the right thoughts. It is making the right choices. It is developing the right habits. I think it is critical for our kids to know these things. As coaches, we need to spend time with our players talking about these points. If you will do this, it will pay dividends in your program, big time.

I think strength and speed development are important. But if you can get the other aspects in order, all of the other things will take off.

Despite all of the overwhelming evidence that supports the importance of a proper mental attitude, our educational system ignores, or is unaware of, that vital factor. This is where I believe our athletic programs can become a very important part of the educational process. As coaches, we have the opportunity to teach those things more than any other place in education. The only exception would be in the home.

In the book *See You at the Top*, Zig Ziglar points out that over 90 percent of our education is directed at acquiring facts and figures, with less than 10 percent aimed at our attitude. Simply stated, we are spending 90 percent of our educational dollars and time developing that part of us which is responsible for 15 percent of our success. We spend 10 percent of our time and money developing that part of us that is responsible for 85 percent of our success. The majority of that 10 percent comes from our athletic programs.

I have always been impressed by the ancient philosophy that says, "A man becomes that which he thinks." A man's character is the outward expression of his inward thoughts. This builds on that attitude. You can trace that philosophy all the way back to the sacred Hindus. I have accumulated several quotes related to the power of thoughts.

The Power of Thoughts

"Man becomes that which he thinks." (Hindus)

"The mind is everything; what you think you become." (Buddha)

"Your life is what your thoughts make it." (Marcus Aurelius)

"As a man thinketh in his heart – so he is." (Proverbs 23:7)

"The divinity that shapes our ends is in ourselves... all that a man achieves or fails to achieve is the direct result of his own thoughts." (James Allen)

You can find the same basic ideas in the writings of Confucius, Mohammed, Aristotle, Socrates, and scores of others. Most important, you can find it in its most familiar form, where the wisest of men look for the truth, and that is in the Bible. That is Proverbs 23:7. The Bible tells us: "As a man thinketh in his heart, so he is."

James Allen wrote a small book entitled As a Man Thinketh. The book was written in 1905. It is a very thin book. My wife got the book for me because she knew I was intrigued by this subject. It is a thin book and she knew I could handle that book over the summer. Allen was an educator and a writer. In the book, he makes a very powerful statement. It is a statement that I think every coach should have solid in his mind. It is a statement that can help our athletes understand a very important principle of success in life. This is what James Allen said:

> The divinity that shapes our ends is within ourselves. All that a man achieves, or fails to achieve, is a direct result of his own thoughts. What we need to be successful we already have. Mental training that teaches strong values and principles can have a powerful impact in our programs, and more importantly it can have a life changing impact on our athletes.

Our young people are in need of role models today, more than any other time in history. There is a void for our young people that needs to be filled. It is important that that void be filled with strong and positive thoughts. As coaches, we can be a part of the problem or we can be a part of the solution. It depends on what we teach the young people that we work with. It depends on what we demand in our programs. It depends on what we expect out of our kids as they go through our programs.

I believe our coaches can have a tremendous impact on our communities, and a major impact on the lives of our young people. I think it is critical for our young people that we find ways to teach winning attitudes through character traits.

I have heard teachers say, "Do we have to do it all? Can we just do what we were trained to do? Can we just teach the essential elements of our subjects? Do we have to teach them and raise them, too?" Do you know that the school and family are about all that the kids have? Some families cannot respond, so who else is going to do it. I believe that kids are too precious for us to ignore the realities of our time, and to abandon them. Yes, I guess we have to do it all if that is what it takes. Do you know what? No one in education knows this more than coaches. No one in education does this more than coaches. I have seen it over and over again, and I am sure you have seen this as well.

There are two types of education. One helps us make a living, and one will teach us how to live. I believe we can teach many lessons of life and fill some of that void that so many of our young people have today. I believe interscholastic sports are a very important part of the educational process, as I am sure every one of you does as well.

I also believe we are in danger of losing our athletic programs as we know them today. The only way for us to counter the negative publicity we have been receiving and talking about is to develop the many good qualities of athletics. We must make sure that our programs offer those things. We must have a plan to offer those qualities through our programs.

We need to take a few minutes to cite the value of a sound athletic program. We need to make it a point to speak up for athletics. We need to sell our programs to our communities. We need to point out to our community that our most important job is not in the skills we teach, but it is in the intangibles that we teach, like no other place in education. We need to develop intangibles such as self-confidence, the value of hard work, and developing habits of dedication and sacrifice. We need to develop leadership skills and we needed to develop character traits that would stay with the kids the rest of their lives. We need to teach self-discipline, and the importance of the right mental attitude.

Sometimes as coaches, we pass over these intangibles as being corny. Men, they are not corny. They are the most important things that our programs have to offer the educational process. It is important to our athletic programs that we find ways within our programs to teach and stress those intangibles.

In 1980 when I first went to coach at Converse Judson High School, we had about 4,800 students. It is the fifth-largest 5A school in Texas. After the 1980 season, our staff sat down and talked about the things we felt we needed to accomplish during the next year. We did not feel we were as good as we should be. We wanted to know why we were not getting the job done. As we discussed our situation, we divided our program into four components. We felt these four areas were important to the development of our athletes.

The first thing we did was to prioritize those four areas. We did that to guide us in the use of our time and interest as it related to each of these areas. The four areas or key components were the areas we felt should be taught by our coaches to develop our athletes.

Four Key Components

- Mental Attitude
- Sports Skills and Knowledge
- Quickness and Speed
- Strength and Flexibility

Next, we established the coaching objectives to build our program around. Again, attitude development was our number one priority. We put that component first because we felt that was the one area we needed to develop to get our program headed in the right direction. We listed our coaching objectives to guide us in building our program.

Coaching Objectives

- Contribute to the development of a well-rounded, mature student-athlete.
- Train the student-athlete for leadership.
- Encourage the student-athlete to achieve academic success.
- Make the student-athlete concerned with the awareness of the importance of self-discipline and commitment in all areas of life.
- Develop, refine, and teach ethical values.
- Teach the practice of excellence in competition.
- Encourage student-athletes to be concerned about their attitude toward the overall educational process, the values inherent in sports participation, and their priorities in life.

We did not always get these areas covered, but we used them to keep us on track. They were the things we could always go back to when we felt we needed to do so.

We gave our players self-evaluation forms in this process. We wanted them to put down on the form what they wanted to be doing 10 years after high school. We wanted to get them to think about the future. I believe this is important in getting them to make mature choices. If they tell us they want to be a doctor and they are making an F in biology, we let them know those two points do not go together. We tried to get them to make choices that would get them to where they want to go 10 years down the road.

I do not believe there is a set way to motivate or inspire a team. There are going to be changes from year to year. The way I do it may be the opposite of your way. I do believe there are some absolute truths and some lessons that remain the same for all of us. An example would be the understanding the importance of unselfishness. It is important to help our kids understand self-discipline, sacrifice, commitment, concern, hard work, and strong choices. Those things remain the same if you are going to have championship-type kids.

When we study the great coaches, there seems to be a common thread that connects all of them. They say the key in understanding the game is 90 percent mental and only 10 percent physical. We have all heard that and we have all read that statement. We have all studied that statement. However, there are only a few who make the commitment to do it. In the vast majority of our programs, the majority of work is aimed at the physical skills of the game. It is not easy. It takes a commitment to some beliefs and some values, and then doing those things it takes to teach those lessons to your players. It takes a commitment, not just in the way you coach, but also in the way that you live. But the most important thing is making that commitment.

I am going to share a story with you today about that challenge and about making that commitment. It is a story about tough choices. I am not sure if the story is true or not, but I have been told it was a true story. It is one of my favorite stories. It brings with it a great message.

Here is the way the story goes. Legend has it that many, many years ago, Mohammed set out to find the finest strand of horses in the entire world. To do this Mohammed brought in 50 of the very best horsemen he could find. He sent the 50 men out on a mission. They were to go out and search the world and to bring back to Mohammed the very best 100 horses they could find in all of the land.

It took those 50 men six months to get those horses rounded up. They brought back to Mohammed the very finest horses they could find in the world. Mohammed trained the horses himself. He trained them in only one discipline, and that one discipline was this. He trained them so when he blew his silver trumpet the horses would come to him. It did not matter where he was or where the horses were, when they heard the trumpet they came right to the feet of Mohammed. It took him six months to train them in that one discipline. At the end of six months, when Mohammed was sure the horses had learned that one discipline, Mohammed, and his men took the 100 horses out in the desert.

Mohammed took the horses out in the desert where the temperature never dropped below 120 degrees. They corralled those horses up on a bluff that overlooked an oasis of cool water that was about 100 yards away. They did not give the horses anything to eat or drink for three days. At the end of three days, those horses were frantic. They could not be contained any longer in those corrals. Then came the test.

Mohammed ordered his men to open the corral gates. They horses came out of the corral and headed toward the cliff and the water. When the horses got about 100 yards away from the cliff, Mohammed blew his silver trumpet one more time. Lo and behold, one horse yielded—reluctantly, but obediently. You know what happened to the rest of the horses. However, from that one horse, Mohammed raised the Arabian strain of horses. They are the finest horses known to mankind today.

The message is this. One out of 100 is truly a committed individual. One person in 100 is willing to make the tough choices in life. We have to be willing to make those tough choices in life. We need to hold on to those things that we know to be right, and we need to say no to those things that we know to be wrong.

We teach by example. I think it is important for us to be what we expect our kids to be. Sometimes the tough call is not following the majority. One of the toughest calls for young people is overcoming peer pressure. I believe being a strong example for our athletes helps them to be strong. As leaders of young people, we must realize that what we do speaks so loudly that the kids cannot hear what we say. Leaders are leaders by what they do, and not by what they say they do.

I want to share a poem that I used to share with our coaches every year. The title is very simple. This really speaks to me as a coach and as a parent.

I Would Rather Watch a Winner
By Dennis Watley

I would rather watch a winner than to hear one any day; I would rather have one walk with me than merely show the way.

The eye is a better pupil, and more willing than the ear; Fine counsel is confusing, but an example is always clear.

And the best of all the coaches are the ones who live their creeds; For to see the good in action is what everybody needs.

I can soon learn how to do it if you will let me see it done; I can watch your hands in action, but your tongue too fast may run.

And the lectures you deliver may be very wise and true; But I would rather get my lessons by observing what you do.

For I may misunderstand you and the high advice you give, But there is no misunderstanding how you act and how you live.

I would rather watch a winner than hear one any day!

In closing I want to share some questions I believe a coach should ask himself to determine his worth.

Questions to Determine Your Worth as a Coach

- While teaching your sport, how many young people have you truly taught?
- While winning games, how many athletes have you truly won?
- While developing and improving the skills and techniques of the sport, have you given sufficient attention to the players' attitudes and character traits?
- While teaching the patterns of the game, have you attempted to show your players a better pattern of living?

If we can give the right answers to these questions, we have accomplished a major task of a coach. It is the job of the coach to help young people become the best pupil they can be first, and the best athlete second. We all have a program that is important to the educational process of our school districts. Most importantly, we want to have a coach who is coaching for the right reason.

I think it is important to talk about the issues I have covered today. I wish each of you the best in the upcoming season. Thank you.

OPTION FROM THE SPREAD OFFENSE

Trousdale County High School, Tennessee

Thank you. Many coaches begin by giving some background about their schools, particularly if they are fortunate enough to have a large, impressive facility. In our situation, we are not blessed with a lot of resources in Trousdale County. We are in a very rural community with not a lot of money. Unemployment is high, and people are leaving the county rather than moving in. We lose good athletes instead of gaining them.

Our staffing over the years has been really thin, but I am lucky now to have the best staff we have ever had. With regard to our facilities, we have had to raise money for everything we have (or build it ourselves), and we have had to do it over a long period of time.

We do not have an athletic period within the school's curriculum. All of our athletics happen after school, including the weight program, and that makes it difficult for us.

National Signing Day is this week and I hear coaches talking about which of their best players are signing with which major schools. I did not have one player sign with even a Division III school this year, and yet we won the state championship. My quarterback is a 4.9 guy and the running back beside him is a 4.8 guy, and they busted their tails for six years to get their speed down to that. If any of you are in similar situations, then we can all relate to each other.

Our players and coaches work awfully hard, we have good discipline, and we expect our kids to do things right. Everyone does a good job with that, but the big thing is that we have to be master teachers and master motivators. For us to win, that is what we've got to do.

I have to talk to our coaches and players about our shotgun offense. A lot of people think that this shotgun stuff is a gimmick. Some see it being done on TV and think they have to do it. Others think it looks like it's fun, and it gets the basketball players out for football. Everyone has his own situation to deal with though, and coaches do what they feel they have to do.

On the other hand, some coaches say that they want their team to be physical and they don't want to get away from what has been good to them, and we are the same way. We are not in the shotgun to try to become something that we're not, and I'll talk about that in just a minute.

Another big thing that I talk to our players about all the time, which is essential to our shotgun offense, is that we cannot have fumbles, interceptions, or busted assignments. I constantly stress this throughout practice, and our kids understand it. And then, we are going to keep penalties to a minimum. These are our points of emphasis.

The shotgun doesn't win for us and neither does the no-huddle scheme. Winning is a combination of a lot of things. We are a no-huddle football team and we use multiple tempos. We use three different tempos.

The first tempo that we use is really, really fast. We're going to call it, snap it, and run it like a two-minute offense run out of one formation. We may try to use two different formations in it next year, but we now go two-by-two, and that is our fastest tempo.

The second tempo is a fast tempo in which we get up on the line really quick, line up, get a play called, and then run the play that is called.

The third tempo that we run is a "check-off" tempo. We will do as we did in the second one, in that we are going to run to the line really quick and get our hands on the ground. After we call a play, we will give an indicator. If we like the play called, then we will give a thumbs up and go with what's called. If we don't, we'll dump it, give them another call, and go with it.

Now that's a big thing. I don't think you can run no-huddle with just one tempo. There are teams that run four or five tempos, but we run three.

Why do we run the no-huddle? We hear defensive coaches saying that they want to dictate pace, but with the no-huddle offense, we dictate the pace of the game. We will determine when the ball is snapped. We will snap it at once or we will make the defensive players line up, put their hands on the ground, sit there, and wonder what's coming next, or have to adjust if we move around on them. We are going to be proactive as opposed to being reactive.

I do not like going to the huddle to get the play, coming from the huddle expecting a front, then not getting that front. Then what? Are you going to run a bad play? Are you going to check it off and take a chance on your players getting the new call? Are you going to take too much time off the clock? I do not like all of that.

Instead, we are going to get to the line of scrimmage, get our hands on the ground, and we're going to make you show your hand really quick. If you don't show your hand, then we're going to go faster and we'll make you show your hand. Or we'll make you show your hand and let you stew around, and then we will get the play called that we want, and then we'll go. But in any event, we're going to be proactive as opposed to being reactive.

The next thing that is really big is our conditioning. We don't do a lot of conditioning anymore because practice is so fast. I mean it is really fast and we want to make it fast. We want to make them learn on the run. We will drive kids crazy demanding that they concentrate and listen on the run. We make them do up-downs on the sideline if they fail to get the signals, and we will run everything we do at a very fast pace. Because of the pace of our work, we don't have to spend a lot of time conditioning at the end of practice, so I like that. It fits my personality.

We get a lot more repetitions in practice. I think we can get three plays off in one minute of practice. I remember in the old scheme, when we used to huddle, I would have a script of about 30 to 35 plays and it would take forever, walking in and out of that huddle. When we go no-huddle, all of that walking is over with, and we get a lot of reps.

The next thing about our offense is that we don't make our quarterback do any checking off. No check offs. I don't want kids making decisions for me. So when we make decisions, I have a coach up in the box, and all he does is look at the line. At home games, he is in an end-zone tower and can see every technique across the front. I have another coach who watches the secondary, and he is like a passing-game coordinator. This way, when we go to the line, we are going to get the best call in the secondary with our passing game, or in our run game with our line coach. What I do is call a play and if we are going to go on that third tempo, when we said we don't know exactly what we are getting, then I will just hurry up and get a play called. The team will go to the line and they're going to give a "leg kick," and I'm talking on the phone the whole time. I check with my coaches in the box to see if the play called is what we want against that particular defense. They will give me the okay or they will tell me that the call isn't a good fit for the defense and suggest a better choice. I will signal the play in myself, but I am talking to the coaches all of the time. So that play selection is a collective effort, but everything goes through me. It has worked real well for us.

I am real big on clarity. I want to see it because I am a visual learner. You can't tell me about it. Instead, I want you to show me a picture of it and you have to draw it up. When I go no-huddle and I line up, then you have got to line up. When you line up, I can see what you are going to do and we'll get a good play called.

Another thing that is big with me, and I have to argue this with our coaches sometimes, has to do with wristbands. I know that you have all seen teams utilize wristbands in running the no-huddle offense and that's fine, but I personally despise them. I don't like lining up and looking down at a wristband. Somehow, in or out of the classroom, you have to make kids responsible for learning, so everybody has to see the hand signal, and there is no wristband.

Another advantage of the no-huddle offense is that the two-minute offense is already built in and we don't really have to practice it. We do spend 10 or 15 minutes on Thursday with a clock drill when we talk about spiking the ball, when do they stop the clock, when do they start it back, or when not to flip a formation. That's all we do on the clock drill.

Now, let's talk about why we run the shotgun. Let me explain it by using an example of an offensive lecture we heard the other day. They were under the center in a one-back set, running the zone play and faking the reverse to hold the 5 technique. For us, I can put the quarterback in the shotgun, hand the ball off, and the quarterback himself will hold the 5 technique so that I don't have to use another player to do that.

Every defensive coach knows that if the quarterback is under center in a one-back set, they won't worry about the quarterback running the ball. He is not a threat. There are 11 men on the field, but if you stay in the same perimeter formation with a running back and a quarterback in the gun, it is now a two-back running game. So now I feel like I am playing offense with 12 men. Furthermore, if I'm playing with 12 men, and your 5 technique is no longer a factor, it is almost like I'm playing with 13 men. I hope you can appreciate the math I use in my counting.

I grew up as a wishbone quarterback running the triple option, and I remember being taught that if defenders are hard to block, then they are easy to read. If you have trouble scheming them to block them, or if they are so tough that you cannot block them, then don't try to block them and just read

them. It makes things easier. You know, the guys that are hard to read are the ones that just stand there, like our scout teams do sometimes.

I really believe it was easier when my daddy coached because they didn't see as many games on television every day and then come into staff meetings on Sundays wanting to try to run all the things they saw Oklahoma or Florida do on TV. I am tempted just like everyone else is, so the thing that we are going to do is to have a toolbox. We talk all the time about the toolbox. The toolbox is this:

We are going to run the inside zone, the outside zone, the trap, the counter, the dart, and the power O, and that's it. If it doesn't fit into those blocking schemes, then we aren't going to do it.

Our passing game consists of the quick game, the dropback, the sprint-out, the play-action bootleg, and a screen package or two. That's it, and that's pretty simple.

Now, our coaches don't always like to hear this, and I don't like saying it about myself, but what you see on the film is a result of your coaching. You either taught it that way or allowed it to happen. That is a fact and you have to take responsibility for that—bottom line.

I tell our players all the time, all the time, and it gets really personal sometimes. "What I am seeing on film ain't good. I know there is one of two things going on. Either I can't teach, or you can't learn, and I know dang well that I can teach. So you better start learning!" We put the responsibility on them. We are going to keep it in that toolbox, but we are going to tell them those things right there.

Now, let's talk about our option drill (Diagram #1). In our option drill we put one quarterback in as a snapper, and another in the gun. If you practice the shotgun, the quarterback cannot be standing there and assume that he will get a good snap, and just start with the ball in his hands. The other quarterback will give an underhand shovel, and he has to catch that ball, find the laces, and proceed with the drill.

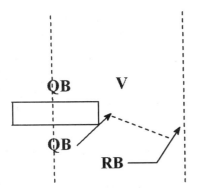

Diagram #1. Lead Option Drill

We take every person we have, every running back and receiver (we only have 27 players in all), and everybody is going to be a runner, so there is a big line of players right there. We will put a coach in place as a pitch read, and we will put a cone on the other hash. We will teach the running back that he will run like a bat out of Hades, parallel to the line of scrimmage, and he is going to run to that hash mark flying. He will open up, cross over, and his eyes will be on the quarterback, and he is going to run to the field as fast as he can run. When he catches the pitch he will come downhill.

To the field, we tell the quarterback to attack the outside shoulder and pitch the ball unless he widens. If he widens and creates a running gap inside, then we will just take it inside, but we want the ball pitched. We are coming downhill, we are attacking the outside shoulder, and we are going to pitch the football.

The big thing here is that I think you have to go to the basketball pitch. When I played, it was all "thumb under." But a coach convinced me a long time ago that it's the basketball pitch, that's the pitch. The reason is that the basketball pitch can be pushed down the line, while the thumb-under pitch is always pitched behind.

We tell our running back to stay on that line, on the "ceiling," running towards the sideline. As soon as that quarterback looks at you and makes eye contact, then you break down, come off of that "ceiling," come down at 45 degrees, and go for the corner pylon. That is the angle, and the pitch will be a good pitch. As you will see on the tape, the pitch

could be as much as 10 to 12 yards. It is wide, it's downhill, and it is really good. That's the first thing we are going to do. We are going to teach that pitch.

The next thing we are going to do is have a dive read key right there, the next defender out will be the pitch read key, and we are going to split our running backs to here and here (Diagram #2). We use the word "phase" to tell our back to get into phase with the quarterback. We put a cone three yards behind the quarterback and we tell that back that as soon as the ball is snapped to run and try to get right behind that cone. His inside foot is up and he is going to drop and he is running for three yards right behind the quarterback.

When he sees the disconnect between the quarterback and running back on the zone play, he will spin, keep his eyes on the quarterback, and get right on the ceiling that he worked to get on when he was in the backfield in the lead option drill.

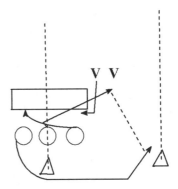

Diagram #2. Triple Option Drill

He has got to learn to get on the ceiling, and he has to learn to stay on that ceiling until the quarterback makes eye contact with him. Then he will break down at 45 degrees and aim at the corner pylon.

Now, the quarterback is working on reading that thing. When the handoff key comes down inside, and I'm going to say more about that in a minute, then he is going to disconnect, attack the outside shoulder of the pitch key, and we are running the triple option.

When we read that 5 technique on the handoff phase of the play, we tell the quarterback to give the ball to the player on or outside the offensive tackle whom we do not block, unless he turns his shoulders and comes down inside. Number one, if he turns his shoulders and just stands there, we are going to give the ball. If he stays square and he just shuffles a little bit, we are going to give the ball. We are going to give the ball *unless* he both turns his shoulders *and* comes down inside, because we want to run the football. We do not want to be pulling it and pitching it out on the ground, but if the 5 technique is going to make the hit on the back, we are certainly going to execute the triple option out of it. That's going to happen.

So we are just going to drill that over and over. We will start with the lead option and then we are going to go to the triple option, and then we are going to do two more things.

We are going to teach the quarterback what to do when he is going into the boundary (Diagram #3). When we go into the boundary, we want the back to run to the bottom of the numbers just flying, and when the quarterback looks at him, he will break down and go for the corner pylon as before. The difference is, when running lead option into the boundary, the quarterback will attack the inside shoulder to force the pitch key to make his decision real quick. If his shoulders turn, then we are going to pitch the football.

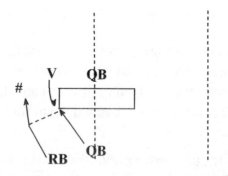

Diagram #3. Boundary Option Drill

If he widens, then we are going to run that gap, but we have got to tell the quarterback that it isn't like running it to the field. When running it to the field, he has a lot of time. He runs it to the outside shoulder, and everybody knows that it is: hash –

numbers – sideline. For example, if the quarterback runs to the outside shoulder, going to the field, and the end man on the line of scrimmage widens, then he gets under that. The next place he's going is to the hash, then to the numbers, then to the sideline. If we pitch the ball, then it's hash, numbers, and sideline for the running back to get away from the free safety.

Now, when we go into the boundary, we don't want to go hash because we are already there. We don't want to be on the numbers. We want the quarterback to come downhill, attack the inside shoulder, and force the issue really, really fast. The quarterback has to make a quick decision when we run the lead option into the boundary.

From there, we get into what we call rocket (Diagram #4). We put a running back by the quarterback and another in the slot and we run what we call a bounce technique. We run the zone play against a dive-read key and a pitch-read key. The slot gets on the ceiling going down, and we're running the triple option.

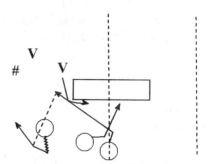

Diagram #4. Rocket Option Drill

We have two-foot spacing across the line, and our back starts out directly behind the tackle. We may fudge him some on certain plays, but when he bounces, his heels will be on the quarterback's toes and our quarterback's heels are five yards from the front point of the football. That way the back is just a little bit ahead of the quarterback, where we get that good across parallel mesh. So we will do this out of rocket.

Then, we'll get in here with our quarterback, and we'll have a runner here, and another runner here, and we'll run the Utah play (Diagram #5). We have a dive read and a pitch read, and we're going to run him on the ceiling, just as he has been taught. We tell the running back to come down to the cheek of the tackle and get with the guard who is pulling. We are going to power 0 it, and we are going to tell the quarterback to replace the feet of the other back, and execute the thumb-under read, or shovel read on the dive read, and the next defender is the pitch read.

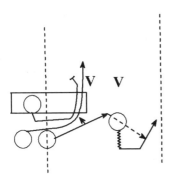

Diagram #5. Utah Option Drill

If the dive read comes up, we will shovel it using the thumb-under pitch, and if he squeezes with the down block, we will execute the pitch read off of the next man outside. If the shovel pitch goes on the ground, it is just an incomplete pass, and we remind the referees of this before each game.

This is our option game, and that is how we teach it. We did not invent it ourselves of course, but we think it is pretty good.

Now I want to talk about how we teach our zone read (Diagram #6). This is an important drill for our running backs. We put a quarterback and a running back in their regular positions here, and we take a bag and lay it right across where the center would be. We have a coach who will snap the ball to the quarterback and then he's going to move that

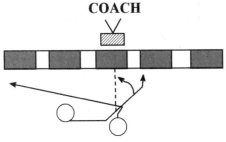

Diagram #6. Zone Read Drill

bag. He has to hold the light bag in one hand and the football in the other at the start of the drill. He snaps the ball, and then either holds the bag where it is, or he will move it.

We tell our back when he runs the zone to read the first down lineman on or past the football. If it is an odd front, that would be the noseguard; if it is an even front, it's the man around the guard area to the playside. We tell the back to be "slow to, fast through." That means we want him slow to the line, and when he makes his decision we want him to be fast through the line. We tell him that the best cut is no cut, so that if our linemen have gotten on that down lineman and he hasn't moved playside, we want to "cram him," and it is nothing more than a dive play. Now, if we get movement, then you want him to get to heel level. You've got one "jump cut" back inside. It is A gap to A gap, and there's your play.

The beauty of the zone play, and it took a while for our linemen to understand this, is that everyone is a frontside blocker. There is not a backside blocker, because that play can go anywhere from callside to all the way back.

In teaching this play, we run the back right across there, and if he can, take two little steps past the handoff. Out of the gun, we press the outside leg of the guard and we want him up in there square. If we happen to be under center for some reason, we would press the outside leg of the tackle, but we are in the gun most of the time. So he presses the outside leg of the guard and reads the first down lineman past the ball. If that guy goes, he's got one jump cut and he's going back behind that dummy and getting north. That's the drill we use to teach the zone.

Another drill that I think you have to have to teach the running back is the jump cut drill (Diagram #7). This is a great drill. These square bags are about two or three feet apart. The back will start in there at the first bag, jump cut it, and then he is going to explode to the next bag. Then, he will jump cut that bag and explode to the next one, and continue past the last bag. Then he will do the drill coming back, developing good habits and switching the ball in his arms.

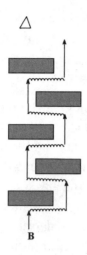

Diagram #7. Jump Cut Drill

He's got to explode, and then he's got to jump, and then he's got to explode. As simple as that sounds, again, it isn't the plays, but it's the techniques that win for you.

Now, let's talk about blocking the zone. The first thing that we've seen this year, most of the time, is the odd-man front. We run a lot of traps and they've gotten those people in 4i alignments, and we do not know where their 9 techniques are going to be (Diagram #8). They are on the line, they're off the line, and they move them around. We have some rules that we use for our lineman that we have to center up the defense. We count the box and number the defense, so theoretically, tackle has number two, guard has number one, and center has zero. But we know that we have to pick up the combinations that we see, so our linemen always talk.

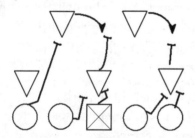

Diagram #8. Zone-Blocking Scheme

The onside guard and tackle make a call and work together, and so do the offside guard and center. The covered guy will take a jab step and go through the outside breastplate, while the uncovered guy will take a drop-step and be vertical by the third step also going through the outside breastplate. They will see how the lineman and linebacker are playing their gaps and they each block the man who plays their gap.

On the backside, we make a sift call. That tells our tackle to take a "subtle" step to the inside and lets the defensive tackle go where he wants to go. If he wants to run around, that's okay, and if he wants to go across our face, we'll just help him. The key for our tackle is that he will sift up to the linebacker and block his backside breastplate, because the defense wants to chase with the linebacker and nest with the tackle. Then, if we get his outside breastplate and the ball is disconnected, there's our dive read. Our pitch read is outside, and we have the linebacker blocked. We really think that is important.

We use a similar counting system on other fronts that we see, and we number the defense to set up our combinations. We will still sift the backside tackle, dive read the 5 technique, and run the option outside, while the running back is reading the first lineman on or past the football. There are a lot of things going on in there.

We tell our quarterback that if they have three-over-two outside, then we want to hand the ball off. Now if the safety is very deep, we may go on and run the option and see if he can tackle in open space.

We can also use the word "load" in our scheme. When we say load, we are going to read the 5 technique and load the pitch-read key. If the 5 technique chases the play, the quarterback just keeps the ball.

Let me add that, on anything we call, we can put the word "option" on it and read the backside 5. We can do that off of counter, dart, trap, or any of our plays.

This concludes my presentation. Thank you.

SUCCESSFUL KEYS TO VICTORY

McGill-Toolen Catholic High School, Alabama

This is my 33rd year of coaching and I know that you guys take this as seriously as I do. I have had the pleasure to coach a good number of great players and be a part of many great football games in my career. To stay in it as long as we have, you have to have fun. We call our staff the geriatric group because we are a bit older than everybody else. I have retired from the public schools and moved to a Catholic school. I am Catholic, so it is a great fit for me.

I want to start with some things we believe in. I want you to understand that I have always coached at the 6A level in Alabama, but I have never had the fortune to coach at a top-five school from a talent perspective. Since we have been in building situations, one of the things we have always done is try to get a number of players to participate. We have only 950 kids, grades 9 through 12. But, because we are a private school, we are considered 6A because of the formula used to calculate students for private schools. Almost one third of the males in our school are playing football. We will have 60 freshmen and right now, we have 117 players in grades 10 through 12. We are tough on our kids. We have a seven-period day, so we cannot use a long block to lift during the off-season. Our players have to come in at 7 a.m. to lift before school every day.

In order to get kids out, I think you have to have a cohesive staff that works together and treats players with respect. The staff has to support one another, especially in public. I am also the athletic director and if I go out to Wal-Mart, someone will always ask me about something going on in our athletic program. I am a company man. I am always going to support our coaches in that situation. We are always asking our players to be great leaders, but you must have coaches who are great leaders.

We do believe in a strong weight program. The weight room is the key to our success and has allowed us to be competitive. We believe in long-range planning. We begin with a yearlong calendar so all of our coaches are on the same page, knowing exactly what we plan on doing all year. I also think you have to get your community to buy into everything you are doing. I will go speak many places in our community. I go to all of our PTO meetings. I go to meetings at our feeder schools. I want to make sure that the moms and dads want their children to play football for us. If you do the right things, the parents will certainly want them to play for you.

When I started 33 years ago, being from Alabama, I thought I was going to be the next Coach Bryant. I also thought I knew it all, but I found out quickly that I was wrong. My first game, we were down 42-0 at the half and we went 0-9 that first season. I have learned so much since then from so many different coaches. The guy who taught me the most about coaching was our head basketball coach. He was my assistant in football and was a great man. He is 69 now and we still talk. He is my hero in coaching and I hope all of you have someone that is your hero in coaching. It doesn't matter what the sport, you can learn from anyone. I went to hear Bobby Knight talk and there is no doubt that he knows how to motivate players.

I also believe you must have a passion for what you do. I realize we don't get paid a lot, but you should be willing to do this for nothing. You also must love your kids. You are going to spend more time with them than you are with your own children. I hope you have a wife that understands that. The willingness to work long hours, holidays, and weekends is a part of success in this business.

Don't compromise your morals by trying to cheat to win. Put in the work and build the character of your team through your hard work.

Every coach has to be ready to make a difference in your program and your community. I am a big community person and I think every coach has to buy into being a part of your community.

As the years have gone by, I have become more understanding as a coach. I have found through the years that being positive gets much better results with the kids than if you are always on them about everything. It has been so much fun to watch my players succeed. I have had five players play in the NFL and I have no idea how many have played in college. The relationships you build with those players and all the friends you make in coaching makes this a great profession. I have been offered a principal's job and I am sure some of my assistants that have to put up with me every day were hopeful that I would move on, but I just could not. I am a coach and I love coaching.

I believe we can all succeed without cursing the kids. I have won over 300 games and have never cursed the kids. You don't have to curse kids to be effective. You can motivate players in different ways. You can be tough without cursing. Cursing tends to take it to a personal level for kids.

There are plenty of kids out there that may not be the glamour players that are the ones that make up the heart of your football team. Many of you may think they are only pre-game meal eaters, but by the time they are seniors, if they love the game, they will help you win football games. I coached Terrell Owens in high school. No matter what he is now, Terrell was a great kid in high school. He was not even a starter until the sixth game of his senior season. As a freshman, he did not even play football. He was a basketball player. I recruited him to play football. He had to overcome a large number of things in his life.

We don't give any awards in our program. I don't believe there is a most valuable player. The New England Patriots stand for team. Banquets are to recognize your team, not the individuals.

Everything we do is highly organized. All of our coaches must contribute to that. We are an I football team. Our philosophy is to keep the ball away from you. We believe we are going to score and if you do not score, we are going to keep the ball away from you. Hoover has won four of the past five state championships and we were the one to beat them. When we beat them, we did so by keeping the ball away from them. I am old-fashioned guy and I believe that a football game is like a prizefight. You must keep punching until your opponent gets tired of being punched. We are very organized in everything we do. We cover every phase of the game on Thursday. From the toss of the coin, to taking a knee for victory, we cover it all on Thursday.

One of my favorite sayings is: "Kids don't care how much you know until they know how much you care." Coaching is a tough job, but you must remember that the kids are the product. You better care for them.

I want to talk about our keys to victory.

Must Play Great Defense

We put our best players on defense after we take our quarterback and tailback.

Run the Football First

We believe that you must control the ball to win games. We believe in running the ball and misdirection.

Must Be Physical

Every Tuesday and every Wednesday we have a period built into our practice schedule that includes one-on-one drills. Our kids love it and they develop a physical attitude. It helps the tempo in practice. We believe in live contact during the week.

Play-Action Pass

We believe in the play-action pass. We take pride in hiding the football and selling the run. We love to throw the football on first down.

Run Some Type of Option

We will keep some type of option in our game. We have gone to a lot of zone option. We don't want to have to spend a great deal of time reading things, so zone option is good for us.

Find Out Who Wants to Play

We are demanding on our players. They don't wear earrings and they don't wear hats. We make them come after school to pride time. We treat every player the same. When I coached in the Alabama-Mississippi All-Star Game, the first thing I told the kids was that we were not going to wear earrings or any kind of headwear. It was going to be the same for Cadillac Williams as it was for the rest of the players. They were all going to be treated the same. We are trying to get them to set a good example all the time. Earrings may not be bad, but we want our players to present themselves like they are in an interview.

I am sorry I have spent so much time talking about this stuff. There are plenty of you who know more football than I, but I promise you that I know how to treat kids, I know how to get them out, and I know how to get them to play hard. If you can do that, you can get them to reach their athletic potential.

As I said earlier, we are an I football team. Our basic formation is the pro I. We can move our tailback out of the I to give us a lot of different looks. It is usually done to get someone out of the box. If we do move him, we like to trap and run misdirection. We can also move our fullback and play him much like an H-back in a one-back offense. We bring our older players in at 7:15 a.m., Monday through Thursday during the season. The time we spend there is to make sure we know everything we are going to be covering in practice that afternoon. We conduct a walk-through on everything we will be doing. We also give our offensive players a blocking sheet each week that defines who will be blocking on each play.

I don't really want to talk about our formations because we have so many formations. We can move our tight end, put him in motion. We have all kinds of places we can put our tight end. We give our backs a look sheet to tell our guys what to do. They get this every Monday morning.

The first play I want to talk about is our lead play out of the I. This is our 20 series. Everybody runs the lead play from the I. We play against the best teams in Alabama. So if we can run this, anyone can. We tell our tight end to step to the playside on our lead play. If he widens, we stay on him and the fullback will stay up inside. Our fullback is a small guy who is the point guard on the basketball team. He is going to block the playside linebacker on our lead play. If we get a 3-technique tackle, we are going to G-scheme block the lead play. We are always looking for angles to use in our offensive blocking scheme. We would block our tackle down on the 3 technique, pull the guard, and kick out the end. We just zone out the backside. You can see that we did not do a good job of getting to the backside linebacker.

I am not going to just show you touchdowns and it is obvious by looking at the tape that we have a number of players who don't always do the right things. Let me give you a little history about our school. We have only won 42 percent of our games in school history and we had never been past the second round of the playoffs. We have improved because of all of our coaches working together. We are in a building process and our kids are just learning how they need to play to be successful.

All of our offense is really simple. In the lead play, we teach our fullback and tailback to read the G block. If the defensive end squeezes and we log him back inside, the fullback and tailback will bounce it outside. The alignment of the fullback and tailback is deep enough to give them time to make this read. The fullback is aligned four yards off the ball and the tailback is six to seven yards off the ball. Sometimes, we will bring our flanker in motion. We love to run play-action off of this look and we have been really good at it. As for the lead play with the motion, we are hoping to slow down the backside flow to the play with the motion.

Depending on the front we see on the lead play, we may decide to base block it and pull the backside guard to give us some help on the playside. Not everything in football is new. Thirty years ago, whenever you ran the off-tackle play, everyone pulled the backside guard. Now, we are back to doing that. We have line calls that are made that will determine how we are going to block a front. All of that is covered in our morning walk-through during the week. Even though most teams are bigger than we are, we feel that if we execute and get to the right people, we can move the football.

We really believe in the fullback trap. We are a big trap team. We have various ways to block the trap and we have a lot of fullback-trap plays. We will run basic trap blocks and we like to run influence block traps. One of our favorite influence blocks is to show pass and get the defensive tackle upfield. Our fullback gets to run the ball on two plays, the dive and the trap. Even with that, I can't remember when our fullback has not gained 1,000 yards.

On our trap play, the check for the quarterback is very simple. We will use an opposite call to run the play to the opposite side than what was called in the huddle. We know we are still running the trap, but we may like the blocking angles better on the other side.

As I said, we are very basic, but we make sure we get kids to know what they are doing so they will play hard. Thank you.

David Sedmak

KEYS TO MAKING FOOTBALL IMPORTANT

Shaker Heights High School, Ohio

Thank you very much. It is a real thrill to be here. I graduated from college in 1991, went to Cleveland, and have been at Shaker Heights ever since. I have been to these clinics for many years and let me say I believe the Nike clinics are the best. I like to come to this clinic because you get so many choices of speakers.

I believe the best people to learn from are the high school coaches. You can listen to speakers from Penn State, Virginia, and Georgia, but what they say does not necessarily apply to my situation.

When you talk to coaches that have the same issues and limitations that we have, it is important. The things they have to say can apply to your situation. What I am going to talk about today, I have learned from other coaches over the years.

The one thing I have learned is that there is more than one way to do something right. I just listened to Ed Nasonti from Bellevue and he gave a great presentation on the off-season program. It was very different from the off-season program we run, but it works for him.

If you can get something from this presentation, that would be great. I want to introduce my staff. We have had a lot of success at Shaker Heights, mainly because of the staff I have.

Let me tell you a little about Shaker Heights. It is on the border of Cleveland. It is both an urban and a suburban school. There are some very rich people in Shaker Heights and there are some poor people there. Racially the school is about 50-50 in its white-to-black makeup. Shaker Heights has been known over the years for it academics. Every year we have about 20 merit scholars. That ranks in the top two or three in Ohio.

We have a tremendous music and drama program at our school. We have people on Broadway that graduated from Shaker Heights. Sports, and football in particular, is not really the thing to do. We are as far from Massillon as you can get.

When we took over the program 15 years ago, it was difficult to make football important. Back then, there were about 40 players on the team. They had just come through six straight losing seasons and had only won five games in the last three years. No one cared about football. The marching band had about 300 members and people came to the game to watch the band march. Football was just a little entertainment before and after halftime.

It was a real chore to try to turn the program around. What I am going to talk about today is what we have done to make football important and keep it important. Football today at Shaker Heights is a pretty big deal.

Our off-season program is the bigger, faster, stronger program. I have talked to many coaches over the years about this program. Some of them like it and some do not. It has worked well for us. We have players from other sports that participate in the program. Sports in general have seen an improvement. Most of our sports are very competitive. Most of them are involved in our weight-training program.

We have developed a program called Spartan sessions. This is a program to make your players tougher. We do not train in the mornings. We do our training after school. That is because of the way the school day runs. We have a seven-hour school day and an additional hour after school for extra help. If we involved our players in a before-school program, it makes their day extremely long.

The purpose of the Spartan sessions is to build mental toughness, cardiovascular conditioning, and team spirit. The format is one hour of grueling physical fitness and team/partner activities. These will be very physical and mentally challenging, and designed to help the individual players and the team to learn to overcome difficult obstacles that will be present in the 2006 season and in other aspects of life.

Once a month, during the off-season, we bring our players in at 6:30 in the morning for an hour-long conditioning session. We do something different each month, but it is a hard conditioning program.

This allows us to get our team together once a month in the off-season. When our players stop playing football, many of them go into other sports. This gives us an opportunity to reunite the players that do not normally see each other until football season starts again. We call it Spartan session because the Spartans were the toughest fighters in Greek history. Webster's definition of the term Spartan fits what we are trying to do. The Spartans were warriors from Sparta in the ancient Greek Empire who would build physical strength, endurance, discipline, and fighting skills through extremely uncomfortable physical-conditioning activities. The purpose was for all to become the strongest, toughest people in Greece.

The players know when they show up for the workout that it is going to be hard. It is amazing how they have come to appreciate the program and their participation has given them a lot of confidence. We have actually had players from other sports come in to work out with this group.

June 8 is graduation day. Shaker Heights is very flat and has only one hill in town. On June 8, at 6:30 in the morning, we run up that hill. At bottom of the hill, we do sets of push-ups and other exercises. We run to the top of the hill and back down. We do 15 sets of the exercises followed by the run up the hill. That is one set for every game in the season. There are 15 games in the season if you get to the state finals.

We have an old trophy from years ago with a football figurine on top of it. That becomes the state championship trophy and it sit on top of the hill. On the 15th time up the hill, the players hold up the trophy and rally around it. We have not won a state championship yet, but this helps the player's confidence.

On July 12 and 13, we have the team sleep over in the gym. Several years ago I heard Al Johnson, the strength coach at Ohio State, talk about their midnight madness. We got the idea from him. We divide our team into five teams. The seniors come to my house for a little cookout and they draft their teams. The teams compete in five events. We add up the repetitions done in each exercise to crown a winner of midnight madness.

They start with dips. Every player on the each team has to do as many dips as they can. The next exercise is the curl station. The players do as many curls as they can in one minute. We do bench push-ups. They see how many they can do in a minute. We follow that with the rope skip. We see how many reps they can do in one minute. Finally, we have a round robin tug of war among the teams.

This is a lot of hard work but it is fun. The players end up getting about one hour of sleep because the screw around all night. They get up the next morning, go home, and sleep all day.

We do a variety of motivational things in our program. Motivation is not what the coach does for the players. It is the ability to create self-motivation in the player. We try to help the players to become self-motivated. The coach provides external motivation with material things, which leads the player to get better. He will feel good about himself because he is getting better and become internally motivated.

The first tool we use is a point system, which awards points for accomplishing certain things over the course of the school year. The purpose of the system is to reward those individuals who work year-round to become better football players, better students, and better people.

We award points for academic achievement. If the player earns a 3.5 or better grade-point average on the second, third, or fourth report cards during the school year, he receives 75 points per report card. If he earns a 3.0 or better he gets 60 points. If he earns 2.5 or better, he receives 45 points. They get no points if they are below 2.5. We award points for every "A" and "B" on the report cards. For every "D" on a report card, they get a 50-point deduction. For an "F" they receive a 75-point deduction. We hope that will encourage our players to do well in the classroom.

We encourage our players to play other sports and reward them on our points system. If they finish the season on the interscholastic basketball, wrestling, swimming, hockey, baseball, track, lacrosse, or tennis teams, we award them 150 points.

I think it is important for our players to play at least two sports in high school. I think the competition they get in another sport will help them in football. It is great to have your players work out year-round, and some of our players do that. However, training in a weight room does not help you psychologically and competitively as having the pressure of a game. I like our players to wrestle and run track.

If they participate completely in a lifting or speed-training workout with the team, or in the advanced weight-training gym class during both semesters, they get two points. They get two points for coming to every workout and if they do an outstanding job, we give them four points.

There are many ways to earn points during spring practice. If they participate in all events of the spring football Olympics, they get 50 points. If they win an event in the spring football Olympics, they get an additional 10 points. If they earn membership in any of our special "clubs," they get 50 points. If they participate in all 10 days of the Shaker Varsity/JV summer football camp days in June and July, they get 100 points. If they miss any days, they receive a deduction of five points per day.

As you can see, there are many ways that they can earn points. In all of the situations, it revolves around our program. They can earn additional points for fundraisers, community service, public relations activities, and many more.

I forget to mention this, which is probably the most important point. When the final point totals are posted on the morning of the first day of official practice in August, the leaders are the starters for the first day. Each individual with the greatest number of points at his position will be number-one on the depth chart at that position on the first day of practice. The number-one position is his as long as he proves capable of getting the job done to help us win. Any missed practice, less-than-adequate performance, or other variables will then give the next player in line his chance to show whey he can do with the first unit.

About 80 percent of the projected starters will be the number-one man at their position. However, 20 percent of the group will be players who outworked the projected starter and are awarded the number-one position on that first day. We have found one or two starters who earned the position on the first day and never lost it throughout the entire season.

We had a player who was a back-up outside linebacker on the JV team. He won the number-one position on the varsity the next year through the point system. We were waiting for the projected starter to beat him out. It never happened. By the end of the year, he was second on the team in tackles and had two defensive touchdowns. The following year he ended up being one of the MVPs on our team.

This helps the more talented players get better because they cannot rely on that talent to make them the starter. The players on the bottom of the points list will be responsible for carrying equipment in and out each day throughout the season. We have to carry our dummies about 100 yards to get them to the practice field; the 15 to 20 players at the bottom do that job.

We added something to that to make it effective. We dress in red or white practice jerseys. The equipment crew wore green jerseys. That prevented someone from trying to slip in and not carry something. Anybody in a green jersey coming off the field without a piece of equipment was in big trouble. The jersey still says "Shaker football" on it. They all knew about the system and if they did not take care of business, they are the ones to blame.

One time in the late 1990s we had a returning all-league football player carrying equipment. If you do not do the work, that is the way it goes.

Players wanted to be involved with our program but did not care about our agenda. Those players did not show up for daily workouts the way our dedicated players did. The players came up with a system to deduct points. The first time a player missed a workout, he lost six points. The second time, he lost 18 points. The third time, it was 24 points. The fourth time he lost 100 points and the fifth time he was dismissed for the off-season. He could come out for football in the fall, but he would be an equipment carrier and start at the bottom.

This got the kids coming every day and it has worked well for us. We had to work up to the point where we kicked players out of the program. We could not have done that when we first came into the program. Once the parents bought into what we were doing and the players wanted to have a good team, things went well.

We have many clubs to reward our players. I try to reward as many players as I can for doing something outstanding in the off-season. If a player attended 90 percent of the off-season workouts, he made the "Ironman Club." Even the players who were little and slow, but tried hard every day, had a chance to achieve. They got a t-shirt and their names on the Ironman board in the weight room.

We give off-season awards in honor of our former players. We give the award the name of our former players. We have the Courtney Ledyard Award for outstanding off-season leader, the Nick Simon Award for the greatest off-season effort and intensity, and the Hassan Adebesin Award for the most physical improvement in the off-season program.

We have a spring Olympics. It is an intra-squad competition in four lifts, two jumps, agility, flexibility, and 40- and 20-yard sprints. The competition occurred between the same class players (11, 10, and 9) and their positions. A two-way player competed within their offensive position. The trophies go to the champions in each event by class and position. Linemen are DE, DT, C, OG, and OT. The skill position players are QB, FB, TB, WR, TE, LB, and DBs.

To win a trophy, they must compete in every event. The players have the calendar of events back in January. There is no excuse for a player to miss for an appointment of any kind. If they do, they forfeit the chance to win a trophy.

We bring guest speakers in to address the team as much as we can. We have used motivational speakers in the past. We have a display case that stays up all year long in the hallway. We give an Ironman of the Week award and put his picture in the case. Any time you can list a players name on a board or a picture on the wall for achievement, it is a great motivational tool.

Fifteen years ago, I started sending a birthday card to every player on our team. I did not think it was that big a deal, but was I wrong. It hit the spot with the players. That is a big deal that you cared to send him a card.

A coach told me a long time ago that five minutes spent in the hallway talking to a player would go a long way. When you meet him in the hall, stop and talk about anything. Show him that you care about him personally and that will go a long way.

Being a teenager is brutal. There are so many choices and so many negative options. It is hard to get them to do the things we want them to do. One way to get to them is show them you care about them. They do not care how much you know, until they know how much you care.

In the off-season, I meet with each player individually. I go over the evaluation sheet his position coach has filled out on him. Before I do that, I ask them what they think their strengths and weaknesses are. The biggest thing is they do not know what their strengths are. Most of them can tell you their weaknesses because the coach yells about them a lot. However, most of them cannot tell you what they are good at. This meeting helps them focus on what they need to work on to become better football players.

One of the best things we do is go to a team camp every year. The last couple of years we have gone to team camp at Mount Union. We had a bunch of poor players on our team and we did not want them to be left out. We raised a lot of money and we paid everyone's camp fee. Nobody paid for the camp and they all had a hand in raising the money to send the team.

You get a lot of practice in July and it is great for the team to bond. It also gets your players on a college campus. Some of our players will never see a college campus unless we take them there. This also gives exposure to your talented players.

If you want your team to be noticed, you have to promote them. We do a lot of promotional stuff. We promote our players to colleges as hard as we can. We send tape and highlight reels whenever they are requested. Coaches are not paid enough to do all the extras that are required to give their players a shot. However, that is the responsibility of the coach to take care of his players.

We send out newsletters once a month to parents, alumni, and supporters of the program. We let them know what is going on in the off-season and how our players are doing in other sports. This is when we publish the dates of upcoming events within the program. This allows the parents to prepare accordingly as far as vacations.

We produce a media guide every year. We send it to the local radio and television stations. We have gotten a lot of media exposure in our immediate area. The football team has been good, but we make it easy for them to cover us. They have all the information right in front of them to write a story if they choose. You cannot imagine how much newspaper reporters and media personalities appreciate having that material.

We try to connect with our alumni. We selected an all-time team. We conducted a golf outing to raise camp money. Our alumni like the idea that we care about them and know they exist.

If you have a booster club, I strongly suggest that you attend all your booster club meetings. Those meetings are not always what they are supposed to be. The booster club is supposed to boost the team, not boost the coach out. If you are at the meeting, there is less chance of people talking about you negatively. If possible, control your booster club. Get them to do what you want them to do. That is what they should be doing. Too many of them have their own agenda and do what they want to do.

We have a junior high and elementary camp. We send out a mailing every year to students in grades 3 through 7 to invite them to camp and to promote our team. I think that marketing our program to the lower elementary schools has helped increase our numbers in our program. In the junior high camp, we give the participants a copy of the highlight tape and a post-season booklet. We give them bumper stickers and t-shirts.

We have three main fundraising efforts. We conduct a lift-a-thon, have a golf outing, and sell coach's choice cards. All the trophies, t-shirts, plaques, and awards we give in the off-season come from fundraising moneys. We also have pregame meals that come from the money we raise in the off-season. The coach's card comes through Varsity Gold fundraising. We raised a lot of money with those cards. It is easy, quick, and beneficial.

After the season is over, I meet with the seniors. We talk about expectations. We try to give them an honest evaluation of where they can play at the next level, if they have that interest. Every player wants to be a Division I player. But we all know there are very few Division I players. It is our job to begin to tell our players what major college recruiters are looking to recruit. If you are 5'9", 160 pounds, and run a 5.1 in the 40, Ohio State is not going to recruit you. Nevertheless, there probably is a school out there to play for if you want to play.

Each year your staff should try to visit and attend coaching clinics, and visit colleges in search of new ideas. Be active in your local and state associations and meetings.

That gets through most of the off-season activities within our program. Our in-season schedule starts in August. The first thing we have to do is make sure we have an installment schedule. You have to plan to make sure you go into your first game with everything it takes to win.

When we go to two-a-day practices, we keep our players there all day. Our players are with us from 8:30 in the morning to 6:00 in the evening. We give them a break in between the two practices.

We do not have lights at Shaker Heights and play our games on Saturdays. On Monday, the offensive and defensive staff meets at 6:30 in the morning to complete the game planning. We begin practice at 3:30 and start with the video of the previous game. We go out in helmet and shoulder pads and work on special situations in the kicking game. We work on onside kick, quick kicks, fake field goal, fake punt, and the hands team.

Tuesday is our offensive day. Anyone who is a two-way player goes to the offensive side during this day. We are a two-platoon football team, but on occasion, we have players go both ways. When we went to two-platoon football, it got more players involved in our program. During our team period, we have our best on best. We have the number-one offense against the best scout-team personnel we can have.

Wednesday we focus on defense. We do the same thing we did on Tuesday except the slant is to the defensive side of the ball.

When we get to Thursday, we have the offense and defense practicing separately working on timing. They are working against the younger groups and timing is the focus for the first groups. The younger player does not give the starter much resistance, but that is fine with us.

On Friday, we work on pregame and kicking game. Everything is repeated for the offense and defense. We walk through all last-minute situations.

Most everyone plays Friday-night games. No one in this room likes to play Saturday afternoon games on the road. We did not like that idea, but we had no choice. We decided a long time ago to turn that to our advantage. We bring our players in at 10 a.m. on game day. We have a pregame meal in the cafeteria or social room. From there, we go into our offensive- and defensive-position meetings. At 11:15, we go through a walk-through on the game field. We play our games at 2:00 and we are relaxed and ready to go.

When we play games on Friday nights, our players get excited about playing at night. They motivate themselves. Saturday after the game, the coaches like to break down the game film. Sunday is a day off for the players.

In our Tuesday practice, we start out with a dynamic warm-up. We do not stretch as a group. We do five minutes of extra point and field goals. The next 10 minutes we practice punting for the 40-yard line. The next 20 minutes are individual group drills. When we go to team drills, we always start out with our goal-line offense going into the end zone. From there, we go to the offense coming off the goal line.

After that, we go to the regular offense for 20 plays. In 2003, we lost our second and third games of the season in the last 20 seconds. We were ahead in both game and lost. We lost the second game on a trick play that is no longer legal. We lost on a double pass behind the line of scrimmage. In the third game, we scored with 30 seconds left in the game. We went into the lead 12-10. The opponent threw a Hail Mary and kicked a field goal as time expired to win 13-12.

Ever since then, we have one play of what we call sudden touchdown. You probably call the play Hail Mary. We practice that play every Tuesday.

Every week during the season, we pick players of the week. We pick an offensive lineman, skill player, defensive player, and three scout-team players of the week. We pick our JV players of the week, also. We try to recognize as many players as we can.

We have a Helmet Decay Award similar to Ohio State's. Most of the decays are awards for team participation and not individual awards.

During preseason and in-season, we have daily character-development lessons. We try to address attitude, responsibility, respect, and character. We spend 10 or 15 minutes and really drive those points home. I am of the opinion that we are the last group of people that have a chance to discipline teenagers.

Teachers have a tough time doing it any more. If you are a good parent, you discipline; most do not. We are the last ones who can. I use football as a way to try to get through to these kids and teach them what it takes to be successful in life. Football is a means to get there.

Most players who play in high school do not go on to play in college. Those that do play in college are finished after they use up their college eligibility. We can teach them what it takes to be successful. You should take advantage of that. My assistant coaches get frustrated that I spend so much time talking about that kind of stuff. Nevertheless, I feel that strongly about it.

We have a Good Deed of the Week program. On Friday, the players stand up in front of the team and tell about their good deeds. That is trying to get them to think in terms of others instead of worrying about themselves all the time. That becomes a character issue.

We do a lot of visualization training. Visualization is important in any activity—especially sports. We started doing something several years ago called "confidence circles." You get all the players in a position and they sit on the floor in a circle. One at a time, each player stands up. Everyone in that circle has to say something good about the player. They have to say something good about him as a player or a person. It gives reinforced positive thoughts about the player.

There is another technique to build confidence and team unity. It is "support squad partners." We have two players working in a pair. Each of them will tell the other what their goals are for the week. The partner tries to help his partner reach those goals. They have a different player each week. As the season goes on, they get to know their teammates better.

The last thing has been the most effective we have done motivation-wise. Late in the year, before our biggest late-season opponent, I bring all the players that will play in the game together for a meeting. This is the "coach's appreciation meeting." I close the door and have them sit down. I go through every player in that room and say something good about him and what he means to the team. I say it aloud in front of everyone. How many times do you do something like that? You might do it at the banquet if you have time.

We do it the night before the biggest game we have in the season. It is amazing each year how the players come out and play their best. You cannot do that all the time or it loses it value. That is why I only do it once a year.

In the post-season, we have several things we have to handle. We have all the media all-stars along with the all-star games. We have to deal with college prospects. We have the player awards named after alumni players and special awards for every senior. We have the appreciation awards given to coaches, parents, and other helpers. We have the banquet and exit interviews with the seniors.

We have a lot of awards we give at the end of the season. We try to keep the tradition of the school alive by naming the awards after former alumni. We give an MVP trophy and most outstanding awards to all positions. We have the most outstanding offensive player, defensive player, back, receiver, O-lineman, linebacker, defensive back, D-lineman, and special-teams player.

Then we go to the specialty awards. We have an outstanding attitude award, highest G.P.A., most improved, 12th man award, perseverance, most courageous, outstanding character, Warrior of the Year, most improved attitude, outstanding team player, and most dedicated in the season.

I give the coach, parent, and people that have helped in our program a special gift at the end of the banquet.

The last official thing I have to do at the end of the season is the senior exit interviews. That is where you sit down at the end of the season and let the seniors vent anything they might have on their minds. We talk to them about college and their goals. It is also a time for them to reflect on their treatment in the program.

We give our players a winner's manual, which I got from Jim Tressel. It has our mission statement and a section about the role of parents in our program. We know what the role of parents is, but they do not. The parents that need to read this do not. The parents that do not need to read this almost memorize it.

Parents
Your Role in Interscholastic Athletics

Communicating with Your Children

- Make sure your children know that win or lose, scared or heroic, you love them, appreciate their efforts, and are not disappointed in them. This will allow them to do their best without fear of failure. Be the person in their lives they can look to for constant positive reinforcement.
- Try your best to be completely honest about your child's athletic ability, competitive attitude, sportsmanship, and actual skill level.
- Be helpful but do not coach them. It is tough not to, but it is a lot tougher for the child to be flooded with advice and critical instruction.
- Teach them to enjoy the thrill of competition, to be "out there trying," and to be working to improve their skills and attitudes. Help them develop the feeling for competing for trying hard and for having fun.
- Try not to relive your athletic life through your child in a way that creates pressure. You were frightened, backed off at times, and were not always heroic. Athletic children need their parents so do not withdraw. There is a thinking, feeling, sensitive, free spirit in the uniform who needs a lot of understanding—especially when their world turns bad. If they are comfortable with you, win or lose, then they are on their way to maximum enjoyment.

- Do not compete with the coach. If our child is receiving mixed messages from two different authority figures, he will likely become disenchanted.
- Do not compare the skill, courage, or attitude of your child with other members of the team.
- Get to know the coach. Then you can be assured that his philosophy, attitudes, ethics, and knowledge are such that you are happy to have your child under his leadership.
- Always remember that children tend to exaggerate both when praised and when criticized. Temper your reaction and investigate before overreacting.
- Make a point of understanding courage and the fact that it is relative. Some of us climb mountains and are afraid to fly. Some of us will fly but turn to jelly if a bee approaches. Everyone is frightened in certain areas. Explain that courage is not the absence of fear, but it means doing something is spite of fear and discomfort.

Communication You Should Expect from Your Child's Coach:

- Philosophy of the coach.
- Expectations the coach has for your child as well as all the players on the squad.
- Locations and times of all practices and contests.
- Team requirements (fees, special equipment, off-season conditioning)
- Procedure should your child be injured.
- Discipline that results in the denial of your child's participation.

Communication Coaches Expect from Parents

- Concerns expressed directly to the coach.
- Notification of any scheduling conflicts well in advance.
- Specific concerns about a coach's philosophy and/or expectations.

Appropriate Concerns to Discuss with Coaches

- The treatment of your child, mentally and physically.
  Ways to help your child improve.
- Concerns about your child's behavior.

Issues Not Appropriate to Discuss with Coaches

- Playing time.
- Team strategy.
- Play calling.
- Other student-athletes.

Appropriate Procedure for Discussing Concerns with Coaches

- Call to set up an appointment with the coach. Contact the athletic administrator to set up the meeting if unable to reach the coach.
- Do not confront a coach before or after a contest or practice. These can be emotional times for all parties involved and do not promote resolution.

If the Meeting with the Coach Did Not Provide a Satisfactory Resolution

- Call to set up an appointment with the athletic administrator or activities director.
- Determine the appropriate next step at this meeting.

We have an off-season booklet for the players. It has everything in it about the awards and points system. It is an inclusive manual of our program.

I give our staff a handbook. When I was an assistant coach, the head coach told me a couple of things and sent me out there to coach. I did not learn a whole lot about coaching from him. I have tried to help my staff become better coaches knowing they will be head coaches some day. I want them to be good assistants until then, but I want them to know how to run a program when they get there.

Football Guidelines for Coaches

Be a role model for our players. Be careful what you say and do in front of them.

- Arrive to practice at least a half hour early.
- *Hustle* on the field. If you walk, your players will walk.
- Be enthusiastic, especially when they will not (two-a-days, in-season practices on Tuesday and Wednesday). Set the tone.
- Severely limit the use of foul language. Use it *rarely* and *only* for its shock value and reinforcing a very important point.
- Dress appropriately.
- Be active and supportive during dynamic warm-up. Socializing, sitting, or not being on the field yet sets a very negative tone among the players. All coaches should be on the field when dynamic warm-up begins, and they should be active—motivating players, setting up drill areas, and so forth. There should be only very rare exceptions to this.
- Take the bus to away games. Exceptions are when the game is near your house or you must make a quick exit for an important event.

Be positive with our players. Calling players names and tearing them down will not get them to do what you want. Correct a player's behavior using the "sandwich technique" – begin with a positive comment, then correct him, and end with another positive comment. This reinforces the correction you are attempting to get across.

- Learn to be a great motivator. Read articles and books, listen to tapes, and watch videos on how to motivate people. (Zig Ziglar, Bruce Boguski, Tony Robbins, Jim Tressel, and Lou Holtz are just some to study.)
- Find something good to say to each of your players every day. Spend a minute or two

daily asking each player about off-the-field things (grades, classes, likes/dislikes, family, girlfriends, jobs, etc.). This shows you care about them and love is the greatest motivator.

Treat all the players fairly and enforce discipline fairly. Keep your likes and dislikes of players out of coaching decisions and do not allow personal feelings to affect how you treat those players. Coach the untalented players just as hard as you coach the talented ones.

- Learn to be an objective evaluator.
- Learn to be an effective disciplinarian.

Teach by showing and drilling, not by "telling." The players will learn by watching you and doing the particular task over and over correctly. You will need to correct it as they drill it, so they are creating a natural (and correct) and response of their body and mind to a stimulus, or key. Practice and repetition make permanent. Perfect practice and repetition make for great performance. Players will never do what you want them to if you only "tell" them to do it, they do it only a few times, or they do it incorrectly.

Do a good job of scouting, studying film or opponents, and grading out film. These are extremely important functions of all coaches with responsibility for players at a particular position. That takes some time on Friday or Saturday nights, Saturday mornings, and Sundays. You are given more time away from school than many other Division I staffs. The trade-off is that you are responsible for squeezing in film study on Sundays. Do not leave it up to the coordinators.

Be the type of coach you will want on your staff when you are a head coach. Care about the program. Take pride in the job you do. Communicate with the players and other coaches. Respect the players and other coaches.

Don't be a "yes" man. Use your brain and experience to contribute to the game planning and season planning.

Realize what you do not know. Your lack of experience or possible inability to see the big picture may inhibit how much your input is utilized. Don't be offended. The longer you coach, the more you study the game, and the greater responsibility you get on the staff, the more you will realize what you *do not* know. You *will* become better over the time.

Attend clinics and college practices, read coaching books, subscribe to coaching magazines, watch coaching videos, talk to coaches from other levels and schools, and join coaching associations. Continue to improve your bank of knowledge as a coach.

Disagreements on a coaching staff are good things. Disagreements within the staff in front of the players are very bad. Keep the disagreements in the office. Never disagree on the field in front of players. The head coach or coordinator will make a final decision. Even if you do not agree with it, support it when you leave the office.

Before acting on your own, communicate with the head coach first. Be aggressive and gung-ho, but do not be a "loose cannon." Be sure what you want to do fits within the philosophy and goals of the program.

Familiarize yourself with the mission statement, program philosophies, team rules and procedures, our X's and O's, and all other aspects of the program.

The head coach will ask a lot of you. He will demand a lot of you. However, he will not ask you to put in more time or work harder than he does. He will set an example for you as he expects you to set an example for the players.

Coach your players every play. Never coach another coach's players. You will be given a job to do, and you will be allowed to do it. Do it well, and do not try to do the "other guy's job."

Be loyal to the program and the head coach. This means refraining from criticizing the head coach and other coaches on the staff, and the decisions those coaches make, and refraining from discussing strategy outside the coach's office. The head coach also owes you the same respect and loyalty.

Enjoy what you do as a coach, where you do it, and enjoy the people you do it with. Many men out there would love to be in the shoes as a football coach. Many of them are in situations where they cannot and must work for a living. Enjoy your coaching experience. Many coaches despise the people they coach with. We have a very professional staff who respect each other and get along well. Appreciate each other. Finally, we are very privileged to be coaching at a place like Shaker Heights High School. We have a supportive administration, a decent but not overzealous fan following, and athletes who are good kids. Appreciate your experience and enjoy it.

Coaches should realize what they do not know. The older you get, the smarter you get, but the older you get, the dumber you get. When we were young coaches, we probably thought we knew everything. They would talk about the old coach not getting it. The best defense to run is the 4-4 or the best offense to run is the I formation. If that were true, every state championship team would run the 4-4 and the I formation. There is no best play. There is no one right way to do things. The more you go to clinics, the more books you read or the more videos you see, the more you realize you do not know.

I want to recommend some books on motivation. I have read all of these books and they have something for every coach. The best one on the list is the first one, by Dale Carnegie.

Books

- *How to Win Friends and Influence People* by Dale Carnegie
- *Bigger, Faster, Stronger: The Total Program* by Greg Shephard

- *Championship Team Building* by Jeff Janssen
- *Coach of the Year Clinic Manuals* edited by Earl Browning
- *Coaching and Motivation* by William E. Warren
- *Successful Coaching* by Rainer Martens
- *The Team Captain's Leadership Manual* by Jeff Janssen
- *Coaching and Winning* by William E. Warren
- *Turning Slumps into Streaks* by Bruce Boguski

Character Education Curriculum

- *Changing Lives* by D.W. Rutledge and Dennis Parker

Periodicals

- *Americana Football Monthly*
- *Gridiron Strategies*
- *Scholastic Coach and Athletic Director*
- *Championship Performance*

What I have talked about helped us build a program. It works for us. You do not coach football; you coach people. The "Jimmies and the Joes are more important than the X's and O's." A perfect practice makes perfect. Practicing the right way makes you learn the skill. If you fail to plan, you plan to fail. Finally, enjoy coaching football. Make it fun for you and the team.

This is America's sport and we are lucky to have the chance to coach it. I am actually leaving Shaker Heights and moving to Dayton. My wife got a great job down there. I will be at Shaker Heights until June. If any of you have any questions, feel free to call. Thanks again for the opportunity.

DEFENDING THE SPREAD OFFENSE

St. Xavier High School, Ohio

I think there is one thing I have learned in the past 20 years. I was smarter when I was younger. I used to soak everything in and everything worked. Nowadays you realize you need good players to make things work. We have been fortunate at St. Xavier High School to have very good players.

I have gotten dumber every year. When I became a head coach, I found that I did not have all the answers that I had when I was an assistant coach. There is a little more pressure on you when you become the head coach.

I appreciate Nike having us here tonight and I want to thank all of the coaches here for your attendance. We used to use a 3-4 defense. With the advent of the spread offense, we shifted and changed a little bit. I am a firm believer in the odd front. Since the spread offense, we have gone to an odd stack.

I am going to talk about defending the spread tonight. I think the key to defending the spread is speed. In 2000, we played Anderson High School. We won the game 40-37 as I recall. It was a real shootout. I was the defensive coordinator at the time. We knew at that time we were going to have to make some changes if we were going to be successful defending the spread offense.

We went to clinics and a number of different colleges. We visited Ohio University, whose coaching staff is now at Wake Forest. We talked about the odd stack or the 3-3 look. That is what we have gravitated toward today. We are still in the odd front and have the stack look, but we play five secondary players.

In the old 50 front, we had three down linemen and a physical linebacker who could play over the tight end. He was a 6'0", 210-pound player. He could not move too well in space but was very physical against the run.

The offense started to take out the tight end and replace him with a receiver that could run 4.6 in the 40. We felt it was unfair for us to ask that linebacker to cover a slot receiver. We shifted and changed.

The first thing we had to do was to decide what we wanted to do with the front. We had to identify the coverage scheme we wanted to "hang our hat on." We had to find one that fit our personnel, that could adjust to formations, and that was simple so we could play fast. We are a three-deep team and always will be one.

I have found out I am a much better football coach when I have good athletes. The essential thing a coach has to do is make sure the good athletes play fast.

When the quarterback comes to the line of scrimmage, the first thing he wants to know is whether the middle is opened or closed. Is it a three-deep scheme or a two-deep scheme? I want to know what the quarterback sees as he looks at our secondary. When we line up, we want to give the illusion that we are both coverages. After the disguise, we align and move to the defense we will play.

In the 3-4, we had a number of checks for our outside linebackers. If the offense displaced a receiver, we had to check out of our stunts. That kind of thinking slowed us down in our defensive play. We wanted to play fast and stay with the defense called.

I have an interesting story. We were getting ready for the state finals this year. We played our stack defense all year and were getting good at it. Our kids played fast and believed in what we did.

Our defensive coaches game planned and thought this would be a great time to go back to some of our old 3-4 scheme. We talked about it, got it on the board, and looked at it. We became convinced it was the right thing to do and shifted back to the old defense. We were going to trick the opponent and run some of the old defense.

That Monday, we went out to practice, installed the old defense, and went over the game plan. This was not something new because we had run it at the beginning of the year. We had a horrible practice. After practice, I had three senior linebackers come into my office. They wanted to know why we changed the defense.

They told me they felt good about the defense we ran all year. If we run the defense we ran the past five weeks, we will win the game. I went back to the defensive coaches and told them we were scraping all the 50 stuff. It made sense to stay with the defense the players believed in and wanted to play.

It was lucky for me that I listen to my players. They are a lot better and smarter than I am as a coach.

When we play defense, we want to take away what the passing game does best. We identify their top passing combinations. The first thing look at is the backside isolation. Every spread team in the world wants to work to the single receiver. He is the playmaker. He is the receiver that is big, physical, and can get deep. The offense puts him to the backside and waits to see how you will play him.

Once we decide how to handle him, we go to the frontside progression routes. We must have an answer for that situation also. We have to stop the go-to receiver. After we decide how to handle the defensive coverage, we adjust the rush according to down-and-distance, red zone, and situation. We use five-man fire zones, four-man storm zone, and three-man two zones.

This is our base alignment against a standard front (Diagram #1). The defensive ends align in a 4

technique, head up on the offensive tackles. The nose aligns in zero technique, head up on the center. The stack linebackers stack behind the ends and nose at a depth of three to four and a half yards.

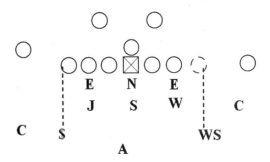

Diagram #1. Base Defensive Alignment

The corners align in an outside shade on the number-one receiver seven yards deep. They have a sideline rule. If the receiver gets within six yards of the sideline, they cheat to an inside shade.

We call our linebackers jet, Sam, and Will. We adjust their alignment to the teams and adjustments we want. We played Colerain High School twice this year. They were an option team and we wanted to press the line of scrimmage. We played our linebackers at three and a half yards. Against passing teams, we play them as deep as five yards.

The safeties align seven yards on the outside shade of the tight end or imaginary tight end. Their alignment against a slot is seven yards deep on the inside shoulder. His hash rules for wide splits by the receivers are three yards inside or outside the hash marks. That is constant with everything we do.

The alignment of the strongside and weakside safeties can vary according to the adjustment we call. We can tag a sparrow call to adjust the alignment of the strong safety or a ninja to adjust the alignment of the weak safety. These names have been with us for a long time. I guess sparrow means strong, but I have no clue about the origin of ninja.

The adjuster varies according to game plan and or defense called. His normal alignment is seven yards deep over the strongside guard. We call him the adjuster because he moves all over the field.

If we call falcon strong, he aligns in a two-by-two adjustment over the tight end. He could be two-by-two over the weakside tight end. In his alignments, he will align in all the linebacker positions. We want to confuse the quarterback and move after his first site adjustment.

We have four alignment adjustments we play. If we call spread, the jet and Will linebackers wall outside the tight ends in a two-by-two alignment (Diagram #2).

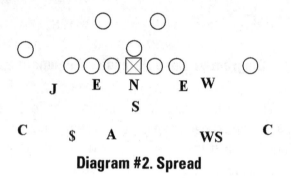

Diagram #2. Spread

The sparrow call puts the strong safety in a two-by-two alignment outside the tight end on the strongside (Diagram #3).

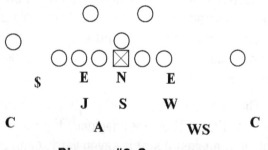

Diagram #3. Sparrow

We can call a bluff and the strong and weak safeties move up the line of scrimmage in a two-by-two alignment outside the tight ends (Diagram #4). That gives us an eight-man front.

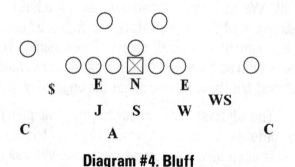

Diagram #4. Bluff

If we align in a ninja adjustment, the weak safety moves down into the box (Diagram #5). He aligns two-by-two outside the tight end or the imaginary tight end.

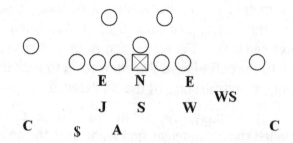

Diagram #5. Ninja

We can get into a bunch of different fronts but for the most part our three down linemen and Sam linebacker do not change. The only time the jet and Will linebacker will change is when we give them a spread call.

I want to talk first about our fire coverage. Everything we do with our coverage is a match-up zone philosophy. When I coached the secondary, the hardest thing I had to teach was how to play the curl-to-flat zone. I coached the defender on his drop. He learned his drop and how to get there. When he dropped into the area, he covered air and the receivers were somewhere else in the pattern.

I could not get the drops over to my players. We went to a match-up concept in our fire and storm coverages. We teach it from day one in practice. Fire and storm are two separate coverages that allow us to play tighter man coverage with outside leverage on the outside receivers. In the coverage, we play a tight match-up zone on the underneath receivers. It enables us to get additional pressure on the quarterback without putting the secondary on an island.

We are not blessed with great speed in our secondary. They are great players and incredibly smart. We have players from our secondary going to Princeton, Cornell, and Columbia. They are well beyond where I am as far as academics are concerned, but they are not great athletes. We give our corners help on the field and coach them to know where the help is.

Originally, the coverage was designed to implement a five-man blitz. However, with the advent of the spread offense, by playing this coverage we have been able to play tighter coverage while maintaining the philosophy of rushing three or four defenders. That is what I want to talk about today.

The rush rules allow you to adapt easily to any coverage scheme, while the progression for our underneath defenders stays relatively the same. The deep scheme in the coverage will change from time to time.

To be successful in this type of coverage you need to have players who can fit certain criteria. You need two cover corners who can match up with speed receivers. You need two athletic safeties or outside linebackers who can run with the slot receivers for 15 yards. You have to be able to route or disrupt all inside receivers. You must have underneath defenders that understand progression reads. You must disguise, mix, and match underneath defenders (Diagram #6). Our variations are simple: we run fire-zone coverage with a five-man blitz, spy with a four-man pattern, or storm-zone with a four-man pattern.

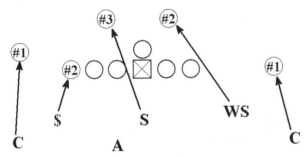

Diagram #6. Fire Coverage

The corners play an outside leverage man on the number-one receiver unless he releases quickly and runs a crossing pattern. That is the only pattern he releases. Anything vertical, the corners lock on with an outside leverage and play loose man coverage. That eliminates the number-one receivers and turns it into a nine-on-nine game.

We have two seam defenders in every coverage we run. It will be a different defender depending on the call.

Seam Defenders

- Read #2 to #3 route progression.
- No immediate threat, get under #1.
- #2 flat-flat man.
- #2 collision the vertical outside in.
- Know where help is (safety inside).
- Carry to 16 yards unless #3 threatens the flat, then play flat man. Read QB outside in and release late. Give up shallow.
- If #2 tries to fight to corner, maintain outside leverage and take away corner route
- #2 cross – carry the cross and deliver to hole.
- Look up #3 out of backfield.
- No #3 think crossing route coming back (dig).

The seam defender, whoever he may be, has the same rules. They read the number-two receiver to number-three receivers. They read the route run by the number-two receiver. If he run a flat route, the seam defender has him man-to-man. He covers the flat route and the wheel route. If he goes vertical, the seam defender collisions him outside in because the safety is on his inside for help. If the number-three receiver releases to the flat, he becomes the number-two receiver. We give up the shallow flat route and react to it late.

Hole Defenders

- Read #3 to #2 route progression.
- Always step with #3, sink 10 to 12 yards.
- #3 flat — deliver to seam and look up #2 on quick cross.
- Carry the cross and deliver to seam defender.
- #3 vertical-collision and sink to 15 yards.
- Keep eyes back on QB expecting underneath threat.

The problem we had in this coverage was on the five-man blitz. The spread teams started to delay the release of the number-three receiver. They would wait until they could match up with the hole defender. That put us in a mismatch in speed. They dump the ball, hit him on the run, and outrun the hole defender. They beat us good with that move.

We adapted and added another defender in what we call storm coverage (Diagram #7). What I like about storm coverage is the corners did not learn anything new. I make fun of them because they line up and do the same thing every day. The toughest position on the field to play is corner. It does not take much to play mentally, but physically it is daunting. Nothing changes for them.

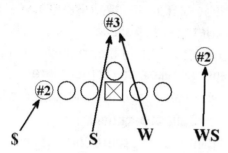

Diagram #7. Storm Coverage

The seam defenders in the storm coverage had similar responsibilities to fire coverage.

Seam Defenders' Rules

- Read #2 to #3 route progression.
- No immediate threat, get under #1.
- #2 flat – man-to-man.
- #2 vertical – collision outside in.
- Know where help is (safety inside).
- Carry vertical outside-in. Rally to anything shallow.
- #3 #2 cross – squeeze and gain depth. Sit on dig coming back.

The seam defender's route read is the number-two receiver. What changes is the vertical route. He plays loose on the vertical and carries the receiver deep if he goes vertical. If he runs a cross, he lets it go. The storm coverage gives us two underneath hole defenders. The seam defender squeezes inside and gains depth to sit down on the dig route by the number-one receiver.

Hook/Curl Defenders

- Read #3 to #2 route progression.
- Always step with #3.
- #3 flat to your side – man.
- #3 flat away – look up, cross back, and lock man.
- #3 blocks – expect check release.
- Do not gain much depth (8 to 10 yards).
- Follow same rules as #2.

This is a sample progression read for a balanced two-by-two formation.

- 10- to 12-yard cross by #2 strong.
- Shallow cross by #2 weak.
- Check down cross by RB #3.

That is what we hope to see in our progression. We have an extra defender sitting on the dig by the number-one receiver and taking away anything vertical from the quarterback. We have the two hook-to-curl defenders jumping the shallow crossing route The weakside safety is leveraging the deep or vertical dig. We think we are sound across the board as far as coverage is concerned. I hope that we can get pressure from our four-man rush with this package.

The cover 2 is the same matching zone concept. It is a change-up to our fire and storm coverage that enables us to play a two-deep safety concept with the matching zone concept underneath. This coverage enables us to play "safer" with pressed coverage on the corners. This provides a tighter coverage on the edge that effectively reduces the quick, three-step game. We can tighten the coverage on widest receivers, while playing a tight match-up zone in the middle.

Originally, we designed the coverage to force an offense to take the short game and waste time. With the advent of the spread offense, we have been able to play tighter coverage across the board and effectively eliminate both the short game as well as the intermediate game.

The progression read remains the same for the underneath defenders. The seam and hole defenders play their progression reads on the underneath receivers. That eliminated more teaching, but changes the corner's assignments.

The corners move from an outside leverage position to a tight trail technique.

Keys to Successful Coverage

- Route disruption of the #1 receivers.
- Athletic safeties and outside linebackers who can run with slot receivers for 15 yards
- Good "trail technique" from the two corners
- Underneath defenders who understand the progression reads
- Disguise scheme and mix-and-match underneath defenders
- Safeties who can cover one third of the field

The rules and responsibilities are the same for the seam and hole defenders. The safeties play deep halves of the field.

The corners change their technique to a trail technique. They funnel the release of the number-one receiver toward the help in the middle of the field. They set on quick releases of the receiver. If they read the fade route, they open to the receiver, collision him, and force him wide. For any other release by the wide receiver, they disrupt the route and sink underneath.

The next thing is the two-by-two adjustments from the storm scheme (Diagram #8). We call this stack-strong edge storm. The strongside end penetrates the B gap. The noseguard penetrates the away A gap. The weakside end penetrates the C gap to his side and contains the ball. The jet linebacker moves to a wide 9 technique and comes off the edge. That is our four-man game.

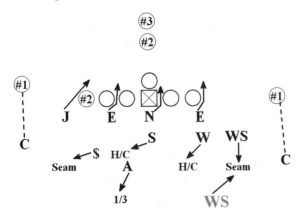

Diagram #8. Stack-Strong Edge Storm

In the storm coverage, the Sam linebacker plays hook-to-curl (Diagram #9). The strong safety drops down, replaces the jet linebacker, and plays the strong seam. The weak safety drops down and plays the seam to the weakside. The Will linebacker plays the other hook-to-curl zone. The adjuster drops into the middle and plays the deep with an emphasis on matching the number-two receiver on the vertical. The corners play loose man coverage.

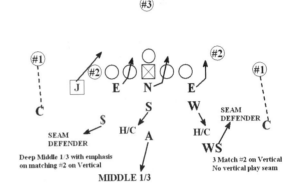

Diagram #9. 2 *2 Coverage Adjustments

We have a "3 match rule." The weak safety matches any vertical from the number-two receiver to his side. The strong safety matches any vertical from the number-two receiver to the middle third. Everyone else plays his normal responsibilities. This defense provides us with an additional hook-to-curl defender. This rule prevents the offense from getting four verticals against the three-deep look. With two slot receivers, the offense can get four verticals quickly.

If we wanted to keep the strong safety in the middle of the field, we call falcon. That puts the adjuster in position to replace the jet linebacker and the strong safety takes the middle third. The adjuster and strong safety switch positions and responsibilities. It is the same concept but a different look for the offense.

If we call the bluff defense, the strong and weak safeties drop down into the box and we have another look for the offense and still play the same coverage. The front does not change. Once they hear strong edge, they run the stunt regardless of what happens on the offensive side of the ball.

If the offense goes to a three-by-one formation with a one-back set, we must adjust. We want to stay with the strong edge call for the front. In this formation, I do not like the match-up we get with the Sam linebacker covering the number-three receiver. It is a long way for him to go to get the coverage on the tight end. We handle that problem with a check we call sling (Diagram #10). We sling the coverage the other way.

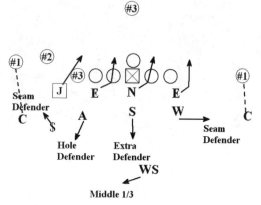

Diagram #10. Sling Coverage

The weakside safety goes from the weak seam defender to the middle third player. The Will linebacker becomes the seam player to the weakside instead of the hook-to-curl defender. He has to get under the number-one receiver to the backside. The Sam linebacker is the extra defender and plays hook-to-curl. The adjuster drops down and plays the sling defender in the hole, reading the number-three receiver to the number-two receiver.

If the offense motions from a two-by-two formation to a three-by-one formation, we sling the coverage. That keeps the front playing fast, because they make no adjustments. The secondary players do the thinking and adjusting. When they get good at the changes and can play fast.

If we have a weakside edge call, it is no big deal because the jet linebacker is in position to covers the number-three receiver. We do not sling the coverage on weakside stunts.

This may seem like a lot to learn, but from day one of our practice, our players rep this defense. They can learn it and you can stay with whatever blitz you want to call.

If we call a strongside nasty, that is basically the same stunt as the edge. The strongside defensive end penetrates the strong C gap and the jet linebacker blows the B gap (Diagram #11). It does not matter what blitz pattern you want to run. The coverage remains the same for the two-by-two and three-by-one formations. The only thing that changes is the blitz pattern on the strongside.

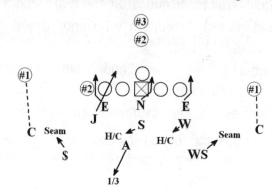

Diagram #11. Nasty

The five-man fire zone is somewhat different. From the stack defense, we run Iowa strong fire (Diagram #12). I think everyone runs this pattern blitz in some form. The strongside end goes into the A gap. The nose and weakside defensive end do the same thing they did on the edge stunt. The jet linebacker comes off the edge and the Sam linebacker fires into the B gap.

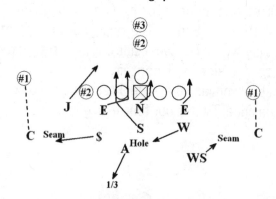

Diagram #12. Iowa Strong Fire

We run fire coverage in the secondary. We cannot run the storm coverage because we lost our extra defender by bring one more in the blitz pattern. The strong and weak safeties are the seam defenders. The Will linebacker drops to the middle underneath and is the hole defender. The adjuster runs to the middle third and the corners play loose man coverage.

From this package, we like to run psycho strong fire (Diagram #13). We walk the jet and Will linebackers up to the outside, and blitz them from the edge. The defensive ends slant into the B gaps. The noseguard reads the center and plays the A gaps. The secondary plays the same coverage they did on the Iowa fire zone, except the Sam linebacker is the hole player.

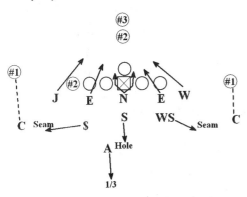

Diagram #13. Psycho Strong Fire

If the offense has a quarterback that likes to run the ball, we play sickem spy 2 (Diagram #14). The ends and noseguard have free rush techniques to the quarterback. They do not worry about containment or lanes in their rush. The Sam linebacker spies the quarterback. He presses the quarterback as soon as he takes a step in any direction. The adjuster and Will linebacker are the seam players. The jet linebacker becomes the hole defender. The corners play tight man coverage on the wide receivers and the strong and weak safeties play the halves.

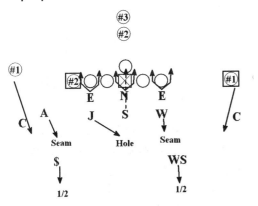

Diagram #14. Sickem Spy 2

There are four phases in teaching our seam defender progression. We drill them in separate drills. In the diagram the coverage not assigned to the seam defender will be most of the inside route and the routes to the flat when the number-two receiver takes the vertical release. In the first phase, the number-two receiver has a flat, vertical, and cross route (Diagram #15). The seam defender applies his technique to each route.

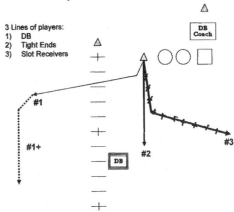

Diagram #15. Seam Defender Phase I

In phase II of the read, we add a backside receiver into the pattern (Diagram #16). The seam defender covers to the flat provided the number-two receiver does not come vertical. If the number-two receiver goes inside and the number-three receiver comes outside, the seam player has the number-three receiver coming outside. The hole player takes the number-two receiver coming inside. The hole player takes the crossing route coming from the other side. If the seam defender has no pattern up the field, he sinks into the dig area. He could help on the cross route from the other side.

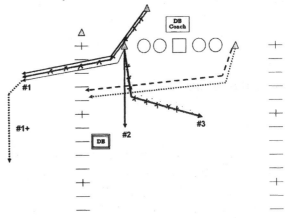

Diagram #16. Seam Defender Phase II

Phase three of the progression drill puts two seam players into the drill and receivers working both sides of the formation (Diagram #17).

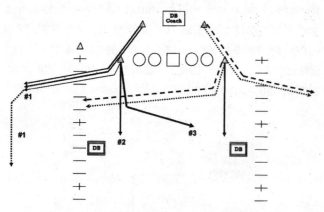

Diagram #17. Seam Defender Phase III

In phase four of the drill, we add the hole defender to the drill and play the entire scheme, with the two seam players and the hole player (Diagram #18).

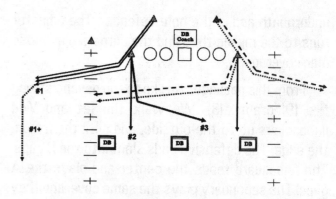

Diagram #18. Seam Defender Phase IV

I am running short on time and I want to show you some film. We can go to the break-out room for any of you who may have question about the defense. I will be happy to continue as long as you want to go. Whatever you need, just e-mail me and I will send you everything we have. Thanks for you time I appreciate it.

THE BASIC 3-5 RADAR DEFENSE

Nitro High School, West Virginia

Thank you. It is a pleasure for me to be here on behalf of Nitro High School and speak to you about our concept of defense. We do some things a little bit different at Nitro, and usually the first thing people ask me when watching our film is about how we came up with this defense.

They call it radar defense but when I think of radar defense, I think of people standing up, moving down the line, picking a gap, and going, and that is not really what we are. We are standing up, but we are not moving around.

We came up with it after we had scrimmaged a wing-T team one year, and they had thumped us pretty good. When we broke down the film and charted all the stats, we found that our down linemen did nothing. They were not helping us at all. At the same time, our linebackers were pretty much getting where they needed to be and making all the plays. We began to wonder what would happen if we just stood our linemen up like the linebackers.

Our problem was that we were not very big. As a school we are not very big and our players are not very big. We only had 33 kids dressed for the AAA state championship game this year and we played with two kids who were less than 150 pounds at defensive tackles.

Anyway, when our defensive linemen would engage with offensive linemen, they would get knocked backwards, and if they finally did get off of the block, the ball was gone. We thought we were asking our kids to do something they could not do, so we tried standing them up.

The following week we stayed in our 4-4 look, but with our 2 techniques standing up, and we had a

lot more success. Our opponent that week was another wing-T team and we shut them down pretty good. I believe that they went on to become the AA state runners-up that year. We thought that maybe we were onto something.

After that week, we went to a 3-5 look rather than a 4-4, but we kept our two tackles and our nose man standing up, with five linebackers standing behind them (Diagram #1). That is how we stumbled into this thing.

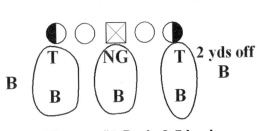

Diagram #1. Basic 3-5 Look

Every offensive line coach spends time teaching the drive block and driving the sled, but against us that is useless. Our defensive linemen who are standing up are two yards off of the ball, and we are not there when the drive blocker gets there to block on us. We are gone and we are someplace else, so we believe that our scheme takes away the drive block from the offensive linemen.

Also, offensive linemen in high school cannot cut any defender not aligning within one yard of the line of scrimmage, so our scheme has eliminated the cut block and the drive block. Now that takes away a big part of any blocking scheme, so that gives us two big advantages from the start.

Strength coaches will not want to hear this, but I have been at Nitro High School for 10 years and we have had some success, and we have never had a weight room. I wish we did, and now that we have been to our second state championship game, they are building us one this year. Hopefully, now we will get stronger.

I do not know how many of you go into games realizing that you are just not as strong as the other team. I read in the paper all the time where coaches say that they got whipped up front, or that they just could not match up with their opponent up front. Well, this is a way of offsetting a bigger team's strength by using speed rather than strength.

The other advantage that we think we have in running this defense is that we have eliminated the guessing game. It was mentioned that we have had some success on offense by going no huddle. No huddle gives us a chance to line up, see what you are in defensively, and eliminate the guessing game. Well, the same goes with our defense.

If you call a slant, an angle, or a blitz, you may have some tendencies on the other team but you are still guessing. Well, this defense has allowed us to not ever have to call any of those things. We feel like we are slanting, angling, or blitzing right into the play on every snap, and I will show you more of what I am talking about. We do not ever have to call that kind of stuff so we do not have to guess with an offensive coordinator any more. Our kids are making their reads and we think we are slanting, angling, or blitzing into the play every time.

There is another advantage we think it gives us. If you put this defense in, people are only going to be able to practice against it for one week. They go out Monday and show it to their kids, they practice against it Tuesday and Wednesday, and they have some kind of pregame walk-through on Thursday. They really only get to block it for two days.

Their offensive linemen are going to be confused at the beginning of the game. We see it in almost every game that they are not sure where the defenders are, or where they are going. I think that any time you make a team practice against something they are not used to seeing, then that is an advantage. It gets their kids out of the comfort zone.

If you saw a team all standing up two yards off the ball and the next level of linebackers five yards off the ball, it may come to your mind offensively that you would just run sneaks and wedges, get your three or four yards, and then do it again. Well, that is not a normal game plan. Not very many people regularly do that.

What we have found out is that almost every coach who goes against us for the first time alters his game plan. He gets his kids trying to do something that they have not been doing the other 10 weeks of the season. We have played teams that have never been in two tights and a full-house backfield before, and in the very first series, here they come. They seem to think that pounding it right at us is the answer. It is yet another advantage for us that we have caused the opponent to alter his game plan.

I do not want to talk about how we read and get there and that kind of thing yet, but we have found that because we are so small and weak, when we were up there in our four-point stances and teams ran right at us, we went backwards every time we engaged. We were going to lose the line of scrimmage and the best thing we could do was maybe try to make a pile.

Now with the quick reads we give our guys, at least we are headed toward the ball on the snap with a full head of steam. That is better than lining up, catching, and getting driven backwards. We get a lot more stalemates this way than we did the other way. The stalemates may happen a yard off the ball rather than the line of scrimmage, but not many teams are satisfied with getting a yard. We are not saying we can stop you from getting one yard. What we are trying to do is keep you from getting three or four yards so you get behind the chains. Then you are playing into our game.

I will say that while we had two tackles who weighed less than 150 pounds, we did have a 300-

pound nose. He was two yards off the ball standing up, but he was a force in the middle. That was another advantage we had.

The other thing that this defense allows you to do is get many, many multiple looks, and it is easy for the kids. Because everyone is standing up and reading, we can move linebackers up to the two-yard level rather than the five-yard level and they are just playing like a linebacker. We do not have to substitute linemen to go from a three-man front to a five-man front because all of our guys are playing like linebackers.

We have gone into many games with two linemen and played a 2-6 look. That is also confusing to the offense. We could also go with three linemen who are playing two 5 techniques and a 9 technique, and no nose in there. It would seem that you would have to run quarterback sneak in there but I will show you film in a minute where, when they do, there are a whole lot of people hitting it real hard. Then again, most people just are not patient enough, I guess, to run quarterback sneak on every play.

It is easy to adjust our scheme to formations. We have five linebackers, so any time we see trips or doubles or anything like that, we do not have to do a whole lot of adjusting to the formations. We have enough skill guys out there that we can spread out with you.

It is also very easy to disguise things. With that many people at the second level, it is easy to roll into other coverages or to bring pressure if we want to, but we do not bring pressure a lot. I say we do not bring pressure, but our game plan in that week may be for our outside backer to have a quick read that automatically brings him off the edge against certain formations. Or perhaps, if he gets a certain look, his automatic read is to come off the backside edge. So, we do bring pressure, but it is all off of the read rather than a huddle call that we are going to send someone. It is coming whenever their read tells them to come.

Now that you know a little bit about how we stumbled into it and what we think the advantages are, we can go a little bit on how we do it.

Every week we come up with a quick read for each lineman and for each linebacker. I will take wing-T teams for example. I want to be careful how I say that no one can do something, but for the last several years no one has been able to stay in the wing-T against us and have success. This defense takes away all the wing-T stuff. They cannot deal with it because of the quick reads it gives our kids.

We may read the guards or we may read the guard that the motion is going to. Some teams read the tackle that the motion is going to cause they will pull the tackle and tight end for that little inside handoff play, but whatever the read is that you come up with that week you have eight guys on that read. When they run the buck sweep and those guards are pulling out there, we got eight guys flying over there to the ball. We will have more people there than they do. It is fun to watch.

Then, when they think we are overpursuing and they try to run the little inside handoff coming back the other way, all eight of our guys are running over there. It has been very successful against the wing-T and I guess the reason is, if you remember when I first started talking, that we stumbled into this because a wing-T team had ripped us up pretty good, and then we stopped a wing-T team the following week.

In the beginning then, it was all based on stopping the wing-T but as we have found, it holds up against all of the offenses that we have faced. I will say that you have to totally buy into this and believe in it or it is not going to work. If you just half way go at it, you will really look silly standing all those guys up. It will either make you or get you fired.

Our kids really believe in this and I know it is not an easy sell. We have had several top coaches come to our office and look at film. Most of them are really impressed by it, but not all come away really sold on it.

If we play a splitback team, we kind of split it in half and offset our nose to either the strongside or weakside, and our Mike backer will be the other way. The nose will have one back and the Mike will have the other one. Everyone else reads his near back. That has really helped us against veer teams.

We play a team that has traditionally been very strong running the veer and since we went to this defense it has really helped us. They have had to go to more of a spread game against us than the veer because it is too easy for us to run and take all of their options away. We have people getting there for the dive, on the quarterback, and on the pitch, and the option game is really easy to defend with all these guys standing up running towards the option.

This defense is really hard on the spread offense and that is funny because we run the spread most of the time. In West Virginia's spread game, they run the tailback one way and the quarterback the other in a fashion that all of you are familiar with. Well, I think that this defense is really hard on that. We would give half of the field to this back and half the field to the other back. Even if they run back in to you, where they take the jab and go this way, our read would take us right into that and we should have them outnumbered on either side of the ball.

Of course, if they want to throw, they are throwing into eight deep. We are dropping eight, so it is hard to throw the ball against eight.

Now you may wonder if we can get any pressure on the quarterback with only three guys up there. All of our defensive linemen use a running-start bull rush. We are two yards off of the ball, so when we read pass we are coming. The offensive linemen are taught to set back, engage the rusher, and stop him. But with the natural separation between the blockers and our defensive linemen who are coming, it is easy for us to set the blocker up with an outside move and dip underneath. We get a full head of steam and we get a lot of pressure with just a three-man rush.

Maybe one of the hardest things for us to defend is just the I formation because it does not give us as quick a read. We always have to decide whether it is the fullback or the tailback we want to read, or if it is a team that is still pulling the guards and taking us to the play that way.

There are some key things that we will take away from the I formation teams. If it is a toss sweep or anything on the perimeter, we have been able to handle it fairly well. If it is the tailback on isolation plays, we have handled that real well. It is the play we call the double dive, that hurts us a little bit where they fake it to the fullback and hand it to the tailback. Usually our first read against I teams is the fullback because he usually takes us to the ball, so double dive gets us out of our lanes a little bit. We got hurt a bit in the championship game with that play.

We have about 50 plays on film here and it should take about 10 minutes to take a look at them. Then Coach Mike Scott will tell you about some technique stuff we use. If at any time you see something you want to ask a question about, feel free to ask a question about it. I will try to go through it with you and tell you what you are getting ready to see.

Okay, if there are no more questions on the film, our defensive coordinator, Mike Scott, is going to talk about our techniques.

Coach Mike Scott

How are you all doing today? At our place, the number-one rule is that we are not going to get outworked as coaches. Coach Tinsley is the chemist and I am his lab assistant. It might be three in the morning until we decide after watching film what we have to do. Coach finally says what he wants done and he tells us to coach it up.

Up front, we want these three guys to eat up these five offensive linemen. That is the basic premise (Diagram #2). We give them the fullback, and then everybody is reading the fullback. They can do it because they are standing up and they are two yards off of the ball. Whichever angle he takes, it is the job of the tackle on that side to meet him. We do not talk about 2 techniques or 5 techniques; we say to go tackle the fullback. The playside guard wants to block a linebacker but he has to do something to slow the nose down. If he tries to check backer first, the noseguard is already flying over to tackle the fullback.

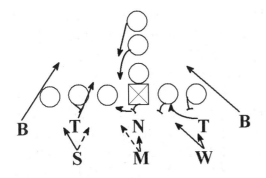

Diagram #2. 3-5 versus ISO

Now when the fullback is your read and you are the backside tackle, you have to go across two faces, but that is easy to do because you are not up on the line. You must make sure you rip across the guard's face so you are taking up two guys.

The center is trying to stop the nose from getting over there, so all five offensive linemen are "eaten up" by our three defensive linemen.

My outside backers are taught to run through. We do not get into a lot of detailed technique about outside arm free, or maintain leverage. We tell them that if anybody comes right at them, whether the fullback or the tailback, they are to run right through his face.

If they are running inside here and it gets all clogged up, the back will bounce and my outside backer will nail him. If they come outside with a lead block, we will run right through his face (Diagram #3). Do not worry about outside contain or any of that stuff. All I want him to do is run through him. Most of the time when that collision happens the tailback will cut back inside where we want him to anyway. If we taught too many detailed contain technique responsibilities, our guys would want to bubble out, and that would just widen the lane.

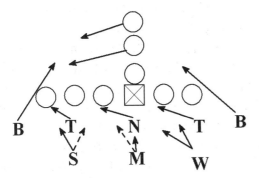

Diagram #3. 3-5 versus Sweep

The key for the outside backers is to run through, and the defensive linemen are each expected to take up two blockers. If they can all do that, then my three inside backers are sitting here untouched and all the offensive linemen are taken up.

They are taught to "hit it from where they are at." If they get in a hurry, I will make them take a read step. I will put them in a closed stance and tell them to read the fullback. As soon as the fullback moves, I want our linebacker to take a read step and then "hit it from where you are at." Do not bubble, and do not try to run out here and do any of that because all of that is taken care of by those outside backers. Hit it from where you are at, and do not go anywhere until you know where your tackle went.

If the ball is at you, and your tackle has crashed down inside, it does no good for you to crash down in there, too. You should come right off that tackle's butt instead, so you can make the play untouched when the back tries to bounce.

Now each lineman and linebacker makes a team. We call the linebackers Sam, Mike, and Will, and we tell them not to go anywhere until they know what their buddy did. If the play starts way outside to Sam's side, our tackle is taught to tackle the fullback whether he has the ball or not, so he is coming outside fighting the offensive tackle and tight end.

Well, I do not need Sam to fly outside anymore because we already have the outside backer out there, so Sam will immediately step right inside off his tackle's butt. The guard cannot really step out to help on Sam because our nose is now ripping across two faces. No one can get to the backers.

The tackle occupies the offensive tackle and tight end. The nose occupies the guard and center, which is easy because he is two yards off of the ball, and Sam has an open door.

You might think counter and other kinds of misdirection would hurt us with all these guys getting these quick reads (Diagram #4). Well, the fullback goes one way on counter and the tailback is coming back, so if everybody is flowing that way we are in trouble. The thing is, everybody is going to the same place regardless, if that makes any sense. If we get counter, our linemen are all reading the fullback. One tackle is probably crashing because the fullback is coming right at him, while the other two are coming hard and fighting across two faces each.

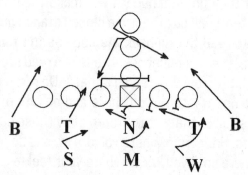

Diagram #4. 3-5 versus Counter

Now to run that counter, they have to pull either the backside guard or backside tackle, which leaves our crashing tackle wide open and they are not going to get anything. Regardless of all that, it is still the front three helping our linebackers make plays.

The backers go through doors. We call them front door or back door. We try to keep it simple for them. If the play starts at Sam he has to know where his tackle is, but once it goes back the other way he goes through his same door regardless of what type of play it is.

Once his flow is gone he does not fit to his tackle. These other two also do not fit when flow is gone. Everybody scrapes back door at the same angle, and there is no place for the offense to cut back. The linebackers are going at the same angles to the same places regardless of what the play is.

I can stand there in practice and watch all five backers and the three linemen all at once in flow and I can see one person that is out of place because he is looking at something he is not supposed to look at. When we started this system, we had to tell our kids over and over again that they had to believe it. They had to trust their reads.

We have been described as an uncommon defense with a new look, featuring the utilization of speed when size is not available. All you really need is a bunch of kids who want to get to the football.

Our time is up here, men. If you are interested in hearing more, we are going down to the Allegheny Room, and we can spend some more time with you. Thank you for your attention.

JET SWEEP AND COMPANION PLAYS

St. Augustine High School, Florida

Thank you. First, on behalf of St. Augustine High School I would like to thank Nike for giving me the opportunity to speak today. I know I am supposed to talk about the speed sweep, but there are some other things I think that are much more important than that. Whether you are an assistant coach or a head coach, there are some things you can take back that I want to talk about before we get to the speed sweep.

Now, as for the speed sweep, it is a particular play that can either be a part of your offense, whether you are an I team, a one-back team, or a spread team, in the gun or under center, or it can be your entire offense, which is the next thing about it. I will go into all of that further, but first I want to say just a little bit about where I want to go, because I do not want to bore you guys a lot tonight. I want to talk a little bit about our program so you will know where we are coming from, and a little bit about the turnaround and how we got that done. I think there are some neat things I can share with you there.

We do not have a lot of bright kids and I am ashamed to say that. Prior to having our second daughter, I probably coached these players a lot differently. If you get one thing out of what I am going to say, this might be the most important thing.

My first daughter is at UCF and she never made a grade as low as a B in her entire life. We had a second daughter and during delivery the doctor, instead of C-sectioning my wife, went ahead and delivered her and she was delivered breech, which means that she came out rear end first. When she came out, she was blue and we did not know how long she was without oxygen. They called for a respiratory therapist and by the grace of God a

therapist was walking by. He came in and got her breathing.

So to make a long story short, I used to think that all kids learned the same way, because if you threw something up on the board, my first daughter would copy it and she would learn it. I now have another daughter who learns completely differently. From that, I think the most important thing is, however you are coaching your kids, make sure that it is not above what they happen to know. It is also important that you teach them differently.

They are not dumb because they do not get it by your telling them how to do it. You might have to show them. You might have to show them or you might have to tell them. You might have to bring them in and show them film, but all kids learn differently.

It used to be acceptable, and I would allow coaches to do it, to call kids "stupid" or "idiots" or things like that. Now, it really turns my stomach. Really, because of my second daughter, I have hopefully become a better human being, and really better for kids.

When we came to St. Augustine, that is the kind of kids we had. We are a D high school. All of our schools are ranked from A to F and we are ranked as a D high school. A high percentage of our kids are having trouble on the FCAT test and things of that nature, so we are continually trying to find better ways to teach our kids.

When they called me to interview at St. Augustine, they had just had a walkout and Channel 12 news from Jacksonville came down and covered it. They had nobody supervising and only about 10 kids on the football team who were coming in to lift weights, and the entire situation was in shambles. It was just a horrendous situation.

I had grown up in Melbourne, coached in Melbourne, and I was at a point in my life where I had decided that it was time for me to leave and go do something different. Whereupon, when St. Augustine called, I said yes, I would go ahead and interview. I went up, did the interview, and I got the job.

St. Augustine had not been to the playoffs since the 1970s. Over the last 10 years, we have won 91 games and we have been to the semifinals four of the last five years and we have won five district titles and finally a state championship. Now, this is not Joey Wiles at all. I believe God placed all the people in my life that have turned this program around, and whether you are a head coach or an assistant coach, you can get something out of this.

I believe the reason we turned it around was because of the coaching staff we hired, and not the X's and O's. Of course you have to have a good guy on offense and a good guy on defense, but it was not the X's and O's. It was the relationship piece to everything.

When I say that, we have a thing that we call "Leadership Monday," which we do every single Monday. I used a book called *The Twenty-One Indispensable Leadership Laws* and I took all of these different characteristics from it. I gave each coach a characteristic and I gave some community leaders characteristics, and it was their responsibility to come in and talk to our team about a particular characteristic.

On our freshmen, JV, and varsity, we have 130 kids. We are a AAA program in a school of 1,400 kids. We bring them all into our weight room on Monday afternoon, and from 3:00 to 3:30 p.m. we have a coach or community leader in and talk about a leadership characteristic such as character, commitment, courage, or generosity. Our speakers are able to model these characteristics through real-life stories for these kids, and they build relationships with them that allow us to lead them as we get on down the road.

So what we did in turning things around was based upon relationships. It was not that we decided to run the speed sweep, or we decided to run what Bob Stoops does on defense. It was not about that. It was the relational stuff first.

The other thing we do that you might consider involves what our coaches do for our players. On every Monday, the coaches have their players over to their homes for dinner after practice. They go over and eat pizza together, and it lets the players see in us models of what it is like to be a husband or a father. Our children are getting to know our players, so it is a big relational thing that is happening.

When we went to play in the state championship game at Joe Robbie Stadium in Miami, we took an offensive bus, a defensive bus, and a special teams bus. All of our coaches, along with their families, rode on those buses with our players. It really calmed our kids and I think it was one of the reasons we went down and upset a team that was probably a little better than we were.

I go back to the idea that it is all relationship based, so if you can start that, I believe it will really help you. If you are an assistant coach, get in there and get to know those kids and get to know their stories. It is probably stuff you are already doing, but I did want to share some of this with you and I do think it is essential.

Next, I think it is really big that you have a plan for everything you do. This is something that I do that you might want to do. We have a football coaches' handbook. In it, I have my philosophy on a varying number of things. Everything from what we are going to do academic-wise, to what our banquet is going to be like, to how we are going to improve our facilities, to having a coach's devotion—all of those things will be touched on in this particular book, and I just want to give you a couple of examples.

First, I will share some of the things we do academically. We will have off-season progress reports and we have academic t-shirts that we give our kids. We have an academic award at the banquet. We have an academic board that lets us know who is in trouble and we have a study hall that one of our coaches runs in the off-season. That is what we are going to do academically to try to improve what we are doing.

Now, we are very simple in everything we do and I want to overemphasize that. I am not at a school with a bunch of bright kids and I do not say that in a derogatory way because I love them. Our strength and conditioning is real easy, utilizing only the four core lifts. Our offense is pretty simple. Our defense is a 4-3 and 50 team, and that is what we do. We do not try to make it real complicated for our guys because for the most part they cannot comprehend it—and again I do not say that in a derogatory way. They just cannot, for whatever reason.

A second example from the handbook deals with travel. This is one that you might take for granted and it is why I say to go through all of the things that you do and come up with your philosophy for them. When we travel, our managers sit in the front. Most of the time they are females, so they sit in the front, then the coaches sit, and then the players sit. When the bus is unloaded, the players help unload the stuff.

Varsity coaches will all ride team buses. I have guys who are always trying to ride the truck to get ahead, so they can go set stuff up and I do not want that. I want every single coach on the bus around the kids, again, going back to building relationships.

Now, I want to get into what we do offensively. I think it is important to have an insertion plan. Without an insertion plan, you are going to leave some things out.

Then, of course, it is essential to have a good practice schedule. We are going to go five-minute periods and we are going to two-platoon. We are a AAA school, middle-of-the-road school, and we completely two-platoon. We will have an offensive side in practice going on over here, while over there we will be running our defensive stuff.

We fill our practice schedule up with five-minute increments, doing a lot of ball security and individual work early on. We will then do a team

pass period, throw some kicking in, and then we always have about 15 or 20 minutes of "stretch-period" offense. You will see as I go through this that you do not have to spend a lot of time coaching the jet sweep.

I did not really believe that at first. We have been an evolving wing-T offense. I visited Herschel Moore at Cumberland University in Tennessee, Bill Zwann at Widener University in Pennsylvania, and Larry Olsen at Navarre High School in Florida. I became convinced that the speed sweep is easy to teach and that it was where we needed to go with our offense.

Why a Coach Should Consider the Speed Sweep Package

- He is able to utilize undersized linemen.
- It is a great misdirection offense.
- The scheme is simple.
- It will fit other offenses.
- It offers a great play-action offense.
- It is a quick way to get onto the perimeter.
- You do not have to block many on the sweep.
- Minimal practice time is needed for sweep.

The jet stuff has allowed us to run even more misdirection than before, and as it says in number seven there, you do not have to block very many people. On the jet sweep, you have to get a piece of the end, you have to get the support player, and be able to get a little bit of a stalk block on the corner. If you can do that, if you can block three people, then you can end up running the play.

We have also learned that you do not need to have "burners" to run the play. A 4.7 guy becomes a 4.5 guy to the defense because he is in full-speed motion when he receives the handoff, and those guys up front cannot take off and go because you have other stuff they must honor.

Reasons St. Augustine Went to Speed Sweep

- It is a quick way to get on the perimeter.
- Minimal practice time is required.

- Extended motion allowed us to run wing-T plays.
- It extended the "life" of the buck sweep.
- Few people were doing it.
- It is a great play out of all sets, including empty.

We particularly like to run the play out of empty. We will go three to one side, two to the other side, and our quarterback will just come up and we will "choice" it. It is just a matter of counting. If they are equal, we have two to block their support guy, and we would run it there. So, you can get into empty, run the play out of empty, throw all your stuff out of empty, and you can still run the counter. You can jet him across and run the counter back the other way, and all kinds of neat stuff that you can end up doing out of it. It is whatever your imagination can come up with.

Before I get into various schemes I would like to discuss some things that I feel are important when organizing and evaluating an offense. I believe that each week it is important to self-scout. It really brings to light what you are actually doing and it allows you to know what your opponents know about you. I also believe it is important to have an insertion plan when you enter fall practice. This helps you to be disciplined in adding plays versus various opponents.

Our base set is a wing with a split end and a wing with a tight end. I will cover the speed sweep against a 50 and 4-3 front, but first there are a couple of key coaching things in the play with the quarterback that I want to go over. The big thing is: when he reverse pivots, he needs to be completely in the playside A gap when he gets around. If he is getting around and stopping early, then the play is too slow. Remember, the wingback has to be in full-speed motion when he receives the handoff.

So when the quarterback is going to reverse pivot, his elbows are going to be tight, hiding the ball just like you do in the wing-T sweep. After the ball is handed, the fullback will stay on the midline and the quarterback will fake to him and continue on the bootleg. If, for some reason, the quarterback misses the handoff, the ball is given to the fullback.

That is built into the play, so the quarterback does not take a hit if he misses the motion from the jet guy.

We do not tell the wingback who is taking the handoff much about the depth he should get. Some backs will belly a little bit and others will stay straight. We just coach them to receive the handoff and run as fast as they can, and we tell them to read the block by the wingback and that is it.

The play is designed to run to the sideline, but because it is now stretching you are going to see that the ball will cut up, maybe in B gap. He takes off and everybody is running, and if he sees a crease, he takes it right now. We would like to try to get to the sideline, but if we do not get there, he is going to cut it up. Being a wing-T concept type of team, they are used to doing that.

I want to show you what the blocking is and then we can get on the film and you can see it (Diagram #1). I will start by giving the rules for running it strong, but we do not run it to the tight end much because it is a longer edge to get to.

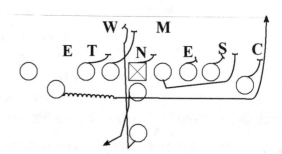

Diagram #1. Speed Sweep Strong versus 50 Front

Strongside Speed Sweep Blocking Rules

TE: Reach man on. Maintain hat throughout the entire block.

PST: Reach man on. If uncovered, pull flat and read TE block.

PSG: Pull flat and read TE block. Turn up inside the first hole.

C: Long scoop. Take angle for Will backer, n/t hash, numbers, sideline.

BSG: Same as center

BST: Same as center

PSWB: Reach first man head-up to outside. Technique same as TE.

QB: Reverse pivot to playside A gap. Hand ball, fake waggle away.

FB: Run through backside A gap. Receive handoff if given.

HB: Full speed when receiving handoff. Read frontside guard.

SE: Stalk the corner.

Timing is the key to the play because we do not block anyone in the B gap (Diagram #2). If the running back is not full speed, he can be tackled by a B-gap player. Our cadence is: "ready, set, go." On the first sound, the running back should be starting to go full speed. When you are running the play from the gun, maybe in an empty set, the quarterback must give the back a foot.

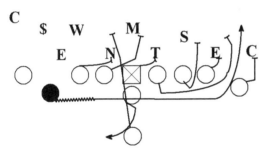

Diagram #2. Speed Sweep Strong versus 4-3

Let us now take a look at the speed sweep to the weakside (Diagram #3). Over the years, this has been our favorite way to run it since you can get to the edge sooner. We like to run it from our base set, out of our empty set, or our empty gun set.

Weakside Speed Sweep Blocking Rules

PST: Reach man on.

PSG: Pull flat and read the OT's block.

C: Long scoop. Take angle to cut off B gap.

BSG: Long scoop. Take angle for Mike backer, n/t hash, numbers, sideline.

BST: Long scoop. Take angle for Will backer, n/t hash, numbers, sideline.

BSTE: Same as BST

PSWB: Reach first man head-up to outside. Technique similar to TE.

QB: Reverse pivot to playside A gap. Hand ball, fake waggle away.

FB: Run through backside A gap. Receive handoff if given.

HB: Full speed when receiving handoff. Read frontside guard.

SE: Stalk the corner.

Again, the big thing is the playside guard (Diagram #4). The playside guard pulls, period. If he has a 3 technique, he is pulling. If he has a 2 technique, he is pulling. He goes, regardless. We do not block a 3 technique in. We will block a 4i, but a 3 technique we will not block. If a 3 technique is making the play, then the jet motion is too slow. Everybody else is just long scooping. They are just turning and running and that is all they are doing. The key block is the block of the support guy by the wingback, and obviously the block by the tackle. Those are the two "biggies," and then of course, the block by the wideout.

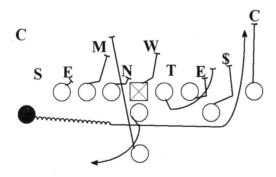

Diagram #3. Speed Sweep Weak versus 50

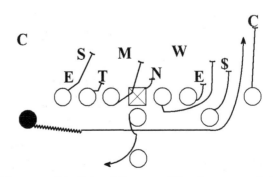

Diagram #4. Speed Sweep Weak versus 4-3

The next phase of our jet series is our fullback trap (Diagram #5). Over the years, it has provided us with our biggest plays. This past season we averaged 8.04 yards per carry on 48 attempts. The trap made up 10 percent of our run-game offense. The key to this play is to have the jet sweep working. The wingback must hit full speed and roll over the ball.

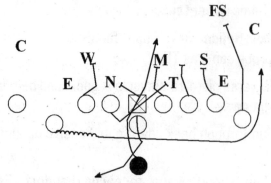

Diagram #6. Jet Trap versus 4-3

I want to show you a couple more of our jet plays, and then we will get to the tape. The first play I will show you is jet belly (Diagram #7). Using our wing-T principles, if the defensive end is sort of peeking out there trying to make a play on the sweep, we will go ahead and run the belly up inside of him. We will block belly just like we do on regular wing-T belly blocking.

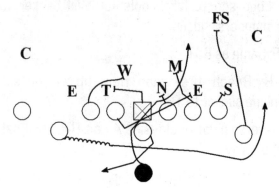

Diagram #5. Jet Trap versus 50

Jet Sweep Blocking Rules

PST: Escape to first inside LB.

PSG: Down to first inside LB.

C: On, away

BSG: Pull, trap first defender head-up or outside PSG. Listen for long/short call.

BST: Escape to first inside LB.

TE: Escape to safety unless Sam LB present.

QB: Reverse pivot, shoulder fake to jet back, hand to FB, fake waggle away.

FB: Dive on midline. First step with playside foot. Read block of guard.

WB: Run jet sweep fake. Roll over ball and carry fake to sideline.

HB: Inside release and block FS.

Again, if you get your jet guy going, and you will see in the tape that the backers will be going, and then the trap hits right up the gut (Diagram #6). Everybody in here probably runs trap, so you do not have to change your trap. You do not have to change any blocking on it. You can run jet trap and use your own trap-blocking scheme.

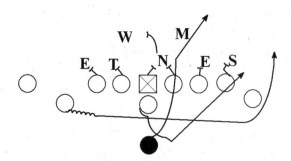

Diagram #7. Belly versus 50

Jet Belly Blocking Rules

PST: On, down. 1 tech: base. 2/3 tech: X block. 50: fan (G calls).

PSG: On, down. 1 tech: base. 2/3 tech: X block. 50: fan.

C: On, backer, listen for fold call.

BSG: Fire, backer

BST: Fire, backer

TE: Fire to safety

QB: Reverse pivot to midline, hand ball, fake load option.

FB: Open crossover, square shoulders, make cut in LOS.

WB: Fake jet sweep, carry fake to sideline.

HB: Block PSLB.

If we get a head-up or a 3 technique, we X block it (Diagram #8). If we have a 1 technique, we block down, turn out, and run it up inside. That is what we do if we get an end running outside.

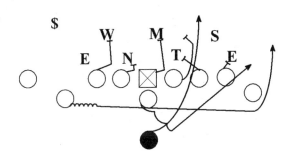

Diagram #8. Belly versus 4-3

One of the great misdirection plays off of the jet sweep is what we call handback. It is a counter trey concept type of play (Diagram #9). Full flow is in the direction of the jet sweep with the fullback taking the ball back away from flow. This is a play we run three to five times per game to help slow pursuit down.

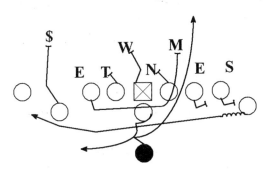

Diagram #9. Handback versus 50

Handback Blocking Rules

TE: Step and hinge, sell pass. Invite DE upfield.

PST: On, down, backer

PSG: Gap, down, backer

C: On, area, away

BSG: On, area, away

BST: Pull, lead through hole. Do not get much depth.

QB: Fake stretch, put ball in wingback's belly. Take ball to fullback.

FB: Crossover, plant, aim at inside foot of tackle.

WB: Fake jet, roll over ball, carry fake to sideline.

HB: Block jet sweep.

The handback is a great play for us against the 4-3, and you will see it on tape (Diagram #10). The quarterback actually puts the ball in the wingback's belly, our fullback is just going to take his steps, and then we are going to bring the ball back the other way. We pull the backside tackle, everybody else hinges, and it is almost like Sally. When you see it on film, it will make a lot more sense to you.

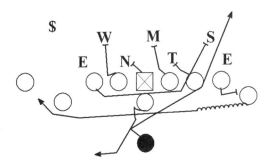

Diagram #10. Handback versus 4-3

We run a double handoff play that we call jet joker (Diagram #11). If you are a wing-T team, it is like crisscross. We are going to hand the ball to the jet guy and he is going to hand it back off to the wingback going the other way. I will show you that play on the tape as well.

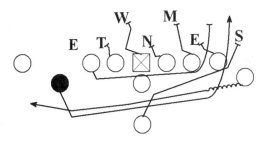

Diagram #11. Jet Joker versus 50 Front

Again, this is only if you want to make it your offense. If you just want it to be a play, the jet sweep, being under center and one back, you can run jet, you can run trap, and as much or as little of this as you want to.

You also have all of the pass routes off of it (Diagram #12). You go ahead and run the jet sweep across and you have high-low routes, flood routes, and all kinds of things that you can do off of that as well.

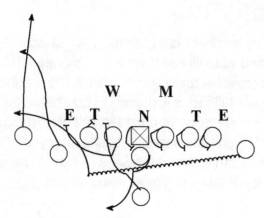

Diagram #12. Jet Belly Pass versus 50 Front

The blocking is pretty simple. We belly block it up front, everybody pass sets backside, and we keep the tight end in for maximum protection.

Okay, I know I went through a lot of stuff, and I will stay around to answer any questions. If anybody wants any of this, if you want the tape or if you want a packet of the plays, just give me your address and I will shoot this up to you as soon as I get back to school next week.

Thanks for having me. I enjoyed being with you.

Rob Zvonar

WINNING WITH CHARACTER

Lincoln-Way East High School, Illinois

I appreciate the opportunity to visit with you today. I want to share something with you in the next few minutes that is outside of the normal X's and O's that we see at clinics. This was a big reason for our success this past season. It was instrumental in helping us win the Class 8A for Illinois.

Last winter our staff was doing our self-evaluation for the past year. We had a lot of discussion on the things we needed to do to become a better football team. For some reason, we go on the topic of things we hate the most about our program. We came up with three points on this matter.

The first thing we did not like was losing football games. The second point we did not like was for our players to sustain injuries. We did not like it when players got hurt. The last point related to our kids getting in trouble.

Obviously, we came up with a plan to keep us from losing. We set up a program that would help us guard against injuries by developing the strength and conditioning program. The third area we wanted to improve on was to prevent our kids from getting into trouble. We talk about making good choices and doing good things, but we did not have a plan to assist the players in this area. So one of our goals in the off-season was to try to find a program for our kids that would help them in making better decisions. We did not know where to look for help on this topic, but we had to start somewhere.

One day I typed in a couple of key words on a search engine to see what was out on the market on this subject. The first article to come up on the Internet was an article by Mark Richt of the University of Georgia. The article was about a new educational curriculum that he had developed for his players at the University of Georgia. I was excited about the article because this was what we were looking for. The program was specifically designed for football players. We liked the article and decided to investigate the program more in detail.

We made a few phone calls to the University of Georgia, and last May five of our coaches went to Athens, Georgia, to train in a seminar related to the enrichment of character. We implemented the program with our varsity players in June and our lower-level players in August. It is something now that is going to be a part of our program, just as with offense, defense, and all of the other areas of football. We have had some positive feedback so far, but it is still too early to tell the effect this program will have with our athletes at this stage of the game.

I can tell you there have been some notable changes. We have had fewer problems down in the dean's office, and we have had fewer complaints from the teachers in our building about our players. Our players seemingly are handling things with a little more humility. In addition, I think they have more respect for each other as well.

The program does contain pre- and post-test, an evaluation form about the curriculum. We will measure our progress in June with these evaluation tools. The kids want to keep doing the program. We meet with the kids individually, and we have to fill out evaluation forms on each player.

Our coaching staff has embraced the program and they have bought into the program. They believe in what we are doing. Is this program filled with soft, fluffy, educational rubbish? No, it is not. If it were, our coaches would not buy into it. We are very demanding. We feel as if we coach our kids as hard as the other programs. If anything, we coach them harder now because we take a personal interest in them off the field.

We have received positive feedback from different people. Our administration loves the program. The parents have endorsed it, and the teachers in our school support us in this program. It has changed the perception of the entire football program that many faculty members see as a problem in their classes. The community recognizes that we are not going to school just to play football. We have been a positive influence in our community. They know we are not at Lincoln-Way High School just to win football games.

I want to show some slides on the program that is a review of the program. This is what the program is all about.

Core Values

- Responsibility
- Self-respect
- Work ethic
- Teamwork
- Discipline
- Integrity
- Courage
- Power
- Truth
- Honor
- Humility
- Honesty
- Diligence
- Strength
- Leadership
- Self-control
- Accountability

What Is Winning with Character?

- Winning with Character was founded in 2002.
- The curriculum was designed for Mark Richt, head football coach at the University of Georgia.

- It was developed out of a desire to provide a structured character-development training program for the University of Georgia.
- The program is taught in 30-minute lessons by members of the coaching staff. We have the class every Monday. We are teaching it now to the varsity on Tuesday before we go into our weight room. On Wednesday, we are working with our young kids on the program.

Program Purpose

- Challenge student-athletes to reach their full potential in the classroom, on the field, and in society.
- Promote values that allow the players to handle all responsibilities with excellence.
- Develop the athlete's body, mind, and spirit to their fullest potential.

Anticipated Achievements

- Building teamwork
- Leadership development
- Character development
- Change thinking and reasoning skills
- Continuously teach honor, respect, and responsibility
- Provides basic foundation for ethical and moral standards
- Influence and encourage positive behavior improvement

Why Is Character Education Important?

- We are fully committed to making our student-athletes better football players, but also to helping them become better young men.
- High School Years
  - ✓ Sons
  - ✓ Friends
  - ✓ Students
  - ✓ Peers
  - ✓ Role models
  - ✓ Teammates

- Post-High School Years
  - ✓ Husbands
  - ✓ Fathers
  - ✓ Employees
  - ✓ Employers
  - ✓ Citizens

Sample First-Year Curriculum

- Foundations of character
- Character in the classroom
- Character and the law
- Being a good teammate
- Peak performance
- Making the grade
- Life beyond the playing field
- Fiscal responsibility
- Community responsibility

Examples of First-Year Topics

- Moral character
- Cheating
- Punctuality
- Pre-martial sex
- Honoring Women
- Drug and alcohol use
- Controlling anger
- Humility
- Responsibility

If you want to know more about our program, I would be glad to share our ideas with you. I hope this tape helped you to understand what we are doing in our program. Winning with character is a never-ending challenge to all coaches. However, we can see the positive changes in our program since we have been using it. Thank you, and good luck next season.

2006
CLINIC NOTES
Lectures by Premier High School Coaches

Edited by Earl Browning

$32.00 • 256 pages • 1-58518-982-0

Also available:

2005	**2004**	**2006**	**2005**	**2004**	**2003**

1-58518-934-0	1-932540-16-4	1-58518-969-3	1-58518-932-4	1-58518-896-4	1-58518-856-5
264 pp. • $25.00	224 pp. • $20.00	304 pp. • $32.00	288 pp. • $25.00	280 pp. • $20.00	288 pp. • $20.00

Title	Item #	Price	Qty	Total

PLUS	KY Tax 6%		
PLUS	Shipping		
	TOTAL		

Kentucky residents only include tax form 51A-126 or pay 6% sales tax.
Shipping & Handling: Included in cost for orders within the USA;
$5.00 for orders in Canada; $7.00 for international orders.

Name _____ Organization/School _____

Address _____

City _____ State _____ ZIP _____ Phone ( ) _____

Method of Payment: ☐ VISA ☐ MasterCard ☐ AMERICAN EXPRESS Cards ☐ DISCOVER ☐ Check # _____ ☐ P.O. # _____

Account # ☐☐☐☐ ☐☐☐☐ ☐☐☐☐ ☐☐☐☐ Expiration: _____

CVC # ☐☐☐ Signature: _____ Email Address: _____